Teaching and Learning *in* Adult Education

by HARRY L. MILLER

ASSOCIATE PROFESSOR OF EDUCATION
HUNTER COLLEGE OF THE CITY UNIVERSITY OF NEW YORK

THE MACMILLAN COMPANY, NEW YORK
COLLIER-MACMILLAN LIMITED, LONDON

First Printing

Library of Congress catalog card number: 64-10583

THE MACMILLAN COMPANY, NEW YORK
COLLIER-MACMILLAN CANADA, LTD., TORONTO, ONTARIO

Printed in the United States of America

Teaching and Learning *in* Adult Education

TO MARILYN

Who made it possible in the first place, and though engaged in her own act of creation, helped with this one.

PREFACE

Adult education is a broad and varied field containing many highly specialized activities. Since this book is addressed to teachers and lay leaders as well as to administrators, it is likely that the reader may be interested in only one or two of the major instructional formats and will look at only the chapters devoted to them. I have tried, consequently, to make each of the chapters on small- and large-group formats self-contained units, at the risk of occasional repetitiveness. They are *not,* however, independent of the first three chapters, which provide orientation often referred to in the materials following. These first three foundation chapters, and the final one on evaluation, constitute a frame for each of the others.

So specialized a field inevitably develops special areas of practice applicable primarily to specific groups of professionals. The book concentrates on what appears to be the most widely useful core of methodological principles and consequently cannot pretend to be comprehensive. Such fields as the education of the foreign-born or the illiterate are not specifically covered, for example, except as the general principles of teaching adults apply to them. Community development raises such distinctively complex issues of techniques that the person interested in the field has available a large body of literature devoted solely to its problems; any decently adequate treatment of them here would needlessly overbalance so modest a work.

I am indebted to A. A. Liveright for suggesting that I write this book as part of a series originally planned by the Center for the Study of Liberal Education for Adults, plans which unfortunately failed to materialize. Roger DeCrow and his staff at the Clearinghouse of the Center provided invaluable assistance and enthusiastic encouragement. I am most grateful to Paul Sheats for his critical reading of the manuscript and for his many suggestions based on his long experience and wisdom about the field.

CONTENTS

• •

1

THE SPECIAL PERSPECTIVE OF THE ADULT

THERE: East of New Guinea, in the southern Pacific, lie the Trobriand Islands. The people who live there are great mariners, lively and active. But they take no interest in things changing. If a thing changes, then it becomes something else, and they call it something else.

HERE: Just as we do not introduce an old gentleman with a long white beard as, "the bouncing baby boy, Jim Jones."

JIM: (a very old man) Very pleased to make your acquaintance.

THERE: (confidentially, to HERE) Buster here isn't any more a bounoing baby boy than I am.

JIM: Ah, but you see, once upon a time I was, in the long, long ago.

HERE: (dismissing him briskly) But he isn't now. In fact, we don't think of him as a kind of modified infant, but as something else—an old gentleman, a different kind of animal.

LISTER SINCLAIR, *A Word in Your Ear*

The dilemma of adult education is precisely that when people think of education, their images are taken from their own memories and from the urgent need to induce the young to take on the responsibilities and burdens of adulthood and the behavior appropriate to that status. To the extent that the adult educator, at whatever level he operates and whatever his purposes, sees clearly the special problems of teaching the already adult as special, the more effective he is likely to be. The cynicism about teaching adults one finds among some university people, as well as the indignant, sentimental defensiveness once common in adult education itself, equally miss the educational point. There are considerable, and valid, differences between the enterprise devoted to the large and necessary task of socializing the young and that which pays attention to the learning needs of the world of adults: differences in purpose, scope, intensity, and available resources, and, consequently, wide differences in the appropriateness of the methods.

THE LEARNING PROCESS

The baby experiences the world, in the phrase of William James which psychologists never tire of quoting, as "a booming, buzzing confusion." His reaction to that world consists in the main of a glassy-eyed indifference to anything which does not immediately meet the demands of his stomach for food, his nervous system for warmth and stability, his psyche for love and attention. In the normal course of development he very soon begins by himself to sort the confusion into a series of recognizable "things," but it is up to his society to tell him what those things are for and what their values are. He must modify his monstrous egocentrism into forms of which the particular time approves and learn to give up his individual, often bizarre, ways of perceiving the world in favor of common agreements about what things mean. He must work out his adjustment to the boundaries of the particular life chance provided by his historical era, his social class and skin color, the local rules of the power game, and his own native fund of energy.

The educational methods of the public school system and the undergraduate college grow out of those tasks involved in becoming a social being, tasks which often grossly distort both the logical and psychological fabric of the learning task itself. These distortions are instructive for adult educators, since in the heat of getting our jobs done, we accept too often the methods with greatest currency as those with the highest intrinsic value.[1]

The Child's Learning

In the early years of life, generally at least until the age of eleven, the child "sees" a world which is very different from the one the adult perceives. By the time he goes to school, to be sure, he has reduced his booming confusion to a certain degree of orderliness. He knows a great deal about the important other people in his life and he can correctly name a large variety of objects and events he meets. But until he is almost ready to become an adolescent, his most important cognitive task is to see the world correctly, that is, realistically rather than magically.

Children, for example, tend to be unable to distinguish clearly distinct parts but to see things as part of a large, global situation. Early in life, when a child says "chair," he might be trying to communicate a variety of things: "I should like to be lifted," or "My chair isn't here," or any number of other meanings. The thing and the word itself stand for all the other meanings which have been at one time connected with it. This kind of confusion persists for longer than one might think. Piaget asked children between the ages of four and twelve what one thinks with, and whether one can see or touch "thought." Children under seven said that "we think with our mouths." "As for animals," said a little boy of six, "they think with their mouths, too, all except the horse, and he thinks with his ears, because he hears when you speak to him but he doesn't talk himself." In the later stage, adult influence is felt, and the child says that we think with our heads. "But under these words the child's conception remains spontaneous and in complete continuity with the answers of the first stage. We think with 'a little voice inside our heads,' says a boy of nine, with 'a little mouth.' "[2]

Because this is a normal pattern in the development of children, the schools can easily organize their methods at these levels on the assumption that almost all the children they will deal with will have basically the same learning problem, distinguishing between themselves and their feelings, other objects, and the situations they are involved in. That the atmosphere of the primary school often seems like a rather genial psychiatric ward is not an accident; most forms of serious mental disturbance exhibit the same distortions and magical elements of the normal childish perceptions.

The second stage of the education of youth is dominated by very different tasks. We expect the school and the college to work on at least two major ones: prepare the child to accept the responsibility of adult roles he will have to assume later, and orient him to the much larger world of time, space, and human relationships. Now that he sees the world about him with some accuracy, he must find out at least sketchily how it got that way, what levels of social and political authority he must respect, which he can reject without fear of punishment, and which he *must* reject.

The school during this stage becomes quite a different one; its major teaching goal is to help the student recognize and respond correctly to a great variety of events, objects, simple relationships, and socially shared values: the American Revolution, which began almost 200 years ago, was a great milestone in man's freedom; South America is a mass of land vaguely south of us and contains many simple-minded people who for some reason do not like Americans; Shakespeare wrote many widely admired plays at a time when people went about in tights; and the like. The school's atmosphere changes considerably to a predominantly paternal one—the tone of most elders in most cultures inducting the young into the mysteries of the society, performing the *rites de passage;* at higher levels, the master and the apprentice.

The Adult's Learning

Adult education has only recently begun to seek a separate and special identity for itself, and although there has been a strong current in the field toward the building of totally separate educational aims and methods, notably in community development, the practice in the larger institutions carrying on adult education has been "adoption without adaptation." Historically, the education of adults has tended to develop as a series of offshoots from institutions or organizations whose major function continues to be some other activity; the public schools, universities, the army, and industry are obvious examples. Little wonder that they should find it convenient and economical to transfer the methods already in use.

But even the cursory examination of the normal patterns of schooling in the preceding paragraphs suggests at least several very important differences between the youth and the adult which ought to concern the programmer of adult education:[3]

HETEROGENEITY. The rather primitive learning tasks which the child must tackle—and which are *common* to all children—find no substitute in the adult world. The normal adult's perceptions are stable, at least relatively so, which is why most laboratory experiments in the psychology of learning must use either animals or young chiidren. The things the adult needs to learn or wants to learn are so wildly various that the traditional pattern of group instruction has difficulty fitting itself to so different a task. Nor does adult heterogeneity relate only to his motivations or to what he will attend to in the learning experience. It arises as a problem very sharply indeed as variations among individual members of a group in knowledge about and previous experience with almost any possible topic.

STRUCTURE. For the child, in very significant measure, learning is the job of identifying new things, events, or relationships which he has never before come across. He is like the inexperienced birdwatcher for whom every bird is a "first." The adult is the experienced veteran, who approaches each sighting with a highly complicated set of expectations and a great deal of experience against which to check what he sees; every field identification for him is structured by these past experiences. For the learning adult as well as the veteran birdwatcher there is always a danger that his previous experience may distort as well as enrich. The hope that one will some day see a prothonotary warbler may lead to a triumphant identification on the basis of very little evidence; so the adult learning a new concept in the social sciences may change it to fit into his own organized body of ideas about society.

MATURITY. Someone else is always "in charge" of the youth. The adult, if he wants to, makes his own decisions; his mistakes are his own, his achievements his own. The distinction is the one between guidance and counseling; we speak of guiding the young because they are not yet equipped to make wholly rational choices, but few of us are willing to take the terrifying responsibility of "guiding" a mature person. The appropriate counterpart is the process of helping the adult see more clearly what it is he *does* want and the realistic alternatives from which he can choose. But the practical consequences of this distinction are not easy to deal with. There is something grand about taking an extreme stand on the matter and saying with Carl Rogers, "It seems to me that anything that can be *taught* to another is relatively inconsequential and has little or no significant influence on behavior. . . . Truth that has been personally appropriated and assimilated cannot be directly communicated to another" or "It becomes teaching and its results are inconsequential."[4] Unfortunately this view is not very helpful to those who bear some institutional responsibility for communicating important concepts and skills to others. In particular it does not help solve the practical problem of the degree to which one ought to permit adult students to decide what it is they wish to learn and how they should go about learning it. Later chapters will take a much more flexible position on this issue and suggest that the degree to which maturity must be taken into account is almost invariably determined by the overriding goals of the particular program.

SOME SIGNIFICANT DIMENSIONS OF CHANGE

Framework #1: Subject Matter

The adult educator works in so many different fields and at so many levels that it is difficult to designate the basic units for an orderly view of the learning problems which need discussion. One common way of dividing up the field, for example, is to consider it as a series of roughly similar institutions: universities and colleges, public schools, associations, and so on. Such a division is ordinarily very useful for considering administrative problems, but there is so much overlapping in the actual operations which the institutions perform that the methodologist must look for other categories.

We face an even greater variation among the types of change which different adult education enterprises seek, to be sure; the bewildering diversity of subject matters and levels at which instructors or leaders deal with them is staggering. But the *nature of the change desired* is obviously our particular appropriate building block, and to deal systematically with adult learning experiences one must impose some kind of order on the wildcat diversity which the field exhibits, whether or not that order introduces a degree of artificiality.

Using Whiting's categories,[5] adult behavior is based either on a technique, a belief, or a value. A *technique* is a known relationship: to start a car, turn this key; to bake a cake, take three eggs, a cup of flour. . . . *Beliefs* are culturally shared notions of relationships, with no really well-tested basis necessary: spare the rod and spoil the child, for example. *Values* are shared judgments of goodness and badness or preferences for one kind of behavior over another: one ought to have fun with one's children, criminals should be punished for their sins, and so on.

A change from one state to another of any of these bases for behavior requires some conviction that present techniques, or beliefs, or values, are in some way inadequate; the crucial educational point is that each of them requires different tests of adequacy. We subject techniques to pragmatic testing. The easiest way to find out whether a recipe works is to try it and see, and few of us in the ordinary course of events have any emotional commitment to any particular technique.

Indeed, men discard old techniques and acquire new ones so readily that in areas where such technical change involves values, such as the maintenance of a given number of jobs in the building trades, artificial barriers to change are erected.

We test the adequacy of beliefs first by whether or not they fit well with our other beliefs and second by whether they correspond to reality. That we are inclined to test beliefs with less rigor than we do techniques is a fact well-documented by the mutually contradictory beliefs all of us live with, as well as the persistence, even in such a highly urban and well-educated culture as the United States, of folklore and superstition.

Finally, values present the most difficult testing task, because they cannot, of course, be "false"; they can be accepted or rejected. We test our values either by examining their goodness of fit, as we do beliefs, or by following out their logical consequences, but we cannot fail to be impressed by daily evidence that the most horrible consequences will often fail to deter people from behavior rooted firmly in value systems. ". . . while to my shame," says Hamlet, "I see the imminent death of twenty thousand men that for a fantasy and trick of fame go to their graves like beds."

The sociologist prefers to work with patterns of techniques, beliefs, and values as they cluster in and connect with social institutions, but the adult educator may find it more useful to view them in the context of *the worlds which the adult directly experiences and out of which his needs for education emerge.* The following set of broad categories is intended to supply a subject-matter framework within which one can identify relatively specific behavior changes which set problems for education.[6]

PERSONAL AND SOCIAL WORLD. Programs which fall in this class include those devoted to examining interpersonal relations in the family, the social problems of the local, national, and international scene, and the moral and ethical problems of the individual.

Example: A short course given at a local high school on child psychology, conducted by one of the counselors on the staff of the school system, attended by a group of mothers from the surrounding area and by a scattering of fathers.

Example: A series of television programs on the problems of the St. Louis metropolitan area: transportation, taxes, crime rate, etc.; beamed particularly at small groups previously organized to discuss these problems, meeting in living rooms around the city, and provided with special materials and an opportunity to call in questions.

Example: A semester-length class on U.S.-Soviet relations, with particular attention to problems of the missile gap, presented by a university extension division on campus in the evening, taught by a professor of political science.

Example: A series of meetings on world politics, organized by an evening college but held off-campus in the living rooms of the participants, provided with special discussion materials but using nonprofessional leadership for the discussions.

Despite the diversity of programs in this field and the vast differences in institutional orientations, they exhibit some common elements of considerable interest.

1. Programs are based on confused or uncertain bodies of knowledge, on disciplines which are for the most part in early stages of development. Psychology, sociology, and political science have grown as scientific disciplines only in the past century and are characterized by the early science's contradictory evidence, premature theorizing, ambiguous findings, and relatively uncertain conclusions. Yet it is an area in which people want most desperately to have unequivocal answers to the problems which perplex them.

2. The area tends to include issues about which people feel very deeply and toward which they have attitudes firmly linked to significant early experiences: feelings of patriotism or of political cynicism; negative attitudes toward those of another color or accent; motherhood, real estate taxes, parental authority, living next door to a Negro family, love, censorship—our attitudes toward all of these are important parts of us and our self-image. It has become clear in recent investigations, for example, that attitudes on such matters are to some degree influenced by whether one's father was employed in an "entrepreneurial" occupation or a "bureaucratic" one: on the one hand, independent small farmers, businessmen, doctors and lawyers, or other professionals on their own; on the other hand, civil servants, salaried workers in large companies, big-business executives, or school janitors —those with jobs which are part of a large complex of relationships. Whether we catch the actual attitudes or merely take over a predisposing personal and social orientation does not matter for our purposes. It is a very uncomfortable area of change for adults.

3. The discomfort relates not only to the early anchoring of these attitudes, but to the probability that people are often in conflict about the desirability of changing their behavior in this area. A mother may feel uneasy about her present relationship with her children, for example, a feeling which may motivate her to attend a series of lectures

on child-raising. But her present behavior satisfies some need of her own and consequently represents a resistance which an increase of information in itself is unlikely to change. This area, pre-eminently, is one of superficial change on the verbal level, often detached from any real change on any other behavioral level.

Programs in the personal and social area, whatever their subject-matter specialization, usually concentrate on attempts to change people's values or to improve their techniques of social interaction. The adult does not need to know about his culture so much as he needs, on occasion, to puzzle out its contradictions, to find out why his habitual attitudes no longer work, or to learn why other people's reactions to him are not as he might wish them to be.

A case in point is the recent change in the beliefs about child-rearing. Wolfenstein's amusing and instructive study of the advice given to parents in the bulletins of the Bureau of Child Study[7] from the First World War to the present makes dramatically clear the successive waves of very different feelings about maternal behavior. It is not merely that in the early period the mother was expected to treat the child with much more systematic care than in the later period; she was also instructed to develop a different relationship with him. The bulletins in the early period told the mother to refrain from too much contact, to set up rigid schedules for feeding, and to restrain any of the child's exploratory activity; they told her in the later period to enjoy fondling and playing with the baby, to feed him on demand, and to remain unworried about his playing with his own body. But all of the prescriptions for individual acts of child-rearing add up to a good deal more. They demand of the mother a different style for playing her role; they emphasize the satisfaction of significantly different needs. In the one case the mother is to view the child as a bundle of strong impulses, some of them evil ones, which must be tamed and kept under control; in the other the child is a mild, harmless, playful creature whom the mother should enjoy and play with.

Juvenile delinquency is another public concern which is often a subject of adult education programs and which similarly includes both of these levels of change, though in a broader context. In considering it as a community and to some extent a national problem, one needs, to be sure, to confront questions which are either factual in character or which make almost purely logical demands of the students. How much juvenile crime is there, for example, and should one make a distinction between actually criminal behavior and delinquent behavior? Is delinquency primarily behavior of lower-class boys, or do the ambiguities of police reporting of crime conceal a proportionately equal share by middle-class boys? Such questions, although they may be usefully considered by the citizen, are problems for the social scientist.

The *public's* problem is centered in the feelings of people toward delinquents, feelings which are inappropriately shifted from the authority situation of the family to the society at large. To a person who grows up in a patriarchal family, anger, followed by punishment, is the proper response to a misbehaving child; but the community is not merely a primary family unit grown large, with the police acting as a collective paterfamilias, and the application of righteous anger and punishment does not control the boys or solve the situation.

In general, then, the education of adults in the personal and social area inevitably emphasizes the examination of beliefs and the adjustment of values which are often lagging behind a changed reality. There are few techniques in the world of social relations, and those that exist demand a special, complicated educational program to communicate adequately. The methods of group dynamics, which do deal directly with techniques, some of them verging on the borderline of group therapy, will be described in a later section, but they demand highly skilled personnel and are unlikely to take a substantial position in adult education for some time. The major emphasis in the personal and social area as a whole will probably remain on the need to change belief systems of adults to enable them to make social responses relevant to changed relationships.

THE WORLD OF WORK. This area without question dominates the activities of the field, as it dominates and overbalances the institutional range of the society at large. The spectrum of the courses, curricula, institutes, conferences, and workshops offered to help people learn new skills, brush up old ones, or keep pace with a technology which is changing with fantastic speed, is as broad as the range of work itself.

Example: A high school in a small industrial city offers a group of a hundred or so courses primarily for young adults, those who have finished high school but have decided not to go on to higher education.

Example: A private university with a city campus offers certificate programs in business as well as full B.A. and B.S. degrees in business administration, given in the evening. It might offer a partial or complete degree in journalism or law, too.

Example: An industrial company of considerable size runs a large training program in one of its major plants and offers instruction in industrial skills to upgrade workers, introduce new techniques, and improve supervisory performance. The training division might also offer a special program in human relations or communications for executive personnel.

Example: The extension division of a large state university, as part of its general program, operates a large hotel with special conference rooms. Groups from all parts of the state come to the campus to spend from two days to several weeks to work on special problems of their profession or trade, to catch up with new developments, or to plan Association activities. The resident faculty is called upon both for program planning and for teaching.

Example: A university offers a ten-week summer program in the social sciences for a small group of labor officials; similar shorter programs are offered in many parts of the country for executives of business and industry.

Example: A university extension division organizes a three-day conference of scientists engaged in work on missiles in order to bring them up to date on the meaning of new technical developments.

In an era which features a demand for increasingly technical skills for an automated economy, accompanied by what appears to be a permanent pool of unemployed, many of them functionally illiterate, adult education faces a challenge of great magnitude. But the challenge is to develop ways of identifying needs, measuring workers' potentials, counseling, and finding instructional resources, rather than to find new techniques of training. The early pilot studies in this field support the view, for instance, that many blue-collar workers are capable of acquiring white-collar skills if we employ reasonable screening procedures.

Despite the extraordinary range of courses and programs which one can consider to be vocational in intention, these activities pose few serious problems for adult education. One need only contrast their general characteristics with those of the preceding area to see why this is so.

1. Above all, the adult student brings to vocational education a consistently high level of motivation. His purpose is generally clear and the rewards for effort are usually fairly visible. Often a promotion, a new job, or a raise in salary is directly linked to his completion of a particular course. Even when the connection is not so immediate, however, the goal may be so powerful in promised social status or economic reward that the motivation to reach it can sustain long years of persistent effort. We see this often astonishing persistence mostly in the college degree programs, but it exists in other fields as well. As the once free-wheeling economy turns into vast hierarchical organizations, shutting off previous opportunities for the ambitious

and energetic, education remains as one of the few means for upward socio-economic mobility.

2. Most education in this area also appeals to what is apparently a widespread characteristic of Americans—an overwhelming absorption in the practical, the useful, and a corresponding suspicion of the abstract or theoretical. It makes *sense* to spend time and effort learning something that will put a little extra on the paycheck or help one advance generally, but businessmen and trade union officials alike seem suspicious of programs in the social sciences, for example, which are often planned for them. "What is this stuff supposed to *do* for us when we get back in the office?" they protest. Of course, the dislike of the abstract stops at their technical specializations; chemist, engineers, doctors, and other highly trained professionals gather happily at adult education centers to discuss the latest esoterica of their fields at levels of abstraction that would make a social scientist airsick.

3. The fields which make up the vocational programs are, for the most part, well-organized bodies of principles and relevant application. Teachers are usually experts in the particular field, and in adult education particularly, they are often experts with a great amount of practical experience behind them. Whatever their actual teaching experience or teaching skill, they usually have a relatively precise image of the objectives of their programs and of how to go about getting evidence of the students' achievement of those objectives. This concern does not even emerge as a problem at all at the level of machine skills; the test of whether a student can run a lathe satisfactorily is simply whether he can demonstrate that he can. Students and teachers alike have considerably less clarity at, say, the upper reaches of business administration, but even here there is considerably less ambiguity than in the personal and social area.

The vocational area is predominantly one of the transmission of techniques. For the most part the belief systems of students are subject to some kind of empirical check, sometimes disastrously, as in the case of some small businessmen whose test of their beliefs about consumer preferences ends in the bankruptcy courts. As for values, many teachers in this area appear to prefer to leave them alone and avoid even the discussion of these values involved in the social roles of the particular vocation or profession.

THE WORLD OF FORM. Adult programs in this area include all of those we might loosely categorize as the humanities, the study, or the creation, of works in which the formal elements are primary. This area may well constitute the second largest of the general program categories in adult education, though it is difficult to find hard and fast evidence for such a belief. It certainly involves some of the most imaginative programming in adult education.

Example: A large suburban high school presents a wide variety of courses in the plastic arts—painting, sculpture, print-making—all of them focused on learning to create rather than on appreciation. Classes are kept small, and so are fees.

Example: An extension division of a large city university presents a two-year program of study of the performing arts: theater, opera, and concert hall. Emphasis is on formal analysis of the arts involved and on raising the level of sophistication of the judgments of the participants.

Example: A university college offers a weekend program, in a mountain lodge setting, consisting of the analysis of one Beethoven quartet.

Example: A midwestern small liberal arts college holds each summer a writers' workshop on its campus, at which aspiring writers gather to work and to submit what they produce to critical analysis.

Example: A large university holds each year, in cooperation with the city in which it has its campus, an arts festival which includes the presentation of concerts and plays, as well as public discussions of issues in the arts.

The examples selected give a hopeful rather than a quantitatively accurate impression of the arts in adult education. The applied arts, such as interior decoration (and cake decoration), jewelry design and construction with major emphasis, apparently, on how to apply enamel to copper, and pottery, dominate the field in number of courses and volume of students. Some aestheticians reject the inclusion of these educational efforts in the arts proper,[8] but all questions of snobbery aside, it is difficult to know how to categorize them otherwise. Whether or not courses in crafts are trivial compared to those dealing with great painting, the former do deal with the aesthetic impulse on some level, with the desire that things should be beautiful. It would be difficult to deny the cultural value of the years of work by Cooperative Extension in helping rural women beautify their drab farm homes. This would be, to be sure, a social value rather than an aesthetic one, if the only product of the effort were brighter slip covers throughout the land, but not if it also raised the level of sophistication with regard to color and pattern of the women involved in the effort.

On another issue, the ideas about education of adults in the arts are sharply divided, as indeed arts education is in many other areas: should we emphasize creativity and teach people to *do* in the arts as the best way of teaching them to appreciate, or should we help them understand by verbally exploring and analyzing the art product? Of course, there is no way of deciding which is more effective without a fairly elaborate study in which the many variables involved, such as the aptitude of the students and the length of time devoted to study, could be held constant for the purpose of comparison. In the absence of such experimentation it is perhaps futile to speculate; one possible hypothesis, however, is that people with some already existing flair for painting, for example, might learn a great deal by spending time at the act of painting itself, but that other students might learn no more than do children at their finger paints. As matters now stand, the issue is largely a theoretical dispute; most adult programs which stress creative activities do so with no more complicated a motive than to provide people with an opportunity for self-expression or relaxation.

Turning to characteristics which programs in the arts for adults have in common, one notes the following:

1. It is above all a woman's world. Traditionally American men have regarded the arts with some suspicion as a display of unmasculine interest. Though this attitude no longer persists so widely as it did, it has by no means disappeared. We find a preponderance of men in the mobility-serving programs in the vocational area, and the reverse is true in this field, as though most people in the culture still maintain the belief of the pioneer days that women are the culture-bearers and men the stern, super-masculine denizens of the out-of-doors.

2. The concepts and the objects of study in the area are least of all close to the familiar or the sensible; they do not follow the rules of logic and order so basic in Western industrial society. Children are not particularly interested in logical relations; their perceptions of the world often proceed on their own logic, and more than one student of child development has pointed out the similarity of the child's conception of the world to that of the twentieth-century artists's. But the adult is emotionally committed to a stable perception of life, and a great deal of his security is associated with that stability; if things are not really what they seem, then where will it all end, after all? Such insecurity poses very difficult problems to overcome in an area which demands of the learner some willingness to relinquish his sense of the familiar in language or in the visual world in favor of spending a great deal of energy in perceiving the shape of complex relationships which move under the surface of the art object.

3. The arts in general also provide a few practical problems of some magnitude. Large metropolitan centers have museums and art

galleries, an orchestra, perhaps a few chamber groups, several theaters, and at least one semi-professional theatrical company, but outside of these metropolises programs may have trouble with providing objects of study. The written word is everywhere available and technical advances in fidelity help make up for the sparseness of live orchestras; but many art educators find reproductions a bad substitute for actual paintings or sculptures. The performing arts, of course, require a real stage and a group of people with considerably more training than most communities are able to afford.

Arts education in general, and particularly for adults, deals fairly evenly with all three bases of behavior—techniques, beliefs, and values—but in very different kinds of programs. Where programs concentrate on the development of creative skills, they work mainly with techniques; where they attempt to raise the level of appreciation or analytical skills, their objectives are almost exclusively changes in beliefs or values, and for the most part, the latter of those two.

THE PHYSICAL WORLD. The physical sciences occupy an uneasy position in adult education, perhaps because of all the areas of developing knowledge and experience, they are most remote from adult role performance. Two major exclusions from the following examples of this area must be justified. One is a very large amount of programming that goes on in the upper reaches of mathematics, physics, and chemistry, programming whose purpose is purely vocational. Doctors, engineers, and working chemists attend such courses not out of an interest in the science but because they must keep up with their fields; these courses, consequently, belong in the vocational area and are noted there. The second omission is those programs arising out of a need to inform the public of, or to help people think about, the social consequences of scientific advance. Automation in industry arises from technical changes which now encourage the building of certain kinds of machines, but the only reason this constitutes a problem is that our social machinery is not adequate to adjust to the change without affecting adversely a good many people. Extraordinary advances in theoretical physics and mathematics permit us to build machines which have the capacity to blow up the planet; whether we are foolish enough to use them constitutes a problem of social and psychological dimensions. In the last instant of atomic annihilation, the person who understands the structure of the atom perishes along with the one without any knowledge at all.

Without these two major groups, adult programs in science are rather sparse. They include such programs as:

Example: General education courses in science, patterned on those developed for undergraduate curricula, are offered for adult students working on college degrees in evening colleges.

Example: Chicago's Basic Program includes a series of texts, examples of very high-level scientific reasoning, which students read and analyze in order to grasp the logical structure.

Example: A high school adult program includes as parts of its general short-course offerings several lecture courses on the new advances of scientific discovery.

Common elements among such programs as these are not difficult to see, and a look at them reveals many of the difficulties with present programming in science:

1. In no other field is the distance between the expert and the curious or interested layman so astronomical. The social scientist, however infatuated with new terminology, talks about phenomena which are thoroughly familiar to any lay person in the same culture. However exasperated the art specialist may be with the layman's preference for the homey simplicity of Norman Rockwell, he still deals with the same kind of object—paint arranged on a surface. But as soon as the scientist penetrates to matters which interest him at all, he leaves behind the person who is without rigorous training in mathematics.

The common solution to this difficulty involves the scientist's finding a way of explaining complex mathematical relationships in relatively simple verbal formulations. The science survey course usually results from such attempts, and it is hard to find anyone who is very satisfied with this answer. The scientific knowledge one gains from such programs can easily be equaled by an interested reader of such first-rate popular treatments of science as *Scientific American,* the science articles in *Life,* or some special television programs. There is little reason to wonder, consequently, why there is so little formal programming of this kind in adult education.

2. Other programs have tried to stress the learning of scientific methodologies as the most significant objective for learning in science, particularly for the layman. One immediately bumps into the same barrier as before. The methods of modern physics or, for that matter, modern biology are so complex and specialized that the layman is lost almost immediately. But if one means by scientific method the approach to the finding of explanations for phenomena or relation-

ships, an approach which is empirical, which works tirelessly to eliminate biases in both the material and an investigator, which is, when it can be, experimental, and which insists on impeccable logic in making inferences from the results of investigation, then the data of the physical sciences are not absolutely necessary.[9] One could use the more familiar material of the social sciences or the earlier and simpler discoveries of any of the physical sciences.

In adult education, consequently, programs in the pure sciences are relatively scarce, even after the Sputnik-aroused surge of public interest at the end of the decade of the 50's. Perhaps as a generation schooled in the new mathematics and provided with new and stimulated physics texts reaches maturity, they will try to keep up with new developments through adult education channels. The chances are that any such demand will be met by TV rather than by any of the small group methods.

To generalize, this area involves no problem of values at all, but predominantly deals with techniques and with beliefs about the physical world and man as a physical being.

SOME GENERAL DIFFERENCES. It is clear that each of the four areas emphasizes a different pattern of subject matter, which considerably influences the desirable features of the learning situation. Learning recipes is a different matter entirely from shifting the orientation of our value system or testing the consistency of our beliefs. There is another dimension along which these areas vary, and that is the extent to which they need to be modified to meet adult needs. They have been discussed here in the order of decreasing need for modification; the approach to a student in the area of science, for example, depends less on his age than on his scientific sophistication, and many parents of this generation are baffled by scientific achievements which their twelve- or thirteen year-old sons understand immediately. At the other end of the scale, the social idealism of some undergraduates rests in some measure at least on their lack of experience with the extraordinary complexity of modern social life; it is easy to talk about sweeping social change if one has not even had the exasperating experience of trying to change the coffee-break habits of a typist pool.

At the science end of the scale, methods appropriate for children need little modification for adults; there is no reason, for example, why the new physics and biology textbooks for the high schools might not be used with groups of adults who would, without doubt, get the same pleasure from doing the ingeniously contrived little experiments.

But as we move toward the personal and social problem part of the scale it becomes increasingly necessary to take fresh approaches to method and to relate materials and activities to the special purposes and experiences of the adult and to the requirements of the special characteristics of the content area. To summarize this discussion in a general principle: decide *how much* modification of methods is necessary by considering the content area in which the program falls; then, determine the general direction of program planning by deciding which of the three elements (technique, beliefs, or values) of the culture complex we want primarily to deal with.

Framework #2: Behavior

Many definitions of learning exist, developed for a variety of purposes: some to guide research, others to complement educational theories. Those interested in the practical problems of increasing the effectiveness of learning experiences for adults can probably most usefully view learning as *some form of change in the behavior of those participating* in the program, primarily *cognitive* behavior, that is, behavior that has to do with knowing or recognizing, attributing meaning, and other intellectual operations. The elements of framework discussed in the preceding section represent a background, a broad field of operations; the more immediate question now arises of what we wish people *to do* with the subject matters relevant to the field, *what behaviors we wish to change.*

The question suggests a number of relatively specific problems which the chapters immediately following this one will discuss. A more general answer at this point requires a broad look at what the adult educators do along two major axes: the type of change they try immediately to achieve in student behavior and the long-range educational purpose that lies behind the effort toward change.

"KNOWING" AND "DOING". Any observer of the broad scene of adult education soon notices that programs differ significantly in whether they conceive of the student or audience as an active organism which must be trained in some desired behavior (whether it is analyzing a poem or running a lathe) or as an empty cup which the instructor must fill with knowledge. We have chiseled "knowledge is power" into the stone of most of our libraries and schools, and our firm commitment as a culture to the idea undoubtedly accounts for the dominance of the "empty cup" theory of method.

In a sense, "knowing" is a behavior, too. To demonstrate that we know something we must go through some act of recognizing it or calling it back into memory. And if everything we know were made relevant use of in our behavior, knowledge in general would indeed be power. A laboratory rat which has been given the opportunity to run around in a maze days previous to the actual test will learn the maze quicker than his fellow who had not been given the opportunity to "know" the general environment of the maze. But humans are considerably more complicated and unpredictable. We unconsciously rummage among the knowledge available to us in any situation to find those bits that fit in with our desires or our preconceptions and to reject the ones that contradict them. The knowledge we have often has little effective relation to our behavior; we know that a significant percentage of automobile accidents are rear-end collisions, but we continue to tailgate the drivers in front of us.

In the face of a truly extraordinary mass of empirical evidence that the passive reception of statements of facts, opinions, or argument by itself has a very low efficiency if one desires change or growth in the recipient, by far the most common method of adult education is the assigned reading and unadorned lecture.[10] From the beginnings of the early lecture series in the nineteenth century to recent national televising of popular charmers such as Baxter and Bernstein, telling people about things has been the easiest way to promote public enlightenment, particularly after the invention of instruments which carry the human voice to a mass audience. Although the lecture is far from being a useless tool for teaching, there is no question that we overuse it, that we use it inappropriately, and that, seduced by the ease of arranging to have an expert talk to people, we often neglect to think through the particular problem of method for our particular purpose.

The opposed conception of the student as a live organism who must be changed in some way by the process of learning and who needs an opportunity to practice new intellectual skills or insights is also firmly present in adult education. One finds the conception most prominently in the vocational area and the arts; few teachers of accounting would consider that they had succeeded at their job if they ended a course in elementary accounting after acquainting their students with the principles of the field but without requiring all the students to perform the necessary operations many times and submit their exercises to critical evaluation.

The problem is not that administrators and teachers of adult programs fail to recognize these elementary and obvious truisms of learning, but that they see the necessity of applying them only in certain areas. The special conditions of the adult as student are influential, too. Active learning processes take time, more time than many adults are willing to give, and they make demands on the energy and concentration of the student which many busy adults find impossible to meet, except under conditions of very high motivation. These conditions occur mainly in the vocational area, and it is in that area, consequently, that one finds most appreciation of active methods in adult education.

LONG-RANGE OBJECTIVES. A second major determinant of method develops from the educator's conception of the purpose of the program.[11] A considerable part of the formal programs of adult education, particularly at the university level, seem merely remedial; that is, they adopt the educational purposes and methods of some other sector of education so that some adults may make up what they missed. Such programs face mainly administrative, rather than educational, problems, as they apply already formulated curricula and bodies of method to different times of day and to students with lower energy levels, using faculty whose basic loyalties lie with other divisions of the enterprise. But a majority of adult educators build their programs to fit some perception of the needs of an adult clientele which they have chosen, or have been hired, to serve. We can generally see in these programs two different kinds of purposes, whether or not they have ever been explicitly formulated.

The first of these purposes is to help the adult adjust to some facet of change in the society which affects his performance in a social role. The concept of role is particularly useful in this context because it specifies a pattern of behaviors and attitudes attached to a particular status in the society, shaped by the expectations of other people. For example, over the past generation the role of the supervisor in industry has radically changed; the people who matter once expected their supervisors to be tough, decisive men committed to carrying out their specific part of the enterprise at whatever cost. They now expect them to be understanding, considerate of the human relations problems involved in the groups they supervise, and committed to the organization rather than to the task itself. These changes in expectations create a considerable amount of tension in the system at large, as those playing supervisory roles begin to feel the pressure to change behavior patterns which they have grown up conceiving as right and proper ways of carrying out that particular role. It is at this point that adult education of some form becomes necessary to train people in the new behaviors demanded of them.

Thus do the relatively sudden changes in technology, beliefs, and values in the culture create demands for change in those who are beyond their formal schooling and consequently for novel educational formats for adults. From this viewpoint, adult education is a kind of vast, unorganized, flexible trade school for social role improvement and adjustment, as the accelerating tempo of social change in an overwhelmingly industrial and urban society demands quicker adjustments from its members. Historically, we can perceive this process occurring many times as adult education grew erratically in response to changes in role patterns. The rapid shift from a rural to an industrial society and the rate of technological innovation after the Civil War demanded a dazzling variety of new work skills, particularly of the white-collar kinds; a host of educational mechanisms sprang up to meet them. Similarly, following the peak period of immigration into the United States, adult education assumed the task of preparing the new Americans for their novel citizen role, mainly through the night-school settings immortalized in the incomparable figure of Hyman Kaplan. In recent decades, under the impact of changing roles in marriage, adult programs have paid increasing attention to marital adjustment and child-rearing problems. Sharply increasing amounts of leisure available in the society find their reflection in growing numbers of programs in both fine arts and crafts, as the role of "consumer of leisure" begins to take on definition.

Of the many social roles which adults in our society must play, Havighurst and Orr have discussed ten to which adult education must pay particular attention:

Parent	User of Leisure
Spouse	Church Member
Child of Aging Parent	Club or Association Member
Home Maker	Citizen
Worker	Friend

They have gathered and evaluated data relating to the extent to which middle-aged urban Americans see the need for change in themselves in relation to these roles, and suggest for adult educators to use in selecting program emphases an approach which has significant implications for the selection of materials and methods.

To illustrate, they define specifications for both an adequate and an inadequate fulfillment of the parental role during the middle years of life as follows:

Setting Adolescent Children Free and Helping Them to Become Happy and Responsible Adults

Nature of the Task

Children are reaching adulthood and establishing their own homes, families, and careers. Parents can help in this process or hinder it. The task is hard for some parents, particularly women, because they have invested so much of themselves in the parent-child relationship, and have gotten so many satisfactions out of having children dependent on them. The artistic performance of this task includes giving the children a lift even though they do not realize it; enhancing their self-confidence by being confident of their success; supporting their efforts to prepare for and assume their positions as adults.

The major qualitative factor in a high level performance as a parent is that of growing toward a less dominant position in relations with one's children while maintaining a relationship which continues in an affectional way to be close but not binding.

High

Gets along with children on terms of growing equality. Has aided or permitted children to make independent choices of: place to live, job to take, person to become engaged to or marry, clothes to wear, college to enter, special field in college. Has become less dominant in relations with children during past 10 years. Spends less time with children than 10 years ago. If he supports children financially, does so unobtrusively and in a matter of fact way, without using this as a means of subordinating the child.

He does not interpret children's independent activities and choices as indicating a loss of intimacy. Rather, he gives evidence of his own confidence in the fact that there are ways in which he can depend on his children to meet his needs—to let him know what is happening to them and that they are actively interested in what is going on in his life.

Medium

Has definitely encouraged or permitted children to become independent in one or more areas, such as choice of friends, job, vocational choice, place to live; but retains a strong, almost compulsive interest in these matters and seeks, often by subtle means, to influence children. Feels that his judgment is better than that of children on important topics. Occasionally gives unasked advice, based on his wisdom or superior power.

Low

A. Dominates children, seeks to make decisions for them. Tries to keep them at home. Prevents them from having independence-building experiences—such as buying own clothes, choosing school or college courses, choosing friends, taking separate vacations from that of family.

B. Indifferent to or rejects children. Sees little or nothing of them. Does not give them emotional support. Takes no responsibility for them.[12]

The specification of high-level competence in the role obviously suggests the objectives for an adult program. This general approach to the purposes of the adult educator, as a diagnostic middle-man operating between new social role demands and the resources which may help people adapt to them, has the great virtues of directness, relative simplicity, and obvious appropriateness. The voluntary character of most adult education, the difficulty of persuading adults to commit blocks of time over a long period, the enormous individual variations in experience and intelligence among any adult group—all argue for the usefulness of this model, which permits us to be highly specific, short-run, and focused on areas of highest immediate motivation.

The success of this model, however, has led adult educators to pay less attention than it deserves to an alternative possibility which shifts the emphasis of program development from the social situation, demand, or problem to growth in the general abilities of the individual. Adult educators, to be sure, take pride in their careful attention to the individual student through their response to expressed needs and by their admirable sensitivity to individual difficulties with the learning situation. But the social-role argument suggests that in a very important sense we are interested in chemists and accountants, fathers and mothers, citizens and consumers of leisure, rather than individuals.

Even as a minor strain in the total effort of adult education, there have been a number of interesting efforts to build programs directed at improving the general abilities of individuals. Because the programs have, in a sense, cut across the grain of adult education and the circumstances which shape its normal patterns, they have had great difficulty in surviving; they are significant enough as a potential in the field, however, to merit attention in a discussion of methods, where they represent a real challenge to ingenuity.

Most efforts so far expended in this attempt to develop basic cognitive abilities have concentrated on training people in formal rational processes. The best-known example, perhaps, is the Great Books program, which organizes groups of adults for the relatively informal discussion of the enduring, recurrent ideas in the intellectual history of the West, sampled from the majestic literature of that history. This is far from "training" in any formal sense; the Foundation does not prescribe any rigorous approach to the ideas under discussion, taking instead the Athenian model of free men enlightening one another in the course of serious talk.

All such programs are deeply influenced by academic philosophy and particularly by the discipline of formal logic, but it would be surprising if the pragmatic American temper had not produced experiments with more informal approaches to thinking, and there has indeed been in adult education a lively history of attempts to deal directly with basic problem-solving abilities. Few of these have developed into extensive or lasting formal programs; the tendency has been to consider training in problem-solving as one aspect of helping people solve immediate, specific problems with which they are confronted. Agricultural Extension occasionally claims improvement in general problem-solving ability as an educational byproduct of helping American farmers improve agricultural methods; community development specialists make similar assertions. Indeed, the one assumption in the field held most widely with great firmness in the face of almost nonexistent evidence is that helping people to find solutions for a specific problem will somehow teach them to solve *any* problem better. Later chapters will examine such beliefs critically.

Behavior Models

As adult educators plan their programs, they select methods and materials on the basis of a series of preconceptions and purposes related to the formal set of categories described above. Program planners may be more or less aware of such formal conceptions, or they may perceive them in quite different terms, but this particular framework works very usefully in suggesting some ideal models toward which programs in the field appear to be moving.

If the two major continua are shown in relation to each other, the following scheme emerges:

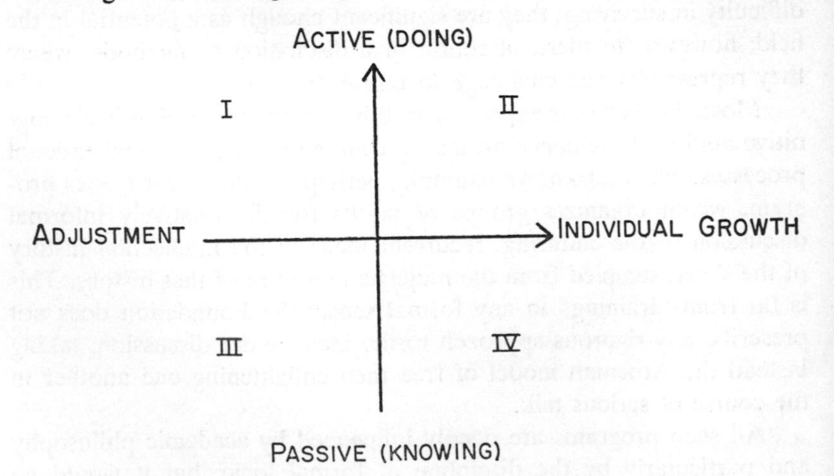

To locate any specific program along each of the axes results in placing it in one of the cells, which may ideally be characterized by the dimensions which produce them, and which make different demands on methodology.

THE EFFICIENT MAN. Programs which emphasize the aim of adjusting adults to some dislocation arising out of social change, and which want to make a real difference in behavior, seem to be interested in producing an efficient person, one who now measures up realistically to new circumstances. A good example is the dramatic shift in the field of mathematics teaching following the public outcry after the first Sputnik. Teachers of mathematics in the public schools were not merely expected to learn new mathematical theory to replace the traditional mathematics they teach but had to be retrained to do a different kind of teaching task altogether. Another example of this active training for efficient adjustment is the ubiquitous training workshop in human relations for supervisors. Changes in the conception of the supervisory role have been met by constructing experiences in which supervisors not only learn new ideas of human relations but are required to practice the skills necessary to act them out.

The desirable image of the person we are seeking to produce in this area is the rational and efficient adjuster. A logical danger, of course, is that we may instead create the other-directed person, who shifts his behavior to conform to demands of others whether or not these demands represent serious needs in the society. As adult educators develop habits of looking more critically at the immediate aims of their communities, where these influence demands for new educational planning, such a danger perhaps becomes more remote.

THE INTELLECTUAL. Adult educators aiming at behavioral change in basic cognitive abilities of individuals, without regard to affecting specific social role activities, wish to produce people with a primary interest in ideas and the skills of manipulating them. The habit of detachment, the formal processes of logic and rhetoric, and the exercise of rational judgment are skills and attitudes which, once acquired, may be applied in any area of social life or, indeed, purely for one's own amusement. The parallel danger in this model is that we produce sophists instead, for whom social reality is merely a convenient source of stimulating problems for discussion.

THE WELL-INFORMED. Programs which stress the passive acceptance of knowledge related to social role problems seem to be striving toward a model of the well-informed citizen. We think immediately of the early days of adult education and the Chatauqua lectures, as well as the early university ideal in the nineteenth century of humanizing knowledge, a noble aim which the practitioners reduced to the dispatching of lecturers out on a circuit. There is no question that the lifeblood of a democracy is a well-informed citizenry, but there is little doubt also that this particular model more often than the others tends to break down into its counterpart, the encouragement of dilettantism. Look, for example, at the steady growth of parlor psychoanalysts who need only an acquaintance with the terms "id" and "superego" to go into informal practice immediately.

THE EXPERT. Finally, the concentration on individual growth through the relatively passive acquisition of knowledge seems aimed at producing the expert. The common model for adult education is the intensely technical three-day- or week-long institute at which changes in the tax law, for instance, are communicated and expounded at Talmudic length and complexity to people who are already tax experts. This is a service function which adult education as an institution can hardly fail to play in a society which increasingly needs it, as professions of all levels become more complex, and perhaps it is almost inevitable that such a model ends up producing the over-specialized person.

PURPOSES AND METHODS

Most adult education programs approach, at least in the intentions of their creators, one of these models or some combination of several of them. As sets of general purposes operating in response to expressed needs in the society, the methodologist cannot question them; what he can usefully do is to indicate the problems of finding methods which are appropriate to each one of them. Many of the present practices in the field create methodological dissonances with program purposes, for the following reasons:

Inappropriateness

The most common disparity of this kind occurs when program planners and teachers assume that methods which are most useful in producing experts also are ideal for the development of intellectuals. The expert usually demands to be brought up to date in one way or another, and as he is in possession of a large body of already well-integrated knowledge, he is capable of sitting passively and absorbing and integrating floods of new information and concepts. If we aim at developing intellectuals, however, the range of knowledge they have is really of a low order of importance; what they need is to practice intellectual skills, and no amount of listening to experts or to other intellectuals will substitute for active practice. The evening colleges are properly cautious about mixing credit students, who are aiming at becoming experts in some field, and non-credit students, who want to sit in out of intellectual curiosity. Faculty complaints in this situation commonly focus on the problems this presents for the credit student, but the non-credit students get considerably the worst of the bargain; as would-be intellectuals they are likely to get almost no help from the traditional methods of the college credit course. Even more striking is the tendency to plan elaborate institutes for adults in which no academic requirements are involved at all and fill the program with session after session of lectures. In the context of this discussion a little learning may or may not be dangerous, but it is not very useful.

Inadequacy of Available Teaching Skill

Often enough, we select a method appropriate to the purpose of the program, but the teachers lack the necessary skill. A most interesting instance of this difficulty may be found in the numerous attempts to develop informal discussion programs, based on important problems and ideas and led by lay discussion leaders. Such programs propose to help the adult citizens who participate think through public issues to much more sophisticated positions, help them evaluate current policies, and understand more completely the complex relationships involved in the social and political scene about them. Group discussion, conducted as disciplined exploration of problems, as a thoughtful exercise in cooperative inquiry, is a method precisely shaped to help people change in these directions. But such an enterprise demands a high order of skill from its leader or an extraordinarily well-trained group of participants. Much to the credit of most of the agencies which have attempted to develop such programs, they have experimented with a number of training devices for improving the discussion-leading capabilities of the lay citizens involved in the programs, but this, in itself, is a very difficult training task.

Inadequacy of Method to Purpose

Sometimes we hope to bring about changes in adults which no educational method, no matter how active, is likely to achieve. This particular discrepancy between purpose and method is most likely to occur in programs seeking to develop behavioral changes or attitude changes strongly linked to established personality patterns. The best developed area, methodologically, in adult education is the one devoted to improving human relations skills in industry; for over a decade some of the most ingenious psychologists in American universities have devoted themselves to the planning of educational experiences which would most powerfully affect attitudes and behavior related to interpersonal cooperation and conflict. No matter how well thought through and scientifically based such teaching is, however, a considerable number of adults remain relatively untouched by it. Their resistance to such change is so strong that one suspects that only psychotherapy could manage it, if, indeed, they were ever motivated enough to seek therapy.

As adult educators develop clearer and more coherent images of particular purposes with particular groups of adults and adopt more experimental attitudes toward methodology, we can make such analyses as the one above sharper and more detailed and advance toward an established set of methodological principles for adult education. For the present, a rough framework such as this, constituting a general perspective, must serve the need for theoretical background for the specific chapters to follow.

NOTES

1. Adult educators commonly look only at the education of adolescents when they attempt to formulate critical differences between childhood and adult education. As I suggest in the distinction made here, the demands which shape the schooling of the child and adolescent differ considerably, shifting from ones which are based on the psychology of the pupil to his social context. This may be one of the reasons behind the concentration of the adult educator on the social setting of his students rather than their psychology and, consequently, what seems to me the rather cursory attention to method in the field when compared with our (mainly sociological) preoccupation with purposes. But many of the problems which teachers of adults must struggle with, particularly in life areas where attitudes tend to be strongly developed and deeply rooted, resemble those of the teachers of children. Many adults, who have led busy lives immersed in an often narrow sector of the larger society, have grave difficulty in the learning situation adjusting their perspective to a broader gauge, cling to comfortably familiar sets of verbal symbols almost as if they were magic amulets, or have difficulty substituting analysis of problems for "devil theories" of social evils. Adult educators should find it rewarding to become familiar with such studies of the cognitive processes of childhood as J. Piaget's *The Child's*

Conception of the World (New York: Harcourt, Brace, 1929), and Heinz Werner's *Comparative Psychology of Mental Development* (New York: Science Editions, 1961).

2. Piaget, *op. cit.*, p. 229.

3. This view of the special nature of adult education is, of course, only one of many, and I claim no particular virtue for it beyond its usefulness for the general purpose of this book. Most such analyses concentrate on drawing distinctions between the characteristics of the adult and those of the child, particularly as those characteristics are modified in the adult by life experiences. Whipple's monograph is the most carefully thought-through of these attempts, and I agree thoroughly with his conclusions. The reason that I did not use such a framework here is that arguing from differences in experience seems to me to lead primarily to formulating different curricula or to selecting different materials for educational use. But aside from such reasonable generalizations as that people with greater experience ought to be given a chance to relate that experience to the educational process, such an approach has little to say for the methodologist, or, at least, what it contributes lacks the necessary precision. I have concluded that considerations of method develop more fruitfully from an analysis of the aims of the adult educator as they differ from setting to setting and from those of the educators of children. But, see James B. Whipple's *Especially for Adults,* Notes and Essays No. 19 (Chicago: Center for the Study of Liberal Education for Adults, 1957), and also Jack R. Gibb's "Learning Theory in Adult Education," in Knowles (ed.), *Handbook of Adult Education* (Chicago: Adult Education Association, 1960). Most of what Gibb says about the adult learner, it seems to me, can be as readily applied to the learner at any stage or age; it is the ingenious application of learning theory to specific aims of varieties of adult educators which provides us with a more fruitful approach to method.

4. Carl Rogers, "Personal Thoughts on Teaching and Learning," *Improving College and University Teaching,* Vol. VI, No. 1 (Winter, 1958), pp. 4-5.

5. Whiting's view of culture as essentially a system of symbolic and cognitive systems of techniques, beliefs, and values seems to me to provide a very useful set of terms for the adult educator, however objectionable it may be to the anthropologist who prefers to see culture as patterns of behavior. In the first place, the framework provides a neat way of linking the socialization of the child to the world of the adult: the three elements of techniques, beliefs, and values in combination form what Whiting calls the "custom complex," a blueprint for action which the culture transmits to each child through his parents. In a rapidly changing culture, by the time the child has grown to adulthood his cognitive maps often need considerable adjustment, which is essentially the job of adult education.

In the second place, Whiting's scheme links culture with the social order, the institutional complex around which adult education tends to organize its activities. "The custom complex, however, is but a beginning. It describes the blueprint for but a single action of a single category of persons in a single situation. Custom complexes are, however, organized into roles that are played in institutional settings. . . . We would adopt, with slight modification, Malinowski's (1944) definition of an institution as being a group of people occupying different statuses (personnel), who are expected to perform certain roles defined in terms of techniques (norms and rules), agreeing upon certain values, and accepting certain beliefs (charter). . . . In sum, a culture consists of a set of customs which may be divided into techniques, beliefs and values that are in turn integrated into the systems of ethnoscience, ethics, and pragmatics. Customs are combined into roles, that are combined into institutions." See J. W. M. Whiting and I. L. Child, *Child Training and Personality* (New Haven: Yale University Press, 1953); J. W. M. Whiting and Beatrice B. Whiting, "Contributions of Anthropology to the Methods of Studying Child Rearing," in Mussen (ed.), *Handbook of Research Methods in Child Development* (New York: John Wiley & Sons, 1960).

A schematization of this conception which relates social change to adult education might look like the following:

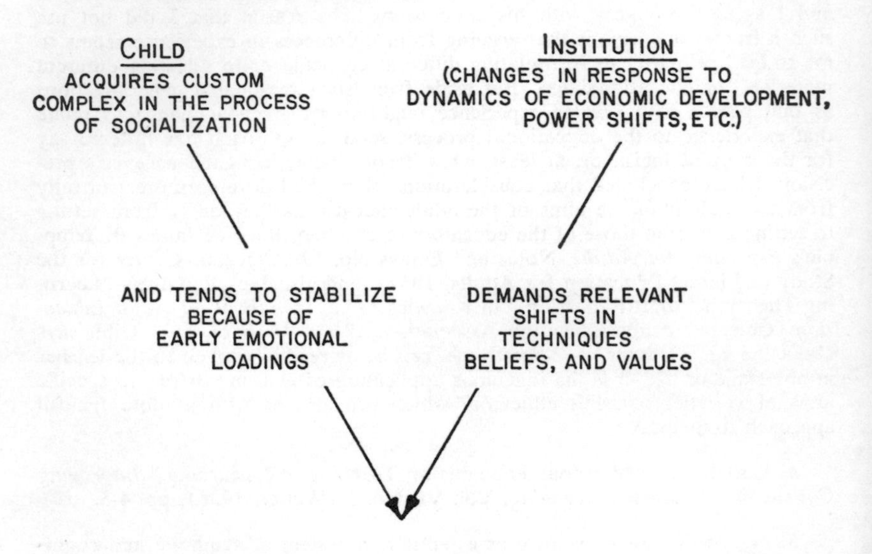

6. Another possible set of categories, of course, and one frequently used by adult educators, is based on special groups in the population—young adults, the aging, and the like. This conception seems to me useful mainly as an administrative convenience, and I have restricted the framework to the four worlds of experience suggested in the text in order to keep the conceptual framework as clear as possible. It fits the available interest areas of adult educators fairly well; see, for example, Part IV: "Program Areas in Adult Education," *Handbook of Adult Education, op. cit.*, pp. 393-550.

7. Martha Wolfenstein, "The Emergence of Fun Morality," *Journal of Social Issues,* Vol. VII, No. 4 (1951).

8. The general issue here is not entirely peripheral to the problem of method, because it involves the formalization of training processes for low-level skills which once were transmitted directly from one person to another in very informal contexts. The clearest example I know is the course successfully given for many years at a midwestern university to train people in church ushering, which is a remarkable illustration of how far the role of adult education can go in a society in which institutions are rapidly changing. If the tempo of social change is slow, institutions can take care of their own training needs. Fathers can transmit their vocational skills to their children, and some children will pick up the know-how of church ushering as they grow up attending the same church in the same town. If institutions change, and the personnel in them shift rapidly, too, then formalized training begins to seem necessary. The question is whether a total adjustment to such blind social demand does not make dangerously trivial the educational institutions and divert the energies of their personnel.

Where such programs are justified as contributing income needed for self-supporting divisions, one can hardly argue with them. But often enough, adult educators argue for them as providing an educational contact with a clientele; "starting where they are" it is often put. Partly as an expression of a strain of social evangelism which entered adult education in its early years, and partly as a reflection of the egalitarianism basic in American values, this doctrine has its usefulness, but not if it becomes the sole criterion for programming in adult education. The field as a whole would benefit from a somewhat clearer division of labor among its separate institutions than it now enjoys and, more important, from an agreement on some rough criteria for the involvement of specialized educational resources. There are many areas of needed training which are best handled by using simple "apprenticeship" methods, and there seems to be no reason why we should not encourage their use.

9. The argument for the inclusion of science in any general education curriculum needs, it seems to me, considerable scrutiny, as the questions raised in this section indicate. All members of the society, presumably, ought to be free of superstitions involved in cause and effect relationships in nature, but my guess is that by high-school graduation most adolescents these days are as rational about nature as they are going to be. We must suppose that there must be a greater virtue in the study of science beyond this, and it is often suggested that knowledge of science helps people become more rational, that practice in the rigorous scientific approach to phenomena and to the generalization of their relationships spreads to other areas of the individual's life. No one, of course, *really* believes this happens, and the general principle is seldom supported by someone's experience with some actual group of scientists who approach the discussion of politics or socialized medicine with a great show of rationality and the spirit of inquiry. Indeed, the intrusion into science itself of related social problems of belief or value may be sufficient to modify not only rationality but basic scientific attitudes. Some scientists with considerable background in biology, for example, believe firmly in the constitutional racial inferiority of the Negro and argue for it on the historical basis that no Negro civilization ever produced spontaneously a complicated, industrial culture. On the whole, I tend to view with some equanimity the relative absence in adult education of programming in this area, until someone presents a more convincing case for a need for it.

For evidence of a recent revival of interest in this area, however, see the summary of recent activity in science programming in the newsletter, "Continuing Education for Adults," of January 29, 1963, published by the Clearinghouse of the Center for the Study of Liberal Education for Adults.

Eric Ashby does a fascinating dissection of the problem of how much science the administrator of scientific research enterprises should know, in "The Administrator: Bottleneck or Pump," *Daedalus,* Vol. I, No. 2 (Spring, 1962).

Ashby argues wittily that the administrator needs to know about scientists rather than about science, and the same may be true of the layman in general.

10. Although some of the associative theories of learning do not stress the need for the learner to be active, all cognitive theories do. The learner must be involved and active, either in practice or in an active search for meaning, a point which will be considered in greater detail in Chapter II. The most important drawback to the passive learning role is suggested not by learning theory but by the work done on memory and perception; what the student retains is a selection determined by his preconceptions. See Frederick Bartlett's *Remembering* (Cambridge: Cambridge University Press, 1954), or the section devoted to perception in any social psychology text.

11. I am aware that the categories of aims suggested here are not the usual ones, nor are they justifiable on any particular philosophical grounds. In the *Handbook of Adult Education* Powell and Benne argue for the existence of two major schools, the *developmental* and the *rationalist,* with community development and group dynamics falling in the first, and liberal arts, humanities, great books, and the like falling in the second category. They freely admit that this distinction omits from consideration most of what goes on in adult education, which considerably reduces its usefulness (see pp. 41-53). For other attempts to categorize aims in adult education over the past ten years, see Chapter II, "Philosophy and Issues," in *The Review of Educational Research,* Vol. XXIX, No. 3 (June, 1959). I would defend the sheer empiricism of the approach in this chapter on two grounds. One is that a book addressed generally to the improvement of methods in the field as a whole must relate its framework to the broadest possible activities in the field. Secondly, it seems to me that a fatal tendency in adult education has been toward a "premature crystallization of theory" (the phrase is Norman Maier's) which invariably isolates or rules out large segments of activity. I think we have a considerable way to go in developing as a recognizable field of education before such clear definition becomes either feasible or desirable.

12. Reprinted by permission from Robert J. Havighurst and Betty Orr, *Adult Education and Adult Needs* (Chicago: Center for the Study of Liberal Education for Adults, 1956).

2

●●●●●●●●●●●●●●●●●●●●●●●

SOME CRUCIAL CONDITIONS FOR LEARNING

> I say moreover that you make a great, a very great mistake, if you think that psychology, being the science of the mind's laws, is something from which you can deduce definite programmes and schemes and methods of instruction for immediate classroom use. Psychology is a science, and teaching is an art; and sciences never generate arts directly out of themselves. An intermediary inventive mind must make the application, by using its originality.
>
> WILLIAM JAMES, *Talks to Teachers on Psychology*

Definitions of subject-matter areas and educational aims on a grand scale must, sooner or later, be made realistically usable; if we have defined those aims primarily as change in behavior, then we need some assurance that adult education's resources and skills can bring about such changes. This chapter, consequently, turns from the general to the very specific act of inducing behavioral change in humans.

Most of what we do know about learning applies equally well to skills of physical action and intellectual behavior, but since our methods of teaching motor skills are far more effective than those we develop to teach cognitive processes, the concentration here will be on the latter. If we taught the skills of logical analysis as carefully and as well as we teach dancing and swimming, adult education's methodological problems would all be solved.

For the purposes of this chapter and the next, *cognitive behavior* means the individual's response to the flow of information coming to him through his senses, how he selects from the flow those items to which he pays attention, how he applies meaning to it, and how he manipulates it. Part of this working with the flow of stimuli coming to one's senses consists in feelings about it, for which a useful term is *sentiments,* the feeling tone associated with our beliefs and values. In very general terms, education addresses itself to the problem of changing cognitive responses and their related sentiments. It is crucial, at the outset, to investigate the conditions under which such changes are likely to occur, so that in later considerations of specific program formats and methods we can be both realistic and creative; the best way to begin is with at least a brief look at basic learning experimentation and theory.

Psychologists approach the problems of how people acquire new and appropriate responses (how they learn) with two different major assumptions which have in the past created two theoretical camps, often totally opposed to one another but at times able to find common ground in their explanations of the facts of the learning process.[1] The behaviorists, the dominant school among academic circles, stress the bonds created, in one way or another, between the repeated association of a particular stimulus with a specific response to it; one controls learning behavior largely by controlling the nature or the strength of the relation between the stimulus and the correct responses. Cognitive theorists, on the other hand, insist that individuals do not merely "respond" but that they react to and organize the information which comes to them, and that it is in this shaping of the environmental stimuli that one finds the most significant fact for learning. Consequently, they stress the control of the conditions under which stimuli are presented and whether they help the individual to make the proper organization.

SKINNER AND THE REINFORCEMENT SCHEDULE

The work of B. F. Skinner at Harvard illustrates the ideas of the first school neatly and more simply than many others, and it is particularly interesting because it is currently being applied directly to public-school classroom methods. It has the admirable simplicity of almost totally ignoring the environment and the nature of the stimulus and concentrating on the response aspect of the learning situation. Skinner starts from the principle that any live organism will tend to repeat a particular bit of behavior if that behavior has been accompanied or followed by a reward, or reinforcement. He argues, therefore, that the way to teach an organism to do anything is to wait for the random occurrence of the particular behavior you ultimately want (or arrange for it to occur), reward it immediately, and keep rewarding it until the organism performs it habitually.

One sees the meaning of this principle most clearly by watching some of Skinner's ingenious and spectacular laboratory demonstrations with animals. Thus, a pigeon in one of his cages is randomly going through its ordinary repertoire of movements—pecking, turning, and walking, as pigeons will. Skinner decides to teach it to turn around clockwise in a complete circle and waits for the pigeon to make even a slight movement in such a direction. In the course of moving about, the pigeon does turn slightly clockwise, and the experimenter immediately presses a button which operates a shutter covering the food box in the cage. The pigeon has the opportunity to eat furiously for a second or two before the shutter comes down again. The same turn, slightly more pronounced now, occurs very shortly thereafter, in confirmation of the principle, and again is immediately rewarded. The next time it comes sooner and more pronouncedly, now almost a half turn, and is again rewarded. Within a few minutes the pigeon is turning a complete circle in the desired direction and happily gorging itself at intervals in the food box.

Skinner and his enthusiastic students consider this process the model for human learning as well, although they have had some difficulty accounting adequately for many of the complexities of the human animal and the social context of his learning experience. Indeed, the recent surge of interest and activity in teaching machines developed directly from the kind of work described above. These machines, which a later chapter will consider more thoroughly, depend on three conditions: first, they present materials which have been broken into many small steps; second, they demand from the student some response, an answer to a question or the filling in of a blank in a sentence; and third, the machine itself immediately reinforces the correct response by telling the student that his response *was* correct. The reward consists in the pleasure of being right. The machine is a sort

of indefatigable and unemotional tutor, constantly questioning the student and saying "correct" when he makes the appropriate response.

COGNITIVE APPROACH

As there are many different sub-schools among the behaviorists, so there are a number of cognitive theories. The important characteristic of the former is an emphasis on the role of reinforcement, of the latter an interest in learning as problem-solving and in how the individual "goes beyond the information given" in approaching a set of data or a learning task. The most widely-known early experiments within this school were those conducted with primates by Kohler. In a typical one, the experimenter hung a bunch of bananas from the ceiling of a cage, out of reach of the animal, and he also provided a few boxes carelessly disposed in the cage. The animal tried jumping for the fruit only to be frustrated; it was out of reach of any point to which he could climb as well. At some point, however, he "saw" suddenly that if he stood on one of the boxes directly under the fruit he might reach it easily, and without wasted motion he pulled the box over and got the reward.

This immediate, sudden grasp of the solution of a problem the gestaltists call *insight* and suggest that it consisted of a rearrangement of the significant elements in a situation into a successful organization. The boxes were no longer nailed-together-pieces-of-wood-for-playing-with, but things-which-if-I-stand-on-them-will-permit-me-to-reach-high. Furthermore, when the animal who had developed such a principle was put into another, slightly different problem situation, he applied the principle immediately, without going through trial and error again. What he had learned was the *principle,* he had learned it without practice, and he did it by going beyond the information given and by selecting from and giving structure to that information.

The early psychologists of the cognitive school never made much of an effort to apply their work to formal education beyond suggesting that we ought to present material to the student in a form which encourages him to find the relevant principles which organize it meaningfully. Recently several experimenters have turned seriously to the study of the process of thinking as primarily one of recognizing or forming concepts. In this view, the way in which we basically and habitually "go beyond the information given" to our senses is by grouping them and from then on remembering and working with the group name, or concept. Every time we see an apple we do not go through the fatiguing and time-consuming process of puzzling out what it is and what it is good for; we long ago learned that most things which are red and relatively round and have a certain aroma and a particular set of indentations are to be classed in a group of phenomena called apples. From then on we can assume without further effort that when we encounter one of these objects, it will be good to eat, juicy and crisp-textured, and will have a host of other qualities.

Concepts, we may suppose, are developed at first as hypotheses; the first apple we eat encourages us to hypothesize tentatively that an object with the attributes of redness, roundness, and particular aroma will have the accompanying good effects of taste, crispness, and so on. Each time we eat another apple it either confirms the hypothesis, negates it, or changes it. We soon learn, for example, to modify the hypothesis to include the possibility that the color might be yellow.[2]

Though we would be unable to survive without such concepts, a difficulty, which the adult educators readily recognize, arises out of the operation of these hypotheses. The semanticists see this difficulty in the uncritical application of verbal symbols to the particular phenomenon; the therapist sees it in the unrealistic responses of the emotionally disturbed (for example, the child who operates on the hypothesis that all people are to be included in the group things-that-are-going-to-hurt-me). On the social scene we have to deal with people who, once they recognize the single attribute "critical of U.S. foreign policy," put the article or book or person immediately into the class of "communist." This approach now obviously begins to be of practical importance applied to the educational enterprise, which particularly for adults requires for success the presence of "open hypotheses" rather than "closed hypotheses."

SIX CONDITIONS FOR LEARNING

Both the behaviorist and the cognitive approaches have much to contribute to the operation of programs on a broad scale. The cognitive theorists tend in general to pay little attention to processes of acquiring and retaining information or to concepts which have already been developed, in favor of having the learner, through search, build concepts himself. But, however demonstrably better it may be to stress methods which force the learner to discover the concept himself, few educational institutions in the society are prepared to spend the time required to do so. The approach also tends to neglect the importance of practice to the development of intellectual skills.

On the other hand, the behaviorists insist on a description of motivation in the learning process which is difficult to apply sensibly to adult learning. In their view, learning may be traced to some fundamental imbalance in the body which sets up a need; such a need-state sets the stage for learning, because its satisfaction provides the conditions of reinforcement necessary to the learning.[3] It is difficult to reconcile the obvious importance of such human motives as curiosity, or what one psychologist calls the manipulation drive, with such theories, or to explain the common instances in which adults learn very complicated things indeed in only one exposure. There is some evidence for believing that the kind of learning which is described so adequately by the stimulus-response model occurs at the early stages of human development, but that at higher levels we must shift gears and adopt an explanation which is distinctly closer to the cognitive model. This, at any rate, is the view which this book proposes to take, as it draws eclectically upon whatever work in the field of learning seems useful to define below the conditions which encourage learning.

Condition I. The Student Must Be Adequately Motivated To Change Behavior. All educational institutions concern themselves over the problem of what impels their students to learn. Learning is work, sometimes very hard work, and it looks easy only when it is either not going on at all and the students are merely being entertained, or when motivation is so high that the work involved in the learning task becomes enjoyable as well as arduous.[4] Adult educators must worry about it on two levels: first, because theirs is a voluntary institution and people must be motivated to come in the first place, and second, because once they participate, they need motivation to change appropriate behavior.

There is no question that some of the important motivations of the first kind have little to do with a desire for learning itself. Neither, of course, do they in formal education, where the desires for social mobility, higher status, and material rewards must be very strong indeed to drive youth through the hard grind of professional school. Vocational programs for adults draw people by appealing to essentially the same motivation, but we have recognized for a long time the rather more complicated nature of the needs which people seek to satisfy by enrolling in programs in some of the other areas.

It is usually the administrator who concerns himself with such needs in the recruiting of students, but the methodologist needs to ask about them: what is their strength and what their appropriateness to the actual learning task? Motives which are strong enough to bring an individual into the learning situation may be too weak by far to keep him in it for very long or to keep him at work; the very high drop-out rate in adult programs which are not vocationally based is in part a measure of that motivation strength. By far the weakest seems to be pure intellectual curiosity, a lusting after knowledge for knowledge's sake, probably because such a motivation is relatively easily satisfied or well enough met for most people by less formal and briefer experiences.

There is a fair amount of nonsense talked about some of the other motives which lead people into adult education programs, as though these extrinsic drives were somehow dishonorable. The two most common of these probably are the need for human relationship and group belonging and the desire for status recognition. Many people appear to enroll in programs at least partially because they are lonely and want the warmth of relating to others on a level which does not threaten too much closeness. Others come in response to a wish to approximate some image they have of the intellectual, a wish arising, perhaps, out of the very real connection between schooling and upward social mobility and continually reinforced by the sham worlds created by advertising and the mass media. In both cases the motive often bears little immediate relationship to the kind of learning which the program aims at, but it serves to bring the individual into the field; whether his motives change to more appropriate ones depends at least in part on instructional skills.

Another general category of motivation is one which often seems more directly relevant than those above, but, the academic world being what it is, sometimes turns out to be just as irrelevant. Wayne Leys[5] has described it as well as it can be:

> There is another kind of interest that is not an interest in knowledge for its own sake . . . it is an interest in *rationality*. . . . I refer to the adult's desire to talk things over. This desire has been misrepresented as a desire to learn something in the ordinary sense of learning. It is not that. The adults want to clarify their thoughts, but not as scholars clarify things. They want to talk out their worries and untangle their deliberations. . . .

This motivation, too, needs to be transmuted into one more appropriate to the educational contexts in which it often appears, but such transformation requires direct, conscious effort.

Part of the difficulty lies in the vagueness of the term *motivation* itself, which leads us often to think of it as a sort of force of nature which cannot be understood or analyzed. But one can approach it analytically and begin to deal with manageable parts of the problem. For any general learning task, for example, we might suppose that there are many identifiable psychological forces, some encouraging the student to change in relevant ways, others acting negatively either to lead him out of the field altogether or to resist change. Planners and teachers seldom have much control over the presence of positive forces, but they can do a good deal to identify and try to remove the resistant forces.[6]

In many adults resistances often take such forms as these: the student is not involved and thus is unable to see the learning task as personally important or significant; the student's objectives have little to do with the instructor's objectives—we have all known students who really are attending another class while sitting in ours; the student's fear of failure results in an unwillingness to attempt certain kinds of changes; the student may find change itself threatening, not only because he might fail in achieving the desired behavior, but because his habitual behavior is part of him and consequently valued—people tend to see any attempt to change them as an attack, which inevitably arouses defensiveness.

The presence of such resistant forces explains a great many of adult education's major problems. The vocational area is the only one in which motivational forces outside the learning field itself are strong enough to overcome the resistances within it. If instructors in the other areas do not deal adequately with the resistances, there is nothing to help them, and the group easily disintegrates or lapses into passivity. One can see, too, why adult students generally tend to prefer methods which permit them to be passive; such a state arouses none of the conflicts which may lie beneath the surface waiting to be mobilized by the challenge of real learning achievement.

The really challenging question, then, is what can be done in organizing the experience itself which will reduce the resistances to change inherent in learning. We can do some things relatively directly, for example, in both small-group and large-group situations, by making the materials as relevant as possible to the live concerns of the students, thus increasing the chance for individual involvement. The experienced adult education teacher tends to do this without much conscious effort. Or he tries to bridge the gap between his objectives and the student's different ones by organizing activities in such a way as to increase the possibility that the student will begin to derive satisfaction from new ways of behaving before relinquishing his previous patterns. Thus, if we want people to be able to suspend judgment while carrying on critical analysis, it is possible to have them do so as part of the rules of the game and hope that some will find it rewarding in itself.

But we have available to us another resource which is often overlooked or used without much skill: the forces of the learning group itself arising out of its attractiveness for the members of the group, and the quality of their interaction. There is no question at all of the power of the group to reduce individual resistances to change if properly mobilized; but pious insistence on rituals of informality and first-name calling will not necessarily ensure its mobilization on the side of effective learning.

Two conditions at least are necessary for harnessing group forces, the first of which is that the opinion of the group as a whole must *matter* to the individuals who compose it; technically speaking, it must be a *cohesive* group. We all belong to many groups membership in which we would relinquish at the drop of a hat, and these groups have little influence on our behavior or attitudes; but we do tend to conform to the expectations of those groups which we value. Many adult education enterprises have attempted to make use of this principle, with varying success.

Often their informal groups of students achieve cohesiveness, but the emerging group goals emphasize social rather than learning tasks. Thus, the second requisite for the successful use of group forces is that the group develop shared values which are hospitable to educational change in the desired direction. One sees this process at work in the academic world in an extreme form among graduate students; the culture of the graduate department develops as a number of settled expectations about how a successful physicist or psychologist behaves and how he feels about important issues; the young graduate student senses that he had better change to conform to this image or that somehow he will never get his degree. And change he does.

One might suppose that this motivational force could only be tapped for small, face-to-face groups, but this is not necessarily so. It is possible that the audience of the early morning television programs on "Sunrise Semester," for example, have a feeling of group membership with their fellow early risers; several adult programs which use television organize the mass audience into small, cohesive listening groups. We need to experiment with a variety of methods for making use of whatever group cohesiveness we find, whether it appears in our small groups or in mass audiences, and find ingenious ways of encouraging group adoption of values favorable to behavior change and growth.

Condition II. The Student Must Be Aware of the Inadequacy of His Present Behavior. When humans are faced with the necessity of learning a wholly new set of behaviors, they often accept it with equanimity. The child learning to walk doesn't feel badly about not knowing but plunges eagerly into the attempt to master the new skill. The adult who sets out to learn calculus for the first time is not ashamed of his ignorance—he has just never learned it before. The problem of learning new behaviors of this kind begins with an acceptance of the need to do so, requires an ability to deal with inadequacy during practice, but seldom involves any initial emotional difficulty.

But adult education, by its nature, deals much of the time with changing behavior patterns which are already organized and habitual. To say that a major condition for learning is that the student recognize the inadequacy of his present behavior is to put in particular and concrete form the problem of motivation for this kind of learning. The major resistance to change in this context is the defensiveness aroused on behalf of already established behaviors, and the fundamental requirement for success is the provision of sufficient security for the student to permit him to relax his defensive posture.[7]

We need to face squarely at some point, however, that defensiveness sometimes is realistically rooted in the incapacity of the individual for the particular achievement level which a given program has set for its students. This problem is seldom discussed in adult education circles, partly because it offends our basic democratic values to exclude some people from participation in an educational program and often because it is unpolitic to do so.[8] The dilemma has been a chronic one for the public schools, of course, ever since schooling for all was accepted as a principle of the democratic society we claimed to be, but long and bitter experience with the problem has forced most public schoolmasters to recognize its reality and the necessity to deal with it. It is hard to escape from that reality, that substantial differences in learning capacity do exist among people and that the quality of the educational experience is affected by too wide a range of such difference. If we are unwilling or unable to screen those who come to our programs, then we somehow must provide for the presence of wide variations. It is not enough to say, as we often do, that everyone will develop according to his capacity, some more, some less, because if the level of the experience is pitched too high, the less capable might find it only a terrible frustration, and if too low, the most capable will find it boring. We must plan the activities themselves to provide rewarding experiences for both groups.

However, aside from this somewhat separate issue of individual capacity, it is clear that we must find ways of dealing with the more common defensiveness aroused by the threat of change, which appears rather differently in each of the life areas with which adult education deals. Thus, a good deal of the formal instruction for adults in the vocational area teaches new skills and consequently has to meet little defensiveness. But a growing number of programs are attempting to change established patterns: supervisory behavior, teaching methods, the attitudes of teachers. The defenses aroused here by the suggestion of inadequacy are very powerful indeed, anchored as they are in primary economic maintenance needs which are in modern society a relatively constant source of insecurity.

In programs of this kind, instructors who try the logical-sounding plan of asking people, for example, what their problems are in dealing with their subordinates may get nothing in response but a sort of bland, "Problems? Who in the world has problems?" Or he might tap an apparently inexhaustible catalog of problems having to do with the way the organization is set up, the impossible superiors one has, the laziness and incompetency of one's subordinates, and the exasperating stupidity and difficulty of one's clientele. All of which may be true, but none of these people are in the class or at the institute, and the only behavior we can readily change directly is the student's.

Instruction must be exceedingly sensitive and flexible in this kind of situation if it is to succeed in helping students to recognize their own inadequacy. Some groups are willing to do so directly, but others need to approach much more indirectly the analysis of what constitutes adequacy in their particular context. Case studies from some not-too-closely connected field might be a better start for some groups; or, if the particular instructor happens to be skilled enough, he can start by accepting the group's definition of their problem as belonging primarily to "all those other people" and help them to arrive at some insight into their own part of the problem.

In this area even instruction in the more impersonal skills is very threatening. It is easy enough to talk about the process of decision making in an objective way, but to ask a group of executives to agree that their ability to make decisions needs improving is to suggest inevitably that they are not performing their most important function well enough. Here again we may need to start at a point somewhat removed from circumstances with which they identify themselves.

Behavior in the personal and social world, and the learned meanings on which we base it, is anchored in the early developmental circumstances of the individual or to very significant events in later growth and maturity. Voting behavior can be accounted for to a considerable extent by the party affiliation of one's family; we are apt to be more suspicious of foreign nations if we grew up in one region rather than another; our settled opinions about human nature and our hypotheses about how to deal with other people form not only at early stages but in very definite forms.

Although inadequacy in this area can be just as threatening as in the world of work, the defenses against perceiving the inadequacy are somewhat different, often consisting of an unshakable conviction of our own correctness and a puzzlement over how any one could have fallen so miserably in error as those who do not see the matter our way. One has only to contemplate the difficulties of making a first approach to peoples' beliefs and sentiments about lower-class members of other nationality or skin color to appreciate the magnitude of the problem in general.

Perhaps the most important problem to be solved in helping students to see their need for change and growth in the social and interpersonal area is the inability of some instructors or lay leaders to avoid the tone of moral condemnation as they deal with beliefs and attitudes. This creates a pressure which can only lead to a stiffening of resistance. Evidence from the field of intergroup relations education suggests instead that people need to feel that their present feelings are accepted, even if not agreed with, before they can proceed to a rational examination of their consistency or their consequences.

Adult education in the arts faces much easier problems in creating this initial tension. Indeed, most people come to such programs with very conscious feelings of inadequacy; if they had not already overcome the common defense—". . . but I know what I like"—they are not likely to enroll in the first place.

Arts programs tap a very powerful motivational force, however, which other areas do not have available to them in the same sense. "Proper" behavior in this field, an interest in the fine arts, museum- and theater-going, well-expressed appreciation, and the like, are linked to upper-class status. People who aspire to social-class mobility, consequently, have little difficulty in perceiving their present inadequacy in relation to the arts because it is one of a complex of behaviors which they must adopt in order to move upward. We adopt the values of the class above in anticipation of moving into it later, beginning to change ourselves into images acceptable by those who we hope will later be our class peers.

Science programming, on the other hand, meets what constitutes almost a built-in inadequacy. If it deals with new developments in science, thus enabling it to attract the science buff, it deals with students who realize and accept readily their present inadequacies and are capable of dealing with them. If it is pitched at lower levels of competence, the students who come also accept their inadequacy cheerfully; part of the folklore of American schools is the dictum that science is difficult for all of us non-genius folks.

Condition III: The Student Must Have a Clear Picture of the Behavior Which He Is Required To Adopt. Here is the heart of the matter, for, if people do not know what kind of behavior their new learning is to result in, how can we expect them to achieve it? For adult education in particular, there are a number of problems related to the presentation of such models; some we share with all other educational fields; one at least is peculiarly ours.

PROBLEMS OF ABSTRACTNESS. Where the behavior model one is teaching is at the lowest level of abstraction, a skill involving mainly muscular coordination, for example, there is little difficulty in presenting it. Watch a golf instructor teaching a person to use a putter; he demonstrates with his own body the proper stance and the position of the head and calls his student's attention to the way he holds the club and the most effective movements of the wrist. He can, if he wishes, dispense with words altogether in presenting his model, although they help a good deal in focusing attention on its significant parts.

At a somewhat higher level of abstraction we also do a fairly good job of modeling the desirable behavior in many vocational programs. Good examples abound particularly in such business courses as insurance fundamentals, where the object is to train people new to the business. The instructor is invariably a skillful insurance salesman, and he knows with a considerable degree of precision what constitutes effective behavior. If an aspect of that behavior includes the ability to apply accepted principles of insurance coverage to complex individual cases, as indeed it must, he demonstrates the steps an agent goes through, pointing out the significant features of what he is doing as he goes along.

We do a consistently poor job, however, at the stratospheric levels of abstraction at which we commonly work. A sociologist giving a special course for a group of labor leaders, for example, might well be interested in increasing their awareness of the complexity of the social judgments they commonly make about events; the behavior which must be modeled here is the reflective habit of taking account of a number of social perspectives on the event, of asking how the perceptions of a variety of social groups appear to be influenced by their peculiar position in the society. But under the pressure of time and the belief that the important pedagogical task is to "cover ground," the behavior which the instructor tends to model can only be described as "ground-covering behavior."

Similarly, how many of us have observed at one time or another a psychologist telling a group of mothers with a great positiveness which barely hides a certain amount of contempt that their behavior toward their children ought to be accepting. It is hard to see where the audience can find out what "accepting behavior" looks like. The field of interpersonal relations, however, does have available to it an extraordinary resource—the film—for the purpose under discussion, and it is used by some adult educators with great skill and ingenuity.

The arts often do a very skillful job of presenting desirable models, too. The teacher who analyzes a poem before a group says, in effect, "Notice now what cues I watch for in the language and the way in which I search for meaning and relate the elements of the poem to that central meaning." One of the most significant aspects to this kind of teaching, as well as some of the best of the human relations programs, is that the model is presented *consciously* and deliberately as something which the student knows he is later to do himself.

It is hard to overemphasize the importance of the student's need to be sharply aware of the fact that he is now being introduced to a kind of behavior which he must later adopt, because we commonly assume that people somehow "catch" the meaning we wish them to acquire from an activity we involve them in. But there is an accumulation of evidence from a variety of sources to suggest that this is far from the fact. The issue is one closely related to the problems of transfer of training in learning psychology: the extent to which people are able to transfer abilities learned in one context to another different context. The idea of transferability of training became somewhat disreputable after modern psychologists proved incorrect the notions of "developing mental faculties"; training in mathematics helped a person do math but had little to do with making him a more rigorous thinker in other fields.

Some more recent evidence suggests, however, that transfer is possible under conditions which encourage the formulation of some verbal generalization or principle.[9] One need only extend the meaning of such evidence one step further to suggest that, on the highly complex cognitive level at which much of adult education operates, people must see clearly what it is precisely that they *are* supposed to be learning. The claim that adults learn about democracy, for example, merely by being involved in an activity in which they must help develop group consensus about some problem is a most unlikely one.

PROBLEMS OF COMPLEXITY. The most common difficulty, however, and the one with the most drastic consequences, is that beyond the skills of muscular coordination we seldom define our learning objectives with enough specificity to make them readily perceivable by our students. Returning to the previous example of golfing, it is easy to see that although competence consists in a mastery of a whole battery of complex skills, both instructors and students ordinarily have a clear idea of what each of the interlocking separate skills looks like. Each is therefore amenable to separate demonstration and practice at appropriate points.

Many of the cognitive changes which every one of the areas in adult education stresses in one way or another are enormously complex but seldom specified in any detail. We often undertake, for example, to improve the skills of making judgments as though this were a unitary behavior, when, in fact, it involves at least these very different ones: (1) an awareness of our own prejudices, values, and psychological sets involved in the particular issue about which we are to make the judgment; (2) the ability to control these at least to the extent of temporarily suspending their full play; (3) a range of skills involved in assessing the validity and reliability of evidence bearing on the issue; and (4) an ability to discriminate among the various elements involved in the issue in order to sort them into categories of their significance to the issue. Faced with such a complex series of behaviors, there is little reason to wonder why so few courses or programs succeed to any significant extent in showing improvement in their students. The next chapter will attempt to take the most common cognitive models in adult education and analyze them into the specific sub-behaviors which compose them.

THE PROBLEM OF VEHICLE. The question of how we should present the behavior model still remains, and it is one that provides some problems peculiar to adult education. The captive, docile pupil of primary and secondary schools and the competitive, highly motivated student in both undergraduate and graduate programs can be induced to do a great deal of concentrated work at something which he does not at the time see as particularly relevant. The adult student, except those enrolled in regular undergraduate university programs for remedial reasons, insists on immediately relevant activity. "If the program deals with international affairs, why aren't we discussing these affairs," he is likely to demand. "It's a free country and everyone is entitled to his own opinion, so let's just express them." We can seldom induce him to read much, carefully and analytically, because his participation is almost always a peripheral part of a busy life.

Recognition of such a state of affairs leaves us with little recourse but to use meeting time for the important business of presenting models or of helping the group develop them through rigorously controlled discussion. Fortunately, the range of pedagogical techniques for such an activity is wide; demonstration, role play, and case analysis, supplemented by lectures or controlled group discussion, can be adapted for a great variety of adult education formats, and for even such a remote relation as the correspondent student the techniques of the teaching machine are useful and relevant to this problem.

Condition IV. The Student Must Have Opportunities To Practice the Appropriate Behavior. It is remarkable that a principle so generally recognized in many fields of commonplace learning should be so often ignored in more formal educational contexts. Any observer of a wide range of adult programs, however, must conclude that in many cases it is the instructor or leader who is practicing the behavior which he wishes to get the student to adopt, rather than the student, who presumably is the one who needs it.

Part of the difficulty, of course, is time. Adults are often unwilling to practice on their own, generally speaking, and it is often exasperating to go through the slow process of working through exercises or examples in periods set aside for contributions from often expensive instructional talent. But practice is so crucial that we must begin to apply ingenuity to the solution of this problem, perhaps, as later chapters will suggest, by developing special kinds of material and by modifying some types of group activities already generally in use in adult education.

Furthermore, the concept of practice, once we go beyond the simple and obvious examples such as running a machine or learning to play golf, must involve the student in an active search for meaning. As Getzels[10] points out:

> Search for meaning may entail a period of fumbling akin to the so-called blind or random trial-and-error behavior. Present theories, however, hold that if the learner is truly searching for understanding in the problem situation and not only rote remembrance of steps in the solution, his apparent trial and error is not random and certainly not *blind*. He is making a real "try" for the solution and is not going through just any behavior of which he is capable. The try is the best hypothesis the learner is able to make at this particular time, and the instructor should not treat it with disdain—even when the hypothesis is wrong.

Thus, the student needs to have time and the opportunity to make mistakes as well as time to work through the behavior model correctly, which further complicates the difficulty cited earlier. Whatever the problems, however, the basic issue remains clear and emphatic: If we are interested in having the student learn, he must be *active* in some appropriate fashion; he must have the opportunity to do what he is supposed to learn to do.

Condition V. The Student Must Get Reinforcement of the Correct Behavior. During the course of practice the student must get feedback as continuously as possible about his progress. All theories of learning tend to subscribe to the idea that report on one's progress is necessary to continued motivation toward a learning goal and that reinforcement of the correct behavior increases the chances for its reappearance at a later point. Reinforcement, as a technical term, arose as a substitute for the idea of "reward," and, fortunately, we have available a range of psychological rewards to substitute for the grain and bananas of the animal experimenters.

Given an adequate level of motivation, both children and adults accept the knowledge of being correct as reinforcing. Indeed, without indulging in theoretical flights into the other-directedness of our culture, one might almost view with alarm the extent to which this can be demonstrated to be true. Recent studies, for example, create a situation in which the subject, sitting opposite the experimenter, is asked to talk about some personal experiences. If the experimenter, at well-defined intervals, nods his head, the subject keeps going; if, after a time, the experimenter stops nodding altogether, the subject tends to peter out and stop; the talking response is simply extinguished. All teachers, of course, are aware of how useful the nod is as feedback to a student that what he has said is correct; few of us, however, are aware of how necessary it is to provide some form of consistent reinforcement.

Condition VI. The Student Must Have Available a Sequence of Appropriate Materials. Here is a principle which bears with particular force on the education of adults because we too often tend merely to import materials from other educational contexts without regard to the particular needs of the adult student. Many adult programs use instructional help from the high school and the university, and the instructor is apt to bring with him the materials he is most familiar with. The university teacher in particular often assigns to a group of adults with a wide range of capabilities and personal objectives a most fantastic series of readings, inappropriate in both difficulty and quantity, apparently under the delusion that because they are mature one ought to treat them as graduate students. The most satisfactory development of materials, not surprisingly, has been done by agencies whose programs eliminate the trained teacher; the extraordinarily careful compilations of political readings and cases developed by the Foundation for Continuing Education is a case in point.

The need for intellectual appropriateness of material requires some amplification. The fault lies, often enough, not only in the assignment of impossible amounts of difficult reading material but in the failure to make clear to the student what the purpose of the reading is, what its relationship is to learning goals which he can comprehend and find personally meaningful. Some programs which have troubled to work through courses specifically for adults have, for an opposite example, re-developed the old method of *explication des textes* in a most satisfactory way.[11] The students read aloud in the group a difficult text and discuss, sentence by sentence, if necessary, the author's intention, the precise shades of meaning, and the structure of the idea or argument he is building. This process does not substitute for the broader discussion of the ideas of a particular writer, but it is excellent training in the several basic disciplines necessary and preliminary to good general discussion.

NOTES

1. The division of learning theorists into two camps is, of course, somewhat oversimplified, but it is a useful distinction often adopted in the literature. The reader interested in some further exploration might try Roby Kidd's recent *How Adults Learn* (New York: Association Press, 1959); the more serious student of adult education will find Hilgard a most useful introduction to the tangled world of learning theory [E. R. Hilgard, *Theories of Learning* (New York: Appleton-Century-Crofts, 1956)]. As I have tried to make clear in the text, it seems to me undeniable that the work on cognition has far more meaning for adult educators than the stimulus-response systems, and I suggest, therefore, Scheerer's very well-organized review of learning theory from the point of view of the cognitive theorists: M. Scheerer, "Cognitive Theory," in Lindzey's *Handbook of Social Psychology,* Vol. I (Reading: Addison-Wesley, 1954), pp. 91-142.

2. The view of the thinking process as essentially one of the categorization of sensory data is as old as the Greeks, but until recently the process was surprisingly little studied by modern psychologists. Bruner and his associates at Harvard revitalized the area in a five-year study of concept formation characterized by an exceptional ingenuity. Some of the findings of that study are cited in Chapter 3. Bruner went on to suggest applications to public-school education in a report he wrote of a conference on science education, a small book which has had more sudden impact on the thinking of public school people than any other I have ever seen. See J. S. Bruner, J. J. Goodnow, and George A. Austin, *A Study of Thinking* (New York: John Wiley, 1956); J. S. Bruner, *The Process of Education* (Cambridge: Harvard University Press, 1961). Also: E. C. Tolman, "Cognitive Maps in Rats and Men," *Psychological Review,* Vol. LV, No. 4 (1948).

3. One of the sharp areas of disagreement in learning theory is still the question of whether or not it must depend, directly or indirectly, on drive-reduction. The case for the irrelevance of such a theory for adult learning is made bitingly by Harlow: "There are logical reasons why a drive-reduction theory of learning, a theory which emphasizes the role of internal, physiological-state motivation, is entirely untenable as a motivational theory of learning. The internal drives are cyclical and operate, certainly at any effective level of intensity, for only a brief fraction of any organism's waking life. The classical hunger drive, physiologically defined, ceases almost as soon as food—or nonfood—is ingested. This, as far as we know, is the only case in which a single swallow portends anything of importance. The temporal brevity of operation of the internal drive states obviously offers a minimal opportunity for conditioning and maximal opportunity for extinction. The human being, at least in the continental United States, may go for days or even years without ever experiencing true hunger and thirst. If his complex conditioned responses were dependent upon primary drive reduction, one would expect him to regress rapidly to a state of tuitional oblivion. There are, of course, certain recurrent physiological drive states that are maintained in the adult. But the studies of Kinsey indicate that in the case of one of these there is an inverse correlation between presumed drive strength and scope and breadth of learning, and in spite of the alleged reading habits of the American public, it is hard to believe that the other is our major source of intellectual support. . . ." Harry F. Harlow, "Mice, Monkeys, Men, and Motives," *Psychological Review,* Vol. LX, No. 1 (1953), p. 25.

4. Harlow, in the same article cited in the previous note, points out that "there was as much evidence to indicate that a strong drive state inhibits learning as to indicate that it facilitates learning," and there is a fair amount of support for his opinion in the literature generally. The consequences of very strong drive states appear to be, as one would guess, a focusing and narrowing of interest to the particular satisfier of the drive and a neglect of every other feature of the field. It would not be too far off the track to suggest that an adult education analogue might be concentration of the adult degree student in business education on those courses which are relevant to the degree he needs and his impatience with what he often sees as the humanistic "frills."

5. Wayne A. R. Leys, "The Two Roles of the University in Adult Education," *Journal of Higher Education,* XXVI (January, 1955).

6. The approach and the terminology here are recognizably Kurt Lewin's conception of the force field. This view might suggest that we approach the adult student's motivation as a field of both positive psychological forces moving him toward the learning goal and negative ones taking the form of various resistances. The option of attempting to increase the force of the positive vectors, one we tend usually to take, often results only in increasing the opposing forces. Lewin's analysis, instead, leads one to try to remove the resistances.

The whole problem of the adult student's motivation, I am convinced, has been so far treated most superficially and needs re-examination in the light of somewhat more complex conceptions. Murphy's discussion of the affect of the early canalization of fairly broad drives deserves some study, for example, and even more so do McClelland's studies of the achievement motivation. As a field we tend to be about a generation behind the available body of information and theory relevant to our purposes in the behavioral sciences. See D. C. McClelland, *The Achieving Society* (New York: Van Nostrand, 1961); G. Murphy, *Personality* (New York: Harper, 1947); K. Lewin, *Resolving Social Conflicts* (New York: Harper, 1948).

7. For a discussion of this problem with specific reference to the training of adults, see L. Bradford and P. Sheats, "Complacency Shock as a Pre-requisite to Training," *Sociatry, 2*:1, *2*:38–48 (April, August, 1948).

8. The difficulty adult education programs have in setting up any sort of screening procedures arises from two sources: one is the financial necessity of getting as many students as we can for a program which must pay for itself; the other is the political embarrassment of asking sponsoring or cooperating organizations to screen their own members. So, we almost never introduce screening devices. Neither do the public schools, because by law they must accept all comers; but once the schools get their heterogeneous population, they proceed to recognize pedagogical realities by devising a wide variety of groupings to prevent the ability range from getting too unmanageable. In our case, it does not seem to me a necessary part of the democratic dogma to insist that somewhat dull-normal individuals be forced or lured into situations of intellectual demand which their own pride prevents them from leaving and in which they are miserable.

We should not confuse this issue of individual differences in what is essentially a verbal or conceptual capacity with the old argument about whether adults can learn or not. Though we know better, we often talk as though people learned only in special kinds of situations, and as though the rest of the time they were static dischargers of previous learnings. For years we defensively used the work of Thorndike in the thirties to *prove* that adults can learn, as though it were a momentous discovery to find that adults were able to commit nonsense syllables to memory almost as fast as a child can! The rapidity with which any normal adult on a new job learns the subtle and complex informal social systems of the new group to which he comes, a task which a social psychologist may spend weeks on; the ease with which we learn our way around a new town, both geographically and socially; the amount of information which the sports buff integrates and retains comfortably, on *one* reading, every time he reads a sports page; the concepts gained and the slight shifts in attitude arising from a talk with a stranger on a bus, a shopping trip, a movie, a family crisis—people do not move through such experiences without drawing conclusions, making generalizations, reaffirming or rejecting previously-held opinions, and storing and integrating relatively large amounts of information.

To ask the question *whether* adults learn, consequently, seems to me nonsensical. We do need, however, to ask what kind of facility with the special world of verbal symbol systems our particular program demands and to deal realistically, either before admission or after, with the corresponding range of ability of the students.

A symposium on adult learning sponsored by Syracuse University in the fall of 1962 focused a variety of contemporary views on the issues of the adult's capacity to learn, motivation, and similar topics. The conference papers will soon be available from University College of Syracuse University.

9. The professional reader interested in the problem of transfer should look at George Katona's classic study, *Organizing and Memorizing* (New York: Columbia University Press, 1940), and E. R. Hilgard's survey of learning theory cited previously. Hilgard and his colleagues did some follow-up work on Katona's experiments which introduces some notes of caution: see, for example, their article, E. R. Hilgard, R. D. Edgren, and R. P. Irvine, "Errors in Transfer Following Learning with Understanding," *Journal of Experimental Psychology,* Vol. 47, No. 6 (June, 1954). The optimistic view of this chapter toward the generalizability of learning is based on such relatively recent work as that reported in D. H. Lawrence and J. DeRivera, "Evidence for Relational Transposition," *Journal of Comparative and Physiological Psychology,* Vol. XLVII (1954), and particularly on Harlow's work with monkeys reported in "The Formation of Learning Sets," *Psychology Review,* Vol. LVI (January, 1949). The suggestion that in humans such transfer of learning is facilitated by the ability to make verbal formulation of the principle can be held only tentatively in view of such evidence as that in H. S. Stevenson, Ira Iscoe, and Claudia McConnell, "A Developmental Study of Transposition," *Journal of Experimental Psychology,* Vol. XLIX, No. 4 (April, 1955).

10. J. W. Getzels, *Learning Theory and Classroom Practice in Adult Education* (Syracuse: Syracuse University: University College, 1956), p. 5.

11. Galway Kinnel, The Basic Program at Chicago, *Notes and Essays No. 11* (Chicago: Center for the Study of Liberal Education for Adults, 1955).

3

SIGNIFICANT BEHAVIORAL CHANGES FOR ADULT EDUCATION

. . . Acting with an aim is all one with acting intelligently. To foresee a terminus of an act is to have a basis upon which to observe, to select, and to order objects and our own capacities.

JOHN DEWEY, *Democracy and Education*

Assuming the general validity of the scheme developed in the previous chapter, we can argue with some confidence for the importance of having clearly in mind some clear and definite model of the behaviors we are most interested in seeing our students change toward. In the absence of such a clear image we are likely to hope that any thing we do in the classroom which expresses our own needs at the time will somehow result in the students' learning what we wish them to. If we want to help people improve their ability "to think," but provide them with no opportunity to practice whatever behaviors we designate as part of that ability, it is no wonder that we end so often in frustration.

Adult educators, of course, have a wide variety of such behavioral objectives, working as they do in a field which is widely sensitive to public demand, and it would be impossible to do more than discuss generalities if the total range were to be considered here. Instead, this chapter selects five major sets of behaviors which, in relation to different bodies of subject matter or areas of human experience, adult educators most often cite as important learning objectives.

I. DEVELOPING INTERESTS

Interests, of course, are essentially emotional and consequently need a somewhat different approach than one can take to cognitive objectives. But, as Asch points out,[1] one can conceive of emotions as having a cognitive base: "To have an emotion is to perceive agents acting upon us or others, *i.e.*, to apprehend causal relations. Emotions are, as a rule, directed toward their perceived source—persons or objects. We are angry at, or because of, sorry about, happy over, grieving for, and so on. . . . Emotions are the way we react directly to the relations between given conditions and ourselves . . . they are immediate cognitions of the state of affairs of our motives. . . ."

That this is particularly true of the motives we call *interests* would be apparent if we followed a person about for a day and observed his behavior closely. Of the thousands of objects, people, and events which come within the range of his senses, only a tiny proportion will truly gain his attention; he will either ignore all the other phenomena or, if he must recognize their existence at all, will do so with a vacant eye, a restlessness, an air of obviously not being, in the beautifully precise French term, *engagé*. Real interest must have something in it of this ego-involvement, which is why actual behavioral observation at a superficial level often misses in reporting the true state of interest. The gentleman's attendance at the ballet is not necessarily an expression of interest in the dance but in the maintenance of a relationship with his wife; the hundreds of thousands of people who visited the Metropolitan Museum during the weeks following the purchase of the $2,300,000 Rembrandt were not necessarily interested in art.

What we see as interests in adults may lead back in devious ways to very early satisfactions of primary needs. The child's very early need for nourishment will at first be satisfied by any edible material, but the need will shortly become *canalized* in the direction of those particular foods which repeatedly bring relaxation of the tension created by the hunger.[2] He becomes a carrot-eating, a milk-drinking, a meat-eating child, rather than a rice-and-beans-eating child. Similarly, his particular immediate culture establishes a relatively narrow range of other satisfiers: faces, tones, pictures, physiological movements, and stories. Later motives, then, seem to depend on early selectivity of satisfiers and on the frequency of opportunity for the specific response, but it is not the sheer familiarity of a stimulus which is important; it is the satisfaction derived from it which must be emphasized.

Unlike conditioning, canalizations do not appear to be susceptible to extinction. A dog which has been conditioned to salivate to the sound of a tuning fork, because the sound has been presented repeatedly for a time in conjunction with food, will lose the response after enough presentations of the tone by itself. But men in an army camp will discuss the delights of a week-end at home endlessly, regardless of the time away from that satisfier. Canalizations which persist as part of the personality appear to go on without being satisfied for long periods of time; thus, Welles in his "Citizen Kane" has the old man on his death bed utter, as his last word, "Rosebud," which turns out at the end of the picture to be the trade name of the sled in which he delighted as a happy child.

Canalizations, formed early or late, seem to be free of interference with one another. A love of Bach does not destroy a love of Shakespeare, nor does it necessarily interfere with a delight in jazz. We appear to be able to form almost infinite numbers of canalizations in our search for specific satisfiers of what were once global and diffuse needs. Perhaps this arises in part from our ability to generalize or transfer already existing canalizations to others which resemble ones we already have. Lovers of New Orleans jazz find it possible to get new satisfactions from modern jazz, as indeed do Bach lovers, who find in it many of the same musical qualities. A person who likes one mystery story is likely to seek out new ones to read, even, as Thurber's American lady in England did, make to do with the murders in *Hamlet* when he can't find the real article.

New canalizations are constantly added, of course, as the individual grows and develops, but old ones, rather than disappearing, seem rather to be overlaid. The adolescent gives up his play with toys as childish and not appropriate to his new image of himself, but a quarter of a century later, when he buys a set of electric trains for his son, he may be found on the floor playing with them in utter absorption. Indeed, Murphy[3] suggests that the key issue in the area may relate to the involvement of the ego with particular satisfiers, that the infantile absorption with one's own physical self centrally influences all later canalizations. " 'I like it not only because I am used to it, *but because I was always fond of it. It is mine.* It is my own favorite book; my own favorite music; my own way of greeting people or of phrasing my thoughts.' "

Consequently, although it is true that there is room for an almost limitless number of canalizations, as soon as the self intrudes, another situation is created. "If I pride myself on my love of Beethoven, I may turn up my nose at all modern music, the appreciation of which might imply that I was giving up my idol or recognizing that I had missed something. 'I simply am not the kind of person that would like Shostakovich—I am a Beethoven sort of person.' Similarly, 'Give me a hot dog; I'm not the sort of guy that you find eating pink tea refreshments.' "[4]

If this is a fair statement of the problem of interests, then the adult educator may view his task as primarily one of helping individuals transfer an already existing interest to another which he might find more rewarding and of providing activities which will deepen and intensify present interests. The enormous advantage we have is that we deal with adults at a variety of developmental levels and as they are confronted with shifts in their social roles; if we are lucky enough, or perceptive enough, we can grasp and use the presence of the "teachable moment" in the life of our students. In the most general behavioral terms, such objectives can be stated as:[5]

The individual continues to read widely in the field or begins to read in new fields; he increases the level and scope of his reading in the field.
He participates in activities to which he was previously indifferent or hostile.
He seeks new learning experiences in the area.
He initiates discussion and attempts to persuade others to share his interests in the field.
He gives more time to thought about problems or issues in the field.
He changes his perspective on familiar concepts and activities and develops new modes of thinking about familiar problems.
He participates at a different level in activities in the area.
He attempts to make independent judgments in the area.

The specific methodological problems we face in achieving such objectives through the variety of formats characteristic of adult education will be discussed in succeeding chapters devoted to those separate situations; for the present, a few general observations may locate some of the general issues in the development of interests. Our professional dictum that "we must begin where people are" is excellent advice leading to a search for present interests which we can use to lead to other, more desirable ones. Too often, however, we end by "leaving them where they were." Program construction must specify the linkages between early interests and advanced ones. A good example is the discussion course Smith developed in literature;[6] he grouped a series of readings, short stories, poems, and plays around central enduring human themes such as war and peace, the battle of the sexes, and the like. But having provided a focus which people would grasp as related to their interests, he formulated a series of discussion questions which confronted them with the literary task of perceiving contrasts in the forms.

Furthermore, if we want to focus the amorphous interest of a student in political events on such specific interests as that of reading a particular type of material in the field, then it must be made easy for him to read that material consistently, so that it becomes a familiar activity and a satisfying one. It is not enough to assign such reading and then assume that the student's reading it, even if he does, will automatically create the desired end. It is much more likely to do so, for example, if he has the opportunity to discuss it with small groups of his fellow students with a prescribed end in view. If the experience proves satisfying, he is more likely to do such reading and subsequent discussion on his own.

II. CONCEPT ATTAINMENT

The act of *thinking* is made up of a number of complicated behaviors of very different type, and the task of specifying those behaviors is not an easy one. It is not made easier by the existence of a number of overlapping general categories involving the act of thought, such as problem-solving, decision-making, and judgment. In this chapter, the term "judgment" will be reserved for the behavior involved in giving phenomena different relative value weights in the act of making choices. "Thinking" is considered as two separate levels of process: the first is concept attainment, that is, the fundamental process of organizing our information about the world in such a fashion that we can *generalize* validly from our experience, and the second is problem-solving, the searching for acceptable solutions to problematic situations. To adopt this set of terms does not leave us unembarrassed by ambiguity, by any means; as the scientist searches for increasingly precise general statements about the natural phenomena he studies, he is, of course, engaged in problem-solving. On the whole, however, the ambiguity arises from a clear difference in emphasis, and need not confuse.

The ability to develop concepts and to use them flexibly is at the root of man's ability to think about the world, to use language, and to learn. James points out that the first actual step in the baby's becoming human is his beginning to *identify* objects by dimly recognizing that $Object_2$ today has the same attributes as $Object_1$ yesterday: "Hullo, thingumbob again!" A concept is a category or class invented to identify objects or events, any phenomena which have the same or equivalent attributes. There is obviously nothing new about this classifying and categorizing ability of man; Western philosophers have been discussing it since Aristotle, and the linguistic experts have lately joined the discussion. Despite the evident fact that conceptualizing lies at the basis of cognitive behavior, however, psychologists have done remarkably little exploration of the laws governing such behavior until the recent brilliant work by Bruner and his associates at Harvard.[7]

Bruner suggests that we categorize in a number of different ways and for a variety of reasons. We often classify things and events as equivalent because they *evoke similar feelings*, and indeed, many psychiatrists argue that psychotherapy is largely occupied with the task of bringing to verbal awareness such of those emotional categories as "people with these particular characteristics who always make me feel angry." Osgood's semantic differential technique,[8] which gives people the task of recording their feelings about any concepts desired by categorizing the feelings themselves into such adjective groupings as "happy-sad," "beautiful-ugly," and the like, has had some remarkable successes in picturing shifts during therapy of the patient's classification of feelings about important factors in his world.

Another large, and important, type of categorizing we do is intended to be *functional*. It identifies and groups those things which fulfill a particular task—"things strong enough and hard enough to hammer this nail with." This everyday conceptualizing activity may be our most flexible and common form, as we straighten out paper clips to clean our nails, improvise funnels out of sheets of flat paper, use lipsticks to write messages, and develop all the ordinary ingenuities and "making-dos" of life.

The third type is the construction of *formal categories* by specifying attributes required by members of a particular class. This activity is, of course, essentially the making of a science, but any living-room discussion of a political event, if it is not merely classifying the feelings of the participants, usually involves an attempt to set up some scheme of categories. Science itself begins with the act of classification, and indeed some, like zoology, seem still to consist mainly of the refinement and elaboration of the attributes which determine the categorizing of any specific natural phenomenon.

Such a basic classifying activity of science as the building of categories for natural phenomena moves through the construction of much more abstract categories to one of the great achievements of scientific thinking, the suggestion of categories for things which are not known to exist, the "empty category." Physicists postulated the existence of a variety of elements which were only theoretical concepts until methods were developed for getting evidence of their existence. The neutrino was postulated first on logical grounds, and so was Neptune. On a practical scientific level, every doctor who makes a diagnosis is, of course, doing a very important and complex act of categorizing: Are these symptoms, taken together, the attributes of the concept "cold" or of the concept "flu"?

Bruner suggests that the categorizing act achieves a variety of ends for the human organism. First, it reduces the complexity of our environment by categorizing as equivalent many of the different stimuli present around us. Second, categorizing provides us with a way of identifying phenomena; that odd noise in the night is "the house settling," but if it were "burglars prowling" we would be far from able to go back to sleep. Third, it helps us reduce the necessity for constant learning; the child does not have to learn anew each time that the white, sweet fluid is milk; if it exhibits the proper defining attributes, it *is* milk and therefore good to drink. A fourth achievement is that it provides direction for instrumental activity. It permits us to know *in advance* about appropriate actions to take. A particular series of physical symptoms are recognizable as a "cold" and we trot dutifully off to bed and drink liquids; banks lend money without security to individuals who exhibit the attributes they have come to label as "sound risks." A fifth achievement is that it helps us order and relate *classes* of events without the necessity of finding relations between individual ones. The child learns that "matches" will "cause" a set of events called "fires." Within such systems, once we have categorized an object we are able to go far beyond the specifics to construct a whole range of possibilities.

Viewed in this way, categorizing is the fundamental and crucial behavior through which what we call thinking and learning proceed, and a knowledge of how the process works can, consequently, enormously increase the effectiveness of teaching. Bruner's ingenious experimentation now provides us with a good deal more information about that process of concept attainment than we have previously had available. The process may be generally described this way: In the attainment of concepts, individuals meet a number of *instances* which may or may not be examples of the concept; they may be characterized in terms of their *attributes,* e.g., color, weight, and in terms of attribute *values,* that is, the particular color, the particular weight. Think of the child who first meets a dog and is told by his parents, "That's a dog." It is characterized by various attributes: relatively small, furry, moves about, has four legs, and so on. The next animal the child encounters is a cat—"Look at the dog," he says. But, no, he is told that this is not a dog. He must now adjust his original hypothesis to the view that only a special kind of fur, tail, and shape of head denotes "dog." As the number of instances increases, his original hypothesis about the attributes which define the concept "dog" changes further and becomes more refined.

Or, consider the example of a person unfamiliar with American culture who comes to live in a small city. He is taken about by a trusted friend and introduced to a number of people and told before each meeting that "he's an influential person" or "a nice fellow, but not very influential." Again, the process is one of meeting a series of instances, some of which are positive examples, others negative. The people he meets are characterized by a large number of attributes: intelligence, wealth, conversational facility, friendliness, and so on. His task is to decide which attributes define the concept "influential," and he begins to do so for reasons which he would perhaps find difficult to state himself. But on the basis of the first few instances encountered, he begins to form a tentative hypothesis which subsequently leads him to make judgments even before his friend identifies succeeding instances for him. It is in this fashion, we must suppose, that adults form new concepts and revise old ones to make sense out of the world they live in. Here are some generalizations about the process as they emerge from experimental work:

1. In forming concepts, individuals employ a variety of *strategies.* Some people are *focusers.* They tend to adopt all of the attributes of the first instance they meet and, using this as an hypothesis, change the hypothesis when necessary with each succeeding instance. Thus, a

doctor encounters a patient who has aphasia with a badly damaged brain—Areas I to VI destroyed. He takes as an hypothesis that destruction of all six areas must be responsible for aphasia. If the next instance he meets is another aphasic with like destruction, he maintains his hypothesis. If he should meet a non-aphasic with all or some of the areas intact, he maintains it. The only time he changes is the occasion of his meeting a positive instance which invalidates his original hypothesis, an aphasic, for example, with Areas I and III intact. He then takes as his present hypothesis what the old hypothesis and the present instance have in common, that is, that the destruction of Areas II, IV, V, and VI is responsible for aphasia.

Others employ what Bruner calls a *part-scanning strategy*. These individuals tend to take as an hypothesis only part of the attributes of the original instance, for example, that aphasia is due to the destruction of Areas I and II. When he meets a new positive instance, he proceeds as the focusers do and maintains his hypothesis. But when he meets a positive instance which contradicts his hypothesis, an aphasic, say, with Areas II, III, and IV damaged, he must depend on his memory of all past instances to make a present modification of his hypothesis or to adopt a new one.

There is, clearly, a considerably greater amount of cognitive strain in the second strategy. All that the focuser need do is remember his present hypothesis; the part-scanner must keep in mind all of the preceding instances and accurately recall them in order to make modifications in hypotheses. It is no wonder that prejudiced persons, who have picked out some few particular attributes of the first examples they meet of another racial group, for example, find it easier to cling to that hypothesis in the face of instances which contradict it.

2. When the material to be conceptualized consists of familiar or feeling-evoking symbols instead of abstractions, the effectiveness of categorizing is diminished. When the individual must learn the concept "large black triangle and small yellow triangle," he is much more effective than when he is faced with stylized drawings of adults and children, even though the drawings exhibit the same systematic variation in attributes. People tend to depend on cues which have past associations, if they are present, rather than sticking with methods of evaluating information which are more efficient. Many of our difficulties in adult education clearly arise out of this tendency, because adults have many more firmly entrenched associations with cues which can become misleading, and these findings in particular suggest

the need for great care in the selection of materials for use in helping adults attain novel concepts.

3. Conceptualizing behavior is strongly influenced by the strains imposed under particular conditions and by what the individual perceives as the outcome, or payoff, for a categorizing decision. Bruner suggests as a model for this process the case of the sentry who hears a noise and must decide whether or not to shoot. His problem is to categorize the noise as a "friend" or as a "foe," and on that classification base his judgment. The following possible outcomes play a role in that judgment:

Anticipated Events and Outcome Values

Decision Alternatives	*Foe*	*Friend*
Categorize "foe" and fire	Alive and highly regarded	Alive, regretful but duty fulfilled
Categorize "friend" and not fire	Dead or wounded	Alive, but feels both lucky and neglectful
Estimated likelihood of events	0.50	0.50

Observation and experience suggest that there is a considerably higher probability that the sentry will categorize as "foe" under such payoff conditions, and experimental evidence supports it. This formulation of the problem is an interesting one for explaining behavior of daily life, but it also has much to say for the more artificial life of the classroom. The use of case studies in the personal and social areas, for example, often presents quite different feelings of risk for students and may inhibit the appropriate handling of information. Indeed, the concentration of adult education on problems which are close to the learner suggests that we search for ways of creating situations in which, temporarily at least, the student feels free to make otherwise risky categorizations.

If, as educators, we are interested in the deliberate and planned attainment of concepts, these data have much to contribute to the teaching of concepts from one such as "need" to that of "abstract expressionism." The presentation of concepts, as such, is no guarantee that the student will be able himself to judge appropriately future instances of the concept, which will have validity for him only if he has had the chance to encounter a number of instances under different conditions. It is obviously desirable that these conditions include simulation of situations which are likely in real life to impose cognitive strains of one sort or another. Stated as educational objectives, then, concept formulation involves the ability to:

1. classify different phenomena into appropriate subject classes and/or concept classes;
2. recognize that the same phenomena can be classified a number of different ways, some of which are more significant than others for a particular purpose;
3. discriminate among different kinds of relationships, e.g., causal, both related to the same or other cause, co-variance, coincidence, pattern similarity, sequential;
4. formulate hypotheses to account for connections among phenomena;
5. apply concepts of one field to the interpretation of phenomena in another.

III. PROBLEM-SOLVING

There is considerable distance between the specifications for problem-solving behavior set down by logicians and the empirical findings about that behavior arising out of research. They agree, however, on the importance of problem-solving as an educational objective, a happy accord which most educators join. The "problem" is the central focus of most daily activities of life and is the most commonly used device in education, not only for practice and for measuring the effectiveness of instruction, but as a form of interest-provoking material to engage the learner.

Dewey's famous analysis of everyday thinking is a description of the way in which people tend to deal with commonplace problems and thus comes considerably closer than many others to the later empirical investigations of the psychologists.[9] Thinking, or reflection, does not begin for Dewey until an individual is facing a difficulty. The difficulty sets up a barrier to some goal or creates some other frustration which leads a person to reflect on how he may overcome it, and the process of reflection begins. Commonly, as Dewey outlines the process, it begins with a search for those features of the difficulty which constitute the problem; thus, for a man walking in the woods whose progress has been stopped by a ditch, it is the width of the ditch and its slippery sides which constitute the problem, not the ditch itself.

Once the problem has been located or defined as some special feature of the general difficulty, the process continues as an exploration of the problem and its context in a search for possible solutions. Once we have hypothesized a solution, the thought process is basically concerned with the evaluation of the solution for its adequacy in solving the problem, trying it out in imagination or testing it in some other fashion. At this point we often engage in further search activity, as a proposed solution raises questions about some feature of the situation which had not previously been important. Finally, we select the solution which appears to be the most adequate, and if the situation permits, try it out.

Psychologists' investigations of the problem-solving process by experimentally setting tasks for subjects, both children and adults, yield results, by and large, which present a remarkably similar picture. The clearly distinguishable phases in a typical human approach to a problem consist of these:

1. The subject must recognize and fixate the problem. Animal problem-solving behavior often begins as a series of blind, random searchings set off by frustration (hunger, pain). Humans spend a good deal of time pinning the problem down to trying to conceptualize it, that is, fit it into a category of problems so that they can bring their past experience into play.

2. Following identification of the problem, we begin exploration of the situation or field within which it exists. Wertheimer[10] considers this phase a most important part of the problem-solving process, because out of a grasp of the peculiar structural and functional relationships of the situation arises the problem-solving dynamic suitable to the particular problem. Thus, Wertheimer, in his informal experiments with school children, first demonstrates for them the process of obtaining the area of any rectangle. His demonstration is itself devised to give the children insight into the structure of the situation; he shows that if the height of the rectangle is conceived as a column of little squares, then the area will be equal to the total number of vertical columns of little squares, thus illustrating the principle of $a \times b$. Once this is achieved, Wertheimer sets the child the problem: find the area of any parallelogram.

A five-year-old child asks for a pair of scissors, proceeds to cut the parallelogram into two parts, ADE and DCBE, moves the triangular piece to the right of the figure, and obtains the area of the resulting rectangle by the method now familiar to him. When the children verbalized their process of arriving at a solution, they tended to talk about "filling up the empty space," indicating that they perceived the equivalence of the two triangular spaces. The grasp of this crucial element in the problem can come only from a search of the whole context and a recognition of the important relationships involved in it.

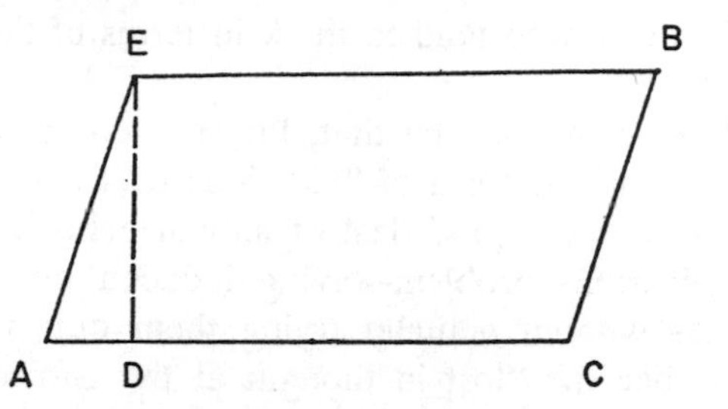

3. Following search comes an analytic phase. This often consists of conceptualization in the sense in which the preceding section on categorizing behavior described it; the recognizable attributes of the problem now permit us tentatively to identify it as one of a group of problems of a particular kind. Our ability to classify the problem of course, provides an enormous advantage, because we can then bring to bear upon it solutions worked out for previous, similar problems. Indeed, Duncker suggests that most solutions are achieved through what he calls "resonance," the relatively automatic application of previous experience to present problems based on a perception of similarity between the past instance and the present one.

It is this phase which formal systems of thought emphasize, because it is here, in complex problems whose parts are not all immediately perceivable, that logical relationships are so important. What can we safely infer from our identification of the nature of the problem? Is our assumption about causal relationships among certain parts of the problem correct, or is our evidence strong enough to support only the view that they are merely associated? How valid is our evidence for generalizations about the problem?

4. When one emerges from the analytic step finally comes the attack on the problem, which may involve taking care of subproblems, or other preliminaries, before proceeding on the plan. Earlier investigations of problem-solving as a part of studies of learning tended to seek some basic way of characterizing the effective attack on the problem, but few psychologists today would deny that individual differences exist and that there are several approaches, none of which is a particularly pure type, and one might find them all present in a particular example of problem-solving:

Insight—this approach, discussed earlier in this chapter, is a type of problem attack which one might suppose is characteristic mainly of those problem-solving situations in which all of the important relationships in the problem are known to the individual, and perhaps typical of certain individuals who tend to think in terms of the whole rather than of its parts.

Trial and error—it may be that, facing a complex problem, we inclined to credit, in the form of "vicarious trial and error".[11] Some psychologists interpret a good deal of animal behavior in laboratory situations as vicarious problem-solving induced by a need to test two possibilities without actually trying them out; whether or not laboratory rats become "lost in thought at the choice-point," as an opponent to this theory once sarcastically observed, no one doubts that *people* spend a great deal of their time in daily life doing precisely that. If, in the face of every small problem, we were forced to try out all the possible solutions which occur to us to discover which one works, life would be intolerable. In reality, most of us do very well by trying them out vicariously, by saying to ourselves, "Suppose I try such a course of action, what is likely to happen?"

Analysis—a third approach emphasizes step-by-step efforts to handle the problem, a mixture of insight, trial and error, and logical thinking. On higher levels, it probably adequately describes the way in which the scholar proceeds to handle a problem in his field, as he develops a logically exhaustive series of explanations for a phenomenon, then carefully assesses the weight of the evidence for each one. Most everyday attempts at problem-solving certainly lack this rigor, which is probably just as well, or *we* should be lost in thought at every choice point; but, as a model for the kind of behavior which adult educators have always viewed as greatly desirable in the social and political world of the citizen of a democracy, it occupies an important position in any hierarchy of objectives.

Although most of the work cited has been done with what one might call "problem-objects," specific puzzles and the like, the behaviors listed below which specify the general objective refer to situational problems, a form more appropriate to the worlds of action and role of adult education. Such problems, of course, have many possible solutions—"What can we do to reduce juvenile delinquency?" cannot be solved, obviously, through insight into the "correct" solution—and therefore require an analytic approach and the choice of the best, or least bad, of the possible solutions. This is true also of less global problems with which we struggle: "How much freedom shall we give our teen-age son?" "What kind of car shall we buy?" In all such complicated problems, the primary requirement is not so much to determine what the problem is, as in the simpler puzzle problems, but to determine, of all the points of disagreement or variance in the situation, *which* are crucial and must be attended to. The behavior we are interested in, therefore, includes the ability to:

1. identify and state crucial issues;
2. rank various statements of issues according to their relevance;
3. state the presuppositions involved in accepting a particular issue as crucial;
4. avoid accepting irrelevant issues as if they were crucial;
5. cite evidence relevant to the issue or issues;
6. assess the validity of evidence by making or recognizing distinctions between fact and opinion, evaluating or rating alternative sources or authorities of particular evidence, and evaluating the weight or significance of particular evidence;
7. state or recognize statements of alternative hypotheses which would account for a given situation;
8. formulate or recognize statements of probable consequences of a given situation;
9. arrive at a position, or "best solution," and support the position with valid evidence.

Experiments in recent years have not only provided us with a detailed picture of adequate problem-solving behavior but have also added information about the conditions which favor that behavior. At least several of these are crucially important, among them the past experience of the individual and his motivation to solve the problem.

The Role of Experience

N. R. F. Maier experimented some years ago with people's ability to integrate previous practice on *part* of a problem with a situation in which they confront the whole problem itself. A typical experiment presented subjects with the task of constructing a "hat rack" with only two lengths of wood and a clamp. The solution to the problem is relatively simple, as in the diagram below. One of the groups which faced the task had previously helped the experimenter construct a piece of laboratory equipment which included a structure similar to the hat rack. Specimens of this equipment were placed in the experimental room to serve as a visual reminder of the previous experience. A second group had also helped construct the apparatus but were given no visual cues to remind them of the previous experience. The third group

had no previous experience at all. In the experiment, 72 percent of group I, 48 percent of group II, and 24 percent of group III were successful. The help provided by the "set" or direction supplied by previous experience is quite clear, and these results have been confirmed many times; in fact, in a number of other experiments, Maier's subjects had great difficulty finding the correct solution without cues of some kind.

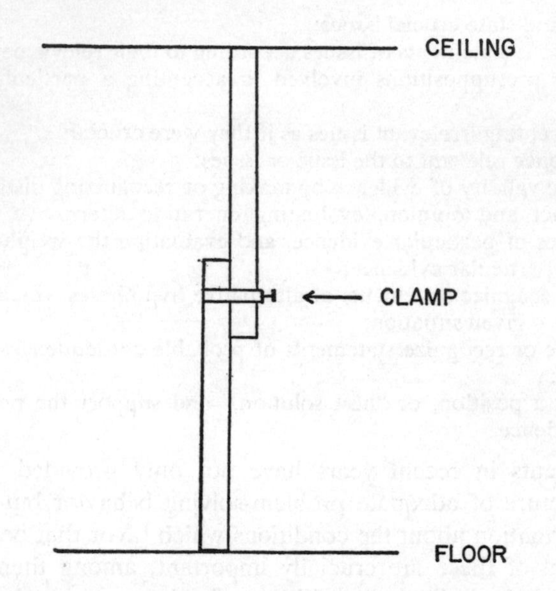

Such findings have several, and rather contradictory, things to say to the adult educator, whose students commonly have a wide and varied background of experience. Where the learning task consists of relatively coherent, one-solution problems, we need to be sure that all of the important elements of the problem are fully in view and that students get training in the process of seeking connections between the present problem and past experience. In complex, multi-solution problems, they need to be restrained from too facilely applying solutions transferred from experience; instead, they need training in what one might call problem discrimination.

A previously-stated generalization about the conditions of learning applies here particularly as a special case: If motivation is too high, too urgent, the student is less likely to solve problems successfully. Indifference, of course, is equally ineffective; problem-solving is best carried on under conditions of moderate involvement and concern.

This principle, supported by a considerable body of evidence, raises significant questions about some of the most cherished beliefs of adult educators. Indeed, the claims of workers in community development for the educational results of group problem-solving in the community rest on an assumption of intense involvement in the life problems which make up the content of the activity. To take a case in point, consider the community that decided it must have a bridge which a state commission had decreed would be erected at another site. The town organized a caravan to the state capital, insisted on another hearing, and created enough pressure to force a change in the original plans. To argue that the community participants had learned anything about problem-solving in any but the purely political sense would be nonsense. They were obviously too involved to spend any effort in seeing the whole problem.

IV. MAKING JUDGMENTS

The final step in the purely "puzzle" problem is the selection of the effective solution, the one which answers the condition set by the problem. The only value involved is effectiveness. But the end to the analytic steps in a complex problem in most of the areas of human activity which form the content of adult education is never so simple and usually confronts us with a choice among values. A group analyzing the national problem of education in the United States might conclude that the solution to many existing difficulties is the assertion of federal authority over the educational enterprise. But this is an effective solution which many Americans feel would violate a fundamental value of local control over the schools. On a considerably more trivial level, we make scores of judgments every day, about the behavior of other people, our environment, the significance of public events, and almost every other facet of life.

The basic element to such everyday judgments is that people do not make them in a vacuum but within some established framework, a reference scale which automatically comes into play for any particular object or event calling for a judgment. In terms of our previous discussion of concepts, people have a set of categories in which to place the phenomenon; where judgment is involved, however, these categories are closely related to one another; they are related points on a scale which lies between fixed points representing two extremes.[12]

One sees the dynamics of this behavior most clearly in types of objective judgment called for in sensory response to phenomena. Thus, if one presents a series of weights, ranging from two pounds to ten pounds, and asks a subject, as he lifts them separately, to judge whether they are heavy or light, he soon learns to discriminate accurately; he establishes for himself an internal scale along which the weights are distributed. One can similarly train individuals to discriminate among tones of different pitch, between, say, a range of 250–550 cycles. One can speak, then, of a scale of values, anchored at each end, which constitutes a reference scale for each judgment.

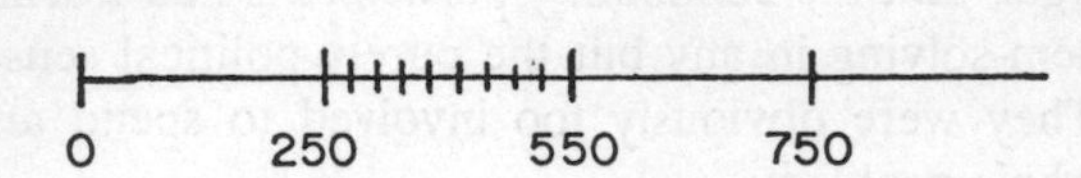

What are the consequences of training one person to discriminate a series of tones between 250–550, training another to discriminate a series between 750–950, and then presenting to both of them a series of tones between 550–750? Obviously, the first individual will judge them "high" and the second will judge them "low." One can do the same thing by holding one's left hand in icy water and one's right hand in hot water, then plunging both at the same time into warm water. This is precisely what happens when people argue about the goodness or badness of an action; they are judging from different scales.

It is, in fact, the end anchors which control the properties of judgment, and they, in turn, depend upon the range of relevant stimuli to which a person has been exposed. The difference, now rapidly disappearing, between the judgments of urban and rural people frequently can be accounted for by this fact. The limited range of social behavior open to the rural individual's notice produced a narrow scale, with bottom and top anchoring points relatively close to one another; the city dweller sees a wide variety of social behavior, and consequently his anchors are farther apart. In a narrow range, there can be very little judgmental difference between different stimuli; thus, in some villages, the elders might see little to choose from in their schoolmaster's taking a drink or beating his wife.

An interesting quality of judgment scales is the effect of establishing an anchoring point *outside* an already-established scale. If a person has been trained on a series of tones from 250–550 cycles, what happens if we instruct him now to consider a tone of 900 cycles as his reference point for "high"? The result is that he displaces his future judgments in the direction of the new anchoring point. One sees analogous judgmental behavior in such social areas as women's styles. A skirt which is two inches below the knee may be considered as low as one wishes to have it, until Paris decrees that the proper length is really four inches below the knee, at which point even the cautious woman will tend to expand her scale of judgment upwards, toward the new anchoring point, though to go all the way might be a little too much. A new anchor thus tends to pull the entire scale loose toward itself, as the former scale assimilates the new stimulus. One sees the same effect in more important social areas. Some years ago, the average Southerner's scale of social distance stopped short of "having my children go to school with Negroes." The Supreme Court decision set an anchoring point outside of his scale of permissible interaction and, if it persists, will gradually change the entire scale. It should be noted, however, that if the new anchoring point is too far from the top of the existing scale, its influence on the scale as a whole suddenly comes to an end.

The application of findings in the area of musical tone stimuli to social behavior is not a mere fanciful extension; precisely the same relationships have emerged from studies using reproductions of art works and ethical judgments. It is quite clear that we are dealing with what educators call *perspective* and with what teachers usually describe as a hope to *broaden* the student.

Volkmann suggests certain desirable features which scales of perspective might possess. First, they should be long, as long as they can be for any given range of stimuli. Narrow perspectives rule out accurate discrimination and leave one unable to perceive the validity of other persons' judgments.

Second, judgment scales must be well-anchored. If a scale is relatively long, it needs not only anchoring points at the ends but intermediate anchoring at various points as well, to permit it to extend toward the extreme anchoring points without pulling loose. The judgments of a middle-class person regarding juvenile behavior, for example, should indicate awareness not only of his own childhood but of various extremes arising out of different social-class backgrounds at the present time; within that total scale, a set of anchors might outline a limited range for judgment of children's behavior in his own social milieu, and other ranges, depending on the range of stimulation he is likely to encounter.

Third, the scales should be flexible. As Volkmann points out, "at different times, anchoring agents could be selected to determine the position and width of a scale. The man who has a long, well-anchored scale, should be able to shorten it for a particular purpose of discrimination. In this way, man A, who has a long scale, can make the same discrimination as man B, who has a short scale; in this sense, he can "understand" the attitude of man B. Temporarily, he shares his discrimination. This is a very interesting case; it might be called *displaced perspective*. Conflict between groups frequently calls for the exercise of displaced perspective. Note, however, that only those people with relatively long scales have the privilege of shortening them."[13]

The life areas representing major foci for adult education suggest a number of perspectives necessary for the average adult. *Cultural* perspectives arise out of the area of personal and social relations, as well as perspectives of *group* interaction and values. *Time* perspectives are useful in any of the areas, as are *space* dimensions. In the natural science field, we must use specialized perspectives, such as the evolutionary scale, for making certain kinds of judgments. And perhaps most important of all to the development of the kind of judgment we call maturity, we need a perspective which places the individual himself and his personal and physical characteristics on a scale with his fellow creatures to give a realistic basis for self-judgments.

V. RELATIONAL SKILLS IN SOCIAL ROLES

An objective which tends to be distinctive for adult education is the improvement of social role performance. Marriage courses in high school and business administration programs in college are, to the extent to which they touch on role adequacy, still preparatory. Adult educators face the tough job of changing role behaviors which have become habitual and settled.

It is impossible to discuss this objective as a body of relatively coherent behaviors, as one can the previously-described cognitive objectives, because of the wide spectrum of social roles with which adult educators must deal—parental, community leadership, supervisory, and others. Problems of behavior change in this area are closely linked to format and are reserved for a later chapter. But there are several issues which consistently demand attention and clarification for the instructional personnel who directly confront the task of role behavior change; they arise out of the often uncomfortable implications of the concept of "adjustment."

Social roles involve not only action but feelings. Training programs for supervisors, parents, or community leaders in neighborhood conflict situations require changes in the conceptual systems and judgments on which role behavior is based; do they also demand that existing feelings tied to present behavior be changed? Some programs for adults appear to assume that they do. Consider an extreme example, for the sake of illustration: training programs in community human relations aimed at helping to solve conflicts over white and Negro housing problems. Many white participants in such a workshop are rationally committed to solve the problem by maintaining an integrated community, despite their feelings of general prejudice about Negroes. In a democracy, should we be educationally committed to try to change their feelings, as well as their acceptance of social reality and the need for cooperative community action?

Apart from the issue of the technical difficulty of changing feelings is the ethical question of whether we should aim at doing so. One can only answer such a question by referring it to values which also strike deeply at the core of democratic ideology, at fundamental beliefs in individual integrity. There is no question that, as a society, we have the right to regulate *behavior* in the public interest and, as educators, the responsibility to help people examine the basis in reality of some feelings and their consequences for the taking of intelligent action. That, as external agents, we also have the right to try to change them is doubtful.

Educators can do much worse than take as a model the way in which psychotherapy tends to solve the problem. Therapists deal much more centrally than we do with the feelings of patients, but they aim at helping them to recognize and accept them and to free them from the necessity of acting upon them when it is destructive to do so. What therapists do in the domain of "private" feelings, educators can do in "public" feelings. Lawrence Frank distinguishes between the task of the therapist and that of the teacher[14] by suggesting that therapy concentrates on "how we feel about what we think" and education on "what we think about how we feel." The distinction points to a way out of the ethical dilemma.

A second issue is closely related to this one. Social roles consist of common expectations about how a person occupying a specific social position should act. When a position is occupied by many people, but the prescription of role is a relatively narrow one, only those whose personality "fits" the role will find such behavior comfortable. In an era in which the masculine role stresses aggression and strength, what happens to men with strong dependency needs? When the role of wife stresses submission and weakness, what does the temperamentally aggressive woman do, besides finding ways of subtly, rather than openly, manipulating others?

In periods which encourage the development of clear images of the self and permit expression of even bizarre personalities, the uncomfortable ones who do not fit into the available social roles can reject them. But in eras like ours, the problem of the fit between social role and personality is a much more complex one. In the first place, we do not encourage the development of clear, strong self-images by adolescents, who are going through the period which should be devoted to developing those self-concepts.[15] Secondly, and presumably the reason for the discouragement of clear character development, the adult finds himself facing a world of corporate and governmental bureaucracy in which the best chance of success goes to those without very firm convictions of very definite character, who shift role behavior very easily as they sense the changes in expectation in others.

That adult education finds itself designated as a social agent for pressure toward role uniformity is inevitable, given its general social function. But we do not need to carry it out blindly. We can make sure that our programs devoted directly to helping people understand or adapt to changes in important social roles, roles in work and personal and social life, emphasize the need to retain an integrity of self-concept, a willingness to be original, and an opportunity for rational assessment of how well one fits into a particular role and how necessary it is, in any given circumstance, to do so.

OBJECTIVES FOR THE FUTURE

The educational aims chosen for discussion thus far are the persistent and well-known ones in adult education. There are several general areas which merit considerable thought and exploration in the future, though at present they exist only as beginnings. One of these is the hope, arising from increasing research during the past decade into the nature of the creative process, that we can significantly improve the individual adult's creativity. A second consists of a current interest in the possibility of infusing into vocational teaching objectives which are essentially liberal.

Creativity

Many of the investigations of creativity have started out, reasonably enough, by examining in depth persons who are recognized by others as exhibiting high-level creativity in some particular field. The results of these studies build a fairly definite picture of the characteristics of the very creative person, the extreme case.[16] Whether his field is one of the arts, or experimental science, or architecture, he has in common with others of his kind an unwillingness to go along with the judgment of his group, if his perception of the situation happens to differ; he tends to be the maverick. He has greater than normal access to his own unconscious processes, such as fantasies and dreams which many reject because they often represent impulses which appear to threaten social adjustment. He is cognitively open and does not screen out experiences or ideas which are unfamiliar, even bizarre. He may have more intense emotional problems than others, but he also seems better able to handle them.

On the face of it, these data seem to discourage any effort to improve creativity in the ordinary individual. If creativity is linked to psychic processes so deeply embedded, it seems likely that only through psycholanalysis might one lower the barriers to creative expression in a particular person. Perhaps for this reason the only popular effort to devise educational method in the field does not attempt very seriously to improve individual creativity but instead teaches a group technique. This method, of course, is Osborn's "brainstorming."[17]

Osborn's system is an interesting example of adult education, particularly because his Institute has developed and distributes widely a packaged teaching program that, with little difficulty, may be adapted by any relatively knowledgeable individual and presented as a course. The technique itself is simple and aims at training any group of individuals in a method of producing the largest possible quantity of original ideas for solving a specific problem as a group. The group agrees to observe a set of rules governing individual contributions of ideas, the most important of which is that *any* contribution, no matter how zany or impractical it may appear to be, is accepted without immediate evaluation. A brainstorming session lasting for 15 or 20 minutes might produce 50 or more different ideas for the possible uses of some new plastic, for instance. Sober evaluation of the ideas comes later.

There is some evidence that such a course increases the chance that individuals who have the practice it affords will respond to problems with more originality than they previously did. Whether the group technique itself produces more original ideas than the same number of individuals working alone might do is another matter; a carefully designed experiment to test Osborn's faith in the group produced convincing evidence that it does not.[18] The work in brainstorming, at any rate, has demonstrated that one can improve people's ability to make original responses to stimuli, and other laboratory work confirms it.[19]

If we assume that, although the educational process is unlikely to produce the really superior creative person who is the object of most study in this field, it might nevertheless succeed in modest improvement in the level of creative response of the ordinary adult, we do not have to invoke therapy as the only answer. There are at least two methodological directions open to those willing to explore them:

1. An increase in awareness of one's own cognitive style and of the extent to which one screens out certain classes of stimuli or perceives things in conventional relationships instead of seeking the unusual. The assumption is that bringing cognitive processes onto a conscious level for examination may change habitual responses. To hope for such changes in students, we would have to employ fairly powerful and involving situations. Thus, to demonstrate the effect of previous set on our ability to find novel solutions to a problem, we might put students to work on a series of problems each of which depends on an ability to overcome previous experience with the materials, helping them become aware as they proceed of the basic nature of their difficulty. At the end of the series it will have become natural for them to ask, at the point of frustration, "Aside from the fact that this object is a key, what more general properties does it possess? . . . Can I use it as a pendulum bob?" In general, one would hope to bring to awareness the particular cognitive habits which the individual has established, so that he can take account of them consciously. (See Chapter VII for a more elaborate proposal which might include this type of training.)

2. A related procedure would train for originality by reinforcing

original responses. Such training might begin with a series of responses to inkblots; when each member of the group has exhausted his responses, the group can examine them to identify those which are common and those which are unusual. Then they can try again, this time encouraged to do their best to see more than they saw before. Or, one can begin with the "Unusual Uses Test": "How many ways can you think of to use a safety pin (or a paper clip, etc.)?" When preliminary ideas are exhausted, encourage additional responses to the limit.

The question of how effective these or other training devices may be is an open one; cognitive habits are difficult to change. The objective is important enough, however, to make any experimentation worthwhile.

Liberal Objectives in Vocational Education

Although there has been a steady increase of interest in liberal education for adults, the proportion of such programs remains, for good and sufficient reasons, fairly low, despite the interest of professionals in the field and the encouragement of grants from the Fund for Adult Education. An alternative possibility, consequently, deserves serious attention: we can try to make existing vocational programs more liberal. To consider such a possibility, of course, demands that we accept an assumption that there is a difference between "liberal arts" and "liberal education." Arts are traditionally disciplines, coherent bodies of knowledge, conceptual systems, and methodologies slowly built up about some area of natural or human activity. If the teaching of the liberal arts is what we mean by "liberal education," then we exclude teaching vocational skills and subjects by definition, as Mortimer Adler and others explicitly do. But we can also take "liberal education" to mean a way of helping individuals grow in basic human intellectual skills, in social understanding, and in insight, which transcend immediate application to a specific job. To be sure, it is considerably easier, not to say more likely, to achieve the objectives of liberal education by teaching Shakespeare than by teaching accounting. But if it is possible to teach accounting and achieve liberal as well as vocational objectives, it is surely useful to try.

Even Adler admits that many of the professions, law, for example, may enter his rather lofty class of liberal subjects,[20] and few people would disagree, for legal training puts heavy emphasis on developing the time-honored liberal skills of intellectual analysis and rhetoric.

Most of us, when we read speeches by Congressmen, are apt to reserve judgment on the issue of how successfully such training transfers to other fields, but will grant that legal schooling develops crucially important intellectual skills. The significant question is whether it is possible to achieve similar results at any level of vocational preparation; can business, accounting, secretarial, and other such programs incorporate gains in more generally applicable skills and understanding?

In the technical realm, engineering schools in particular have attempted to develop methods of teaching aimed at precisely these objectives; Carnegie Institute and MIT have succeeded notably in infusing their curricula with undeniably liberal skills. In adult education, where administrators tend to be on the periphery of curriculum-making and the development of teaching methods, they will often assert that teachers in *their* schools do indeed teach vocational courses liberally, but they are seldom able to provide specific illustrations.

In a recent questionnaire study, more than a hundred university instructors of adults, in business, engineering, education, and like fields, attested their belief that they do introduce liberal elements into their courses and described the way they did it. These responses yielded some remarkably consistent dimensions which provide an excellent summary of most of the possibilities.[21]

The clearest of these dimensions, and the most obvious one, results from an attempt to relate the vocational discipline itself to other essentially subject-matter areas. This approach assumes that to help people understand the general context of a field of work and its connections with other fields is more liberal than to focus narrowly on matters of competence strictly within its boundaries. It is easy to visualize the categories into which the examples submitted fall as a series of concentric circles, with the vocation itself at the center and the teacher undertaking to show relationships to surrounding areas, some of which are fairly close, others quite distant.

At the core is the vocation or particular discipline; let us say accounting. It has a history, a very long one, and an accountant who knows how some of his techniques developed out of ancient Egyptian life is presumably a broader person than his fellow accountant who does not. Accounting is embedded, moreover, in the vast field of business itself and is significantly related to business decision-making. At still further remove, it is related as an applied discipline to mathematics. Finally, the kind of culture we live in influences the problems which accountants face, and they, in turn, influence it in many ways. Awareness of all these expanding and overlapping relationships clearly frees the individual from the limitations imposed by the rigid life boundaries set by routine activities at which he spends most of his time.

The second major system of categories emphasizes, instead of the subject matter of the discipline, some element of growth in the individual which transcends the particular skills or insights necessary to practice his vocation efficiently. This is a considerably more complex objective than the first and divides into two separate dimensions: individual growth or change, and socially-oriented growth.

The first of these can be visualized as a continuum on which one can order a series of categories which vary from feeling states of the individual to very complex general cognitive abilities. At one extreme is the aim of awakening real interest in a field as such, which one can call "liberal" with some justification; there can be few activities more dehumanizing than to spend one's time at routine tasks without ego-involvement. Next is "tolerance and receptivity," which is surely liberalizing, a freeing from the bondage of pre-judgment and the closed mind. It was not, however, a very frequent response. The "skills of communication" come next and are perhaps on the borderline, primarily cognitive but involving some degree of empathy. Finally, the skills of critical thinking or analysis, sometimes treated in the responses as equivalent to an ability to follow "the scientific method," is by far the most popular category on this dimension.

The social dimension is slightly more complex. The continuum itself, in this case, might be thought of as a measure of distance from the concerns of the student. Thus,

Insight into the vocational role (close to ego)
Insight into views of other groups
Value perspective
Citizenship perspective
Historical perspective (far from ego)

Closest to the self is an understanding of the vocation or profession as a role which must be congruent with self-concept. Next is an understanding of the way in which other groups in the society perceive one's own vocational group, and an ability to evaluate these perceptions. The third lays emphasis on the social consequences of the way in which the vocation or profession operates, the ethics, morality, and the like which form a value perspective. Somewhat related to this is our interest in one's citizen role, particularly as it might conflict with the demands of the vocational outlooks. Finally comes an historical perspective, which is different from the historical category considered under the subject-matter orientations. There, history meant the history of the vocation itself, its origins and development; on the social dimension, it comes closer to meaning a relationship of the vocation to the history of man and his future.

We need to explore a number of questions raised by these suggestions for the broadening of vocational work with adults. Are particular liberal objectives appropriate to certain vocational fields rather than others? What are the most effective ways of incorporating the objectives into student activity in class and out? Further data on these and other questions can obviously come most frutifully from experimentation by those who are actually teaching adults.

NOTES

1. Such a relationship between motivation and cognition has also been made part of Rogers' system, who postulates self-concept as the link between the two. Thus, "interest," in his sense, is learning what the "I" values; and by internalizing the experiencing of others as if it were one's own, for example, it can be experimentally demonstrated that the tension induced by an unfinished task begun by a person can be lowered when *someone else* finishes it. Scheerer suggests, however, that Rogers overemphasizes the "private world" centering of motivation and that he overlooks the extent to which motives can arise from the demands of the task. For a general discussion of this point, see M. Scheerer, "Cognitive Theory," in Lindzey's *Handbook of Social Psychology, loc. cit.,* from which the quotation from S. Asch is taken.

2. My view of interest is adapted from Murphy's discussion of canalization, which, although any behaviorist would find it shockingly lacking in rigor, has a profound appreciation of how complex the human behavior we call "interest" really is. See Gardner Murphy, *op. cit.*

3. *Ibid.,* p. 187.

4. *Ibid.*

5. This specification of the intensive objective, as well as those specifications quoted later in the chapter for other objectives, is a group product developed out of the cooperative evaluation project of the Center for the Study of Liberal Education for Adults. Work groups of teachers of adults, administrative personnel, and research people, over a period of several years, agreed on the important objectives of adult liberal education, specified the objectives operationally, and worked out a considerable number of devices for gathering evidence about their achievement. For a progress report of the project, including all of the so-far developed evaluation instruments, see H. Miller and C. McGuire, *Evaluating Liberal Adult Education* (Chicago: Center for the Study of Liberal Education for Adults, 1961).

6. Russell F. W. Smith, *An Invitation to Literature* (Chicago: Center for the Study of Liberal Education for Adults, 1952).

7. Early studies of concept recognition depended primarily on subjects' recognizing a particular element present in some relatively hidden way in a complicated design. Bruner's design, on which this material is based, permitted a great deal more flexibility. During his five-year study of concept recognition and formation, he used abstract design series consisting of systematically varied geometric figures, sketches of adults and children, varying their dress and attitudes, plane silhouettes, and stylized sketches of faces. The experimenter could decide in advance what particular combination of attributes he wished to designate as the concept, and show the subject a series of items, some exemplars of the concepts, others not. See Bruner's *Study of Thinking*, cited previously, for the details of these experiments; I strongly urge the reader, even if he is not interested in the technical details, to go over Bruner's introductory and concluding sections for a brilliant discussion of the thinking process. The table of decision alternatives in this section is reprinted with permission from J. Bruner, *et al., Study of Thnking* (New York: John Wiley and Sons, 1956), p. 76.

8. See Osgood's *The Measurement of Meaning* (Urbana: University of Illinois Press, 1957). His semantic differential measure permits one to see the differences over time in peoples' conceptualization of any part of their world by obtaining their responses to the words which represent the concepts. This seems to me, consequently, to offer to adult educators particularly a remarkably useful tool for evaluating the effectiveness of many of our programs, because our aim so often is to change the perceived relationships of already familiar concepts. In the book cited, Osgood describes several studies of patients in the course of psychoanalysis, in which the gradual shifting of the interrelationship of such relevant concepts as Mother, Father, Love, Sin, and the like, can be diagrammed.

9. The process conceptualized by experimental psychologists as "problem-solving" is essentially the same as the one educators have often referred to as "scientific method." In a sense, the latter term is a better educational one because it specifies a particular approach as more rational and efficient, an approach which must be learned. Problem-solving is a more general term, however, and avoids the implication that rational thought-processes are employed only by scientists.

10. The discussion of problem-solving is adapted from Robert Thomson's *The Psychology of Thinking* (Baltimore: Penguin Books, 1959), an admirably written summary of the complicated literature of this area. Thomson also deals lucidly with Bruner's concept formation experiments, which those who would prefer a briefer description to the original may find more useful.

11. See E. C. Tolman, "Cognitive Maps in Rats and Men," *Psychological Review*, Vol. LV, No. 4 (1948), and I. Krechevsky, "The Genesis of 'Hypothesis' in Rats," *Publications in Psychology*, University of California, Vol. VI, No. 4 (1932).

12. The discussion of scales as perspectives is based on J. Volkmann's chapter in J. Rohrer and M. Sherif's *Social Psychology at the Crossroads* (New York: Harper, 1951). The reader interested particularly in the application of judgment-scale theory to verbal materials might look at H. R. McGarvey's "Anchoring Effects in the Absolute Judgment of Verbal Materials," *Archives of Psychology,* No. 281, (May, 1943).

13. Rohrer and Sherif, *op. cit.,* p. 291.

14. In an unpublished communication.

15. This general view, of course, is developed at length in Riesman's *The Lonely Crowd,* but this statement refers more particularly to Edgar Friedenburg's early chapters in *The Vanishing Adolescent* (Boston: Beacon Press, 1959), which, because it deals sensitively with adult education's future clientele, every adult educator ought to read.

16. The literature on the study of creativity is extensive. A good place to start is M. Stein's *Creativity and the Individual* (New York: The Free Press, 1960). A remarkably interesting report on a very important five-year study is at present available only in mimeograph form in *Conference on the Creative Person,* October 13–17, 1961, published by the Institute of Personality Assessment and Research and the University of California University Extension at Berkeley.

17. Alex F. Osborn, *Applied Imagination* (New York: Scribners, 1957). The Creative Education Foundation publishes a wide variety of materials, both hortatory and scientific, on its work. Write to the Foundation at 1614 Rand Building, Buffalo 3, New York.

18. D. W. Taylor, P. C. Berry, and C. H. Block, "Does Group Participation When Using Brainstorming Facilitate or Inhibit Creative Thinking?" *Administrative Science Quarterly,* III (1958), 23–47.

19. Irving Maltzman, "On the Training of Originality," *Psychological Review,* Vol. LXVII, No. 4 (1960).

20. Mortimer J. Adler, "Labor, Leisure and Liberal Education," *Journal of General Education,* VI (October, 1951).

21. A complete report on the study is available, in mimeograph, from the Center for the Study of Liberal Education for Adults: H. L. Miller, *Liberal Orientations for Vocational Teaching.*

4

• •

SMALL GROUPS: IN THE CLASSROOM

Teaching may be compared to selling commodities. No one can sell unless someone buys. We should ridicule a merchant who said that he had sold a great many goods although no one had bought any. But perhaps there are teachers who think they have done a good day's teaching irrespective of what pupils have learned.

JOHN DEWEY, *How We Think*

It is not surprising that the formal class comes closest to being the standard format for adult education, even when a particular program is sponsored by institutions outside the common academic range. We are so accustomed as a culture to the tidy rows of chairs (25 to 30 of them is a good, satisfying number) facing the desk where the authority sits or stands behind his protective lectern, that we are suspicious of any deviation from an apparently God-given norm.

The external format is a perfect expression of the underlying authority situation of the classroom for children. The master is in the best position to see and to control the individual's behavior, and there is no reason why the children should not be firmly fixed facing him, because he is the source of learning. Long years of schooling spent mostly in such a situation led adults, until recently, to accept it without much question. But the ordinary classroom poses severe problems for an adult education program interested in the objectives which are most appropriate for it:

1. It assumes by its arrangement that the major form of interaction will take place between individual students and the instructor and encourages such a pattern. As in the regular schoolroom, this arrangement can only result in an increase in individual competitive behavior among the students and makes it difficult to set up group activities devoted to such purposes as practice.

2. The formal classroom encourages passivity in the students because they can too easily perceive themselves as an audience. As an earlier section pointed out, when learning involves a threat of change, many students express resistance to such change by embracing a passive role.

3. The same resemblance to the "performance" setting makes shy instructors uncomfortable and brings out the "ham" in others. In the first case, admittedly, few adult students must cope with any teachers like those legendary ones in graduate schools who build little screens of books and briefcases on their desks to protect them from the gaze of their students; most teachers who cannot relate readily to a group do not find themselves with adult classes for long. And, in the second case, there is no doubt that some dramatic emphasis in teaching serves at least to hold interest and keep the group engaged; one wonders, however, whether the importance of holding-power in adult classes does not encourage the hiring of a greater proportion of pure showmen than the field ought to have, teachers who are really a form of popular entertainment and not particularly interested in what students learn.

Despite these drawbacks, the traditional formal class is not very likely to disappear as the dominant teaching format in American education, institutionalized as it is in hundreds of thousands of rooms with the proper furniture facing in the proper directions. Because much of adult education is carried on inevitably in institutions whose major task is the education of the young, who pose problems of order and discipline as well as of learning, we often find ourselves conforming to the traditional teaching pattern whether we like it or not simply because our physical context makes it easier to do so. The public school and the college are at the core of adult education programming, and to some extent at least, they subtly impose their major format on the field as a whole; thus, one sees such non-academic institutions as the YMCA providing much the same classroom patterns as its neighboring evening colleges and night schools.

The formal classroom and the relationships between teacher and students which it assumes can be made a flexible instrument for a variety of learning objectives, but to do so requires the exercise of some imagination and a considerable amount of effort. Lacking this, its range, considered against the complexity of the objectives described in the previous section, is likely to be very narrow. It encourages passive taking-in rather than active search, discovery, and development of cognitive skills. The instructor in such a setting, particularly because of its evocation of his own past schooling, finds it easiest to emphasize the process of exposing the student to bodies of information and concepts which bear on the life areas of adults but which seldom are vitally connected with them.

MODELS OF TEACHING STYLES

Because the structure of the formal classroom makes the role of the instructor a dominant one, we find in it the greatest variety of teaching styles. Evolutionary studies demonstrate that in a given environment species tend to develop into forms which will fit into each possibility offered for life, each niche open to their existence; the formal classroom setting, perhaps, analogously permits a wide variety of personalities to survive because there is so little external prescription of what is acceptable teaching. A large proportion of the considerable number of studies of teaching behavior, in fact, attempts to analyze teaching into a number of empirical patterns descriptive of particular groups of roughly similar teachers.

Such studies assume that the most significant element in teaching, that is, the one most likely to produce different results, is what the teacher himself does, or what he is. They concentrate on studying the kind of control which the teacher imposes, the emotional climate of the classroom, and other variables arising directly out of his personality or habits. Current studies of teachers of adults give evidence of a patterning in teacher style, as many factor analyses of public school teaching have in the past.[1] Our own experience with teachers often gives rise to more empirical typologies; models of teaching styles suggested by acute observers such as Thelen, for example, are instructive:[2]

The Socratic

"The image is of a wise, somewhat crusty philosopher getting into arguments with more naive people." This model assumes that both the teacher and his students have relatively the same background of knowledge; the teacher asks questions which force the student to generalize and which require the group to test the generalizations or the logical analysis which leads to them. The teacher has a central role, and the discussion often takes on a good deal of emotionality.

The Town Meeting

"The image is of a group of citizens whose lives are interdependent meeting together to decide on courses of action required to solve problems." In the experience from which this model is drawn, the citizens are vitally concerned with the issue and draw on their own experience; in the classroom, the teacher who approximates this model uses case materials which can seldom be as urgent or real as a comparable group in life, and he plays the analogous role of a moderator, injecting himself as expert to a much greater extent than the real town meeting chairman.

Apprenticeship

"The image is of a young person's life being 'taken over' by an older one." In the apprentice system not only was the particular trade skill taught, but an attitude toward life and an internalization of a complex of role behaviors was inculcated. One sees this style particularly vividly in the graduate schools, but it is not uncommon at all levels of teaching—even in adult education, where so many instructors are younger than many of their students. The respect for the authority of knowledge among many adults helps keep this style viable despite disparities in age.

Boss-Employee, or Army

"The image is of the person of higher status and the authority to reward and punish who knows what there is to be done and sees that it is." He is not necessarily harsh in carrying out this role, but the relationship emphasizes dependency of the student in all the important elements of the learning process, including the evaluation of results. As it is the dominant model of the public school, so it is the most prevalent one in adult education for the formal classroom.

The Good Old Team

"The image is of a group of players listening to the coach between quarters of the football game." The coach's aim is to get the highest achievement possible, and he uses any means of persuasion and motivation he can. This is a model which, in adult education, one finds less often in the classroom than in more informal settings, but it is not entirely absent even here.

One supposes that styles such as these somehow affect the kinds of learning which students achieve in a classroom, though there is little evidence one can present; one study of teachers of adults indicates, for example, that the more flamboyant styles appear to result in a somewhat different kind of achievement than the quieter ones, analytic abilities rather than information acquisition.[3] But in the absence of a greater body of generalization we can at least point out several obvious advantages and disadvantages to the prevalence of such styles of teaching. (For detailed descriptions of three very different teaching styles, see Chapter V.)

For the teacher, they serve as a coherent guide to behavior, and to the extent that consistency is a virtue in teaching, they provide a steady image for students to respond to. Styles of teaching are, as Thelen points out, realistic ways of handling the problem of teaching, for at least two reasons: by concentrating on teacher behavior, we underscore the fact that his own behavior is, in fact, the only behavior the teacher can directly control in the classroom; secondly, the teacher, by his choice of a style which emphasizes a relatively narrow range of behavior and attitude, effectively prescribes the limits of student behavior.

However realistic such a view of teaching may be, it unhappily ignores at least one important aspect of the total problem: *what the students need to do to achieve a particular learning objective.* The view of learning presented in the first section demands student activity to achieve the more complex cognitive objectives, and particular types of needed activity would clearly be inappropriate for certain teaching styles. It is difficult to see, for example, how one can provide a situation in which students can practice independent, critical thinking where the teacher's style makes the students overwhelmingly dependent upon him. The major problem of the classroom teacher of adults, consequently, is to find a way of integrating his own needs into plans for activity which have some realistic connection with the specific learning objectives he has in mind.[4]

Much of the advice which classroom teachers of adults receive threatens their basic styles, which have been developed through years of adjusting particular personal needs to the teaching situations they face, and consequently meets determined and often hostile resistance. For example, discussion, the experts suggest, is more appropriate for adults for a variety of reasons; "a pooling of ignorance," the teacher replies, and in many cases he is correct. Discussion is a technical device and we mislead ourselves and others if we assume that it has some intrinsic worth. If we begin with a clear and operationally stated idea of what we expect the student to be able to do at the end of a particular learning sequence, we can choose the technical means most likely to bring that end about. Discussion might well be one of those means, but it is then a particular kind of discussion, in which the participants clearly perceive the desired nature of their contribution and in which the responsible instructor is acutely aware of the roles which need to be played, either by himself or members of the class, depending on the demands of his natural style.

An Illustration

The following description of a particular class in an adult program serves as a convenient device to make concrete the relationships among objectives, class activity, and teacher style. It is by no means the best instruction one can imagine, but neither is it intended as a horrible example. As an illustration, it is fairly typical of the adult education range: one session in a course which is part of a certificate program offered to supervisory personnel working in federal offices in a large city. The program was developed by a university but carries no academic credit; the participants, however, perceive their achievement as a step toward promotion within the systems, and extrinsic motivation is consequently relatively high.

The course from which the illustrative session is taken is called "Human Relations" and must fit into the general framework of the entire program, which adopted as its focus "the act of decision-making." In his general scheme for the course, the instructor has arrived at the point at which he thinks it is useful for the class to examine bureaucratic structure itself. He has a number of objectives for the session, but primarily he intends to help the group understand the relationship between the way in which bureaucracy is organized and the types of problems which people often attribute to the personal faults of personnel in the system. A grasp of this relationship will presumably improve their ability to analyze and solve human relations problems they meet daily on the job.

At the beginning of the class the instructor suggests that they are all working members of one of the largest bureaucracies in the world and are consequently in the position of expert resource persons. He asks them to reflect on their own experience for a moment and to supply, as they think about it, the following information:

Any important rule of organization which seems to be characteristic of the agencies they work for.
When such a rule or general intention of the organization doesn't work, how this malfunction is evidenced.
What is the probable cause of the malfunction.

The instructor writes the three headings on the blackboard and notes each contribution in the appropriate column as the student offers it. A typical exchange:

STUDENT: Well, you're only supposed to communicate with people on higher echelons through regular channels. If you need something, then your request is submitted and bucked up through the people above you. But there are many times when I just don't bother to go through channels and just pick up a phone and call a friend of mine in the bureau in Washington.
INSTRUCTOR: Then the evidence for the breakdown of this particular rule is the common short-circuiting of official communication channels. (To class in general) Is this a general state of affairs?
CLASS: (Nods and laughs. Several members contribute examples from their own agencies.)
INSTRUCTOR: What are the reasons for the rule's breaking down?
SECOND STUDENT: It saves time, mostly. When you need to get something done in a hurry, it takes forever, so you just go around the rules to the person who can help you.
THIRD STUDENT: Sometimes, too, you feel that you can get a more sympathetic ear from someone you know. When you've been in the system a long time, you have friends in various places, and a good deal of communication goes on between them.
INSTRUCTOR: So, one of the causes you suggest arises out of the demands of the task of the organization, getting things done, and the other relates to the fact that humans are running the system and develop typically human forms of interaction.

As various members of the class make contributions, the columns on the board grow. Several times a rule is suggested which the class as a whole considers not common enough to be characteristic, and it is eliminated. The reasons for some breakdowns are not so simple to determine, and numbers of suggestions are made and evaluated. At the end of this phase the blackboard is fairly well filled and has on it the data presented on the following page.

The instructor now suggests that they might like to take a look at the results of a more systematic view of bureaucratic structure taken by a social scientist. He interposes a five-minute lecture at this point, whose main burden is that the common public image of bureaucracy as some devil-inspired system which, if we willed it we could get rid of, is far from rational. On the contrary, as soon as any social task becomes large enough in scope and effort, it must inevitably be broken into smaller parts and, whether governmental or private, assume the form of bureaucracy. He proposes that they now check their own observations against Weber's pure model of bureaucratic organization.

The next phase of activity is the presentation, by the instructor, of the major elements of Weber's theoretical model:[5]

1. The regular activities required for the purposes of the organization are distributed in a fixed way as official duties.
2. The organization of offices follows the principle of hierarchy; each lower office is under the control and supervision of a higher one.
3. Operations are governed by a consistent system of abstract rules and consist of the application of these rules to particular cases.
4. The ideal official conducts his office in a spirit of formalistic impersonality, "without hatred or passion, and hence without affection or enthusiasm."
5. Employment in the bureaucratic organization is based on technical qualifications and is protected against arbitrary dismissal.

As each of the elements of the model is explained and noted on the board, the instructor raises questions about:

Which of the students' contributions are similar?
If it was not mentioned by the class, is it absent from 20th-century bureaucracy?
Do the malfunctions the students noted mean a breakdown of Weber's model or merely an adjustment?

The major discussion is stimulated by the students' somewhat indignant response to the model's insistence on bureaucratic impersonality; it seems alien to them. The instructor agrees that it sounds un-American and describes the feeling-tone in Kafka's *The Trial* as an example of the response to European bureaucracy. He adds, however, that he will proceed to argue for Weber's suggestion, to make sure that the class is aware of the meaning of the term "impersonality" as Weber

Organizational Rule	*Malfunction*	*Reason*
Standards of performance are set by the system	Inflexible standards of quantity may result in lower quality	
Complete and uniform communication is required	Sometimes communication doesn't go all the way; different groups interpret the same communication differently	Groups are separated; people have different perceptions
Equality of treatment	But people do get differential treatment	It's hard for people to be properly objective
Policy-making power is located in definite centers	But operators make policy sometimes	Needed policy may not exist, may be unclear, or remote from reality
Staff and budget are centrally allocated	Sudden needs for funds or for additional staff cannot be met	Reorganization; work fluctuates
Work is specialized in planned ways	When workload is heavy, people get pulled out of their job	Over-separation of function
Cooperation, teamwork is necessary	Individual initiative or ambition may disrupt cooperation	Human element—some people work better alone
All jobs classified uniformly	But people supposedly having the same classification are doing different work	Personal interpretation again
Authority fixed by the system	But sometimes informal leaders are important but not officially recognized	Just so many places at the top
Chain of command	Sometimes necessary to bypass it to get a job done	Individual personality of the authority
Promotion is by merit, judged objectively	Not so, sometimes	Difficult to be objective when relationships have already been established
Exceptional initiative should be recognized	Suggestions sometimes not put in operation	Someone in authority doesn't like it; general resistance to change
All activities to be coordinated	Sometimes lags develop	Lack of communication; difference in interpretations
Policy-makers and operators are separate groups	Sometimes policy people operate	Policy makers afraid of loss of prestige, have feelings of insecurity —habits of operation

uses it and of the consequences of *not* maintaining impersonality in bureaucracies.

The ensuing discussion is fairly emotional; the issue has obviously touched a nerve. There is finally some general agreement that impersonality does not necessarily involve unfriendliness or hostility; that personal relationships with clients certainly, and with subordinates possibly, would create difficulties.

The instructor provides a rapid summing-up, referring to material on the board, and the class ends.

Comments

Among the elements in this session, note first the extent to which it takes into account the adult status of the students. The generalizations being taught are, of course, just as appropriate to any number of undergraduate courses, but an instructor would be unable to take this approach. In this case the experience of the students is used not merely in an attempt to increase interest by making the problem more real, but to provide essential data for analysis and a rough conceptual framework which prepares for acceptance and understanding of a more rigorous one.

This approach strikingly illustrates the learning process which Bruner[6] calls "discovery," a process which is particularly appropriate for adult education in many areas because they are fields in which adults have had unexamined life experience. The classroom setting has the unique advantage of providing expert guidance for such a process in a situation which permits flexible interaction. The informal adult discussion group, commonly intended to encourage discovery of concepts and structures of knowledge, just as commonly fails to do so because of the absence of expertness.

Arranging the conditions of learning to facilitate the process through which the class itself discovers some of the structures of the body of knowledge they are dealing with is easier to do in some adult life areas in others, to be sure, but we can hope to accomplish it more than we often attempt to do. As a technique it is appropriate for some bodies of principle or generalization at varying levels in all of the areas suggested as central to adult education in the earlier chapters. If it can be used with children—for example, presenting them with a physical map of the United States and having the class locate, and justify their choices, the points where they think large cities *should* be—it is surely even more appropriate for adults in dealing with social and political relations, their world of work above the levels of skill training, and science. Application of the method to esthetics is perhaps less certain, because the principles we rely on in the arts are formal constructions which are difficult to deal with inductively.

Second, the major activity of the class is clearly an exercise in concept formation and generalization. The students were engaged in identifying the attributes of the concept *bureaucracy* and, therefore, detailing the assumptions which may correctly be made once one has made such a categorization. Another objective which the class aimed at falls under the improvement of the ability to formulate relationships, involved in their evaluation of causes for the breakdown of bureaucratic rules.

Another important aspect worth noting is that the class time is divided into distinct phases and into relatively clear-cut activities within those phases. The construction of generalizations about bureaucratic structure, and within it the assessment of malfunctioning, constitutes one such phase; the evaluation of a systematic model is the second. The resulting clarity does more than merely avoid possible vagueness and confusion for the student; it has a positive motivational value by providing cues for a shift in the kind of participation which now has relevance. Knowing what is expected has considerable influence on whether or not one *will* become involved.

Finally, an analysis of the class illuminates some of the earlier remarks about teaching style. The description suggests that the instructor is chiefly preoccupied with the problem of setting conditions which would maximize the achievement of some relatively clear objectives he had for the session. Within that structure it is entirely possible to play widely divergent roles and to permit great variations in emotionality and in the kind of interaction between students and instructor, and even some differences in the degree of dominance exercised. The role flexibility is not, of course, infinite. Some basic dominance, for example, is suggested by the imposition of a plan for the session which originated with the instructor.

Some of the persistent problems of teaching-style components, for example, the familiar issue of whether teachers should lecture or conduct discussions, take on another aspect. Obviously, from this viewpoint, the question is settled by reference to the particular objective one has at the time. The instructor in the example did both, in response to the demands of the situation and his objectives. A later chapter is devoted largely to the problem of discussion leadership, and the general question of participation and the structure of discussion may be found there. But in the classroom, and in the presence of a teacher who must take responsibility for what goes on in it, the problem is considerably simpler. The teacher lectures when some direct communication from him contributes to the achievement of a specific aim, and he encourages students to interact with one another when there is some point to their doing so.

The major criticism of the lecture as it is commonly used is precisely that its purpose is not clear. To use it to convey information readily available elsewhere is a waste of valuable class time; there is good evidence that students pick up no more information from an oral presentation than they do from a written one. If the information is necessary but not readily available, it is quite another matter. To use the lecture to analyze or interpret or evaluate, if the teacher can find a way for the students *themselves* to undertake those activities, is to ensure that the teacher learns more than the students possibly can. If the teacher knows fairly precisely what his objectives are, confusion over when and in what fashion he ought to allow group discussion is similarly reduced. The exchange of experiences or personal opinions related to some broad question is unlikely to be useful, though it is seductive to most groups in the classroom. A particular objective may demand that the class be aware of the range of opinion about a given issue, and it is then reasonable to collect them because it serves a specific purpose. But the general principle insists that discussion have a particular function to serve, and that function is most likely to be to provide the students with an opportunity to practice some well-defined process related to a learning objective of the class.

In the light of these general comments, it is clear that the teacher in the illustration given might have improved the class in several ways. He could have helped the students to become more sharply aware of the processes they were going through, of generalization and evaluation, in the hope of increasing the possibilities of transfer of whatever improvement they might have achieved in those skills. He might have considerably increased the chances for participation and thus spread the opportunity for practice by dividing the class into small groups, each with the assignment of developing and evaluating the rules of bureaucracy, and then collecting the data from each. The analytically-minded reader will doubtless be able to think of other possibilities he missed.

VARIATIONS ON THE MODEL

Small Discussion Group in the Classroom

A favorite practice of many teachers is to divide the class, particularly if it is fairly large, into a number of smaller groups for brief periods of discussion. This is a useful device, when appropriately used, not only because of its contribution to the learning process but as a change of activity particularly welcome in evening classes of weary students.

As a procedure, it is so simple that it hardly needs comment here. The important question is whether, at the point at which the teacher employs it, it performs a useful function. There are few things more futile than finding oneself in an intimate little group with the assignment "to discuss the problems of teen-agers." Such small groups often have a good time chatting or arguing but are not likely to make a very substantial contribution to some general result the instructor may have had in mind.

The value of the small discussion group is directly related to the clarity of the task people are given to perform. The discussion topic above may, for example, be transformed into: "On the basis of your experience as parents, try to agree on the five things that *most* worry teenagers." The statement of the task makes clear what is meant by "problems," and it requires the group to discriminate between trivial and important concerns. The brief small group discussion lends itself best to work on such processes as problem identification and particularly to providing practice in specific intellectual skills, such as analysis of a specific situation or forming hypotheses for the solution of a problem.

When small groups are given a more general discussion task, the instructor will do well to provide training in the processes of productive discussion. See Chapter VI for a detailed presentation of a discussion model and some suggestions for training the group.

The Seminar

Presumably to remove some of the curse from the traditional, formal classroom, adult educators in recent years have turned to providing new names for programs; among the more popular ones are seminars, workshops, and institutes. The degradation of the seminar as a teaching format is perhaps the most dismaying of these trends, although what has happened to the seminar is representative of a general movement to destroy any characteristic identity each of the academic formats may have had. The seminar in many adult programs turns out upon investigation to be the formal class itself, except that the students sit around a table instead of in rows of seats. The interaction between student and teacher differs in no way, students are perhaps more comfortable but often find it more difficult to attract the instructor's attention for a question, and the instructor himself tends to lecture from a sitting position instead of a standing one—a loss, generally speaking, in dynamism and in the tendency to use the blackboard.

Granting the advertising value of the term *seminar,* with its overtone of mature, high-level deliberation, and consequently the unlikelihood of anyone's succeeding in reversing the present trend toward making it a meaningless word, it is possible to turn it into a format which retains some of the purposes of the original but adapts them to the clientele of adult education. The seminar is pre-eminently a tool of the graduate school (where it is probably just as badly distorted as in adult education) intended to provide the young scholar with the opportunity of practicing, under the critical eyes of his peers, the skills of scholarship and the methods of contributing original ideas to the field.

As a mature instrument of small-group learning, the seminar makes two basic demands: that each member contribute materials representing his own original thought or research, and that the group utilize these materials in an act of cooperative reflection. The graduate seminar often requires individual research; the less formal seminars, so popular recently, which bring together people of high status in science or politics, often ask their members to contribute papers which express a range of opinion on a particular issue. There is no reason to suppose that in adult education we cannot vary the type of production required while retaining the essential character of the format.

As an educational tool, in contrast to its policy-making use, the seminar provides a first-rate opportunity for giving students practice under appropriate conditions of reinforcement in the complex cognitive skills described earlier. Two of these objectives are perhaps particularly suited to the seminar form: problem-solving and the improvement of perspective. The climate of small-group deliberation favors the discussion of a particular problem, a process which is improved when an individual member of the group contributes a preliminary analysis and a personal judgment. In the second instance, if each of the participants is working on aspects of the same area, the group has available over a period of time a wider range of viewpoints than any one of its members had previously been forced to consider. The opportunity for the seminar leader to help the group construct an image of a broad judgment scale which includes all of their judgments and to lengthen it further by inferring positions which are not present within the particular group, is an obvious and extremely valuable one.

The personal and social relations area, of course, is a particularly appropriate one for this kind of seminar method. An example from the extreme end of the personal scale is the assignment made by one instructor of adults in a "seminar in self-awareness" to have a dream about the class and be prepared to submit an account of it for group discussion.[7] Rather more prosaically, a group of supervisors in a human relations seminar might write brief descriptions of consistent behavior patterns of a person with whom they work, and attempt to infer the need which the behavior apparently meets. As students report these to the group, the instructor has the opportunity to guide discussion toward a wide variety of useful generalizations. Or a seminar group of active community leaders studying problems of education may devote a large proportion of the total seminar time to the discussion of extensive case studies of individual schools prepared by the participants and based on interviews and studies of budgets.

The world of work presents similar opportunities for adult education above the level of pure skill training. The fact that much adult education consists of job upgrading means that students in many instances are already working in the setting in which they hope to increase their competence. They can carry out assignments of a wide variety of analytical and data-gathering tasks to provide material for seminar discussion. The application of the principle to many courses in business is obvious, but teachers of professional and sub-professional seminar courses may use it just as readily.

The seminar format appears less often in the worlds of form and science, perhaps because the demands of these fields do not lend themselves to the method. Where the objective in one of the arts is individual competence in producing works, the workshop is a more appropriate tool; where the aim is to appreciate or develop analytical skills, it is useful to concentrate the attention of the group on one or several works of art. In those areas in which it is particularly appropriate, however, the seminar format, modified to fit the peculiar demands of the adult student, is an excellent device, if we can learn to use it properly, for focusing on the acquiring of particular intellectual skills.

LEARNING MATERIALS

The selection of appropriate learning materials depends to some extent on the particular variation in format selected; the more special the format, the more likely it is to make demands for a particular type of material, as the discussion of the seminar indicates. But there are some more general problems and opportunities within the formal classroom situation which deserve discussion within the particular framework of the education of adults. Perhaps the most important of these is the crucial use of the experience of the adults who are members of the group; this is such a central issue, however, that consideration of it permeates the description of each of the formats.

Books and the Use of Libraries

Inexperienced teachers of adults, particularly university personnel, tend to overdo the assignment of reading material and provide lavish bibliographies which get tucked away and forgotten. The assumption of the undergraduate college that students will do long reading assignments, whether or not they are related to actual class activity, is seldom justified even there except as a pleasant fiction; in adult classes, particularly outside of the credit-degree framework, the assumption is even less trustworthy. The teacher of adults who uses books as a resource must, in most cases, heed two fairly obvious principles: assign only a few really important books or parts of books; be certain that the material assigned is used in the sessions and that the class understands the reading.

The availability of high-quality paperbacks provides an enormous advantage. Even in an era of sharply rising book costs, the paperback is substantially cheaper than the equivalent bound volume; it is convenient to carry around, which is important for busy adults, and it looks considerably less threatening to an older person who is not accustomed to doing much serious reading. In regular bindings, the current popularity of collected journal articles and short theoretical pieces among publications in the social sciences make available an astonishing variety of original source materials on many important social problems. The propositions advanced by earlier chapters on the conditions for effective learning suggest the importance of this type of material as a substitute for the pre-digested, bland textbook. If students are to engage in an active search for meaning and in practicing such skills as analysis and judgment, materials which do not do all the work for them are a necessity.

At some levels of adult education, and for many subject areas, such materials are simply not readily available except in a library. Because the classroom format is characteristic of programs which ordinarily have some connection with established educational institutions, libraries are often enough available; the problem is to find ways of helping adult students make use of them. Librarians are notorious for a compulsive need to keep books on their shelves, few adult students can find time during the day to spend in the library, and on the evening of the class itself general weariness is usually a sufficient deterrent to scholarship even if library closing hours were not.

One teacher of adults at the university level has developed a systematic way of dealing with the problem. At points where it seems useful to do so, he plans sessions which have three phases: the class begins with a discussion of a particular problem or issue, a brief one which attempts primarily to expose its major dimensions; the entire group then moves to the library, with individual assignments of materials which they can read in a relatively short time; at a definite time, they reconvene in the classroom to report their results briefly and undertake the necessary discussion. The fact that evening classes often meet only once a week in a long session makes this scheme feasible and, in fact, adds to its desirability because it provides a welcome change of pace in a long evening.

Another possibility which is too seldom employed is to build a classroom library, a small but varied collection of books and pamphlets which the class can circulate among themselves. If each student were to buy several books recommended by the instructor and agree to pool them for the benefit of the entire class, even a small class can put together a useful collection, particularly on a relatively specialized field of interest. Even if the instructor decides to use a basic text, the students might buy different supplementary books and circulate them among the group.

The Case Study

Among the variety of learning materials which education has experimented with during the last several decades, one of the most popular and useful is *the case.* It is particularly appropriate for study in the personal and social problem areas but has been used advantageously even in science. The concentrated analysis of case materials has, of course, time-honored origins in both law and medicine; the method is more difficult to apply in other fields, but its advantages repay the effort necessary to develop good cases.

As those who try using impromptu cases soon discover, materials which have not been fairly carefully tailored for a particular use may not accomplish much. It is important particularly here to specify the learning objective, or we find ourselves without some crucial element in the materials, a lack which is not exposed until a group is engaged in discussing them. Each of the following purposes for which cases are commonly used, for example, impose somewhat different requirements on their construction:

APPLYING PRINCIPLES. Mere ability to recognize or recall a generalization or a theory is scarcely very good evidence that the student has achieved understanding; if he can apply the generalization accurately to a particular instance, we not only have reasonable grounds for assuming understanding but practice in doing so enlarges that understanding. In fact, in a society becoming increasingly bureaucratic, the skill of application itself is an important one; a fundamental characteristic of bureaucratic structure is the existence of abstract rules which the bureaucrat must apply to concrete instances. Case materials used for this purpose educationally do not require a high degree of complexity and may often be constructed out of events reported in news stories or may simply be contrived instances.

The opposite process, that of building principles or generalizations from the consideration of particular instances, is considerably more difficult. Critics of the case study method often point out that much discussion of this type stays on the particular issue or circumstance and seldom rises to the more abstract level of generalizations. One of the problems, clearly, is that it is difficult, if not impossible, to generalize on the basis of a single case, and if we are interested in developing principles we had best provide enough examples.

IMPROVING DECISION-MAKING SKILLS. Recent adaptations of the case study method in business education have stressed this purpose above all others, the famous Harvard School of Business cases being a notable example. The requirements imposed on a case by the need to base a decision on it are severe. The student must know with whom he is to identify in the case and what the pressures are which generate the necessity for a decision. Above all, he must have available all of the relevant data, which is the real difficulty in case construction of this kind. The instructor must carefully think through the possible lines of discussion and provide answers for the whole range of questions which students are likely to raise. This very difficulty, however, suggests a method of case presentation which might considerably enhance its learning value; if we present the bare bones of a situation and the kind of decision demanded, we may require as a first step that the students indicate what further data they find necessary before they can come to a decision, thus providing for one of the crucial skills in decision-making.

Adult classes offer opportunities for the use of cases of this type which are not available in other milieux, in that the students are usually involved in real situations which are likely mines of source materials. Students can be assigned the task of constructing a case of their own by selecting a relevant incident, gathering data about it through interviews and documentary research, and tracing the natural history of a decision with which they had some connection.

POWER ANALYSIS. Faultily-constructed decision-making cases often turn out to be useful only by providing an opportunity to examine the role of power relations in a particular situation. To avoid confusion it is best to present them as such in the first place. A case which presents the dilemma of a teacher who is ordered by his principal, backed by the school board, to remove certain books from a list of recommended reading does not present many decision alternatives; desirable alternatives are clearly fantasies involving the elimination of real facts of organizational life.

VALUE CLARIFICATION. Case materials often provide dramatic examples of value conflicts, which enable a group to think through the structure of values embedded in a situation without the confusion produced by their own ego-involvement. For this purpose, even the simplest outlines of a situation are sufficient to produce lively and useful discussion.[8] One instructor of adults, for example, as an efficient way of getting a class to achieve awareness of the fundamental value-system differences which underlie many of the more superficial opinion clashes in discussion, presents this little case: "If a man is shipwrecked on a desert island, how is he to determine whether what he does there is right or wrong?" The often rather heated discussion of this problem usually produces very quickly a number of basic orientations to ethics, which can usefully be referred to class discussions of other issues. Generally speaking, case materials for this purpose are the least difficult to select or develop.

An Illustration

Because the decision-making case is the most difficult to construct, a case of that type is presented here as an illustration. Note the careful attention to detail, which the student might or might not want to pay attention to, the way in which the locus of the decision is clearly specified, and the mixture of both technical and human factors which must be considered for a rational decision.[9]

LAMSON COMPANY

The Lamson Company was a small independent oil company, producers of a variety of oil products which they distributed throughout a midwestern territory covering parts of three states. The headquarters and refinery of the company were located in Cincinnati, Ohio. Part of the refinery equipment of the Lamson Company consisted of two distillation towers, designated as Towers 1D and 2D. These towers served the function of distilling crude oil under heat and pressure into a variety of petroleum components, which were, in turn, further refined and processed with other equipment. The operation of each of the distillation towers was controlled by means of semiautomatic equipment that was housed in a control building adjacent to the towers.

Each tower required for its operation a three-man crew for each eight-hour shift. The units were run not only three shifts a day but seven days a week. The crew spent most of their working time in the control house, making adjustments to the control apparatus, doing minor repair work when trouble arose, and performing routine maintenance work.

Henry McMahon, crew foreman, supervised all the crews working on Tower 1D. Andrew Kirk supervised the crews on Tower 2D. Both of these supervisors, in turn, reported to the distillation foreman, Samuel Wood.

In 1941 the Lamson Company decided to make certain changes in the plant which entailed training some of the personnel for different types of jobs. The company decided to construct a new distillation tower, incorporating many new technological improvements that were not present in the older existing towers. Among other innovations, the new installation was to include a radically different type of control equipment which was both more intricate and more fully automatic equipment than the older equipment. Because of these modifications in the new tower, the management decided to give a training course for the crew members who would be selected to operate and maintain the new equipment. The training course material was prepared and presented by one of the company's younger engineers, William Downes, with the constant help and guidance of the engineers designing the new tower.

In the selection of men for this course, Samuel Wood made a careful canvass of the entire operating and maintenance force throughout the refinery, and, in general, chose only outstanding men, since higher management, based on information from the designers, felt that a new unit of this type, which was of such vital importance in its functioning, should be well handled. Also, since the equipment was the first of its kind in the country, it would, no doubt, receive considerable attention. He finally selected 12 crewmen to take the course.

During the extended course the entire group, including the instructor and the representatives of the designers, became very closely knit. Changes were constantly being made by the designers which added to the problems of the students. At the completion of the course, the students and the instructure held a "graduating" dinner among themselves. This "graduation" was subsequently celebrated every year by a dinner sponsored and attended by the original group in the course.

After several delays, due to war conditions, the new equipment was finally placed in service. It was operated as Distillation Unit 3D under the supervision of William Downes, who, in turn, reported to Samuel Wood.

The type of work required on the new equipment was considerably different from that on the older units, being more in the nature of a white-collar job. For example, work on the new equipment was cleaner than on the old equipment, as a considerable amount of dirty routine maintenance work was eliminated. Another new feature was that special ventilating equipment was installed to provide filtered air in the control house in order to keep down dust and dirt. Fans were also installed to give additional circulation of air.

As the work proceeded, Wood noticed that the men seemed highly interested in their jobs. They made many suggestions for improvements in order to eliminate some of the "bugs" that showed up in the equipment in the early stages. The designer accepted many of these suggestions. Some of the men felt that they were "even doing engineering work." Wood was pleased with the operating results obtained from the new unit.

After some months' experience in operating the new unit, the management felt that it would be necessary to train six additional men on this type of equipment to care for turnover, absences and vacations of the regular crew. Such a plan, however, meant that since 18 men would not be needed, at all times, some of the group would have to spend part of their time working on the older type towers.

After plans had been discussed, and the training program for the six new men had started, Wood received the following letter addressed to his home and signed by the 12 original crewmen of the 3D unit. In addition to the letter to Samuel Wood, copies were mailed out simultaneously to William Downes, as well as Wood's superiors in the next four higher levels of authority. In each case the letter was mailed to the home address, signed personally by all 12 men and bore the names of all the recipients.

December 7, 1944

To: MESSRS. LYNCH
YOUNG
TURNER
STEPHENS
WOOD
DOWNES

GENTLEMEN:

This letter is being addressed to you to direct your attention to a problem confronting the crew members at the 3D Distillation Unit.

Plans are being made to combine the operating work of all three distillation units. We believe a proper understanding on your part of our feeling toward these plans will serve to circumvent what possibly could become an unpleasant situation.

First. We are agreed, that had we known three years ago, when we were informed of this job, that such a proposition as the above was contemplated, we surely would have made every effort to stay where we then were. Because of the fact that the type of equipment was new, the methods, the whole job itself modern, we were led to believe a chance to work in such would be an advancement.

Second: On the day of our induction into the training course for the new unit, we were informed that the system was so unlike anything we had ever experienced that a close application to the job, frequent "refresher courses," and much diligent study would be required of us in order to stay on top of the job. In the 33 months since that day we have experienced nothing to disprove this statement. To the contrary.

Third. Not one of us feels that he has mastered all parts of his job to such a degree that he could retain the knowledge he has acquired, if forced to divide his attention between two other dissimilar units. None of us feels sufficiently experienced in all normal job assignments in the new unit to merit the title of "all around men." Add to this the fact that no training has been given on many miscellaneous and routine problems of the job, and it will become evident that further dilution of job contact is inimical to giving the kind of service that all informed persons declare is imperative with this type of equipment.

Fourth. If we consider the money spent on training men for this job as an investment in good results, then any plan that would tend to depreciate that investment prematurely would be, to say the least, unwise and inefficient.

However, we realize that the training of additional men for the new unit is good insurance, and we believe that the six men now in school can receive their "on the job" training and at the same time be used to relieve the present force for refresher courses and during vacations. We have been given to understand that it would be dangerous to spread our 12 men as thin as was done last summer. So it would seem that more men could be used to advantage.

Finally, while not wishing to appear critical of a proposal which, no doubt, is well meant, we do not want to minimize the intensity of feeling which this proposal has aroused in our group. We trust that you will take this letter as it is intended, that is, as a sincere expression of a group of workmen having the best interest of our job at heart.

Respectfully submitted,

Role Playing

As a device for classroom use, the role play has become popular only recently and is perhaps the only innovation which is adult education's own. From Moreno's sociodrama and the early days of human relations training for administrators it has spread experimentally to a number of other areas; if used with skill, role playing is a very powerful instrument for achieving some types of understanding and insight and should be in the repertoire of every instructor of adults who might find it relevant to his field.

The role play is, in a sense, an animated case study. A problematic situation is presented, but instead of discussing it, part of the group takes over the roles of those involved in the situation and acts it out to some resolution. Its use as a tool in psychotherapy has no place in this book, but as an educational device, one might consider three major forms:

IMPROMPTU HUMAN RELATIONS SITUATIONS. In many programs within the personal and social relations and the work area, problem situations arise for discussion in which the central issue is the effect of particular kinds of behavior on others or on the situation. Problems of community group action, supervision, and parent-child relationships are the most common examples in the broad field of adult education. The group can use the role play to provide an immediate, dramatic experience with the dimensions of the particular problem, one which is shared by all present. The class itself shapes the dimensions of the situation and suggests the cast of characters; thus, in a discussion of teen-age reactions to parental supervision, the instructor might suggest that a role play involving a parent attempting to set rules for late hours for a teen-age daughter be acted out several times with different types of parental behavior. Not only do the directly visible consequences of each method become material for later discussion, but the actors themselves are available for questioning about how they felt at certain points during the role play. If they become involved in their characterizations, their reactions are relatively accurate and useful data.

This type of impromptu role play often appears to be the easiest to do and is, in fact, probably the most difficult. Instructors who attempt it need a considerable amount of skill and some experience to make it an educationally useful device. Assuming the presence of a competent professional, however, such role playing can contribute a great deal of insight in a way which case study discussion seldom can achieve.

CONSTRUCTED HUMAN RELATIONS SITUATIONS. A less risky approach to the method involves setting up a role play in advance, planning the situation and writing the roles. This can be a very useful pedagogical device indeed, because one can thus build into the roles in advance significant problems of which some of the players are unaware and must therefore respond to spontaneously. One report, for example, describes a class demonstration of the effects of status, which sets up a meeting of a school faculty to consider how to allocate a special fund to the school.[10] One member of the group has been told separately that several people at the meeting are members of the school board and that the others are teachers. When he joins the meeting, his deference to the two people whom he perceives as having status is in marked contrast to his behavior toward the other members of the committee and sets up ripples of adaptive reactions in the meeting as a whole. Class analysis of this kind of situation, starting with attempts to describe and account for the variety of behavior observed, can help students to a dramatic sense of social psychological concepts.

Norman Maier has constructed more elaborate role plays for the communication of important insights into industrial situations presenting problems for supervisors; an example is presented at the end of this section to demonstrate how ingeniously and elegantly the possibilities of the role play can be exploited. But the work and social relations areas have produced some experimentation with even more elaborate forms of role play, suitable only to the residential program. In these forms, all of the participants in the program are assigned roles in a company, or a government agency, or a community, and work together over a period of days in an attempt to solve a given problem situation. The chapter on the adult residential, following this one, will consider this format in more detail.

OTHER OBJECTIVES. The real learning potential of the role play for objectives other than human relations ones has been sadly neglected. It is a very useful method for dramatizing the interaction of forces in any dynamic situation in which we want to help people grasp relationships of a complex order. One instructor, for example, in dealing with comparative economic theory, has the class act out a meeting of a high-level planning commission in the Soviet Union. Members take on specific roles of commissars responsible for separate sectors of the economy, familiarize themselves at least slightly with the problems of that sector, and then together try to work through a plan for the coming year. The resulting insight into the problem of planning in a monolithic state is hard to come by in any other way. A noted American political scientist once played with the idea of presenting a year's course for adults in which each member of the class would take on the identity of one of the members of the Constitutional Convention. He would be expected to do a good deal of reading about the actual life and character of his other self and try to feel his way into his skin. Class sessions would re-enact debates and committee meeetings in which students would work on the crucial issues faced by the framers of the Constitution. It is hard to imagine a more exciting way of coming to understand the issues of the time which echo in major conflicts in our own day.

Here, finally, is an example of a first-rate constructed role play, one of a considerable series which Maier developed for human relations training courses in industry.[11] Notice that it demands not merely the presentation of a situation which the group observes, but splits the group into teams for what Maier calls *multiple role play*. Having 15 or 20 such couples acting out the scene simultaneously does not, as one might expect, produce utter chaos, nor does it take an extraordinary skill or training either to carry out the instructions or to manage the subsequent analysis.

ROLE FOR JIM WELLS, DIVISION SUPERVISOR

You are the supervisor of a division employing about 75 men and women and six first-line supervisors. You like your job, and the supervisors and employees who work for you, and you feel that they cooperate with you in every way.

This morning you noticed that one of your first-line supervisors, Bill Jackson, was rather late in getting to work. Since Bill is very conscientious and was working on a rush job you wondered what had happened. Bill is thoroughly dependable and, when something delays him, he always tries to phone you. For this reason you were somewhat concerned and were about to call his home when one of Bill's men, a young fellow named Joe Blake, came in. Joe is a good-natured kid, just out of high school, but this time he was obviously angry, and said that he was not going to work for Bill another minute and was going to quit unless you got him another job. Evidently Bill had come in, started to work, and then lost his temper completely when young Joe didn't do something quite right.

Although Bill occasionally has his bad moods, it is unlike him to lose his temper this way. This latest rush job may have put him under too much pressure but even so, his outburst this morning seems difficult to explain on any reasonable grounds. You feel, therefore, that something must be seriously wrong and if you can get Bill to talk about whatever it is that is bothering him you may get the situation straightened out. In any case, you are determined not to get into an argument with Bill or criticize him in any way. Instead you are going to try to get him to talk about his troubles, listen to what he has to say, and indicate that you understand how he feels about things. If Bill seems more angry than Joe's mistake would reasonably justify, you might suppose that there is something more behind all this and Bill would probably feel a lot better if he got it off his chest. If Bill is thoroughly angry with Joe, you may suggest that Joe be fired in order to demonstrate that you have not taken Joe's side in the matter.

You talked with Joe for several minutes and, after he had told his side of the story, he felt better and was ready to go back on the job. You just phoned Bill and asked him to drop around when he had a chance. Bill said he'd come right over and is walking toward your office now.

ROLE FOR BILL JACKSON, FIRST-LINE SUPERVISOR

You have just come to work after a series of the most humiliating and irritating experiences you have ever had. Last night your next-door neighbor, Sam Jones, had a wild, drunken party at his house that kept you awake most of the night. Jones is a blustering, disagreeable man who has no consideration whatever for others, so when you called him at about 3:00 A.M. and told him to be less noisy, he was abusive and insulting. Things quieted down later on, but when you finally got some rest you overslept.

Since you were in the midst of a rush job at the company, you skipped breakfast to hurry to work and, as you were leaving the house, you noticed that someone had driven a car across one corner of your lawn and had torn out several feet of your new hedge. You were certain that Jones or one of the drunks at his party had done it so you ran right over to Jones's house, determined to have it out with him. He not only denied everything, but practically threw you out and threatened to knock your teeth out if you didn't shut up and behave yourself and you know that he is big enough to do it.

When you came to work, more than an hour late, your nerves were so ragged that you were actually shaking. Everything conceivable had gone wrong, and then the last straw was when you discovered that Joe Blake, a young high school recruit, had made a mistake that delayed you several hours on your rush job, or at least it would have if you hadn't caught him in time. Naturally, you gave him a good going over for his carelessness. Blake said he wouldn't take that kind of abuse from anyone and walked out on you. You noticed that he went in to see your supervisor, Jim Wells. Obviously he is in there accusing you of being rough on him. Well, you don't like that kind of an attitude in a young squirt either, and if he has gone in there squawking you'll make him wish he'd never been born. You have had all you can stand and the big boss had better not get tough with you because he'll have one hell of a time getting the job done without you.

Jim had that snivelling brat in there and talked to him for quite a while before he phoned you to come in. Gabbing when there's work to be done—that's certainly a hell of a way to run things. You are on your way to Jim's office now and have no intention of wasting time on words.

(Try to get into the spirit of this case and feel some of the emotions that would ordinarily be present.)

MULTIPLE ROLE PLAYING PROCEDURE PREPARATION

1. The members of the class should pair up with a person next to themselves, one member of each pair calling himself Jim Wells, the other, Bill Jackson.
2. Persons taking the role of Jim Wells should study the instructions on page 109, while persons taking the role of Bill Jackson should study their instructions on page 110.
3. The members of the pairs are advised not to discuss their roles with each other. They should try to imagine their positions and get in the spirit of the problem.
4. When the Bill Jacksons are ready to begin role playing they should stand up to indicate their readiness to meet with Wells. The instructor will give the Jacksons the signal to begin, which should be taken to mean that all Jacksons have arrived at the offices of their respective Jim Wellses.

PROCESS

1. The instructor signals the Bill Jacksons to approach their Jim Wellses. Each assumes his role and conducts himself as in a real-life situation of this kind. It would be natural for Wells to greet Bill and invite him to sit down.
2. All groups role play simultaneously.
3. Between 15 and 20 minutes usually will allow sufficient time for the interview to be completed. The instructor should terminate the few incompleted interviews after about 20 minutes. A warning of one minute is desirable.
4. During the role playing process the instructor should prepare headings for the tabulations he will make on the blackboard when he supervises the general report from the pairs of role players. The reports from the Wellses require three columns with headings as follows: (a) Jackson's trouble; (b) action to be taken; and (c) assistance offered. The reports from the Bill Jacksons require the form shown in Sample Table 1, Bill Jackson's Report, page 112.

GENERAL REPORT AND ANALYSIS

1. The Jim Wellses in turn should report (a) what they found Bill Jackson's trouble to be; (b) what action, if any, they think Jackson should take; and (c) the kind of help, if any, they feel they should give Bill. These reports should be listed in three columns on the board. The instructor should tabulate briefly each new item and place a check mark after dupli-

Sample Table 1, Bill Jackson's Report

(Use Table for Recording Class Data)

	1 Feel no better toward Blake	2 Feel better about Blake	3 Want Blake in unit	4 Intend to apologize to Blake	5 Feel better about neighbor	6 Will apologize to neighbor	7 Felt criticized by Wells
1. Number of Jacksons							
2. Wells scolded or lectured							
3. Wells gave fatherly advice							
4. Wells listened and advised							
5. Wells listened and got Bill to tell everything							
6. Wells took sides with Blake							
7. Wells took sides with Jackson							
8. Wells remained neutral							
9. Wells brought up problem of how to talk to Blake							

cate suggestions. (When possible the Wells reporting should indicate when his opinion agrees with a report already given by a previous Wells. This will reduce the number of entries.)

2. When all of the Wellses have reported, the instructor should summarize briefly the trend in results.

3. The responses from the Jacksons may be quickly obtained by the leader if the Jacksons indicate, with a show of hands, their reactions to the following questions:

a. How many feel no better toward Blake since talking to Wells?
b. How many feel better toward Blake now?
c. How many want Blake back in their units?
d. How many intend to apologize to their Blakes?
e. How many feel better about their next-door neighbor?
f. How many will apologize to their neighbor?
g. How many felt criticized by Wells?

The instructor should enter the appropriate number in line 1 of the table, arranged as in Sample Table 1.

4. The Bill Jacksons should consider the manner in which Wells dealt with them. He might have scolded or lectured; given considerable fatherly advice; listened but with some advice thrown in; and listened as well as responded to feelings so effectively that Bill found himself telling everything. These four classifications are shown on lines 2, 3, 4, and 5, respectively, of the sample table. The instructor should determine the number of times each type of interview occurred in connection with each of the kinds of feelings listed for Jackson and write the appropriate number in each of the columns.

5. Whether or not a given Wells intended it, he may have caused his Bill Jackson to feel that he was against him, on his side, or neutral. Lines 6, 7, and 8, respectively, allow space to record these feelings of Jackson, under the various column headings.

6. Table 1 should be discussed and conclusions formulated as to the procedure used by Wells that seems to attain the most worthwhile objectives.

DISCUSSION WITHIN PAIRS

1. Each Bill Jackson should tell his Wells what he liked most about how he was treated in the interview.

2. Next the Bill Jacksons should tell their Wellses what they liked least about the treatment they received in the interview and why they reacted as they did.

3. The members of each pair should privately discuss the situational factors (such as rank differences, Blake's bypassing Jackson, work pressure, Jackson's expectations of criticism, etc.) that made for possible misunderstandings between Wells and Jackson.

DISCUSSION ISSUES

1. Is Jackson ready to deal with Joe Blake without embarrassment? Should Wells have covered this problem in the interview? Discuss.

2. A former Wells should play the part of Joe Blake. The Bill Jacksons who believe that Blake is entitled to an apology should be given an opportunity to demonstrate. Blake should indicate what he likes or dislikes in each apology without bothering to respond to the apologizer. The group should discuss and evaluate several kinds of apologies.

3. How does Jackson feel about his neighbor? Is this important? Discuss.

4. How should higher supervisors deal with employees who bypass their immediate supervisors? Discuss.

NOTE: Class members and role players will raise many questions. These should be discussed and the instructor should avoid supplying answers.

GENERALIZATION OF CASE

1. Develop a list of situations which participants have experienced or observed that are basically like the case presented.

2. Discuss differences in opinion. Revise list as seems indicated by discussion.

Other Resources

The formal class for adults may be enriched far more than it often is by bringing into it other sources of life experience. The most neglected of these is probably the individual human who is shaped by particular role circumstances. Often enough we import into the classroom the expert in a particular field who, by interacting with the students, can provide a much more dramatic sense of a body of knowledge than reading can produce. But we seldom use the ordinary person, the civic official, the policeman, the teacher, the businessman, the practicing artist, the assembly-line worker, who can provide at appropriate points a sharp awareness of points of view outside the often narrowly-segregated interest boundaries of the middle-class Americans who constitute the bulk of adult education clientele. If several members of the class are appointed as an interviewing committee to prepare a series of questions in advance and to conduct the interview in front of the class, such confrontations can be exceedingly useful.

There is, of course, the enormous resource of audio-visual materials to which teachers of adults have access in common with all other educational enterprises; regrettably, access is not equal, because the structure of the producing industry servicing the audio-visual market is determined by the needs of educating young people. In some cases this makes little substantial difference; the areas of art and science, for example, can use the often superb films produced for children in these fields. Our other major areas of adult education have less to work with.[12]

Lacking a comprehensive and reliable evaluative listing of audio-visual materials from the point of view of adult education, the instructor of adult classes who is ordinarily devoting only a fraction of his time to adult students must take on the job of hunting out the films and tapes and recordings which will prove to be truly useful for what he is doing. He may well decide that the results do not justify the effort, particularly if his objectives are fairly sophisticated ones. The film and recording can dramatize and clarify concepts and often convey the human significance of a problem in a way that no other material can, but they are seldom capable of being as complex as we need to be, and they inevitably impose a kind of passivity which the instructor must be prepared to overcome. Audio-visual resources take on a quite different significance in adult education formats in which the trained instructor is not present, of course, and Chapter VI will raise the question again in that context.

We give too little consideration, however, to the possibility of creating our own materials, as we complain about the difficulty of using a film or a tape which is commercially available and is therefore likely to be too general for some specific application we had in mind. Medical education is, perhaps, the only field which assumes as a matter of course that one can build one's own library of visual materials to do precisely what one wants it to do.

It is not easy, to be sure, to produce a polished 16-mm. film to one's own specifications, but flexible 8-mm. cameras are now on the market which will produce good enough film for most purposes. One can put together a film of a special neighborhood for a sociology course, photograph a role play for class analysis, or take children at play for illustrative purposes. The new Fairchild 8-mm. camera permits one to take sound films much more inexpensively than has ever been possible before.

Filmstrips or slides are far less expensive and require only a good 35-mm. camera and some ingenuity in plotting the sequence of still shots which will clarify or dramatize a process or a situation or illustrate a principle in fields as widely different as architecture and biology.

In the personal and social area, tape recordings may be invaluable. Played for a class, brief interviews with a random sample of people on some topic of interest may make excellent discussion material on the way people express values. An interview with a boy in trouble, in which he is encouraged to talk about his neighborhood, his gang, the police, and what he sees as his future, can be a revelation to a middle-class group who may never have met such a boy.

Many institutions now have available elaborate equipment which many instructors seldom bother to use. Yet, with it one can very easily make transparencies of any printed chart, graph, drawing, or text, capable of being projected to a very good size on an overhead projector without darkening the room. One model of this device provides a movable roll of clear plastic on which the instructor can write or draw as he talks, without his having to turn his back to use the blackboard, interpolating prepared charts or drawings as he wishes.

In an age of very rapid technical advance in devices which add richness, variety, and precision to the act of communications, we need only become aware of the possibilties and be willing to spend the necessary energy to develop aids of considerable usefulness.

TRAINING PROBLEMS

Formal teaching in adult education, as in all educational enterprises, is uneven in quality and in the attention it pays to the special needs of the student as an adult. In a sprawling, varied field it probably succeeds, in fact, in being considerably better on the average than in other institutions; one can only surmise this, because there is little apart from individual observation and impression from which to generalize. For one thing, it is probably true that the relatively formal setting with a trained instructor present represents a minority format in the education of adults; in the world of work, by far the largest sector of the field, much of the instruction is carried on informally, by the county agent in agriculture, for example, or by modified apprenticeship procedures in industry. Formal instruction in the latter field usually involves the communication of fairly specific skills and presents few difficulties. Much of it is conducted by the adult departments of high schools under very competent instructors.

Formal instruction in the more abstract and complex skills of work life, as well as the major part of the activities carried on in personal and social relations, the arts, and science, is often under the auspices of the university or uses university personnel. Here the room for improvement is considerable, but the difficulties which beset any attempt to get it are great. Most adult education enterprises have an inherent mechanism which tends to eliminate poor teachers; students simply register their opinions by dropping out of courses. But this is far from being an efficient device, because students are often poor judges of teachers: they don't know anything about teaching, but they know what they like. What they like, in fact, tends to be the dramatic and the entertaining, whether it happens to result in effective learning or not.

Raising the competence level of the formal classroom teacher of adults is a difficult goal to achieve for many complicated reasons.[13] College instructors as a group are research-oriented and often remarkably naive about the processes of instructing and learning. There is every good reason, indeed, why they should conceive research to be so important, because most of the rewards in the academic system are channeled to the industrious and successful researcher; but though the university teacher is sharply aware of the complex skills involved in doing research, it is regrettable that he tends not to recognize skills of a different order which are equally complicated and difficult to acquire.

These barriers of attitude are hard to overcome and are strengthened further by the institutional structure of much of adult education. Most teachers of adults work only part-time, they do not have established lines of communication to the administration, they are not in any real sense a cohesive group, and they are seldom willing to give time and attention to a task which is peripheral to their central concern. On their part, administrators themselves often devote only part-time to their adult education responsibilities, and their own lack of professional training makes them hesitate to take on the training task which is so vitally needed.

Yet, as the disparate enterprise which is adult education slowly moves toward some sense of coherence and professionalization, and its administrative staffs acquire better-trained, more committed personnel, the training of teachers to meet the special circumstances of the adult classroom becomes more feasible and, indeed, more evident. These early steps are, to be sure, tentative and in most cases are aimed at changing the instructor's attitudes rather than actual practice. They consist of relatively informal gatherings of faculty to discuss general problems of teaching adult students and politely assume that the faculty already are fully competent teachers of some other population.

We could, without much effort, make these group meetings more effective by being less wary of faculty reaction and focusing them more sharply on the specifics of the teaching-learning process, but the training problem can perhaps be dealt with more easily by working with individual teachers or with very small groups teaching courses in the same field. Such a training scheme might embody the following steps:

1. Ask the faculty member to write a plan for the course, with emphasis on a statement of his objectives, the work the students will

be asked to do, and the course of events in a typical class session. Some institutions do ask for such an outline, but only a few of them ever do much beyond filing it.

2. Schedule a session to discuss the plan. The questions which the administrator at such a meeting can raise need have little relation to his own knowledge in the particular subject-matter field and in many instances will bear most directly on helping the instructor clarify his course objectives:

> You wish the student to become "more sophisticated" in this area. If he fitted your idea of the sophisticate, what ought he to be able to do? Recognize more elements as related to particular problems in the field? Recall more information about it? Be able to apply a range of particular theories to explain the phenomena of the area?
>
> If any of these meanings fit your definition of the objective, how do you intend to ensure that the student gets a clear idea of what it is you wish him to learn to do? Describe it for him orally? Ask him to read something which is a model of your objective? How will you get evidence that he comprehends the model?
>
> Are all of these objectives achievable in a single course? Are some of them so important that it might be useful to concentrate on them and eliminate peripheral ones?
>
> If these are the terminal student behaviors you want to achieve, will the student have an opportunity to practice them? Is the work which you want him to do relevant to those behaviors? Will he be able to do some of them in class time, so that you can let him know whether he is doing it correctly or not?

3. Ask the instructor, on the basis of the discussion, to revise his original plan for his own guidance and your information.

There is little question that such a procedure would help improve instruction; many administrators would protest that it is far too time-consuming, even if the normal faculty member would stand for it. Some of them might welcome it, others might be persuaded; many instructors recruited from the community would be glad for the help. Whether one is able to free enough staff time to carry out such a program even on a modest scale depends, of course, on the local situation and on where, on a scale of institutional values, one puts effective teaching. Many adult education enterprises earn enough to enable them to plough back a share of the excess into improving the operation; the business world recognizes the need to do so, and perhaps it is time for us to recognize the same logical necessity. There are very few functions of adult education more at the heart of the matter, or more in need of attention, than teaching.

NOTES

1. An intensive study of a sample of teachers of adult classes was undertaken by the Center for the Study of Liberal Education for Adults in 1958. The general categories which directed the collection and analysis of data reveal the conceptual framework as well as the scope of such research:

Goals: the kind of changes in student behavior in which the teacher is primarily interested;

Direction of interest: in which element of the situation is the teacher most interested: the student, the subject matter, or the act of teaching itself;

Class orientation: the teacher's perception of the needs of the students—as individuals, as subgroups, or as a single unit;

Control: the teacher's direction of the class: the amount of dominance, the degree of responsiveness to students;

Emotional tone: protective, relaxed, threatening, etc.;

Methods: of stimulating students, of allaying anxiety, of presenting subject matter.

The exploratory steps taken in this study also have some relevance for the general question of the improvement of teaching discussed at the end of this chapter. See D. Solomon and H. Miller, *Exploration in Teaching Styles* (Chicago: Center for the Study of Liberal Education for Adults, 1961).

2. These amusing types are from Herbert Thelen's *Dynamics of Groups at Work* (Chicago: University of Chicago Press, 1954), a tough-minded, stimulating work of applied group dynamics, valuable for anyone interested in the more informal aspects of adult education.

3. From a preliminary report on the study described in the first note above. Reports for publication are in preparation.

4. The general view of the role of the classroom teacher of adults suggested here, and in the chapter as a whole, does not quite coincide with what I would urge as an ideal role. The latter would be closer to the one described by Nathaniel Cantor which emphasizes the students' struggle to define the problems which concern them within the broad context of the subject matter. See Nathaniel Cantor, *The Teaching-Learning Process* (New York: Drydon Press, 1953). Schueler and Belth have applied this view to adult education in H. Schueler and M. Belth, *Liberal Education for Adults Re-examined, Notes and Essays No. 25* (Chicago: Center for the Study of Liberal Education for Adults, 1959). I am convinced that, despite its merits, most teachers find this an extremely complex and difficult teaching role to play and one which does not fit their personalities very well. The more pragmatic approach taken here leaves considerably more latitude for the expression of individual styles.

5. This outline of Weber's classic model of the bureaucracy is taken from Peter Blau's *Bureaucracy in Modern Society* (New York: Random House, 1956), which the instructor then recommended to the group as supplementary reading. Citing such extra reading at the point at which the group sees its relevance, instead of providing a long list at the beginning of the course, is apt to stimulate more reading in adult classes.

6. J. S. Bruner, *The Process of Education, op. cit.* See also Bruner's article in the *Harvard Educational Review,* "Act of Discovery," Vol. XXXI, No. 1 (Winter, 1961), in which he discusses some of the experiments currently in progress. Professional educators interested in the public schools are currently much excited about the possibilities of Bruner's suggestions and are beginning to test them in both science and English instruction. Critics often raise the question about such approaches: Isn't it likely to be effective only with bright children? It seems to me that the more crucial question is whether or not the average teacher is capable of applying the method. For adult educators it becomes even more crucial; if the schoolmen, with considerable control over teacher training, often fail to make some new methodology come off, we in adult education are considerably less likely to influence our instructional staffs toward the adoption of more sophisticated methods.

7. For a detailed description of the seminar mentioned, now given at New York University's adult division, see Daniel Malamud, *Teaching a Human Relations Workshop, Notes and Essays No. 10* (Chicago: Center for the Study of Liberal Education for Adults, 1955). Many of the ingenious methods Malamud describes might, with some success, be applied to other areas.

8. Short cases which are occasionally developed as research instruments in the behavioral sciences can often be made to serve learning objectives. See, for example, those developed by Jones in an attempt to measure attitudes toward property, in A. W. Jones, *Life, Liberty, and Property* (New York: Lippincott, 1941). Or the cases cited in the final chapters of this book which were constructed for evaluation purposes can just as readily be used for class discussion.

9. The Lamson Company case is one of the Harvard cases and is reproduced by permission of the President and Fellows of Harvard University (copyright 1948). Business education has available many such case materials; for example, R. Dubin, *Human Relations in Administration* (New York: Prentice-Hall, 1951), and most instructors of adults in this area are accustomed to using them. In other fields, one must hunt them out. For some models, see E. L. Hartley and G. D. Wiebe, *Casebook in Social Processes* (New York: Crowell, 1960); George and Louise Spindler, *Case Studies in Cultural Anthropology* (New York: Holt, 1960); *Case Records for Study and Teaching* (Family Service Association, New York); Aaron Sayvetz, *Scientists at Work* (Chicago: Center for the Study of Liberal Education for Adults, 1952).

10. Alvin Zander and Arthur Cohen, "Attributed Social Power and Group Acceptance," *Journal of Abnormal and Social Psychology,* Vol. LI, No. 3 (November, 1955).

11. Reprinted with permission from Norman R. F. Maier, Allen R. Solem, and Ayesha A. Maier, *Supervisory and Executive Development* (New York: Wiley, 1957), pp. 40–45.

12. Standard references to audio-visual materials can be discouragingly misleading for the adult educator. Wilson's *Guide to Educational Films,* for instance, records the hopes of the film maker for an audience by citing many films made for children as useful for adults. Sometimes they are appropriate for adults, but in a good many cases they are not. The time-consuming task of previewing films to decide whether they are relevant is another deterrent, even without considering the difficulties of getting the film and equipment together at the right place in the proper working order. On the whole, where it is possible to follow the suggestions in the text for preparing one's own materials, the instructor is likely to be better off, with the exception of science and the arts, of course.

13. For a collection of varied views of these complications, see M. Miller (ed.) *On Teaching Adults: An Anthology* (Chicago: Center for the Study of Liberal Education for Adults, 1960).

5

SMALL GROUPS: IN RESIDENCE

> The small community as it existed throughout most of man's history and by means of which the greater part of every person's real education was achieved is disappearing in America. It seems unlikely that it will or even can be re-established. Nevertheless the functions that it performed in the education and the maturation of individuals are still essential. Without community man is not truly man. The residential adult school can to some extent give to people that dimension which we call community and which becomes more and more important as society becomes increasingly technological and impersonal.
>
> ROYCE S. PITKIN, *The Residential School in American Adult Education*

Much of adult education is carried on in the relatively formal classroom, in small groups which come together about once a week for several hours over a period of weeks, and there is little question that the format works. Yet, there has been in the past several decades a strong trend toward the practice of getting groups of adults together in a residential setting for concentrated study for periods ranging from several days to several months. We might look for the reasons for such a movement in the problems of getting normally busy adults to maintain a reasonable attendance rate or to fit necessary reading into a crowded life schedule. Perhaps, as adult education increasingly attracts the middle-class business man and professional, it must adapt to the conference-going patterns of such people. Or it may be that the regular evening class still carries the stigma of the "night school" in which the new arrival learned how to be an American or in which the socially striving lower-middle-class person found, and still finds, an opportunity for social mobility.

Whatever the reason, many adult programs above the level of pure skill training or of delayed degree programs are scheduled at residential centers, often on a relatively cloistered university campus, or in frankly resort-like surroundings completely away from the city, at glass and steel conference centers and in converted hunting lodges of now-forgiven robber barons. Because it does not imitate any already existing pattern in the education of youth, the format gives adult educators an opportunity to develop a distinctive education form, shaped to the special needs of its clientele.[1]

Indeed, there is a tendency among some adult educators who are philosophically committed to the residential format to assume that it is the only educational pattern that, historically, is distinctively adult. If the Danish folk school is truly the ancestor of the present American residential institute or conference, then they are correct. But it is hard to see any line of direct development.[2] The Danish prototype gathered together groups of country folk during the hard winter months in an effort to overcome what Marx called the idiocy of rural life; in the communal life of the schools, with their deeply religious tone, the leaders of the movement hoped to raise the level of life of an essentially brutalized and alcoholic peasantry. Nor is there much doubt that the present level of civilization in Denmark owes much to that effort. There are a number of country study centers in Britain today which clearly owe their development to these Danish precursors, and one of the early movements in American adult education established a handful of similar institutions, several of which still exist.

It is significant that these American folk schools were established in areas of noteworthy backwardness, among, for example, the eastern mountain folk who were cut off from the mainstream of nineteenth-century industrialization. They encouraged the development of literacy, better diet, the improvement of local arts and crafts, and the like. To connect the recent rapid increase in residential study for adults to that movement would be a dubious undertaking. The modern phenomenon is clearly an urban one, related to the occupational and interest grouping of American associational life, far removed from a folk preoccupation with land and deeply-rooted tradition. In Riesman's terms, the folk school was an effort to help a population at the stage of tradition-direction struggle out of the bonds of a folk culture no longer appropriate in a society devoted to production and which now demanded a new character type. The new residential movement is a phenomenon of other-direction, a way of rapidly communicating the latest word, the most acceptable life style, or the new fashion in character.

This is why residential programs are attended so consistently by homogeneous social groups, second-level business executives, supervisors, hair dressers, labor leaders, secretaries to executives, community leaders, school teachers, insurance salesmen. Seldom does one find a two-week institute in human relations, let us say, with representatives from more than one of these groups, even from more than one level of the corporate structure. Whether or not one accepts this sociological explanation of the basis for the structure of recent residential education, such relative homogeneity presents both advantages and problems. The instructional staff can often build on common background and interests; they are also likely to encounter a massive resistance to alien concepts precisely because of the common frame of reference. Whatever the difficulties, many adult educators assume that they are outweighed by what are seen as important, inherent advantages in the format.

ADVANTAGES OF RESIDENTIAL ADULT EDUCATION

1. There does seem to be special merit, on the face of it, in getting people out of their normal routines and often harried lives into a new and different setting. It permits them to relax, to concentrate on study as a major focus of activity for a period, and even, hopefully, to be reflective. There is very little dependable evidence, however, that the residential setting itself enhances learning. A recent study compared two programs, almost exactly alike in content and staff, in one case presented for a group in residence at one of the Kellogg centers, in the other given as a series of day-long meetings.[3] Pre- and post-testing of information gain, ability to apply principles to problems, and relevant attitude shifts found little significant difference between the two groups. Any claim against the superiority of residential learning, however, can hardly rest on such fragmentary evidence; we need to do

more research of the same kind in a variety of situations before the issue is decided.

2. Those who are philosophically committed to the folk-school idea stress the advantage in the residential of group interaction. The classroom format of spaced sessions seldom provides an occasion for very extensive personal relationships among the members of an adult group, with the exception of the informal discussion groups which meet in participants' homes. The residential group, on the other hand, constitutes a small, artificial, social world of its own, which often develops an atmosphere of great friendliness and something of the tone of youthful camping experiences or the jollity and good fellowship of the German nature groups. Such an atmosphere is sometimes deliberately encouraged by the staff of the institute, who arrange group sings, folk dances, and the like. This aspect of residentialism has most often drawn the fire of hostile critics, who like to inquire what relation there is between "togetherness" and the process of education. We have widely different capacities for enjoying closeness with groups of others, to be sure, and it is difficult at times not to be repelled by the sometimes unrelenting "we-ness" of modern education. It is equally difficult, however, to brush aside the considerable body of evidence for the linkage between the acceptance of change by the individual and his group membership.

Learning is change in behavior, and we tend, as earlier chapters indicated, to resist change. Desirable change becomes more acceptable to us if other individuals who are important to us are willing to accept it at the same time—if the change is group-supported.[4] A group of individuals who come together for a week at a residential institute find, for the most part, that their acceptance by others is very important. If the group develops norms about the value of certain concepts or the importance of particular patterns of cognitive behavior, the individuals composing the group will find it easier to make such changes. Part of the conflict over this issue arises from a probable relation between the choice of a career as an intellectual and the need to maintain emotional distance in one's relationships with others. The critics of togetherness may be turning a personal preference into a principled objection, a not unheard-of process; a number of intellectuals who share the same basic distaste for sentimental campfire singing will pass out the songsheets themselves, convinced that they are helping to structure a more effective educational situation.

3. A final advantage to the residential is the rather obvious one of

time. The ordinary adult program consisting of separate sessions at spaced intervals seldom can count on very many more hours of student time than are represented by the actual meeting times, about thirty hours for an average adult course at the university level and somewhat less for the short course. But a group meeting daily for two weeks can spend that much time together and still have afternoons and evenings free, even if one provides occasions for relaxation and play. Some experimental evidence suggests that this may not be altogether an advantage. Concentrating learning trials in one massive dose seems to be inferior to spacing the trials so the organism has a chance to consolidate new behavior.[5] But although this principle seems fairly well established in some areas of human learning, it remains to be applied to adult learning at this level; it would suggest, for instance, that in the comparison study cited above, the group who attended spaced sessions should have demonstrated superiority on the criterion tests over the residential group, which was not the case.

In general, then, one can conclude that there are some significant advantages to the residential format, at least in theory, and we must wait for the results of future research to draw any firmer conclusions. Many adults do, in fact, find it more attractive than attending a course, and this alone suggests that it is worth the effort to find ways of increasing the present effectiveness of the residential.

MAXIMIZING THE POTENTIAL OF THE RESIDENTIAL

Residential institutes and conferences are currently presented in all of the major areas of adult education at some levels. The majority of them concentrate in the work area, where it has become the favorite device for disseminating new knowledge and techniques. An inspection of the annual programs planned by a representative Conference and Institute Division of any of the large state universities testifies to the incredible variety and number of such gatherings but also to the domination of the world of work. Increasingly, however, one finds more residentials devoted to social and personal problems and the arts: a week spent studying the modern metropolis and its problems, or automation; a weekend spent on one Beethoven string quartet or learning about modern painting.

In this new and largely unexamined field, generalizations do not come easily, but one can raise a number of questions relating to what appear to be persistent and unresolved problems of methodology.

The primary issue is: Who makes the decision about method? Characteristically, the residential program involves the administrative staff of the adult division more heavily in planning than does the regular course program; it is taught by more than one instructor; and, particularly when it takes the form of an occupational conference, an organizational planning committee takes a strong hand in formulating objectives and methods. The planning committee representing the sponsoring organization knows a good deal about the field of practice and nothing about the educational problems involved; their orientation inevitably sets up demands for a situation in which academic expertise will supply answers to their practical problems or bring them up to date by providing a flow of information. The instructional staff, indeed, usually is composed of experts who are firm believers in the tenet that the educational process consists of telling people what you know or think. The administrator, who may know a good deal about the conditions under which people learn, may find himself too busy organizing the living arrangements and schedules of many conferences to play the role of educator in the planning, or he may feel that his lack of expertness in the particular content of the conference bars him from taking an active role.[6]

The most likely solution for this situation lies in training administrative personnel to play a new role. If they were to be relieved of administrative detail by clerical assistants and encouraged to take a strong hand in planning the educational process, there is little question that we would improve the effectiveness of many residential programs. The preceding chapter suggests what that planning and guiding role might consist of.

Outside of the occupational area another difficulty becomes central. Here the general tendency is to recruit members of the academic profession to play separate instructional roles with little attempt to modify what they do normally in their ordinary classes.[7] A sociologist presents a series of sessions which often condenses his introductory course; a number of parallel sessions at another time of the day are taken by a political scientist, who does the same. The model is the university summer session, in which the student telescopes in time the same activities which he might carry on in a normal semester. Such concentrated residentials for adult groups can often be very stimulating, but the pattern fails to make the most of the possibilities inherent in the format. The approach uncritically adopts the assumption of the traditional American four-year college curriculum and proceeds on the principle that a little bit of a good thing is proportionately as good as the whole. The analogy which comes to mind is that of the physician giving a patient a thousand units of penicillin because that is all that is available, when the effective dosage is several hundred thousand units; one is often reminded of the dosage image in listening to academics planning an educational program: "We'll give them 20 hours of psychology and 32 hours of history."

This kind of planning overlooks one of the potentially most fruitful characteristics of adult residentials—the common background and interests of the students. Members of the same social group or community organization, or persons occupying a similar social status with accompanying role difficulties, inevitably are concerned with common themes or problems. It requires thought and time, to be sure, to transform these themes into curricula and to find ways of bringing to bear on them the compartmentalized disciplines into which we have organized knowledge, but it is worth the effort. The adult is not in the position of the adolescent at the threshold of life; he is already playing a number of life roles and knows at first hand the dimensions of the human condition. Because the residential situation usually involves a temporary withdrawal from activity and routine, it encourages the thoughtful examination of real problems at a much more meaningful level than we can ordinarily manage; it provides the opportunity to develop the perspective which an earlier chapter suggests as a major goal.

One fairly brief residential attended by the executives of a large company, for example, was devoted to an examination of power, a theme which permits the educational planner to draw from a number of disciplines. Literature offers the kind of moving insight into such a theme that opens up new perspectives (in this case, *Antigone*); philosophy provides approaches to the problems of value choices inherent in the theme; sociology and political science contribute hypotheses about the structures in which men wield power, the shapes of power roles, and detailed case studies of social reality. Readings were very carefully selected to illuminate crucial issues of power as they are likely to be raised in the contemporary executive role. Such an approach is consonant with the special character of the residential, not only the common background of the participants, but the concentrated nature of the experience.

If the group is together for a period longer than a week or two, one can plan a funnel-shaped experience. The first part of the program might consist of a separate examination of a number of different topics or themes, with a final three or four days, or a week, devoted to discussion of a major problem which focuses and applies the earlier learning. Thus, a ten-week residential for union officials included separate series of sessions on labor history, sociology, psychology, and political science, and concentrated in the final week and a half on a number of present problems of the labor movement which the group could now approach with a more complex body of concepts and understanding.

Finally, there is the problem of using the available time more flexibly and effectively. The weekend retreat, or even the single week, presents no great problem of timing, but if the program runs longer, it is difficult to avoid either over-programming, with the group sinking into a dull apathy, or providing too little stimulation and encouraging a vacation atmosphere. The first of these risks is probably the safest, *if* the program involves the student in a sufficiently wide range of activities. Prolonged periods spent passively listening can be poisonous, but because it is the easiest way to program, we often subject residential students to them without weighing the consequences for our educational goals.

The task of developing a sequence of appropriate activities for the group is a relatively easy one. It is often possible to adopt in modified form some of the methods of the workshop (see Chapter VIII). The most useful general approach is to include in the preliminary planning an examination of the institute's objectives in the behavioral framework suggested earlier. If our objectives include "an understanding of the major forces which determine political behavior on the community level," and we take the trouble to list the behavior which would demonstrate that the student has achieved such an understanding, we can plan activities which will give him the opportunity to practice those behaviors. We might suggest that the group, at some point, work together on a plan for a campaign for urban renewal in a specific community for which they are provided with a good deal of data. We can provide case studies and the chance to analyze them by applying generalizations which they have now presumably learned.

Adult education objectives almost inevitably include some form of role adjustment or role insight. If the residential hopes to influence such behavior, participants need the opportunity to act out, or see acted out, some of the relevant situations. We can assign groups of students the task of constructing role plays to present to the group at large. Many of the devices suggested in the preceding chapter for the seminar are appropriate with little change for the residential situation, and the limited opportunity for using library facilities which often severely limits the methods of the regular course seldom applies to the residential unless it is held off in the woods.

AN ILLUSTRATION

The most convenient illustration of a residential course is a two-week program held at Vassar College in 1956, because a published description of it is available. It is in some respects atypical; it was experimental, a considerable amount of extra money was spent on programming, and its focus was exclusively a liberal arts one. But many of its features might be duplicated without great cost, and its program represents two of our four major adult education areas, the personal and social, and the world of form. The following description is condensed from a longer account of the Institute.[8]

The Vassar Institute for Women in Business was held at Alumnae House, Vassar College, Poughkeepsie, New York, August 5–19, 1956. The 28 participants were holders of the Certified Professional Secretary certificate conferred by the Institute for Certifying Secretaries, a department of the National Secretaries Association (International) and they were the pilot group for this residential experiment in teaching liberal arts to highly trained and experienced specialists.

The Institute opened officially with an orientation session on Sunday evening. . . . Irving Kriesberg had, during preliminary planning, a suggestion for starting an exchange of personal information among the students, and his plan worked to provide a warm introduction as well as an unplanned, impromptu art class—perhaps because Kriesberg is an artist. He had suggested that each participant bring with her 'something of value,' prized not for monetary worth or artistic merit but for personal meaning, and that each woman describe this meaning to the group.

As the women began to talk, the orientation session became, in small, much of what was to characterize the whole Institute.

A tone was set which was to prevail for two weeks: the women, although occasionally shy, were eager to learn and willing to share, as some remarks about their possessions will show: a diary of a trip to Europe, important to its owner because, 'I am not creative, and people of my economic class do not go to Europe. But this is a diary from someone of the hinterland first exposed to Europe. It may be very naive, and I am sure it reflects all of my prejudices, racial and religious, but it is very dear to me. It may not be true, but it is honest.' A birthday card made by an 8-year-old, brought by her mother because she so liked thinking of herself as the child has described her, 'You're a real nice lady.' Or a pair of opera glasses, a gift from a mother-in-law, lovely in themselves but more prized by their owner because they symbolized a warm and workable relationship created of one which is monotonously reputed to be cold and unworkable. Or a mother's wedding ring, worked into another ring of the daughter's design: for the woman who had designed it, a treasured combination of the sentimental and esthetic.

As conversation buzzed around an object being discussed, Kriesberg questioned the response, beginning the prodding, asking, suggesting, not the telling, which was later observed to be one of the Institute's major strengths. Kriesberg is speaking: 'What does *our* interest in this object mean?' 'This is beautiful, but it is not prized for its beauty. What does that suggest? Or, this is utilitarian; that is sentimental; this is beautiful—these things are not thought of as works of art by the people who brought them. But many have artistic merit. What can these things tell us about art?'

* * * * *

The first regularly scheduled class of the day was Dan Malamud's. His introductory remarks to the class indicated that he wanted, through the course of the program, to help the class better understand people—to discover what moves them, how they meet situations and needs, the influences which make them what they are. Or, as he observed after the Institute:

> . . . I helped the group move step by step towards greater relaxation with each other and with me, toward increased questioning of what they had been taking for granted in the behavior of human beings, and towards more sympathetic awareness of themselves and others as individuals striving to meet very human needs . . . .
>
> Though I had my moments of uncertainty, for the most part, I knew what I wanted to accomplish and how to go about it. My approach was based on the following assumptions:
>
> 1. Developing insight into human behavior is not simply a matter of transmitting facts.
> 2. Group discussions are especially effective when they grow out of commonly shared here-and-now experiences.
> 3. The ease with which a group learns is closely related to its consciously felt need for acquiring such learning. The need for learning, therefore, needs to be stimulated before learning can take place most efficaciously.
> 4. The likelihood of learning is lessened if the group feels itself under attack.
> 5. The likelihood of learning is heightened if the group feels free to express the very attitudes which block receptivity to new concepts.
> 6. When the group itself arrives at insightful attitudes, these atti-

tudes are likely to be lasting and influential in affecting behavior.

To underscore his belief in point #1, above, Malamud observed the first day that he would not do very much question-answering; he might rather answer a question by asking one, to encourage a student to think out her own answer to her question, or to suggest that the class might find its own solution; and such, it developed, was exactly his method. To implement point #2 above, providing the group with 'commonly shared here-and-now experiences,' he provoked discussion through a fascinating variety of classroom material, which encompassed most areas of the women's lives: films for the class to analyze, experiences from the women's pasts which were discovered to be of common concern, and situations at the Institute itself.

He began with films and with fairly straightforward questions about them. He might ask, stopping a reel, 'What do you think is going to happen next?' Having canvassed the class, he'd begin again and when the anticipated sequence had been shown, would remark, 'Did you guess right? Why not, do you suppose? Or, those of you who did, how were you able to?'

From these he began gradually to encourage the women not only to analyze the film but to explore personal reactions to them: 'How did you feel about having guessed wrong?' 'How do you feel about the people in the film?' 'Whom do you prefer?' 'Is there anything about these people which reminds you of your own life?'

Midway in the Institute, he suggested a deeper probing: 'When you watch this film, don't look for a relationship between these characters and, say, your parents; look for a relationship between them and yourselves. If, for example, in this film about a child's relationships to its parents, you relate yourself to one or the other of the people, what does this indicate?' His final film portrayed a patient in psychotherapy; Malamud asked, 'How do you react to these scenes?'

The class moved with amazing speed and probed with considerable depth, perhaps because of the strength of their emotional reactions to the films and to classroom discussion, and despite their unfamiliarity with the field (some had been unable to find the books Malamud had suggested they read before the Institute). Occasionally the class was reticent; but more often students eagerly accepted the challenge of a film's idea and what meaning it might have for their own lives. When, as often happened, there was too little class time to finish a discussion, or when someone was reluctant to bring up publicly a matter of some interest to her, Malamud made himself available—as did the rest of the staff—for appointments.

At first, most remarks were addressed to Malamud, but very soon the group began to interact, an interaction aided by the fifth class meeting. That day Malamud divided the class into four groups, in order of birth—oldest child, middle child, youngest child, only child—and asked them to discuss problems which they had found to be characteristic of their birth station. He suggested some questions they might think about: 'What was the attitude of your parents toward you? of your brothers and sisters? How has this affected your attitude toward your peers, your teachers, your boss, your coworkers, your subordinates? How has it influenced friendships outside school and work?'

Results of the experiment were dramatic both in the class and out of it, for when the women reconvened to summarize their discoveries and to hear Malamud's summary of analysts' findings on the subject, it was clear that the women had by themselves in 20-minute conversations touched on almost all of the conclusions which analysts have made concerning personality traits characteristic of birth station. One group arranged to spend lunchtime further investigating their similarities; over and over for the rest of the Institute and in questionnaires after it one found the gratitude for this class. 'It's so nice to find that other people had those troubles, too. We aren't so much alone after all.'

Other experiments were similarly absorbing. Participants were asked to write down and bring to class their earliest childhood memories along with an analysis of what these memories might indicate. Malamud suggested, 'Sometimes our first memories are signs of important attitudes toward ourselves and other people; notice who's in your memory—are people active or passive? On the basis of one single memory, all we can do, of course, is hypothesize, but this memory may indicate that you've had many such experiences.'

Once the women were instructed to dream about the Institute, to write down the dream and analyze it. Malamud helped their analyses by commenting that dreaming is thinking which goes on without distraction, during sleep, and that a dream is struggling in some way with a crucial, on-going problem; 'Everybody in your dream is you—how does this other person reflect a part of you?' So off they obediently went and dreamed, and had a class session devoted to dream interpretation. Or they considered which member of the Institute they'd most like to have for a mother or a daughter, if ages were to make it possible, and discussed their reasons. And they reflected upon how their initial impressions of each other had changed, and how the change made them feel.

At the end of each class period, each woman wrote Malamud a one-page letter of her reactions to that day's class. They are remarkable letters, remarkable for their frankness, self-analysis and growth. Some letters begin with questions—but later ones tell, instead of ask. Some begin by observing that Malamud's class will certainly help them to understand other people but the last ones often say, gratefully, that it was an even greater help in handling personal problems.

Malamud consistently praised their analyses of the films, the group, and themselves, adding that never before had he had a class where session after session there was no relapse, no retrogression—only a consistent progress both in extent and depth. But much of the power and meaning of the class came of course from Malamud—from his supportive warmth, consideration, and understanding in receiving every comment and every suggestion, both during and outside the class, from the skill and restraint with which he helped the group to do its own analysis, and from his complete avoidance of jargon. He was able to effect his own point #5 above: 'The likelihood of learning was heightened since the group felt free to express the very attitudes which block receptivity to new concepts.'

* * * * *

Morton Gordon's class, in Public Affairs, was as provocative and challenging as Malamud's, but in a totally different way—not altogether because classes in human relations and public affairs often have different subject matter, but because Gordon's most effective classroom manner is as distinct from Malamud's as it is possible to be. Gordon was experimenting, for a while, with 'audio-visual aids'—he played records and had plans for swooping the class down to the Union Building to watch the Democratic National Convention. But it became evident early in the Institute that Gordon is another kind of teacher, and the women were quick to recognize that he was, in a sense, trying to be something he was not. So at their awareness of this fact and his own uneasiness, he stopped experimenting, reverted to his pre-Institute teaching style, and promptly found himself very often in the middle of a spirited, angry, or thoroughly aroused class.

His purpose he described as being to consider not the facts of public issues, for these facts change, but the theories which lie behind them; he insisted upon talking not about descriptions, but about principles, to help the students learn 'the larger lesson.' He warned them that he would do anything he could to open their ears—tell jokes, badger or insult them, flaunt their cherished ideals, make fun of them, fight with them—so long as he could make them re-evaluate and reconsider. So long as he could arouse suspicion or encourage a questioning attitude toward social and political phenomena. Anything—even to espousing a point of view to which he himself did not for an instant subscribe—to make them look behind a fact instead of at it, to make them define, and clarify; to make them realize that other arguments exist; to make them think of public issues in terms of issues, alternative policies, or actions that need not have been taken—'not in terms of sweet smiles, bombast and hot air: vote for Ike, vote for Adlai, fine—but know *why*.'

Gordon made a number of remarks designed to implement his purpose. These are excerpts from a few of them (in response to a question about his opinion) about Richard Nixon made to the class, composed as it was of predominantly Republican women: Nixon is an appalling choice for Ike's running mate because he belongs heart and soul to the isolationist movement, now at a time when the United States is so involved in international complexity and intervention that we must have allies or give the Soviet Union an edge in international affairs. Too, Mr. Nixon doesn't think—he feels, as note his accusations against the Democrats as a party of treason, or his questioning the loyalty of Mr. Truman and General Marshall. He speaks in childlike terms about Red China's victory, when 'there would have been a revolution in Asia even if Marx had been strangled in his cradle.' It is difficult to believe that Mr. Nixon is uninformed; we must therefore conclude that he is deliberately using a terrible calamity to partisan advantage.

Student reaction was precisely what Gordon might have anticipated, and in which he clearly reveled:

A. 'Can we avoid personalities, please?'
B. 'Who knows, maybe I will change my mind!'
C. 'Are you going to balance this conversation by giving us the other side?'
D. 'What does Ike have to say about all this?'
E. 'Democrats say bad things, too!'

Gordon, again: What is the purpose of a platform? To win friends and avoid enemies—to keep the party together, not to state principles. Do issues change in each election? Only slightly. What about newspapers?—They are generally guilty of distortion by omission or commission; news coverage isn't complete anywhere; perhaps the difficulty results because journalism is a profession which has no enforceable professional standards upon it and its outlets; newspapers must be read carefully, with suspicion and with questions.

Sometimes women were furious—one said she went to sleep in class so she wouldn't blow up. Another was overheard at dinner muttering, 'He'll have to prove that to me,' and another, who described herself as calm and even tempered, said angrily in the hall, 'He had me almost ready to fight the War between the States over again,' and at the laughter which greeted this, she remarked, 'He's making me think, though. I don't know what's got into me—I never get this mad!'

However, she didn't stay mad long, nor did many of the others. Because evident through the provocation and comedy and baiting was a clear, considered, forceful, and fair presentation based on thoughtful study and analysis, from a man who had a way, after all, of making one think about something which was once diligently thought through and now comfortably put aside. Some were not, to be sure, convinced that they shouldn't have been lectured to instead of badgered; but of the nine women who thought they would be able to fit evening classes into their full schedules, seven said that they intended to take theirs in political science.

* * * * *

The Kriesbergs' class in Creative Arts followed no fixed schedule—one day Kriesberg painted; the next Mrs. Kriesberg might be playing records; the next Mrs. Kriesberg might for the first hour ask the group to talk about a poem or a story, while for the second Kriesberg showed slides or asked questions about a reproduction. This flexibility and sharing of presentation helped them to indicate that there is much greater similarity among the arts than there is disparity, and that, as Mrs. Kriesberg remarked at one point, 'The goal of art is to increase the limits of experience, and if you fully experience one, you go on infinitely to appreciate all art.' They might, to use only one example, show similarity by pointing out that the development of music from the simplicity of Gregorian chant to the elaborate harmonic of Beethoven is not unlike the development of art from crude primitives to the worldly and technically skillful embroidery of a Memling canvas. Or they tried to show by bouncing the student against a work of art and asking her to react to it—whether a painting, a poem, or a concerto—that the approaches to art are the same, no matter what the art; and they were aided in their attempts by the gratifying articulateness and agreements in principle of guests who had been asked to talk to the group about the creative process.

As Kriesberg painted, and as the women in a short writing assignment stumbled over the difficulties besetting a writer, the Kriesbergs were able to illustrate that an artist has a craft and technique of composition which he must command with skill and efficiency. But the theme which rang most consistently in discussions of the humanities was that although an art object is created by an artist who had some concept which directed its composition, our own appreciation of it is determined not only by understanding the tools and craft of the artist, and not only by comprehending his meaning (these are of course useful), but also by what of our own experience we bring to a work of art. Our perceptions, our experiences, our understandings, can make of each work of art a unique thing for us. Aaron Copland, speaking to the group at Tanglewood: 'I have something in mind when I compose, of course; but it doesn't bother me if you hear something else.' Marilyn Wood, a modern dancer: 'Of course I want to make you see what I am thinking when I move my body in a certain way, but it's to be hoped that you will see something else, too.' George Balanchine, classical choreographer: 'I work out an intricate design for my dancers to perform on stage; it is a clear thing in my eye; but what you may see is another thing again. Or I have a gesture in mind for a dancer; but a dancer's individuality determines how that gesture will be interpreted.'

The Kriesbergs also provided the students with a further glimpse into the variety of teaching techniques which demands of subject make: for art classes, Kriesberg showed slides and prints, and kept up a constantly changing gallery of reproductions from various museums. Mrs. Kriesberg read aloud, and played records of poets reading their own works, to underscore the necessary aid which sound and inflection are to meaning; she played musical compositions illustrative of single, emerging, and combined aspects of music; she was in the library of Alumnae House each afternoon playing records, or discussing music and poetry for women who dropped in; she helped a play reading experiment which several students gave for the group; she posted a list of proverbs and suggested that each woman try her hand at writing a story illustrative of, not naming, a proverb—to learn something of the steps in composition—a session which captured the group's interest as much as any of those devoted to literature.

Kriesberg's forte showed not when he talked about other artists and their work, but when he painted himself, and when he ran his own experimental film; as he tried to verbalize what he had had in his mind when he began to make it, and as he described with a kind of wonder how it became an entity in itself, becoming almost of its own volition something other than he had intended.

The women wanted very badly in this class, more than in any other, to be told—so they wouldn't waste time. But the Kriesbergs were not going to tell them. Mrs. Kriesberg: 'You didn't come here to learn *my* interpretation—you came here to learn how to interpret for yourselves. I want you to fish around, and even waste time, *doing* it yourselves.' And it is very likely that the group would not have accepted the very kind of direction they were asking for, because there was recognition, daily expressed of the truth of Mrs. Kriesberg's credo: 'My concern is not that you learn facts, but that you learn a method of approach. For the humanities the barrier we all face between ourselves and the subject is information—we don't know, so we think we can't appreciate. But I am dedicated to the proposition that the arts may be approached through the heart, not the mind—information *enhances,* to be sure; but naming and defining do not lead to understanding.'

Schedule

The daily program for the two weeks followed this general time schedule:

8:45 A.M.–10:45 A.M.	—	Man and His Behavior
10:45 A.M.–12:15 P.M.	—	Public Issues
12:30 P.M.	—	Lunch
Afternoon	—	Free
4:00 P.M.–5:30 P.M.	—	Creative Arts and Humanities
6:30 P.M.	—	Dinner
8:00 P.M.–	—	Evening Program

Special guests and events were planned as follows:

Sunday, August 5	— Orientation and 'Something of Value' Session	
Monday, August 6	— 5:30 P.M.	Eleanor Roosevelt
Tuesday, August 7	— Oppenheimer Film	
Wednesday, August 8	— 4:00 P.M.	Painting begun by Irving Kriesberg (completed by August 23)
	8:00 P.M.	Marilyn Wood, modern dancer
Thursday, August 9	— Morning classes. Afternoon and evening at Berkshire Music Festival at Tanglewood; session with Aaron Copland, noted composer; symphony concert	
Friday, August 10	— 8:00 P.M.	Ivan Nagy, former Hungarian diplomat, on leave from Department of Political Science, University of Oregon
Saturday, August 11	— Humanities class in the morning, followed by holiday until 2:00 P.M. Sunday	
Sunday, August 12	— 2:00 P.M.	Midway evaluation
	7:30 P.M.	Films: *The City, The River*
Monday, August 13	— 4:00 P.M.	Lewis Mumford, social critic and city planner
	8:00 P.M.	*Pastoral,* experimental film, Irving Kriesberg
Tuesday, August 14	— 7:45 P.M.	Pete Seeger, folklorist

Wednesday, August 15	— 4:00 P.M.	Stephen K. Bailey, Director, Graduate Program, Woodrow Wilson School of International Affairs, Princeton University
Thursday, August 16	— 8:00 P.M.	George Balanchine, choreographer, and his wife, Tanaquil LeClerq, classical ballerina
Friday, August 17	— 8:00 P.M.	Play reading: James Barrie, *The Twelve-Pound Note*
Saturday, August 18	— 8:00 P.M.	Commencement Brawl

Comments

Many of the problems faced by the residential institute in general are illustrated in this example; in some instances the staff solved them, in others they sidestepped them. The easiest way out of the difficulty of influencing teachers to deal directly and appropriately with adult students is to choose able people who happen to *be* brilliant teachers, a luxury we can seldom afford. Politics, self-insight, and the arts are such separate areas that the staff did not have to face the question of helping the students integrate or at least relate different areas of experience. But a number of interesting questions nevertheless present themselves.

1. One has the feeling that the planners deliberately gave priority to first-rate teaching and developed the program on the basis of which teachers they obtained. Since their experimental question was directed toward investigating the acceptability of liberal arts by a particular kind of group, they were justified in doing so, but in a more general sense one wonders whether such a two-week period might not be more effective if it had some coherence to it. There is a danger, presumably, in being too well-organized and interrelated, but it is probably possible to attain some balance between the two poles. A program with the objectives of the Vassar Institute might well wish to avoid too tight an organization, but its designers could have chosen content areas for the seminars that, for instance, separately related to some major theme.

2. If one accepts the view that liberal education is directed at man in his general, rather than his specialized, nature, the educational planner is perhaps justified in ignoring the background of the student group. It might be useful to speculate, however, on how we could plan such a program to be somewhat relevant to the life roles of top-level secretaries. The psychology might more relevantly be social psychology, though one could surely find counter-arguments for justifying the

psychoanalytic focus of the Institute. Perhaps a problem focus, rather than a disciplinary one, might have led to a seminar on "The Woman in American Society," which a subsequent institute for the same group did develop. Such suggestions are not intended to be definitive but to indicate possible approaches to making the program-planning process more relevantly selective. The Institute staff did question the participants in advance of the program to seek their preferences for general areas they would like to explore; it would have been interesting to see the results if the questionnaire had asked them to describe their perception of their life dilemmas.

3. On the positive side, the program is a model in many respects. Its objectives of providing as much stimulation as possible, to encourage the students to select from a wide variety of possible paths for self-development, is well realized in the quality of the one-shot sessions indicated in the schedule. Although the report does not present data on how well these isolated experiences were deliberately integrated into the continuing seminars, they are clearly related to them and play a strongly reinforcing role. The teaching styles of the instructional team provide a variety one seldom sees in this wide a range and, more significantly, encouraged the active involvement of the students in ingeniously contrived situations. There is little question that such methods contributed a great deal to the Institute's impact, which, as spot checks of the students over a period of several years showed, was astonishing.[9]

THE PROCESS ANALYST: A PROPOSAL FOR A NEW ROLE

The discussion to this point has concentrated on the opportunities for improving the effectiveness of the residential format through a more careful application of educational planning techniques and the improvement of instructional resources. The special advantages of the residential as an instrument of adult education, however, suggest the desirability of trying out completely new forms of what is a potentially very flexible structure. One aspect of that flexibility is *time;* the residential provides us with a good deal more time than do other formats. Can we, instead of filling the extra time with more-of-the-same subject matter or with different instructional faces, use it to *deepen* the experience for the participants? A second aspect is *interaction;* living together inevitably creates a special social world, whether or not we have intended to bring it to life. Can we not consciously utilize this social experience as vital material for learning, for gaining insight into one's own behavior and how it affects other people and into the problems of groups at work?

It is reasonable to suppose that we can. This section proposes that, to take advantage of these opportunities, we construct and experiment with a special role for the residential and quasi-residential program for adults; the person who plays it *will have the task of helping the group to learn better to get insight into some of the processes of learning themselves, and to explore the interpersonal relations of the group as an informal part of the curriculum.* One person might fill both of these somewhat different roles, or they could be split; in either case there are probably some advantages in having them performed by someone who is not a member of the instructional staff. We could assign an innocuous title to the job, such as Staff Associate, and eliminate the risk of student misinterpretation of some more definitive term, or we could try to find an accurately descriptive title. For the purpose of developing the theme here, calling the role "process analyst" clearly enough indicates its important elements of concentration on process and its function as supplementary rather than central.

1. The Intellectual Process Role

The development of residential education for adults in this country has occurred mainly under university auspices and with university faculty as staff. Although the proportion of those with some college training in the United States is steadily increasing, the chances are still good that any group of adults, particularly in their middle years, will contain a majority with very little or no previous experience with higher education. As a result, residential institute faculties find themselves facing groups whose scholarly performance never comes up to their unrealistic expectations, and the students find themselves in a situation in which their habitual handling of ideas and concepts is inappropriate and in which they have no access to any clear delineation of the student role that *is* appropriate.

We might specify that role in such terms as these:

1. Insight into the difference between merely voicing an opinion and developing an argument for a point of view. The pattern of everyday adult exchange about events or ideas is that of the bull session, and the average adult imports it into the discussion which is intended

to do something quite different. The necessary insight depends on an acceptance of the facts that opinions are derived from many sources, including early conditioning, feelings, values, one's place in the social structure, and not necessarily on some defensible structure of evidence and rational linkages.

2. Acceptance of the existence of intellectual pluralism, a necessary counterpart of the first specification above, for the reader or listener. One often gets the feeling in listening to adult groups discussing some political issue, for example, that the members regard anyone who disagrees with them as a scoundrel, so unlikely is it that any reasonable person with human impulses should oppose their own settled convictions. The residential situation, providing people with the opportunity to get to know one another, is an excellent opportunity to make the general point.

3. The ability to attend to structures of evidence for positions with which they passionately disagree. While the instructor or another student is arguing an unpopular point of view or the possible solution to a problem, one often sees the rest of the group busily engaged in the internal work of formulating a counter-argument. They might just as well have ear plugs on.

4. The ability to relate any particular discussion of a problem to some general model of problem-solving behavior, so that the group can move from the narrow issue under discussion to seeing it in a broader context, then back to the issue again with increased insight. If a particular group of adults happens to be fairly homogeneous in its social class or background, as often happens, they will tend to focus on a relatively narrow range of possibilities. An awareness of the utility of returning to a reconnaissance of the problem itself for a time in order to frame alternative hypotheses can enormously increase the learning yield of the session.

5. Awareness of how significantly their very basic values and assumptions about the world enter into their judgments and arguments. This not only means that they need to see the reliance on their basic values of statements which they may believe are based only on the facts; they should understand that, though few people would dispute their rights to the values, it is important for the educational process that they learn to suspend their operation temporarily while examining new ideas. It is particularly useful if they can see their own value orientation as a particular position on a larger continuum of values.

6. Insight into the relation between feeling and rationality, and the realization that though anger is an indispensable human emotion

which is very useful to express at times, it is difficult if not impossible to be rational while one is angry.

Are these understandings, and their related behaviors, teachable? Or are they so embedded in basic characterological structures of the individual as to be out of educational reach? There is no question that for some individuals the answer to the second question would have to be "yes." Some people's need for the security of the extreme position under all circumstances, their basic intolerance of any ambiguity, makes them educational untouchables. The rest of us, under reasonably powerful circumstances, are, technically speaking, docile. The insights and abilities indicated are difficult to teach in the abstract but are teachable at least theoretically when we have the chance to communicate them in relationship to live experience, as the results of reflection on that experience.

The task of the Process Analyst (hereafter referred to by the initials), then, is to help the group in that act of reflection. Although he will necessarily sit in on all of the group's sessions, he will not raise process questions during the session itself. One could argue that this is precisely the time when discussion of process could be most effective, because it is as close as possible to the actual experience. Theoretically this is probably so. But few instructors would stand for it, and the group itself would have to bear an enormous load of frustration. Instead, we might schedule at least several meetings a week, of reasonable length, at which the only business would be discussion of the intellectual process problems of the learning sessions preceding.

The PA's problem will be to select those events which will be most fruitful for discussion, but he might well start off by having the group consider general problems of participation, questions of whether members feel they are getting the chance to make a contribution and of whether they are seeing clearly the nature of the contribution desired at various stages of the classes. Beyond this, the course of the discussion is determined by what actually happened to the particular group and depends on the ingenuity of the PA. But the following examples make clear the kinds of activities which might be appropriate; the problems on which they are based are taken from the recent experience of an observer at a residential institute for labor union officials.

The instructor, an expert in labor history, has suggested that one ought to approve of unions raiding one another, because it gives union members an opportunity for democratic choice. The group reacts violently to the idea, pointing out angrily that to permit unlimited raiding merely helps the employer divide and conquer, insures permanent conflict in the labor movement, and keeps unions so busy fighting one another that they have no time left for improving the lot of their members. The group has a fine opportunity for expressing hostility and rage, but it is hard to see what anyone has learned.

The PA reminds the group of this session, hardly necessary because they are still boiling over it, and suggests that they take another look at the issue, this time from a different perspective. He suggests further that one of the difficulties may have been that the instructor's proposal was only a very small part of a larger problem and that what is needed is a look at that problem first.

It may be useful for him at this point to set a tone of objectivity by describing for them the abstract structure of problem-solving, the process of inquiry, using some simple example not related to the current issue to point out how problems arise from difficulties, the difference between a difficulty and the problem itself, the need for exploration and reconnaissance of the facts related to the problem, the development of hypotheses, and the evaluation of alternative hypotheses. A structure of this sort can be outlined on a blackboard fairly quickly, and the present disagreement can be located as the evaluation of a single hypothetical solution.

At this point the PA's job is clear. He must help the group return to a consideration of the difficulty relevant to their present problem and work through the total inquiry process. At the end of such a discussion, the blackboard might look like this:

Difficulty:

Union members often have little opportunity to express discontent with what the union is doing, often have little opportunity to participate *effectively* in union decisions.

↓ →

Problem:

The problem is that union leadership feels that the power of the union depends on unanimity, and to some extent rightly; that there are relatively few realistic opportunities for members to express grievances against unfair treatment, etc.

↓

The situation: ← ↓

To some extent, then, the problem seems to be related to fears of the leaders which may or may not be fantasies; or it may be related to the union structure itself.

↓ Solution (a)	↓ Solution (b)	↓ Solution (c) (etc.)
Give members an opportunity to choose among unions to express their discontent.	Establish a series of informal courts within the labor movement to which grievances can be brought to impartial judges.	A series of conferences at the top level of union leadership to discuss the limits of any structure of union democracy that needs to be set for the protection of the union, to bring fantasy down to reality.
Evaluation of (a)	Evaluation of (b)	Evaluation of (c)
What are the consequences? Are they worth it? Etc. (This is what the group was doing in its class session.)	Can it work? Is it worth the expense; can we learn from the UAW experience or improve on it?	Is such a solution realistic; what pressures could move some autocratic leaders to agree, etc.

If the PA follows this by asking the group to locate other recent institute events within the same framework, without developing each in such great detail, so much the better; perhaps in one case it may turn out that they were merely discussing the difficulty without talking about the problem as such, in another that they were proposing various solutions to a problem but failing to evaluate them critically.

During one session an instructor shows the film "Operation Abolition"; Whether or not they have seen it before, most members of the group have thoroughly pre-judged it one way or another because of the publicity. When discussion is invited, everyone who speaks makes an obviously set speech, ignored by the person who follows him, and so it goes.

The PA decides that this provides an excellent opportunity for dealing with the issue of how much we attend to one another and during his next session reminds them of the particular class and invites their comments on how useful the discussion was. Reactions are likely to be sheepish. He suggests that the group now start the discussion anew, this time with a single ground rule: before anyone may make a statement, he must summarize what the previous speaker has said to the latter's satisfaction. One needs to keep this game going for only fifteen or twenty minutes to make the necessary point as graphically as it needs to be made.

A visiting speaker presents a careful description of the UAW's answer to the problem of union democracy, a panel of impartial arbiters made up of citizens of impeccable national reputation, and suggests it as a model which, with modification, other unions might follow. Most of the group reject it out of hand as a lot of expensive nonsense, nit-picking, and a diversion from the real job of the union.

The PA might pick up this incident as an opportunity to build a group standard for more reflective behavior, as well as group support for the change of attitudes in the course of learning. He asks everyone, no matter what their real opinion of the UAW arbitration panel idea, to spend fifteen minutes writing the most cogent, water-tight, persuasive argument in favor of it that he can manage. Recent work on cognitive dissonance suggests that one can expect under these conditions to get some shift in attitude so long as the dissonance is slight, that is, so long as the PA does not make the situation too threatening. If the student perceives the task as a superficial academic exercise, paradoxically, he is more likely to change his own attitude to conform to the contradictory ones required by the task.

The PA can follow the exercise by asking the students to rate their disapproval of the UAW plan on a scale from 1 to 5 and then collecting the ratings by asking individuals to raise their hand for each number. The PA need only recall the things people said in class to suggest that there has been some shift of attitude and to raise such questions as: to what extent do our preconceptions prevent us from really examining ideas which may be useful and important; what makes us really dislike to change our minds about anything; is it possible to learn anything significant without changing in some way?

In the class on American government, a discussion of balance of power is based on the reading of, among other texts, one of the Federalist papers. It becomes clear during the discussion that students are interpreting the particular reading in a number of ways or ignoring it altogether to ride favorite horses of their own.

The PA uses this session to demonstrate how difficult it is to grasp the development of a complex argument presented by a first-rate mind, to dramatize the effort which is required to do so, and to emphasize the importance of first understanding a position before one discusses it.

With the text of the Federalist paper before each member of the group, the PA calls on individuals in turn to read the essay aloud, stopping each reader at frequent natural intervals to discuss with him and the class the meaning and significance of the particular passage, its relation to the argument as a whole, its logical consistency, or the assumptions on which particular statements are based.[10] No one who has not experienced this exercise can appreciate how powerful it can be and how generally useful for people who have not had prolonged training in verbal skills.

II. The Interaction Process Role

The aspect of the PA's role which concentrates on the understanding of what is happening within the group and on increasing self-insight for individual members bears at least a partial resemblance to the National Training Laboratory's summer workshops in group development, but there the entire experience is devoted to such objectives. There has been little if any experimenting with such an addition to standard adult residential curricula.[11] But in the course of such institutes, whatever their primary objectives, we obviously have an excellent opportunity not only to add a different dimension to the group's learning, but to meet and deal with morale problems which may be interfering with the work of individuals or the group as a whole.

The basic task of the PA in this area is a precise counterpart of his role in the intellectual work of the group. He participates in enough of the informal activities of the Institute to become aware of significant events, those which constitute diagnostic clues to problems of conflict, morale, and the like. At sessions set aside for the purpose, he helps the group deal with them directly and thus either eliminate or reduce the disturbing effect of the problems. If the particular issue is one which provides an opportunity for wider learning, the PA can direct the discussion toward the development of generalizations from a particular incident or situation.

It is difficult to specify this role, because each group develops its own culture, and the problems of members obviously depend on which individuals are at the particular residential. But we can predict with some confidence that some type of clique formation will develop and that members of both in- and out-groups will have significant attitudes about it. There is almost certain to be at least one member whose behavior exasperates the rest of the group. Some feelings of insecurity in the unfamiliar academic atmosphere are bound to be present and will reveal themselves in defensive behavior which impedes achievement either for the individual or the group.

Whether such problems should be handled in a series of informal sessions at which the particular concerns of the group at a given time are encouraged to emerge naturally, or whether the PA should provide more structure, may presumably be left to his judgment. For purposes of clarification it may be useful to describe here a structured session directed by a person playing the PA role; everything he did, however, might obviously have been accomplished using materials arising out of more spontaneous discussion.

This particular session was an actual one, scheduled as a three-hour seminar during a ten-week summer residential. It was conducted by Goodwin Watson, who was not a member of the staff but was visiting as the director of the evaluation team observing the institute. Under these less than ideal circumstances, the session nevertheless had a tremendous impact on the group.

Watson began by pointing out that one of the opportunities open to members of such an institute was to learn more about themselves as persons, and the best way of doing so was to get the reactions of other members to themselves. He asked them to write down the names of all those in the group, either first name, or last, or nickname. (This was the fourth week of the institute, and a majority of the group were living in the same quarters.) After about five minutes of peering owlishly at one another, it turned out that only about half of the group could name *all* the members. They were visibly shocked by this result. Watson then asked them to draw lines connecting the names of those people who seemed to spend a good deal of time together and, after they had done so, asked whether there were some members who were not included in any of these subgroups. There were. He suggested that this might mean that some people felt left out of the group, some who were not relating at any level. Several individuals responded openly and confessed that they did indeed feel left out. Then he asked them to check those names on the list about whom they knew something other than the kind of job they had—an interest, a hobby, or personal life. No one member of the group could do so for more than five others.

Watson then asked them to write the names of three people they considered most important to the group, the ones whose absence they felt would make the most difference. He suggested that it would be very interesting to look at such selections, if they would not be embarrassed about revealing them. The group shuffled their feet and looked nervous, but by this time it was obvious that they felt committed to the game and finally agreed. Out of the total of 57 choices, three members of the group received 30 votes, and the rest were scattered. Watson discussed the results briefly in very general terms of group structure. He raised the question of why no one had selected himself and suggested that this had some meaning for the kinds of thoughts which we consider inappropriate to expose to groups of which we are members.

Next, he asked them what characteristics of people they tended to notice at first meeting. Each member in turn mentioned his particular focus, turning up the expected type of dimensions: bright or dull, open or closed minds, liberal or conservative politically, extrovert or introvert. Watson asked why they avoided such characteristics as sex, or physical attractiveness, and went on to discuss the general issue of what people are embarrassed to reveal to others, relating it to the difficulty they had including themselves among those important to the group.

From these purely interpersonal factors, he turned to examine the characteristic ways of participating in the work of the group, as in class discussions or informal discussions out of class. He suggested a series of three categories which describe dominant tendencies of different individuals and put the following scheme on the board:

	Dimension of perception: what he values most in others	*Method of influencing other people*	*What he dislikes or avoids*	*Rx*
The friendly helper				
The strong achiever				
The logical thinker				

He drew out of the group descriptions of the behaviors of each of these types which are relevant to the dimensions he supplied and their suggestions for the Rx column, for what the person needs to do in order to balance his dominant tendency.

Finally, with all of these conceptual areas open, Watson reiterated his original proposal that each member of the group could learn from others members' views of himself and that the way to get such help is to ask the group for such feedback. After some hesitation, individual members began discussing their own feelings about the group, interestingly enough going back to the earlier focus of the session. For example, one woman who was thoroughly isolated from the group complained bitterly about what she saw as rejection on the grounds that she was trying hard to be a lady and didn't drink or smoke, but no matter how much they looked down on her she was determined not to relax her standards. Several people pointed out to her mildly that they didn't care about her personal habits, but perhaps she needed to be able to accept other peoples', and one member remarked that he hadn't cared much for her at the beginning but his opinion was improving. Watson intervened to ask why she was being so vehement and attacking, but she wasn't quite ready to face that issue. A Negro member of the group talked about his feelings arising out of his being the lone Negro. The general reaction was to reassure him that "we were really color-blind" and it didn't make a bit of difference, he needn't worry about *us,* to which he replied that to believe that was a lot of nonsense and they ought to get to know themselves better.

On the whole, the session stimulated the group as nothing else in the institute did, and they discussed it for weeks. As a single, isolated phenomenon, however, its drawback was that no one could follow through on the avenues to real help which it opened up. The general approach, too, which is dominated by Watson's interest in the processes of group therapy, might seem to some to strike at deeper levels of the person than they would wish to do. Given a choice, however, the group itself selected to discuss these rather than the less threatening area of work-orientation. In the more general context of the present proposal, the question of emphasis would be up to the individual PA; if Watson's approach is not his cup of tea, he might decide to concentrate on more general aspects of group interaction in the work context.

A Note on Recruitment

A number of possibilities for experimenting with the roles proposed here suggest themselves. In many cases, residential institutes are administered by individuals who might themselves take on the task of working with the group in the intellectual area and who are competent to do so either by previous background or by special training. We are less likely to find in such positions people with the background in psychology necessary to perform the second aspect of the role, and in such cases a separate staff member may be hired to fill it.

But, although there are no strong arguments against such a division of the role, there are clear advantages to integrating all these activities in one person. It is more convenient and less expensive; the group is not required to build two separate relationships in addition to those they must have with the instructional staff; and the two areas have obvious points of connection and overlap. One answer to these requirements lies perhaps in experimenting with the two separate functions *as* separate ones, building one of the roles into some institutes and the second into others.

But it is not so difficult as it may seem to find individuals who might competently perform both functions.[12] Those institutes which are held in the summer particularly might find people who are not on the local campus. Where circumstances restrict one's choice to the local area, there are a number of places where one could look. The probability of success is greater if one starts with those who are competent to handle the interpersonal part of the role; on the whole, there are more psychologists interested in cognition and learning than there are philosophers interested in interpersonal relations, although the fact that these two departments are still, in many universities, linked to one another perhaps provides a clue to the essential unity of the two roles. One might rummage among the available educational psychologists, too, as well as in the cross-departmental institutes and committees so common in universities these days. Departments of industrial relations, for example, often attract restless spirits who find regular academic departments too confining.

There is no question that we can find the resources for doing such a job once we decide that it is worth doing such experimenting. And if we are to build effective bridges between the needs of our adult clientele and the resources of the academic community, we must begin to be more inventive than in the past in constructing new forms.

NOTES

1. John Diekhoff has registered a trenchant dissent to this favorable view of the residential in "Residential Education: No Place Like Home," *Adult Education,* Vol. X, No. 4 (Summer, 1960). His witty cost accounting should give program planners pause; if we cannot supply more proof than we now have that the residential setting pays off in greater learning, it is a terribly expensive way of carrying on education for adults. The proposals at the end of the chapter attempt to provide for learning results which would be very difficult to achieve in ordinary class sessions.

2. The best source for this general issue is Robert Schacht's doctoral thesis, *Residential Adult Education,* University of Wisconsin, 1957, which traces the history in detail. His concluding chapter has been published by the Center for the Study of Liberal Education for Adults under the same title. One of the Center's *Notes and Essays* series provides a good example of the American folk-school tradition as it still exists today; see Royce Pitkin's *The Residential School in Adult Education, Notes and Essays No. 14* (Chicago: Center for the Study of Liberal Education for Adults, 1956). The major point I argue here in the text seems to me clear, on the face of it, from the lack of connection between contemporary residential activity and the folk schools themselves; for example, one seldom finds the folk-school people attending meetings devoted to residential problems among the universities. Reports of the annual meetings of the National University Extension Association usually contain material from their Conference and Institute division and give a good picture of trends and problems of the new American form.

3. A. A. Lacognata, *A Comparison of the Effectiveness of Adult Residential and Non-Residential Learning Situations* (Chicago: Center for the Study of Liberal Education for Adults, 1961).

4. Almost any recent text in educational psychology summarizes the evidence for group support for individual change. More relevant for the adult educator is the collection of articles published by the National Training Laboratories as part of its Reading Series: Leland Bradford (ed.), *Human Forces in Teaching and Learning* (National Education Association, 1961).

5. See, for example, Chapter 10 in L. J. Cronbach, *Educational Psychology* (New York: Harcourt, Brace, 1954), for a review of the evidence.

6. A major deterrent to the general improvement of educational procedures in this field is the self-image of the Conference and Institute administrator. If he seems himself as an "innkeeper," he eliminates the only potential force in the situation primarily concerned with process. Reluctance to assume the educational planning role *vis-à-vis* the many determined egos one finds on university faculties is understandable, but it can be met, I suspect, by providing the conference man with relevant training. He tends to be hired out of the business field rather than the educational one, for obvious reasons related to the nature of the programming; only as he shifts his professional identification toward that of educator is the situation likely to improve.

7. Paul Sheats, Dean of University Extension at the University of California, which is famous for its extraordinarily varied and imaginative residential program, dissents. In a personal communication, he remarks, "We are able to get good people in our residential programs precisely because they have freedom in the residential to deviate from normal classroom procedure." California has a large staff of professionals deeply committed to adult education as an enterprise requiring its own methods. My reading of programs and reports of residentials and my own observation of a good number of them lead me to believe that only a few institutions like California make very strenuous efforts to depart from conventional formats within residentials.

8. Reprinted with permission from Marilyn Vaughan, *The Vassar Institute for Women in Business* (Chicago: The Center for the Study of Liberal Education for Adults, 1957), pp. 6, 7, 10–20. The report includes a description of the reactions of participants and a detailed cost breakdown.

9. For several years the students kept in touch with one another through an informal newsletter, a striking example of seeking further group support for personal change. A sizable number of them enrolled in courses in their local communities or became active in other ways related to their experience at Vassar. They also organized educational reunions for several years following the Institute. Some of this enthusiasm might well be due to the well-known Hawthorne effect—a great deal was made of the experimental aspects of the program—but there is little question of its being due in part to the development of warm personal feelings of shared experience, a phenomenon fairly typical of the residential situation. In this case at least, the "glow" had specific educational consequences.

10. Leonard Olsen, *Analytical Reading* (Chicago: Center for the Study of Liberal Education for Adults, 1952).

11. The suggestion for such experimentation comes from Goodwin Watson of Columbia University Teachers College and is here gratefully acknowledged. The only attempt to experiment with the idea that I know of is Dr. Sidney Mailick's, who is director of New York University's program of executive development for high-level New York City officials. He included a process analyst among the staff members of a week-long program which was part of his general offerings.

12. For example, to cite a person well known to adult educators because he was at one time president of the Adult Education Association and editor of *Adult Leadership,* Kenneth Benne could do both with ease. He is both an educational philosopher by training and one of the founders of the National Training Laboratory.

6

• • • • • • • • • • • • • • • • • • • •

SMALL GROUPS: INFORMAL DISCUSSION

> "I don't think they play at all fairly," Alice began, in a rather complaining tone, "and they all quarrel so dreadfully one can't hear one's self speak—and they don't seem to have any rules in particular; at least, if there are, nobody attends to them—and you've no idea how confusing it is all the things being alive."
>
> LEWIS CARROLL, *Alice in Wonderland*

Informal group discussion has been a significant focus of interest for adult educators since the emergence of our identity as a distinct profession, but its roots clearly begin considerably earlier in social history. It seems to be a distinctively American form of social interaction in politics and education, singularly appropriate in a society dedicated to a fervent egalitarianism; if every man is as good as any other, then he has the right to speak his piece and contribute his weight to the group decision.

Discussion, and the problem of making it more effective, is consequently so widespread in the culture that it is necessary to set with some distinctness the limits to the form which this chapter examines. These limits are defined by two major criteria:

1. *The discussion must have a conscious educational purpose.* A great deal of talking together, aimed at accomplishing a number of vastly different purposes, goes on in the society. There is official talk, some of it good, much of it the kind that the *New Yorker* maliciously likes to quote under the heading "Wind on Capitol Hill." An incredible amount of talk is involved as Americans go about the business of trying to achieve their special interests, from running businesses through improving their communities to swapping the best ways of growing prize flowers. All of this kind of discussion is directly *instrumental*; it accompanies personal or social action or is intended directly to cause it.

People *do* learn from some of this discussion, of course, but this is hardly a sufficient basis for considering it an educational process itself. When adult educators set about helping corporation staffs or agency employees improve their conference skills, it is an effort to improve needed vocational skills and can be handled as any other educational problem is. The informal discussion whose basic purpose is learning presents a rather different set of problems.

2. *The discussion group cannot have professional leadership.* This second limiting criterion is intended to differentiate the format from the group discussion which goes on primarily in the classroom, but sometimes more informally, where an expert is perceived as being in charge. He is usually a subject-matter expert and to some extent at least is justified in bringing into the group already formulated objectives. There is considerable overlap in the discussion process involved in these two formats, but there is enough difference in dynamics between the situations to argue for considering them separately. This view does not rule out the use of experts as resource persons in a discussion group, any more than it eliminates using books written by experts.

GENERAL OBJECTIVES FOR DISCUSSION GROUPS

The historical and social basis of contemporary discussion groups is important not merely because it is academically interesting, but because, if we ignore it, we miss some essential clues to differences which exist within the general format. Swapping opinions, or "batting the breeze," can be a pleasant form of social interaction or may be useful as communication, although there are some kinds of verbal communion which are not even intended to communicate; such talk among a group seldom results in any significant amount of learning for the individuals who compose it, however, unless the group has some purpose in talking together. Current interest in discussion for learning appears to arise from three separate streams of tradition with different purposes, and an examination of them sets the major problem of method.

One of these streams connects to the eighteenth-century idea of the democratic state and the way in which conflicting opinions become expressed.

> . . . The public is the loom of classic, 18th century democracy; discussion is at once the threads and the shuttle tying the discussion circles together. It lies at the basis of the conception of authority by discussion, based on the hope that truth and justice will somehow carve out of society a great apparatus of free discussion. The people are presented with problems. They discuss them. They decide on them. They formulate viewpoints. These viewpoints are organized, and they compete. One viewpoint 'wins out.' Then the people act out this view, or their representatives are instructed to act it out, and this they promptly do.[1]

The hope of encouraging grassroots discussion of public issues and improving its quality has been a persistent theme among adult educators, and they tend to reject the statement with which Mills follows his description quoted above: "You will recognize this description as a set of images out of a fairy tale." During the thirties a good deal of energy went into planning public forums at which crucial issues were debated, and we have made repeated efforts to use the modern mass media as material around which citizen groups can form to discuss their common concerns. Recently, James Reston, the nationally influential political correspondent of *The New York Times*, suggested that someone undertake a massive campaign, based on appropriate materials, to get the public discussing the crucial issues we face. He wrote apparently without knowledge of the efforts of the Fund for Adult Education during the fifties to do precisely that, not only through their own community discussion programs but through their support of regular programs of the American Foundation for Political Education and the special Great Issues project.

The purpose of discussion in this case is to help people make intelligent decisions or judgments (see Chapter II for an examination of this objective in behavioral terms). Contemporary proponents of the format assume that the discussion process enlarges the perspectives of the individuals participating as they take account of the range of views present among the total group, and that individual opinions are tested, refined, or changed when challenged by the group. These assumptions are subject to some doubts, when we consider the social-class segregation of American urban society; most discussion groups are homogeneously middle-class without any internal elements making for sharp conflict on some major issues.

Educators involved in administering such programs, however, make honest efforts to compensate for the human homogeneity by providing materials which contain the necessary challenge. Materials appropriate for this type of informal discussion consist, at their best, of collections of separate readings, selected to represent the real diversity of opinions on an issue, and should, logically, avoid any written efforts to resolve the issue or to show how the conflicts might be accommodated. This is the group's task, and they ought to have raw materials to work on.

A second type of discussion has its roots not in the grand social theories of a rising middle class but in the local community structure of early America; the image for this form is the New England town meeting, the gathering of all the responsible citizens to consider and vote on the public problems. The general thesis that all who are affected by a problem should have the chance to participate in its solution has a long and honorable history in America and is, indeed, at the heart of the democratic process. As the frontier spread westward, new communities set their own norms and laws by the discussion of specific problems as they arose; Dewey emphasized the need for skill in problem-solving as the most effective method of dealing with the introduction of change.[2] The basic assumption in this body of thought is that solutions which a group of affected individuals reach may not be the most efficient solutions to a problem, but they are almost bound to be the most *acceptable* ones and consequently the only workable ones.

There have been organized efforts to use discussion for civic problem-solving as early as the Chautauqua movement, and later by the U.S. Office of Education under Studebaker and the Office of War Information.[3] The contemporary educational expression of this stream is the community development movement, a very interesting phenomenon which has yet to work its way through many of its own problems. It is most successful in its pure form of government-assisted village and town work in underdeveloped countries, where trained people help the community improve its own economic, literacy, and health levels; the Peace Corps is experimenting with the form in several countries. In the United States, community development has traveled a curiously rocky road, and its practitioners seem unable to come to agreement on its purposes. Many of the bureaus of community development operated by state universities seem to be devoted solely to the task of helping communities attract new industries; other programs devote considerable energy to community organizations which end, trivially, in a spate of house-painting and garden-beautifying.

But without attempting to evaluate the present state of community development in this country, which has no place in this volume, the relevant question posed by the movement is whether it is or is not education. We could easily regard it as an offshoot of social work; several of the more important books in the field are written by social workers. Empirically, it is often difficult to see in much of the activity called community development any educational process. To the extent that the community developer in the field, however, tries, as he sometimes does, to help the community learn effective problem-solving processes, we ought to assume that central questions of educational method are involved.[4]

This type of informal discussion, then, has as its basic purpose the solution of problems. The materials are the life situation itself, and the group consists of those individuals whose lives are affected by the problems and who are urgently concerned with the quality of the solutions.

The third stream of contemporary group discussion probably has a longer history than either of the others, back to the image of Socrates and the young Athenians inquiring into fundamental matters of life and the state. The aim of such discussion is the improvement of the individual through the exercise of his most important faculty, his rationality. Aristotle argued, to be sure, that the ultimate aim of education is the perfection of the state, but he insisted that the best means of ensuring that goal is to perfect each individual citizen and that we must seek such perfection in rationality.

The contemporary expression of this view comes, of course, from Hutchins and Adler, and the latter has systematized it for adult education in particular.[5] In fact, he argues that liberal education is unsuited to the young, that only the mature person has the motivation and experience for an adequate inquiry into the human condition. Such national programs as the Great Books movement have attempted to realize these aims, as well as local institutions such as The Basic Program at the University of Chicago. One might include in this group the Living Room Learning program at Cleveland College of Western Reserve University and several other community discussion attempts as well; they are not as firmly committed to a philosophical approach, but they do emphasize the development of the individual rather than the improvement of community or political life.

Though they may differ about the preferred books, most of the programs in this category do tend to be book-centered and are committed to the principle of lay leadership. The book is the teacher and provides models for rational analysis, theory building, and the examination of important values. In relation to the scheme proposed in Chapter II, the educational purpose of such groups is to develop conceptual skills. Their basic assumption is that the individual improves through the cooperative enterprise of thinking through abstract issues, though the reason why one needs a group in the first place is not entirely clear. Unlike the other models of group discussion, in which the role of the group is central, the proponents of this type insist so vigorously on the importance of the individual as the educational target that they give the impression that they consider the group setting merely as a convenient way of getting people involved in the process.[6]

In summary, then, all three of these types of adult discussion groups have in common their elimination of professional leadership and their emphasis on learning but differ in their learning objectives and focus separately on:

Judgment
Problem-Solving
Conceptualization

The problem they present is whether one can build a model of group discussion which is appropriate to all three. Generally speaking, the organizers and administrators in this field have tended to believe otherwise; each program builds its own training schemes which are often very different in both theory and structure.

But it is by no means difficult to conceive of a discussion process which would fit them all. First, all of them involve a group of individuals working together, without assigned or official leadership. Second, all of them include movement toward some goal which requires the accomplishment of a task. The tasks are different, to be sure, but they are all learning tasks which we can state behaviorally. In all cases, the basic model is one of *cooperative inquiry,* generally speaking, with different specific ends. We need a fairly rigorous model for it, because it is a process unfamiliar to most adults. They are accustomed to the classroom, in which an expert takes the responsibility for guidance and control; or the living-room bull session, where the winner is the most skilled rhetorician or the person with the worst temper; or, in some cases, the negotiating discussion, in which the object is to come out with the greatest advantage. Cooperative inquiry makes very different demands on the situation and the participant if it is to be fruitful.

A DISCUSSION MODEL

If discussion is, essentially, work on a shared task, it is useful to examine this phenomenon at a general level. When a lone individual is at work, observers usually have little difficulty deciding when he is working at the task and when he is resting, particularly if the task involves a physical operation. The foreman of a pick-and-shovel brigade can apply a very simple criterion: if one of his men is not wielding an implement, he is not working. The office manager can apply the same standard to her group of typists, though with somewhat less confidence; the girl who is busily typing may be writing a letter to her aged mother in Jersey City. But if work involves intellectual creativity and imagination, the problem of judging whether a person is at work becomes more difficult; the young man dreaming at his desk in the advertising agency may be about to come up with the selling idea of the century. His superior, at any rate, may hope so.

Work carried on by a group is at the same time easier and more difficult to observe, particularly when the work cannot by its nature produce something visible. Two different types of work go on simultaneously, for example, in a group whose work is inquiry: work on the publicly stated problem which the group came together to deal with (understanding modern art or agreement on the best solution to a problem), and work on individual learning aims, as some people learn things the rest of the group already knows. But many of the problems which arise when people try to think together are very similar to the general problems of doing any kind of work as a group.

A group of men who decide to build a community tennis court, for example, have first of all agreed on a common goal, as have members of a discussion group. They must then agree on a certain order of work steps—to measure first, then dig, then fill in, and so on. Some members of the group are most valuable during the digging operation, while others have a certain knack with a roller, so that the value of the contribution of each member to the work may depend on what the group is working on at a given time. All of these activities, *including the reaching of agreements about how to proceed,* are work. They move the group along toward the goal of a finished tennis court.

At times the group may tire and stop to exchange comments about some neighborhood event. Or, two members who have a private backyard feud may have an argument which not only keeps them from working but stops the work of the entire group. Or, they may all knock off for a well-deserved beer and exchange sociable opinions about which team has the best chance in the world series. During all these periods, whether the lapse is necessary or not, the group is *not* working, but doing something else: socializing, fighting, escaping, or whatever one wishes to call it.

Discussion groups, in a rather more complicated fashion, operate in the same way. If the group is talking about what it ought to do or how it should go about it or is actually exploring problems it has agreed to consider as a group, it is working. An example of a discussion group *not* working may clarify the picture. Suppose the inquiry has been into the question of whether the United States ought to increase its aid to foreign countries. Two general opinions have emerged: one insists that the U.S. will lose the "cold war" if it does not help build the strength of the underdeveloped countries both economically and politically; the other holds that it makes no sense to give away large sums of money and material, which constitutes a serious drain on the American taxpayer, to countries which are not grateful for it anyway.

The group faces two apparently irreconcilable views, hotly argued. Suddenly, someone tells a joke, which reminds someone else of a long story, which he proceeds to tell, and which in turn recalls an interesting trip another member has taken to California. Even if the group is interested in the stories and laughs at the joke, it has stopped working. One might explain such a situation by suggesting that the group is frustrated because it does not know how to get out of the box created by two such opposite views. Faced with frustration, many individuals either get angry or try to escape from the situation. The way out of the frustration involves a consideration of the question,

"What do we need to do to understand the differences between these policies, or their consequences, or the sources of our disagreement? Set up some criteria in advance by which each can be judged? Find evidence of the results of either policy? Clarify the conditions under which we might all agree that foreign aid ought, or ought not, to be given?" The consideration of such questions is, of course, also work, in the same way that the activity of the engineer in calculating stresses and drawing plans is necessary to the work of constructing a bridge.

Sometimes non-work activity is necessary to relieve the tension of concentrating on a difficult task; no group can be at work *all* the time, because the variety of individual needs which people bring to the group must have some outlet. A group which has worked together a long time and has successfully ironed out its problems alternates between short bursts of sociability, joking, or fighting, and long periods of concentration on the job at hand. The emotional satisfactions in the brief flights from work can, indeed, provide a stimulating push.

Students of group behavior, or, more precisely, of the behavior of people in groups, have developed a useful set of terms to describe the varieties of non-work activity:[7]

Flight—ignoring the problem by joking, laughing, talking animatedly about other things.

Fight—arguing heatedly about an issue instead of finding ways to understand or resolve it.

Dependency—implicitly confessing that the problem is too great by appeals to the leader or to outside authority.

Pairing—acting as though it had met to associate sociably in teams of two.

A considerable amount of research supports the view that individuals have what seem to be natural tendencies toward behaving in one of these several ways, which helps explain why some groups seem always to be fighting or others always break down into pairs; they may have too many of one kind of person.

The Demands of the Task

To say that there is a basic similarity in all groups at work does not mean that the nature of the task has no influence on the behavior of the members. A group of people engaged in trying to arrive at the soundest solution for a local problem must obviously go through somewhat different steps than a group which is exploring the meaning of a Platonic dialog. As a later section will suggest, a clear image of the behavior appropriate to these different tasks gives us a rational means to control the discussion process.[8]

Other problems related to the nature of the task, however, arise from our connection with its content; one ingenious experimenter set his subjects the task of deciding whether or not a series of syllogisms were correct and put some of them in the traditional form of "All A's are B's" and others, expressing exactly the same logic, into statements involving controversial issues; as we might expect, judgments of logical consistency were seriously distorted by the content of the syllogism. Similarly, one can inquire into the problem of the cause of inflation and consider the worth of the various theories proposed with a fair expectation of serene objectivity because the forces under discussion are of such magnitude and are so remote from the control of the ordinary man. But if the inquiry concerns the question of which segments of the society are hurt and which are helped by inflation, the leader might expect at least a minimum amount of hostility if the group consists of mixed economic levels.

Here are four common types of inquiry which impose requirements of very different kinds and pose varying control problems for the group:

The inquiry deals primarily with established relationships anchored strongly in reality. Examples: natural sciences, economics, public health. In this kind of inquiry the group must spend considerable time learning and understanding relationships which operate impersonally, and the usefulness of the discussion depends on how closely they keep to the materials provided. Personal experience may have its place at times, to be sure, but it is important to realize the limitations of single cases and of personal opinions. One's attendance at a few stockholders' meetings is not justification for large generalizations about corporate behavior. Groups tend to dive too hurriedly into arguments over policy or general theory without looking first at the facts; others settle down to a dead-level consideration of facts only, which is boring for many members. The boredom may be expressed in horseplay, irrelevance, or other forms of "flighting." A change of pace may be necessary, or a call for a re-examination of the purpose of the particular phase of discussion activity.

The inquiry deals primarily with questions which are rooted ultimately in individual values and opinions. Examples: social role behavior, politics, questions posed by the behavioral sciences which involve policy choices. Many discussion programs are designed not to settle arguments or increase understanding of the meaning of facts, but to excite discussion, provide practice in critical thinking, and widen the perspectives of the participants. Such discussion easily becomes a kind of bull session, devoted to the unloading of opinions by everyone in the group without critical examination of any of them. Because there is usually a wide range of views on the issues under discussion, such groups may find that a preliminary exploration of the total range of opinions and values is better than settling down immediately to discuss extreme views.

The ambiguity of this type of inquiry can be very disturbing for a group which is not conscious of a very definite aim for its discussion. Members tend to be continually aware of whether they are at a given time doing what they really intended to do. When the group is "not working," participants are likely to be fighting, because the issues strike deeply at people's political or moral values.

The inquiry deals primarily with questions which strongly involve the individual on a personal level, on problems close to the "self." Examples: anthropology, literature, some aspects of psychology and sociology. Problems of family life and child rearing, personal values, ethics, and responses to art all present the group with the extremely difficult task of talking about personal reactions and deeply-felt values and at the same time depersonalizing them sufficiently to find common grounds for inquiry. Discussion must avoid over-easy generalizations of personal experience, and the group needs to realize that some concepts, for example "culture" in its social science usage, seem much more readily grasped than they really are; spending time understanding them pays off in the long run. Some members of the group may feel personally threatened by examination of such ego-involving themes as child rearing, family relationships, and race. The group needs, therefore, to build acceptance of emotional statements which may arise out of such feelings of threat. When ego-involvement is high, aimless recounting of personal anecdotes is a constant possibility, and the group must agree on careful statements of the issue if it wishes to control the flow of participation.

The inquiry deals primarily with questions which have a strong flavor of unreality because they deal with events geographically remote or completely beyond the influence of individuals. Examples: international relations, some aspects of science. Programs in these areas tend to confront an incredible complexity of problems with startlingly simple public stereotyped solutions. The group will not discover the real complexity of the problem without a great deal of patient unraveling of the strands which make up the issues. They must realize the need for challenging stereotypes and attitudes rooted in widespread, often unexplained assumptions, which implies that they must accept, as part of the group culture, the consistent, calm examination of such challenges. When the group is not at work, they are likely either to be fighting, given the presence of a fair number of aggressive individuals, or expressing dependency on the leader or on some authority. Because the frames of reference for judgments made in such discussions are so remote from personal experience, the conflict is likely to be rooted in a battle of authorities. If this becomes a recurrent problem of control, the group needs to develop a method for handling it, perhaps by setting up a number of criteria for accepting or rejecting an authority. Because the problems are so complex, the group will find it easy to lose sight of central issues and wander off into dead ends, not necessarily irrelevant, but fruitless.

The Demands of Cooperation

Individuals working alone at a task can set their own pace, resolve their own conflicts about alternatives, and handle their frustrations in any way they wish. A major source of the problems in group discussion lies in the difficulties people have in accommodating to the demands of working together. In a society which stresses competitiveness, of course, cooperation cannot be expected to occur naturally. Most groups adjust to the requirements of cooperative work only gradually. One-shot discussion group sessions, as everyone with experience will attest, are almost always disappointing; groups with a fairly long life have a much better chance to become productive, and the way in which members participate will gradually change. At the beginning there is likely to be considerable dependence on the leader, and participation will often pattern itself in the form of member-leader exchanges. If this is permitted to become an accepted tradition in the group, the likelihood of developing a cooperative attack in any genuine sense is very dim indeed. Particularly at the start, then, it is important to pay attention to the way in which members of a group are participating.

Some general criteria for cooperative participation are obvious:

FOCUS ON WORK, NOT ON PERSONALITIES. Discussion as group inquiry is a flow of separate contributions, all of them presumably relevant to the task at hand and related to each other in some meaningful way. Expressions of feeling about other members of the group are, therefore, a form of waste motion. If, in response to an expressed idea, one member says, "Anyone who knows the realities of the situation would know that's impossible," he is really saying, "You're ignorant and fuzzy-headed." The Romans had a word for it: *ad hominem,* which they used to describe an argument directed against the person instead of coming to grips with what he has said. A fairly common form, in groups which have spent a good deal of time together, is the irritable remark, "Oh, Charlie's on his horse again!" in reaction to a reiteration of a point of view the group has heard several times before. Freely translated it means, "Charlie's an old bore, so let's not pay any attention to what he says." This may well be true, of course, but even if it were, the progress of the discussion would be better served by some examination of the contribution itself than by a statement of how one feels about Charlie.

DETACHMENT. People have great difficulty detaching themselves from the attitudes and opinions they feel are important. A person may think it proper for women to wear gloves in public and tolerate an opposite view with a shrug of the shoulders. But question his conviction that motherhood is a sacred institution, or that the United States had no other course but to drop an atom bomb on Hiroshima, and he may respond as if not his opinion, but his person, had been attacked. The flow of adrenalin increases, blood rushes to the brain, attack muscles tense, and jungle drums can be heard in the distance. There is nothing odd about this; people's images of themselves as persons consist of the things they value. Self-esteem is closely bound to others' approval of, in this case, one's ideas or opinions.

The tendency to respond to a questioning of one's ideas as an attack on oneself is of no great matter in an informal bull session; that form of discussion is really a kind of competitive play. But participation in cooperative inquiry requires of a group an ability to detach themselves, at least to some extent, from the contributions they make to the general enterprise, so that the ideas may be subjected to critical examination. Nor is this a counsel of perfection. It requires discipline, to be sure, but people in a great many fields of work are successfully trained to do it.

DIFFUSED RESPONSIBILITY. Any cooperative effort demands that the participants not only contribute to the work to be done, but that whenever possible they take responsibility for the organization of the effort and for some forms of work which are ordinarily thought of as leadership functions.[9] Discussion leaders are often expected to supply summaries where needed, clarifying conflicting positions, develop generalizations which might integrate a number of apparently disconnected statements, and so on. But these are all functions necessary to cooperative inquiry generally, and to the extent that group members perform them without waiting for the leader to do so, their participation is on a high level. This, again, is a characteristic of mature groups and hardly to be expected from people who have worked together only a short time.

Judgment of the effectiveness of participation must therefore take account of both the quality and the patterning of contributions. Quality depends entirely on the specific task on which the group is working. If it is problem-solving, and at the stage of collecting all possible ideas for a solution, then contribution of ideas is good participation, and almost anything else at that point is bad participation. If the group is examining a series of opinions about an issue and is working at locating the assumptions which underlie them, an attack on one of them, no matter how brilliant or stimulating, is irrelevant and therefore "bad" participation. Such considerations of the quality of participation are basic to the problem of discussion control and may be found in that later section.

The pattern and flow of contributions is a much simpler matter, and a fairly uncomplicated device, the participation flow chart, can provide many useful clues to the state of group cooperativeness. It provides only limited data on the quantity and direction of participa-

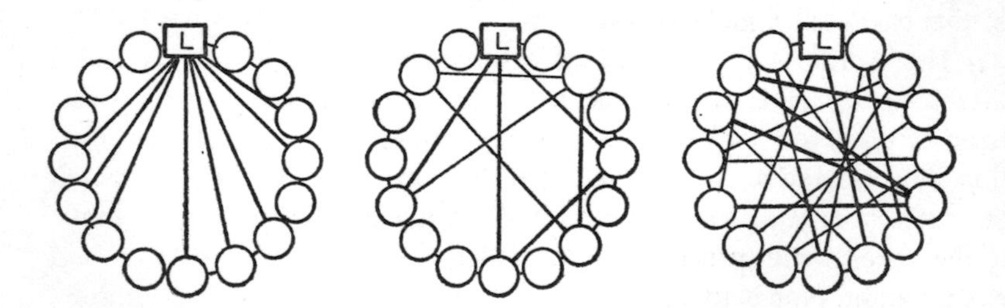

LEADER DOMINATED RESTRICTED INTERACTION GENERAL INTERACTION

tion and therefore has little significance by itself for evaluating the value of the discussion, but it may ring a warning bell on some major difficulties. In the following patterns, for instance, it is fairly easy to observe that for one reason or another Group 1 is centering its attention on the leader, that in Group 2 participation is restricted to only a part of the group, and that Group 3, whatever the quality of the discussion, is probably utilizing all its resources.

It is useful to assign the job of charting the flow of discussion occasionally to a member of the group and ask him to report his observations at the end of the session or at the beginning of the next. The observer may use a large circle with members designated by number, as in the example given below. Make a record of each contri-

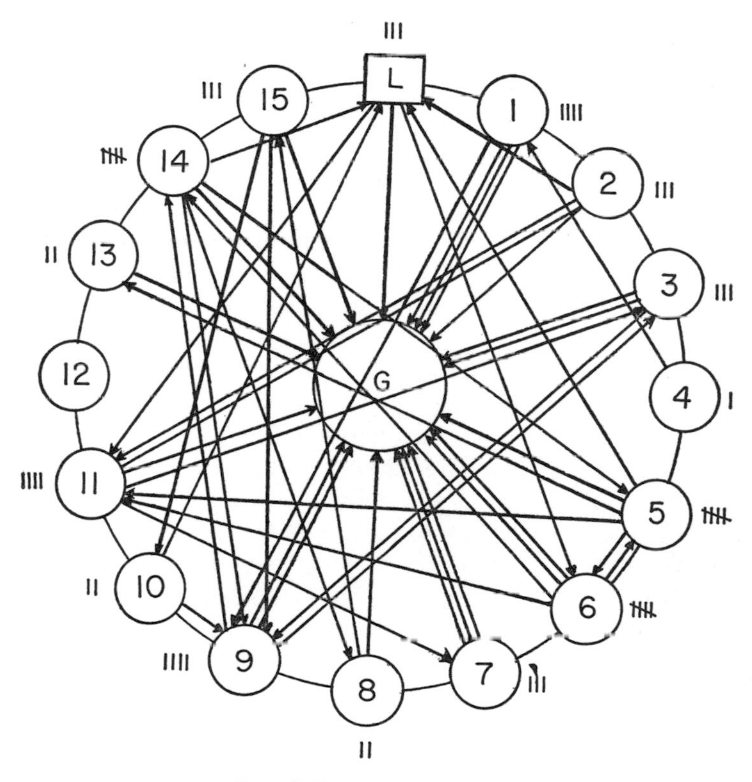

Sample Participation Chart

bution, using a straight edge to draw an arrow from the small circle representing the speaker to the person addressed. If the speaker addresses the remark to the group generally, draw the arrow to the center of the circle. Keep a tally of each person's contributions beside the circle designating him. A report to the group may address itself to answering questions like these:

How general was participation; did most members contribute?

Did anyone talk too much? Why? (It may be that one person had specialized knowledge or experience which made him a resource on a particular problem.)

Are those who talked most sitting together; and do the relatively silent ones also constitute a sub-group? (This might suggest the presence of friendship cliques which are operating to prevent full participation.)

Was the designated leader the focus of participation? Some other person? Why?

To what extent were contributions made to the group as a whole? (A partial clue to the extent to which issues are divorced from persons.)

Flight from Work: Individual Member Needs

The preceding sections suggest that when the group is not working at its discussion task, whatever form that flight may take, they may be reacting to difficult demands posed by either the task itself or problems of working together on it. These elements of the discussion situation may trigger the reaction, but the causes are likely to lie at more fundamental levels: in the relation of the individual to the group, and in leadership climate.

Difficult as it may be to deal with, there can be no ignoring the fact that discussion groups are composed of individuals, and no matter how interested in the topic they may be, no matter how intelligent, polite, and charming, they are individuals with different personalities and histories and widely varying emotional needs. Their contribution to the discussion may, consequently, be of two kinds: it may be relevant and necessary to the inquiry which is going on, part of the group's task, or it may be an expression of an individual need of the person making it, without real relevance to the task.

In its demonstration of the fundamental tension between the individual and the group with which he must make common cause, the discussion group is a society in miniature. Every human society must deal with the problem of how much expression of individuality it will permit and to what extent it will allow those needs of the society which are common to all to override the individual. Our "open" society tends to cut and patch the social order to fit individual preference and need; others make the individual adapt to the demands of the society. But even in our case, the individual must increasingly submit to regulation, as more areas of common concern become pressingly evident. And most people stop at a red light, even though no traffic policeman is in sight; most suburban residents, at times of water shortage, obey irritating regulation of their water use. If they did not, they recognize, everyone might be without any at all.

The tiny social system of the discussion group must face the same problem as the larger society, that of finding ways of participating with others to meet common objectives while recognizing individual differences in motivation and need. If the goals of the individual members overlap to produce a fairly large area of common objective for the group, participation is apt to be relevant and productive; if the overlapping of individual needs and the requirements of the group task is too small, too much frustration and conflict may be present for anything at all to happen.

The term "need" is used in a rather special sense to stand for tensions which lead people to behave in ways which, for them, provide emotional satisfaction. Physical needs, such as the needs for nourishment, for sleep, for balance, are easier to observe; faint, almost unfelt, stirrings in the stomach will lead a person on a familiar route to the refrigerator, and the observer notes that he is hungry. It is useful to realize that this automatic conclusion, in the present case, is usually made without prejudice; unless one feels that the person is grossly over-eating, it is a matter of indifference to most people whether or in what manner he is satisfying his body's need for food.

The expression of emotional needs is a far more complicated matter. Whole systems of psychology have been built on defining the needs which seem to be most significant in most people. It is easy to get fairly general agreement on the existence and importance of such needs, as long as they are on a general level. One social scientist identified what he called the "four wishes" present in all members of our society: security, recognition (status), emotional response, and new experience. At the opposite pole, a psychologist identified as many as 35 separate needs, including needs to aggress, to defend the self, to dominate, to achieve, needs for recognition, for order, for affection, and many others. Or, and perhaps most useful here, need-meeting behavior can be classified as either self-enhancing or self-defending.[10]

Unlike physical needs, the expression of emotional needs tends to arouse value judgments. People see a striving for achievement as a "good" thing, and so also is the expression of the need for order or for affection; dependency is a "bad" thing (one ought to stand on one's own two feet), and so are aggressiveness, dominance, and abasement. But the case is not really so clear-cut as it often seems. Orderliness, in general, is a virtue and is encouraged by all mothers, teachers, employers, and top sergeants, but the office manager who will not provide a paper clip without a signed requisition in triplicate can be just as exasperating as the one who can never find that important paper in the file. Striving for achievement is widely approved by a society which encourages individual upward mobility, but the person who cuts and slashes his way to the top with no compunction about whom he hurts on the way is no more admired than the one who seems completely to lack ambition. Thus, though Aristotle is not widely read, most people appear to agree with his doctrine that the good man is the moderate man.

All of this suggests that any society has some generally recognized standards about how *intensely* certain emotional needs can be expressed without upsetting other people. There is another aspect to the problem of expressing needs which is quite as important—how appropriate to the situation is the behavior? Everyone expects very young children in our culture to be dependent, but when adults express strong dependency needs, people find it difficult to handle. The military, as well as some levels of the economic enterprise, encourages people, within stated limits, to express dominance and aggressiveness, but these same individuals are expected to curb these needs within the family circle or in informal social situations. And, remarkably enough, most people can manage, when it is clear enough to them what behavior is appropriate. There are a number of fairly common situations, however, in which it is difficult to see what *is* appropriate or which encourage the expression of individual needs not related to the task. These tend to appear in the following ways in discussion groups:

THE NEW GROUP. A series of recent studies to gather evidence about what students think about during a class surprised no one by proving that some of the time, when the instructor or other students are talking, thoughts are concerned with matters which have very little to do with the subject of the class. Such "out of field" thoughts may, in undergraduates, be concerned with the date of the previous night or worry about personal concerns and vary in number depending on who is doing the talking, the nature of the subject, and other conditions. They increase, to a dismaying percentage, during the first meeting of the class. Conference experts have observed the same phenomenon whenever a group of specialists are called together to work on a problem; the first session is seldom likely to accomplish much work on the problem, because people are working on their individual concerns arising from facing a group of persons new to them.

These concerns are often in the area of identity and status. People feel more free to interact with others when they know *who* they are: not only what special status they might have, but whether they represent any particular threat to them, what they might have in common, what *kind* of persons they are. This is why first meetings may usefully employ some time having each person identify himself to the group; it is not merely a device to encourage "togetherness," but serves the necessary purpose of accomplishing with dispatch what is going to go on anyway.

THE URGE TO INFLUENCE. When the members of a discussion group think of discussion as a chance to influence others, an arena for conflicting opinions rather than a cooperative inquiry, other participation difficulties due to individual needs arise. The common "problem members" so often the focus for anguish among discussion leaders, the person who talks too much and the one who does not talk at all, may often be explained in these terms.

If the purpose of talk is to make someone see it your way, then the overtalkative person may be doing one of several things: trying to influence the group when they already agree with him, in which case he needs to be informed of the agreement; trying to convince the group of something which they feel is unimportant or irrelevant, in which case there needs to be open agreement by the group on what is relevant to the discussion.

The silent member, similarly, may not participate because he sees that he agrees with others in the group and that every time he is about to make a contribution, someone says it first. Or he may believe that he has little influence with the others in the group, and it would therefore do little good for him to speak. If the need to influence others is not the major concern of the group, then such members may see the possibility of other contributions which they might well make to the discussion, the presentation of needed factual data, for example, or raising a question about the adequacy of an opinion.

One of the most interesting consequences of viewing discussion as a battlefield happens when one member of a group maintains a position or opinion very different from that of all the others. Communication then concentrates on the dissenter, almost all contributions flowing toward him, as the group tries to influence him to change. This goes on until the group is convinced that it is not going to succeed in changing his mind, and communication in his direction is likely to cease altogether.

The preceding section suggested a method for gathering evidence on the general flow of participation without regard to its quality. The discussion of individual needs now provides a starting point for a systematic view of the quality of the participation. Here are some indicators for recognizing the presence of expressions of individual, rather than task, needs:

1. Aggressive expression of disapproval of acts or feelings of other members. This does *not* mean disagreement, differences of opinion, or other contributions necessary to the inquiry process, but the loading of statements of such differences with aggressiveness toward the individual who differs. A manner of delivery which implies "not only is your opinion incorrect, but only an ass would believe in it," directs criticism toward the person as well as the opinion.

2. Attacks on the group or the problem it is working on. These may often be subtle enough to escape general notice. Complaints that "we're not getting anywhere," without indicating either where the group should be going or suggesting a change in procedure which might be more effective; remarks to the effect that "all this talk about democracy is arrant nonsense, because democracy is only a meaningless word anyway"—such attacks may be deceptively mild-mannered, but they often lead the group away from the task to concentrate on the individual who makes them.

3. Disagreement or opposition without or beyond "reason." A stubborn restatement of a position after it has been thoroughly explored makes sense only if discussion chiefly aims to change other people's opinions and beliefs to one's own. The court tradition of the "dissenting opinion" helps the inquiry proceed if everyone is satisfied that further discussion will not bear fruit, and the leader has the often difficult task of deciding the appropriate point to make such a suggestion.

4. Remarks which call attention to the person: accounts of personal achievement or consistently irrelevant contributions. Here, again, the leader needs to make a distinction between individual and task needs but may find it relatively easy to determine when a member is contributing a personal experience as a useful piece of data and when he is merely asking for attention. Consistent irrelevancy, too,

may often result from a misunderstanding of what the group is doing at the time rather than from a personal need, a situation which requires different handling.

5. Horseplay, cynicism, and the like, which display lack of interest in the job of the group. Groups cannot be "at work" all the time, and interludes of fun usefully change pace and relieve tension. Horseplay which does not have this function disrupts work and annoys most of the members of the group; this kind of reaction provides a good clue to the true nature of the behavior.

6. Attempts to assert authority or superiority by giving directions authoritatively or interrupting the contributions of others. This kind of behavior is usually a pure expression of individual need and is easily diagnosed.

7. Special pleading for stereotypes, for example, "the small businessman," "grassroots community," "labor," which hides the member's own prejudices or biases. There is a considerable difference between a contribution which describes the position or demands of a social group as a datum for the group to consider and one which uses such a description to provide a spurious social acceptability for a position.

Flight from Work: Leadership Climate

If the group is to concentrate its main attention on the job at hand, the conduct of the inquiry, it cannot at the same time consistently worry about the individual participation of each member. Some leaders and groups try to do so and no doubt consequently swell the rising tide of tranquilizer consumption. A good deal of evidence exists for a relationship between relevant participation in work and some general characteristics of leader behavior. An understanding of that relationship can decrease considerably the amount of specific attention which needs to be given to the participation level and flow.

The classic study of the effect of leader behavior on the participation pattern of the groups they lead was conducted in 1940; as subjects it used groups of boys who had volunteered for membership in a number of clubs in which the major announced purpose was crafts activity. One of the aims of the study was to examine the effects on group and individual behavior of three variations in leadership.[11] These variations were roughly labeled "authoritarian," "democratic," and "laissez-faire." The roles which were to be played by the adult leaders look something like these:

AUTHORITARIAN. The leader should determine all policies governing club activities and procedures and should communicate the techniques and the steps by which the task is done one at a time, so that the group is in the dark about future steps most of the time. The leader should take considerable responsibility for assigning tasks and companions of each member and, except in demonstration, should remain fairly aloof from active participation in the group. He should keep his standards of praise and criticism to himself when evaluating individual or group activities.

DEMOCRATIC. Whenever possible, policies should be subjected to group discussion and decision with the active encouragement and assistance of the leader. During this discussion the leader should attempt to see that the general steps necessary to reach the activity goal emerge clearly. Whenever technical advice is needed, the leader should try to suggest two or more alternative procedures from which the group can choose. Everyone should be free to work with the person of his own choice, and divisions of responsibility should be left up to the group. The leader should try to communicate objectively the bases for his praise and criticism and should try to be a regular member of the group in spirit, without doing much of the work himself.

LAISSEZ-FAIRE. The leader should play a rather passive role and leave the group complete freedom to decide on the activity they want to undertake and the procedures for doing it. He should make clear what materials are available and be sure that the group understands that he will supply information and help when asked. He should take the initiative for making suggestions as seldom as possible. He should express neither good or bad opinions of either the behavior or productions of the group, although he should be friendly rather than "standoffish" at all times.

These three leadership roles, it turned out, produced not three, but four distinct types of reaction, which the experimenters called "styles of group life." Two of these emerged in response to authoritarian leadership, the other two were reactions to the democratic and laissez-faire roles. An examination of these participation patterns illuminates the general problems of discussion groups.

AGGRESSIVE RESPONSES TO AUTHORITARIAN ROLE. One of the groups reacted to the authoritarian atmosphere with considerable frustration and some aggressiveness directed toward the leader. At the same time, they displayed a good deal of dependency on him. They were more rebellious than any other group, demanded attention more than the others, and spent less time talking about the work they were doing than any but the laissez-faire groups. They shared with the other authoritarian group a high level of irritability and aggressiveness toward fellow members. When the leader was late, or absent from the room, very little work was done.

PASSIVE RESPONSE TO AUTHORITARIAN ROLE. Three groups reacted to the authoritarian situation not with aggression and rebelliousness, but by passively leaning on the leader. They probably felt more discontent than they showed, however; their conversation was considerably more restricted than was the interchange in the democratic or laissez-faire groups. In both types of authoritarian situation, demands for attention from the leader were great; where all power seems to be in the hands of the leader, getting his attention is the only way to achieve recognition. As noted previously, little work was done in the absence of the leader.

RESPONSE TO LAISSEZ-FAIRE ROLE. Groups in this situation were rather more like the democratic groups than the authoritarian. They were less dependent on the leader, less discontented than either of the authoritarian groups, more friendly, but considerably less work-minded than any of the other groups. Their plight is dramatized by the fact that almost 40 per cent of their behavior toward their leader consisted of requests for information, compared to about 15 per cent in the other groups. In the absence of the leader, they were more active than any of the other groups, but not productive. At times, in the absence of the passive leader, one of the boys took over and achieved a greater coordination of group activity than was usually present, and the activity was productive.

RESPONSE TO DEMOCRATIC ROLE. The democratic groups were least dependent on the leader, least discontented, most friendly, and most work-minded. Their demands for attention and requests for information fell somewhat between the laissez-faire groups and the authoritarian ones. They felt much freer and more inclined to make suggestions on group policy than those in the other three atmospheres. Leaders who arrived late found the democratic groups already productively active, and, in general, the presence or absence of the leader had practically no effect on productive work.

The significant findings of this study have since been tested with adult groups as well and substantially confirmed. Groups of adults are of course more complicated worlds, and the results of later studies are in some ways less clear-cut. But the precise data needed by the social scientist is often enough *too* precise to serve as a useful tool for people in real situations. In this instance, the rough generalizations useful for discussion leaders can readily and fairly be drawn from the study described.

And they are reasonably clear. The way in which people who are working together participate in that task is determined to a considerable extent by the atmosphere created by the leader, the *climate* of the group. Climate is a good descriptive term because it implies the pervasive, hard-to-pin-down, feeling tone of a group, detectable in the way the members act toward each other and toward the problem they are working on.

The relation of the climate to the behavior of the leader is also clear. The terms "democratic," "authoritarian," and "laissez-faire" are not necessary; they are political labels which the experimenters found convenient and dramatic. "Participative," "dominant," and "non-directive," or any other set, would do as well. The real meaning of the roles lies in the description of what the leader does in relation to the group and the model of participation which he establishes by his behavior.

A Control System for Discussion

To summarize the argument up to this point: a discussion group is a group at work, whose task consists of one of several well-defined sequences of behavior appropriate to its particular learning objective; it may not be at work because the needs of individual members not relevant to the task have become stronger than the shared need to accomplish the group task, a situation which may or may not be due to the group's response to leadership climate. Any general scheme for controlling the process must rest on a systematic view of the leadership function.

In the ordinary course of events, the person who tends to emerge naturally as the leader in an informal discussion group is the person who makes the most contributions and becomes, consequently, one of the more visible members of the group. When he is designated by the group as leader, he most often sees his role as a dominant one. The term is not meant in the Captain Bligh sense but indicates that the leader concentrates in himself all the necessary functions of inquiry: he sets the objective for the discussion, he decides on the steps necessary to get to it, he evaluates the contributions of the participants, and he sets the standards by which progress or success is judged.

There are, no doubt, many situations in which this particular pattern of leadership is workable, but it is a singularly inappropriate one for conducting discussion groups of the kind under examination here.[12] We are not concerned with producing a perfect final product but with increasing the learning of the individual members, learning which in part consists in change of behavior in dealing with problems and issues. Our objectives are to help people become more skilled in weighing political issues, problem-solving, and the examination of value conflicts, not to achieve consensus on a course of action. The skills are process skills, and if we center the processes in one person, we deprive the rest of the group of the opportunity of practicing them.

The traditional view of leadership as a number of personality dimensions which a given individual does or does not possess simply does not fit the discussion situation.[13] More appropriate is the recent conception, supported by a considerable body of research, that leadership is a number of functions which must be performed if the group is to move toward its objective: suggesting direction for activity, defining goals, and evaluating the performance of the group. Someone must perform these functions at the point at which they are necessary, but there is no reason why they must be performed by any given person; any member of the group may do so, or the group as a whole can cooperate in getting them done. This view of the nature of leadership is functionally suitable to group discussion because it provides for the sharing of those activities which individual members of the group must learn.

Where, then, does the leader come in? Experience with leaderless group discussion suggests that the answer does not lie in that direction; the emergent leader may turn out to be the most dominant member of the group rather than the one most sensitive to the group's learning needs. In its simplest terms, the answer is: *the leader takes major responsibility for helping the group decide, at any particular choice point, what it can most usefully do.* In the military sense, he is not a line authority, but a staff person, who keeps his eye on the tentative goals and estimates progress toward them, suggests the need to assess present activity, proposes alternative goals for consideration, raises questions of whether present goals need to be modified, and performs other such staff activities.

The leader, then, helps the group come to agreements about how to make their work most productive, which often means that he must first make the group conscious of agreements they have already come to without verbal exchange. For, in fact, all groups of people in interaction develop *norms,* agreements about conduct which will be tolerated or encouraged, approved patterns of work, and ways of behaving toward one another.[14] Informal groups develop such norms in very complicated ways, and they are seldom articulated except through disapproval of the individual who violates one of them. But one can detect them by inference. For example, consider these common discussion group behaviors:

1. The leader always starts off the discussion with "I think we ought now to take a look at . . ." and off they go. This group operates under an agreement to let the leader choose the topic and is running the risk of having him choose one in which no one else is interested.

2. After the leader calls the group to order, there is a short silence followed by what appears to be a random observation by one member. This is taken up and becomes the theme for the discussion. The culture of this group includes the agreement that they will discuss whatever question is raised by the first member to speak. They risk complete aimlessness as the discussion runs up and down the back alleys of each one's particular interest or prejudice.

3. No member ever seems to respond to the contribution of the person who spoke before him; the discussion is a series of almost unrelated comments. This group apparently has an unspoken compact to the effect that no statement needs to be responded or reacted to.

These will serve as examples which most discussion leaders will recognize. It is not difficult to construct a picture of the culture of any group by observing its habitual patterns of behavior and inferring the agreements which appear to rule the operations of the group.

The examples above are all horrible ones. Most groups, if they are at all effective, operate under agreements which are helpful, as well as ones which block work. But such agreements, generally speaking, are unconscious; they grow and get accepted just as do the rules which children follow when they play games. But the fact that the process exists provides the basis for a general method for the leader to use.

Discussion leadership operates by controlling the process of agreement, the changes which must be made in agreements and in the conditions under which they are to be made. The leader does this by bringing out into the open and subject to decision by the group, agreements about what questions shall be discussed, in what order, how the group will treat individual contributions, what kinds of contributions are most relevant at a particular time, and all other necessary operations demanded by the nature of the inquiry in which the group is involved.

How does the leader, or the group, know what agreements are best? As we have pointed out, they cannot be determined in advance, because the purposes of each group are different, groups are composed of a wide variety of people, and the task itself imposes different requirements. The only reasonable answer is that *leadership must work by using the experimental method: it must take a first step, then see what happens.*

The leader can maintain the experimental process in several major ways:

1. He must be sensitive to the amount of *confidence* the group has in the agreements it develops about the way it works and, when necessary, check his judgment with the group's.
2. He must help the group recognize the points at which a *choice* must be made about its activity. Such choice points exist, for example, at times when there appears to be a difference of feeling in the group about what it is doing. It is very important that, at these times he take into account the feelings of everyone in the group. It is in this regard that all members are equally respected; despite differences in knowledge, experience, and wisdom, everyone has the same right to have his feelings about what the group should do taken into account.
3. He must find and maintain conditions under which each person who can make a contribution needed by the group will make it. Part of the leader's job is to discover and coordinate the resources available to the group in its members.

Problems of Diagnosis and Control

The proposed model for leadership is necessarily a general one; all models are abstractions, and their workability depends on the ingenuity and intelligence of the person applying them to specific situations. But because some problems are more persistent and common than others, it is possible to suggest some specific applications.

An important task of the leader is that of diagnosis. We have been talking about "the group" working or not working, as though it were a single entity and not a collection of individuals. Without debating the question of whether it is mystical and absurd to regard groups in this fashion, one can point out a useful, practical reason for doing so; it permits the leader to diagnose the state of the group enterprise from clues provided by individual behavior. For example, consider a situation in which two members of a group are arguing: not examining two different points of view in order to advance the general purpose of achieving clarity or more understanding, but fighting to no purpose but their own individual ones. Now, if the other members sit passively and watch, they will be seen as enjoying it or at least as agreeing that the fight ought to go on; if a single member steps in to try to stop it, he will be seen as joining the fight. By permitting the fight to proceed, the group implies its agreement not to work on the problem at hand.

One way of looking at puzzling or disruptive contributions by members of the group, then, is to see them as expressions of the way the group as a whole feels at the time. An irrelevant remark may indicate that the group is not clear about what kind of contribution they should make. A confused and wandering offering may mean that the group has no really clear idea of its purpose at the moment. A fight which the group permits to go on may signalize the presence of a frustration generally felt, which it escapes by enjoying the fight. These sorts of manifestations provide clues for the leader to the possibiilty that the group has lost confidence in its operational agreements or that a new activity is needed.

There will always be periods, of course, when even the most work-oriented groups need to let off steam and relax. Periods of flight from work are necessary and, indeed, should be scheduled. The coffee break is a magnificent and useful institution.

Diagnosis may lead the leader to suggest any one of a number of experimental control devices which the group may decide to institute. One of the most useful of these is the agreement, for a limited period of time, to specify the type of activity it thinks most useful. If they are engaged in working through a problem, they might agree to restrict contributions for a time to suggestions for a solution, without regard to how good or bad someone might think a particular solution is, and follow this period with one restricted to the systematic evaluation of each of the proposed solutions. This type of control often has a striking effect on the clarity of the discussion.

Another useful area of agreement is how contributions of individuals should be treated. The environment of a discussion group is largely made of statements and responses to statements. Because people have a need for a stable environment, it is important that the members have a reasonable expectation about how a contribution will be accepted. If the group has developed no control over this process, a member will have no way of knowing whether a statement will be jumped on and stamped to death or accepted and examined for its usefulness to the problem at hand.[15]

If the group over a period of time has identified some kind of behavior which it agrees should be avoided, it might set up a "watch-dog" to enforce its agreement in the interests of cooperation. Or, more generally, it may decide to take time out for an evaluation session to consider past activities and to hammer out a number of agreements on how to proceed. The purpose of this kind of session must be clear, or, as Thelen points out, "it may become either a festival of politeness or a session wallowing in emotion."

AN ILLUSTRATION

The following is the first part of a transcription of an actual discussion held by a nine-member group which is typical of many informal community groups in having a wide spread of occupational and educational backgrounds. The leader, however, is a highly-skilled professional with a style of his own which does not particularly follow the dictates of the model presented in this chapter.[16]

The group has just listened to a dramatic recording (one of *The Ways of Mankind* series) exploring anthropological concepts relating to the family. It tells the story of a Chinese scientist, raised in the United States, who is assigned to do a job in China after the war and who finds himself by chance living in the small village from which his father came. There he meets a large number of his relations and for a time is enchanted by the unity and closeness of the family group, particularly as he contrasts the dutifulness of the children with the behavior of his own Americanized son and daughter. But as he observes more closely, disenchantment sets in. So long as his old, patriarchal uncle lives, he discovers, his cousins are continually frustrated in their attempts to better their lives; women in particular must put up with a great deal of frustration and emotional pain until they are old enough to attain a respected position. And his own American family, though the price in conflict and insecurity is high, nevertheless gains for its members a valuable freedom to adjust as they wish to a swiftly moving society.

LEADER: Maybe we should try to move into the discussion. Through a discussion of this record we can't hope to bring about any drastic changes in our own family life, or reorganize either our whole social system, or the plans for gerontology. But there were some pretty cogent and fascinating ideas in there, which could provide us with insights into some of our own problems and dilemmas, and help us to a little more self-understanding and self-examination.

I'd like to start off with one question, if I could. As I was listening to the record a thought which kept recurring in my mind is that at the present all of the Freudians, social workers and analysts are talking about the importance of trying to develop security in our children—for after all, they ask, can we be really free people or really individuals unless we have internal security? Let me ask you whether you think our society could usefully borrow anything from the Chinese family life referred to on the record, for it seems to give the child a basic security. From what we've heard about Chinese family life, who do you think has a greater chance to achieve individual happiness and growth, children who come from that kind of family situation, or those who grow from our family situations?

HORACE: I live in a part of the U.S. where this system still exists—Hawaii; and both situations exist there in an odd combination: the parents may be still Buddhist, while some of the children may be Catholics or Protestants, but they all live under the same roof.

LEADER: In other words it is possible there to have both kinds of situations?

HORACE: That's the way it seems to be working there.

HARRY: How are the Hawaiian kids compared to ours? Do they have the same kinds of faults that we are continually attributing to our kids?

HORACE: I think they have the same kinds.

HARRY: In other words, they are more like our children than they are like the Chinese.

HORACE: Yes.

LEADER: If we had the kind of security and cohesion that the Chinese have in their families, would this be basically a good thing for our kids' development, or would it be inhibiting to their individuality?

MARIAN: I wonder if environment isn't just as important—could you take that same Chinese family and put them in the U.S. or Hawaii and have the same situation?—they're living a rural life in China.

HORACE: Even though there is in Hawaii an urban center like Honolulu, there is still a rural life like that in China or Japan or the Philippines.

MORRIE: Actually, China has both rural and urban life—there are villages in China that have as many as 50,000 people, although there is no city as we know it.

ROSIE: I was going to say the same thing—Hawaii is different from China, because Hawaii has an influx of different people coming from all over the world, whereas people don't usually go to visit China unless they have family or business ties. The influx of people coming to Hawaii has changed a lot of people's ideas, whereas they could go on undisturbed for hundreds of years the way they have if there were no outsiders. Maybe *once* in a while there is some little undercurrent of resentment about changes which are happening—mostly among women.

(Laughter)

LEADER: Could I push this back for just a minute, although I do think the environment question is an extremely significant one? Do you think that the kind of situation that traditionally exists in China—the respect for parents, and for family whether alive or dead, and a looking inward on the family—is really a good thing? Imagining that it might be possible, would any of you like to see it for your own children? Would it be a benefit to them or a harm?

ALLAN: I think the children are not the ones who enjoy the most direct benefit from this type of social organization—parents and grandparents benefit the most. I couldn't get a very good glimpse of how this affects the life of children, but since older people get psychic satisfaction and security from it, that's probably the reason it developed as much as it did.

MARIAN: Do you think children can live in that kind of environment and not get *some* satisfaction from it?

EVELYN: Don't you think that with this attitude in the family, a child could look forward to enjoyment of later years and to creating the same situation for his own children or grandchildren, an enjoyment of the unity and respect?

ALLAN: Undoubtedly children participate in that feeling and have a sense of security and satisfaction belonging to this very intimate thing. But children tend to feel a certain rebellion, a certain desire to break away even though the desire may be latent.

EVELYN: Well, I don't know; I think maybe that children could want to break away to a degree but at the same time more than appreciate the unity of the family group and the things they enjoy.

HARRY: I think I'd go along on that.

EVELYN: I'm speaking from experience myself, and from the little I can see of this in my teen-age daughter.

HARRY: I've a feeling that part of the trouble with American kids is that they don't have a well-enough structured life, that they have too much freedom.

LEADER: You mean that there's nothing to break away from.

HARRY: That's right. I think the young kids, Freudian theory to the contrary notwithstanding, really do need a structure. They can't face certain kinds of problems, and they shouldn't be made to face them. It isn't necessary for them to be given choices that are really kind of phony choices. Smith's book, "Where Did You Go?—Out; What Did You Do?—Nothing" makes that point beautifully when he talks about the kids in this generation, which is our generation. . . .

MORRIE: If we go back to the early period in our country's history, we remember that we had that patriarchal situation—there were big families and houses with father or grandfather more or less in charge. When we broke away and started the movement west, we individually were out on our own for the first time. Day's play, "Life With Father," brings out the early phase of American life. A father is in charge, when he walks in the door; everybody in a sense cowtows to make sure that there's no noise and that supper's on time.

HARRY: Yes, well, I think what I'm saying is that certain elements of that situation are good; but it may have its disadvantages, too.

ROY: You think that we might return to this stage?

HARRY: Well, I think this is an open question—as I got the question, we're just talking about the advantages or disadvantages to the child in the two different situations.

LEADER: As you listen to this record, do any of you, as parents, have a little bit of yearning and think, as I did at certain points, "My kids do not have the kind of security that these kids have—there are not as many 'givers.' Wouldn't it be wonderful if they did have some of this close, warm security." Did any of the rest of you react that way?

EVELYN: Well, I think I did. I could understand certain portions of it, like the obligations to family, because I am from a family that is small but close, and I was raised with grandparents and great-grandparents. And since my grandmother is still living, my daughter is now experiencing a great-grandmother's love.

LEADER: When you were a kid, did you like this or resent it?

EVELYN: Well, I resented it only when it interfered with something that was important to me, but I find in looking back that it was usually petty, not important. If it was something that I really wanted to do, they would say, "Well, okay—we don't make demands on you, so don't put demands on us." When I was faced with the problem of giving up my connection with my family, I couldn't because I liked that routine. I try the same thing now, with my daughter, and it really works. I automatically tell her she's not a member of the family anymore and I don't have to argue.

(Laughter)

MARIAN: I read an article the other day that has some bearing on this. It tried to explain the recent increase in large families. One explanation was that in the last two or three generations there have been many families with only one or two children; these children are now grown up and about to have a family; and they feel that since they lack something because they weren't a larger family, they ought to have four or five children.

ALLAN: Now, we assume that the more stable a family is, the more secure the children are going to be: but there are conflicts that arise from this stability as well. What's the problem here? Are there more conflicts in a single family consisting of several generations, where we know there are opportunities for conflicts between the younger and older generations? Is there more security for a family of only parents and children, and therefore less opportunity for conflict?

MARIAN: What's the matter with conflict?

ALLAN: Well, only that we're talking now specifically about security. We were asking where the child is more secure—in the stable family where the family circle is three and possibly four generations? Or in the family where the only important circle consists of only his parents and himself?

EVELYN: I work with a teen-age group and listening to their conversation I think they get a pleasure out of the little conflict that they've hit in life, the tensions and the criticisms from their parents, and the completely opposite viewpoint that their grandparents or great-grandparents have and . . .

HARRY: One minute, Evelyn—I'm not sure I understand what you mean.

EVELYN: The family conflicts you're speaking of are the differences in viewpoint between maybe a mother and dad or between maybe a grandmother and grandfather—is that what you mean?

ALLAN: Yes.

EVELYN: Well, I think that, in the long run, if they're fairly intelligent people they'll come to an agreement in the end. But during the time that the problem is being discussed, I think kids enjoy just a little bit of conflict, because it gives them something to face. It gives them a way to judge in the future.

LEADER: Of course in the Day family that you mentioned, Morrie, there may be eventual conflict, but at least as long as the kid is pretty young, he's not confronted with a question of conflict—I mean, old man Day is the authority. So at least in the formative years there is the security of knowing what's going to happen. I think that one of the questions is whether in the long run this develops individuals who will be autonomous or those who will just get in the habit of being dependent. That's the question that worries me, and I'm not sure of the answer.

ROY: I was wondering if perhaps we could make some practical use of a couple of philosophical conceptions here. One is that the important thing is to learn how to cope with problems as they arise—that since you're going to keep getting into conflicts, you finally come to some sort of happiness if you can cope with these daily problems. Then the opposing theory is the Greek tradition that there is some universal and ultimate good. It seems that the Chinese family situations are perhaps more like the Greek tradition in that they set up what they feel are more or less lasting values for the younger generation to adhere to and to know and love. And I think we can reasonably say that in an American society we have more a Deweyistic type of philosophy, in which we feel that the coping with problems and solving them is the thing.

LEADER: I'm not sure that the American Legion and our President would agree with you that we're based on a Deweyistic philosophy.

ROY: Fortunately I don't have to have their agreement.

LEADER: Touché!

ROY: Well, I was just wondering if this is an unanswerable problem. If you try to take a little of each and blend them into perfect harmony, this is the ultimate solution; so far no one has been able to do it. I'm not saying this *is* an unsolvable problem; I'm saying that these issues have been confronting man since the beginning of time, and that there isn't going to be any resolution. We have to decide what is important to us—whether solving of problems and conflicts is the best way of life, or to hand on a tradition through the generations.

LEADER: I think Morrie wanted to say something; then let's go around.

MORRIE: Returning to the comment that the Chinese family really gives the individual emotional security, I think the issue, then, is what price an individual pays for this emotional security and placidity, for being denied experiences and growth that he would get in another kind of society. Suppose we grant that the individual gets emotional security out of the Chinese structure. Then we look around and observe that the Chinese society is one which is tied to tradition, opposes change, has crystallized and congealed; we then have to argue that if that's the nominal price which the individual has to pay for his emotional security, this very price is denying him a long list of other advantages.

ROY: You're suggesting that there are two main aspects of this, psychological and philosophical.

LEADER: Is change good just for the sake of change?

MORRIE: I think that the kind of changing society which seems to be precluded by the extended family has many advantages for the individual. For example, although the extended family brings him economic security, the more dynamic society can bring him economic security and protection in the sense of insurance and different kinds of economy and so on. A kind of society that releases energy and in an explosive way gives us fast development, gives us scientific institutions, gives us educational institutions. Change may not be good for its own sake, but it is an almost inevitable kind of instrument for the kinds of emergence we have in a society where the individual is gaining much. I and my children can gain a great deal from the emotional security of an extended family; but we can also gain in the kind of a society that produces Salk and other researchers who come out with conclusions that give us physical benefits.

LEADER: I think Horace wants to get in. Let's go down the line.

HORACE: I'd like to ask a question: in what society do we believe there is the greatest amount of conflict for young children—the Chinese society represented on the record, or American society?

HARRY: I don't think there's any doubt that the American family has more open and more emotional conflict. Lynd was very fond of pointing out that in a highly mobile society like ours, in which a terrific stress is on the economic, the kinds of psychological blows that people take get taken out sooner or later. The guy goes off to work and he has to take all sorts of ego blows, and handle all sorts of problems; he comes home and the only way in which he can take this out is on an extremely tenuous marriage relationship. There's nothing else holding the family together except a contract. No land, no property, no tradition, no nothing. There's just the emotional tie between the man and the woman, and that constitutes the only real structure for the family in this society. And when a guy or his wife handle the blows they receive from other institutional areas in this society, by taking them out on the tenuous little institution of marriage, no wonder it keeps dissolving; there's nothing else holding it together.

MORRIE: I'm going to let you come back, Horace, but my question would be this. What is the individual's interpretation of what the family is and what the family is going to give him? You might take the whole group around here, do a little historical background, and I find that each one of us has a difference of approach. For example, I've been away from home since the age of six; which may sound silly, but it is true. Some of us have been gypsies in this world and roamed from place to place. I have a family, Harry; now what *is* family life? You see, I don't know what to do with it. That is, what can I expect from my children? How should I act to them? Because I've been roaming the world, you see—

MARIAN: Why did you assume family life?

MORRIE: Well, I suppose it's quite normal and rather natural and . . .

MARIAN: And now that you have it, you don't know what to do with it, you don't know what to expect of it.

MORRIE: Yes, that's what I say, but I tell you . . .

MARIAN: But didn't you have any expectations?

MORRIE: I know what I'd like to have in a sense of friendship within my own group. You talk about conflicts—there've always been conflicts. The question is can you solve them.

HARRY: I'm not sure that's the question we're really addressing. The question raised first of all was whether there is more conflict in our small families than there is within an extended kinship system. I think I was really challenging you. And making some very definite assertions that inevitably there is more emotional conflict.

LEADER: Horace wanted to come back on that.

HORACE: I would hypothesize that by the very nature of things, the more stable a society is, the more conflict there is, but less opportunity for *manifesting* it. That in the Chinese family, because of the nature of the Chinese family . . .

LEADER: Say that again, and then give us an example of it, Horace, if you will.

HORACE: In the Chinese family, which has absolutely resisted change, when the young desire to change there's no opportunity for it because of the hierarchial nature of the family; so the conflict is present but it's inhibited by the structure of the family. In the American family, there is actually less opportunity for conflict but more opportunity for expressing it and less guidance in resolving it.

ROSIE: In other words, Americans make mountains out of molehills.

HARRY: No, I think I see his point.

ROSIE: I do, too, but whereas there's an undercurrent of unrest in the Chinese family, the American family will always explode. But, too, the Chinese family may resolve some conflicts very quietly and efficiently, while the American one will make a mountain out of a molehill, with each little thing seeming like a great big challenge.

HARRY: I think there's another point to add to this; and that is they picked an unfortunate example in this middle-twentieth-century Chinese family; these conflicts may well have not been there traditionally. The social system on which they are based is changing.

LEADER: I think there are two or three areas of discussion now open and I'd like to try to define them; but before I do, Horace wants to say something.

HORACE: I just wanted to answer Morrie. I think you can have both of these systems operating together in a modified way. I don't think you have to have complete breakdown of the family when there are technological advances.

MORRIE: Yes, I have my in-laws living right across the hall from me, and it is an effort to observe the extended family.

(Laughter)

LEADER: So your mind's made up, Morrie. I do think that we've been talking about two or three different kinds of problems. Let me try to set them out and see if we want to follow through on any of them a little more before we go on. One of these problems was which of the two kinds of families tends to provide the greatest security for children who are growing and developing, and which kind of family system we might select for the development of our kids if we had a choice, which we don't. Very closely related to that was the other question of which one of these systems poses the greatest conflict for the child. An accompanying question is whether conflict is a good or a bad thing for a growing child: should he be protected from conflict situations or should he have to face them? We pushed aside two questions of environment in our present American society: is it possible to push back to any older values, or is it possible to have a mixed situation such as that in Hawaii.

ROY: There's one more I don't think you captured in your summary, and that was the one I expressed . . .

(Laughter)

ROY: Add to the summary, what constitutes the ideal society? What ultimate goals are there? Does man achieve greater happiness through interactions with society?

LEADER: Good—I'm glad you added that, because it is an important one, and we didn't really follow through.

Comments

As an example of the third kind of group discussion, in which a group explores a perennial human problem to learn more of its dimensions, this excerpt is, most people would agree, a good one. The group is amiable and disciplined and present few of the kinds of participation difficulties which normally arise. These circumstances permit a clear view of the role of the leader in relation to the model of leadership and control previously developed.

In this case, the leader has adopted a strategy, often strongly recommended by discussion experts, based on a concentration upon logical progression within the subject matter of the discussion. The leader himself chooses a reasonable issue implicit in the material and suggests it as a starting point to the group. Presumably the group may reject the suggestion in favor of another if it chooses. In the present case, they accept the lead and go through a period of preliminary exploration, during which a number of dimensions important to a consideration of the issues emerge naturally out of the spontaneous interchange, until the leader decides that summary and further organization are needed to clarify the next steps for the discussion. He thereupon restates in an excellent summary three of the important issues which emerged and suggests that the group might want to concentrate attention on one of them. During the exploratory period, the leader, in addition to this content-organization task, has acted mainly as an expediter of participation flow, encouraging maximum participation, and as a clarifier of single contributions.

The role as played here puts a high premium on the ability to organize and categorize complex intellectual material and to some extent on a previous knowledge of the field under discussion. In this sense the leader takes a position midway between the role of the classroom teacher described in Chapter IV and the pure model of the nonprofessional discussion leader suggested in this chapter. It is not a simple matter to achieve improvement of these abilities in most persons.

In the framework of the proposed model, on the other hand, the leader, instead of proposing the subject for the inquiry and testing it through discussion, would instead initiate the process of deciding on the start-off point. If three or four different suggested issues emerged, the group might briefly discuss their priority and agree to explore them in a definite order and then begin on an examination of the first one. Consequently, the group could reap the benefit of having at hand immediately a fairly clear-cut task, and the leader would find his control responsibility simplified. For example, if priority is given to the issue of whether children's emotional security is likely to differ significantly between the two types of family, the nature of the discussion can be fairly well-defined; the group might wish to use itself as a resource for a time and encourage each individual to reflect on his own family structure and its relation to security, thus making more systematic use of the personal references which inevitably arose in the actual discussion, or they could try listing the sources of emotional security and match them against the relationships which each type of family structure encourages.

One could argue, of course, that the actual discussion achieved the same end, and more naturally, by allowing individual concerns to emerge through the spontaneous interplay recorded. Some of the issues raised by the group, perhaps, were suggested by what others said during the course of the discussion. But the model does not eliminate the usefulness of such afterthoughts; they can be added to the agenda as they emerge, for later consideration, and thus be eliminated as alien presences from the current task. In fact, the virtue of the suggested procedure is not only that it clarifies and simplifies the leader's role, but also that it encourages coherence generally; if people expect that the issue they raise as paramount will be discussed in due course, they are more likely to concentrate on the task at hand.

Several other features of the discussion are worth noting. One is that the traditional roles of the leader are obviously taken by members of the group at many points. Individual members ask others for clarification of something just said, ask questions leading to amplification of points, encourage others to speak, reassure others that they will have a chance to contribute shortly, and in general perform many of the necessary management tasks. When the leader participated on other than process matters, it was largely to raise questions of the validity of some conclusion stated by a group member. Now, if the discussion leader is perceived as a controlling force in the flow of ideas, he must be very cautious about expressing his own views, because they will be given more weight than those of other members of the group. If the discussion leader plays the role suggested in the model, however, the situation is dynamically different; from the point at which the group, for example, has agreed that the appropriate next step is to collect all available ideas for solving a particular problem, the leader can toss his suggestions into the pot with all the others. When he is not helping the group come to necessary work agreements, there is no reason why he should not participate as any other member does.

In general, applying the leadership model to this particular discussion tests it at a fairly extreme level; the group is not only articulate but apparently determined to cooperate and eager to participate and has a skilled leader. Experience with more typical lay-led discussions suggests even more strongly the need for the kind of leadership role this chapter proposes, as does the nature of the training problem involved.

TRAINING FOR DISCUSSION

Training the Leader

If we view the task of the discussion leader as essentially one of controlling the ideas or content of the discussion, we face training problems of considerable magnitude. Important sectors of adult education concerned with discussion have attempted to solve these problems in a variety of ways and with varying success. It is by no means simple to provide the average middle-class American with a sufficient grasp of the skills of philosophical analysis, for example, in a five- or ten-session training course. Many of us would consider it impossible. An alternative is to select from among persons interested in a particular program those with better educational background, so that one can start the training at a higher level.

The results are often not particularly happy. The assumption that a B.A. guarantees a better grasp of ideas may be generally true, but this is not so reliable a relationship that we can depend on its being so for any given individual. And like many old saws, the one about the danger of possessing a little learning has considerable predictability. One adult program went somewhat further and favored the selection of lawyers as discussion leaders, on the reasonable assumption that legal training concentrates on appropriate skills of intelectual analysis. Unfortunately, the adversary basis of American law favors the development of a high degree of aggressiveness and a concentration on argument rather than on a search for truth.

The Living Room Learning discussion program at Western Reserve carried this conception of discussion leadership to its logical end by setting up a training course designed to produce substitutes for the college instructor. They selected potential leaders on the basis of their having majored in some relevant discipline in college, favoring those who had actually done some teaching, encouraged them to embark on independent study of recent developments in the field, and sponsored impressive conferences to which they brought leading scholars to talk about problems of teaching their disciplines. This is an admirable program in many respects, but it is an attempt to bring the college classroom into the community rather than a solution to the problems raised by the types of adult discussion programs outlined earlier.

If we see the task of the lay discussion leader within the framework of the suggested model, the training problem is to some extent simplified and subject to some fairly well-understood training methods. Intelligent alertness, an interest in work and in the most practicable methods of getting it done, and a sensitivity to group moods are encouraged by the society generally; persons of such a character are not difficult to locate in American communities, whereas budding intellectuals are.

The objectives for a training program based on the model of discussion leadership suggested arise naturally from the demands it imposes on the leaders:

1. Awareness of the relation to effective discussion of both the nature of the task and the individual needs of participants.
2. A clear image of the leader's role.
3. An understanding of the general procedures of the task of the particular group: problem-solving, or decision-making, or theory building.
4. Practice in controlled situations in which the leader's behavior is subject to critical analysis.

Most of these objectives can be achieved by designing demonstration and practice sessons in which a group of trainees alternate between role-playing discussion and periods of analysis of what happened. For example, the group might discuss for 15 or 20 minutes the issues raised by a view such as that expressed by Jefferson, "Error of opinion may be tolerated where reason is left free to combat it." Immediately following this discussion, the trainer assigns the task of discussing the inferences which might reasonably be drawn from a graph showing the hourly wages and car price per pound in the auto industry from 1925 to 1937. Differences in patterns of participation in such discussions are striking, and the group itself can usually generalize from the experience. Given some awareness of the differential behavior of groups faced with a variety of tasks, the trainees are prepared to look more generally at the leader's role in a theory session devoted to presenting the major elements of the model. This step of the training process might include several fairly long role-played discussions in which the trainer, as discussion leader, demonstrates how the theory works in practice.

The third objective involves the group again in generalizing and may be handled in several alternative ways. If time permits, the group itself can be given the task of specifying the procedures which are necessary to the particular task they are interested in; for example, if the groups they are going to lead will be involved mainly in problem-solving, they can try first listing and then systematizing the steps normally involved in solving a problem. To save time, the trainer might present them with a systematic scheme for problem-solving and devote a session to an examination of the scheme, using a specific problem as an example.

Finally, the trainee should have the opportunity to practice the model of leadership skill under conditions which permit the trainer and the rest of the group to comment on his performance. Ideally, each person in the training group needs at least one such chance, but there seldom is enough time to carry out such a scheme. A reasonable substitute plan is to arrange a series of follow-up sessions to which the trainees can bring problems arising out of their experience in their real community groups.

Training the Group

Leadership training is a relatively expensive process and demands highly-skilled personnel; often enough, neither the money nor the staff is available when a community discussion program of one sort or another is undertaken. The Hills[17] have proposed a detailed scheme for directly training a group during its beginning stages by helping it develop a series of basic procedural agreements. The plan assumes that the group is using readings as the basis for discussion, which is true of so many discussion groups that the suggested procedures have wide applicability.

The Hills' plan suggests that the first several sessions of a new group devote themselves to two major tasks: a review of the kinds of behaviors appropriate to effective discussion of reading material, and consideration of the process problems involved in group discussion. Assuming that the group has not only a series of readings, but a discussion outline for each one, the plan suggests that the first session consist of examining in detail the following outline of activities which each participant should be aware of and practice:

Before the Discussion

Step 1—Preparation

a. Start your preparation with a copy of the discussion outline before you.
b. As you read, jot down ideas wherever you think they fit best in the discussion.
c. Look up and learn to say the meaning of new words and concepts.
d. When you have finished reading, go back through the outline and write down reminders of what you might say during each step in the discussion.
e. Practice saying or formulate questions about material you plan to introduce into the discussion.

During the Discussion

Step 2—Clarification of terms

a. List the words or concepts with which you had some difficulty and ask others to add to your list.
b. Try to define or explain one of the words on your list.
c. Ask the group members if you have defined it as they understand it.
d. Encourage others to practice explaining what it means to them.
e. Restate what someone else has said to make sure you understand it.

f. Give an example to clarify the meaning.
g. Ask someone else in the group to give an example.
h. Ask the group members if everyone understands the new word or concepts.

Step 3—Statement of the author's message

a. State in your own words what you think the assignment was all about.
b. Frame a question that will encourage someone else to state what the assignment was about.
c. Encourage other group members to practice explaining it.
d. Add to what someone else has said.
e. State the ways in which your understanding or interpretation differs from that stated by another member.
f. Ask for clarification on points you don't understand.
g. Restate what someone else has said if you need to be sure you know it.
h. If you think two other members are misunderstanding each other, try to clarify the confusion.

Step 4—Analysis

a. Ask the group to state the essential elements of the author's presentation:
   (1) Hypotheses
   (2) Methods
   (3) Devices
   (4) Techniques
   (5) Arguments
   (6) Sources
b. Practice saying to yourself what the author was mainly concerned with and encourage others to do so.

Step 5—Integration

a. State the meaning or usefulness of the new material in understanding other ideas or concepts.
b. Phrase questions to put to the group members which will stimulate them to see how the new material fits into what they have studied previously.
c. Ask or state how the new material contradicts, substantiates, or amplifies some previously-developed point.
d. Summarize points others have made into compact statements.
e. Listen critically for and try to state puzzling aspects of the material that are giving the group trouble.
f. Ask for or give help in stating the material more concisely.
g. Ask another member to restate what he has said if you think you may have misunderstood.
h. Call the group's attention to and reinforce a comment that seems particularly helpful.

Step 6—Testing, criticizing, evaluating

a. State questions to help the group evaluate the new material, the method of arriving at the conclusions, etc.

b. State points supporting or questioning the validity of the arguments or the reasoning of the author.
c. State why and how you think the new material is or is not useful.
d. Frame questions which will help the group to test the usefulness of specific points.
e. When appropriate, restate, ask for clarification, summarize, encourage others, etc.

Step 7—Application

a. Ask or state why and how the new material can be useful to members.
b. Give examples of how you might apply it or how the knowledge of it may be useful to you.
c. Compare the author's reasons for thinking it worthwhile to your own experience.
d. Test the usefulness of the new material by constructing a situation for which it should be useful.
e. Give examples you know of which the new material helps to explain or helps you to understand.

A second step in pre-planning involves the consideration of problems which are likely to arise in the course of discussion. Most people have had experience with some form of discussion and, consequently, are aware of some of the persistent difficulties which arise. They have seldom given any thought to how these difficulties can be overcome. The Hills suggest that the group verbalize these expectations and develop a consensus about how to handle the difficulties when they arise. The result of one such discussion, recorded on a blackboard as it developed, looks like this:

Problems in Discussion Groups	*Criteria for Learning by Discussion*
1. We may be afraid to talk for fear of showing our ignorance.	1. We are trying to learn and not to impress each other. We should encourage members to speak up —to try to say what they think needs to be said—and we should not belittle anyone's attempt at participation.
2. Some people just naturally don't like to speak in a group. And hardly anyone likes to be put on the spot.	2. Everyone should participate because participation is the way by which we learn. Naturally, quiet members should make an effort to talk without being asked. Others can help keep the class centered on its task rather than conscious of individuals by putting questions to the group at large rather than to any one person.

3. Some people who are better informed than most of the group will dominate the discussion. Other well-informed people may be reluctant to participate for fear of antagonizing the rest of the group.	3. Our reason for discussing is to learn; those who are sure that they already know what is to be known should give others a chance to speak first. On the other hand, any good group uses its resources, and we should make sure that our better-informed members have an opportunity to contribute.
4. Some people don't think as fast as others. Those who talk easily may dislike silence so much that they will try to dominate the group or urge the discussion ahead too fast. The whole group may get bogged down and spend too much time somewhere along the way.	4. Everyone should share responsibility for keeping the discussion moving. We should adjust our pace so that members have a change to think and don't have to shout, fight for the floor, or be left out. Verbal people should frame good short questions to put to the group when they get the urge to talk too much.
5. We could get involved in arguing about where we are in the outline and not learn the subject matter.	5. The outline is a means to the end of learning subject matter and is not an end in itself. We should be flexible.
6. Some people who don't do the reading may try to bluff and get us into unnecessary arguments.	6. No one should feel that he has to talk at each discussion period. Learning takes place by listening as much as by talking.
7. A group like this could become too serious.	7. We should enjoy the discussion. We should be able to laugh at ourselves and to find enjoyment in the learning process.

Some considerations for the leader which can greatly affect the applicability of this method and its success are these:

This method requires that members go deeply into whatever aspects of the material they discuss; preparation for such discussion, therefore, is rigorous and time-consuming. Group members should know well in advance what they must prepare and be given adequate time for careful study.

The materials should be the very best available, because in a sense they become both the expert and the instructor; obviously, if the reading material does not present a challenge, it cannot become the basis for stimulating discussion.

This method involves some rather simple-minded skills, repeating, reciting, and rephrasing, which members may feel are beneath their dignity. The leader may handle this resistance by assuring members that they need to spend time on these elementary activities only so long as is necessary to insure that all members know what they are talking about.

Members will frequently contend that they need formal leadership; when this happens, the leader might suggest that members choose planning committees for discussion from the group itself. As members become more skillful discussants, they will usually abandon the practice of delegating leadership and instead share it very effectively themselves.

A group of 20 or so—or a smaller one—can use this method effectively. If it is larger, the leader can suggest subgrouping into more manageable groups and can himself then either confine his role to that of process observer or can rotate among subgroups as a resource person.

In summary, here are the advantages which characterize the method:

1. In the planning stage, members are helped to understand more quickly why and how discussion aids them in learning subject matter, and they participate actively themselves in establishing procedures to make the learning as thorough as possible.

2. In preparation for the discussion, members learn to read more critically, to select and organize important material, and to assess their own strengths and weaknesses.

3. During the discussion, members learn together cooperatively; they develop skill in asking questions and making comments to test their own understanding; they take responsibility for mature classroom behavior; they evaluate their own excellence in terms of their own goals.

4. The leader's role is clear-cut; he can tolerate initial frustrations without anxiety, because the method has self-corrective mechanisms; he need not be a highly-trained discussion leader, because he shares the responsibiilty for managing the discussion with his group members; he is free to learn as well as lead.

In short, the method creates high morale based on realistic achievement, because members can see evidence that their increasing skill as discussants helps them to progress toward their goals; they are motivated to prepare more thoroughly, because each shares the responsibility for conducting a meaningful and productive discussion.

NOTES

1. C. Wright Mills, *Mass Society and Liberal Education, Notes and Essays* No. 9 (Chicago: Center for the Study of Liberal Education for Adults, 1954), p. 4. Mills' analysis of the role of education in the breakdown of a society of publics and the trend toward a mass society was rewritten and amplified in a chapter in his later *The Power Elite* (New York: Oxford University Press, 1956).

2. A fascinating description of the way new legal norms arose in the frontier community may be found in Muzafer and Carolyn Sherif's *Outline of Social Psychology,* Revised Edition (New York: Harper, 1956). The American philosophers who most influenced adult educators in the formative period of the field were Dewey and Meicklejohn. Dewey's views are too well-known to require mention here, but Meicklejohn goes even further. So important to a democracy is the intelligent formation of public opinion, he argues, that the media of mass communication should be restricted to that purpose. In industrial relations, Lewin's great influence on the field stressed the importance of the development of production norms and the solution of work-group problems by the people involved, not merely because this is democratic but because imposed norms are often a waste of time. For a recent statement of this view, see Maier's *Principles of Human Relations* (New York: Wiley, 1952).

3. For detailed historical background, see Malcolm Knowles, "An Overview and History of the Field," *Adult Education,* VII: 4 (Summer, 1957).

4. The generally confused state of community development is not made clearer by the fact that operations carried out in the name of particular theories often bear no relation to them. Thus, one of the most prominent of these theories, in the book expounding it, outlines the most democratic procedures possible for a community to diagnose its own problems; some observers of the practitioners of the theory claim that in the field the democratic procedures appear to become merely ritual, and the charismatic leader takes over. Recent attempts to take a rational and systematic look at the field show considerable promise of clearing up some of the present confusion; see Kenneth Haygood's most recent monograph, *The University and the Community* (Chicago: Center for the Study of Liberal Education for Adults, 1962). The view taken here that community development ought to consist, educationally of an attempt to develop problem-solving skills among community groups is developed by Jack Mezirow in "Community Development as an Educational Process," *The International Review of Community Development,* No. 5 (1961). It is reprinted in the fourth reading series, *Community Development,* issued by the National Training Laboratories of the NEA. Mezirow's new book on community development is due to be published in 1963.

5. See Mortimer Adler, "Labor, Leisure and Liberal Education," *Journal of General Education,* VI (October, 1951). Also, almost any of Robert Hutchins' brilliant polemics makes the same basic argument; see, for example, his *The Conflict in Education* (New York: Harper, 1953). The kinds of people who participate in these programs, and their motivations, are described for the first time in any depth in the report of the study of the Great Books participants:

James A. Davis, *A Study of Participants in the Great Books Program* (White Plains, Fund for Adult Education, 1960).

6. This distrust of groups, "groupiness," and anything to do with "group dynamics" is such a striking characteristic of this type of adult educator that I will not bother to document it; it is much more prominent in orally expressed views than in written ones. My purely personal view of the basic conflict involved in this controversy would ordinarily be an enthusiastic "Pull Devil!—Pull Baker!" were it not that the "perennialists" on occasion reveal an anti-scientific bias of a kind I find dismaying in the mid-twentieth century and, on the whole, educationally destructive at any period.

7. The general model of discussion presented here closely follows Herbert Thelen's in *Dynamics of Groups at Work, op. cit.* Thelen and his students for some years followed up the implications for group discussion of Bion's work on therapy groups, from which they took such terms as work vs. flight-fight, dependency-pairing, and the like.

8. A. A. Liveright's *Strategies of Leadership* (New York: Harper, 1960), a study of lay leaders in adult education, is based on the assumption that the appropriate leadership role depends on the demands of the objectives of the particular program. My view here, that a single model can fit all three of the types of discussion described, does not conflict with Liveright's thesis; he would probably categorize all three discussion types as having similar objectives, compared to other programs in adult education, such as a Red Cross safety program.

9. For elaboration of this point, see K. Benne and P. Sheats, "Functional Roles of Group Members," *Journal of Social Issues,* Vol. IV, No. 2 (Spring, 1948). Descriptions of some of these roles follow later in the chapter.

10. For this section in general: for a readable discussion of needs as the basis for a theory of personality, Kluckhohn and Murray's *Personality* (New York: Knopf, 1953); B. S. Bloom's "The Thought Process of Students in Discussion," in Sidney J. French (ed.), *Accent on Teaching* (New York: Harper, 1954); "The Individual and the Group," in *Adult Leadership,* Vol. I, No. 8 (January, 1953); "The Silent and the Overtalkative," *Adult Leadership,* Vol. I, No. 10 (March, 1953); Robert F. Bales, "Some Uniformities of Behavior in Small Social Systems," in Guy Swanson *et al., Readings in Social Psychology* (New York: Holt, 1952).

11. This study by Lippitt and White, "Leader Behavior and Member Reaction in Three Social Climates," as well as the most recent experimental data on the effects of various leadership patterns, may be found in Zander and Cartwright's *Group Dynamics,* Revised Edition (Evanston: Row, Peterson, 1960).

12. See the Zander and Cartwright book, cited above, for a thorough discussion of approaches to the definition of leadership. No one argues, I think, that the traditional view of the leader as decisive, aggressive, dominant, magnetic, etc., is not still a viable one in some contexts: running an army, for example, or a large corporation. This conception of leadership, unfortunately, was transferred to *all* contexts, so that it became the image against which the teacher compared her little 7- and 8-year-old charges when she rated them on "leadership qualities," which is manifest nonsense.

Some psychologists have advanced the interesting argument that by keeping all the important decisions in his hands, the dominant leader treats the group as children and thus leads individuals in the group to respond to such authority as they did when they *were* children. Some children are rebellious, and the dominant leader has his rebels who dispute his decisions, whether they are good or bad, as an expression of the need to resist domination. If they succeed in developing a "rebel band," the group may find itself divided into cliques. Other children respond to authority by submitting all, becoming "mother's little helper," the faithful servant; the discussion group equivalent is the person who gains security by dependence on the leader; other members may dislike him, but the dominant leader beams upon him. A third kind of child reacts to authority by competing with other children for the attention and favors of the authority; the "sibling rival" in the discussion group can take up a great deal of time in disputes which get the inquiry no further.

13. Most of the standard books of group discussion come out of speech departments and are written for college students. They tend to emphasize, therefore, rhetoric and the logical analysis of issues. Few of them seem relevant to the demands of the adult discussion group, particularly those with a fairly long life.

14. On the general process of the development of group norms, see Sherif, *Social Psychology, op. cit.*

15. Osborn's brainstorming technique has as its major purpose the avoidance of this particular tendency of groups. See the earlier reference to his book in Chapter III.

16. Some of the group were doctoral candidates; others were typists with a high-school education. The leader was A. A. Liveright, director of the Center for the Study of Liberal Education for Adults, an expert in leadership methods in adult education. We got the group together for one session only, openly to tape-record an illustrative discussion. Everyone was consequently on his best behavior.

17. This section is adapted with permission from Ida and William Hill's *Learning and Teaching Through Discussion, Notes and Essays* No. 22 (Chicago: Center for the Study of Liberal Education for Adults, 1958, pp. 10-13, 15. The Hills' essay was written for the college classroom instructor, but the method they developed is just as useful for informal groups.

7

• • • • • • • • • • • • • • • • • • • •

THE AUTONOMOUS ADULT LEARNER

> An educated person is one who is at work on his own enlargement. If we learn things that become part of us, if we make efforts to develop our own particular understanding of life and of the order of life's goods, it is education we are doing. A person is something that it takes time to make; there is on everyone an invisible sign, "Work in progress"; and the considered effort to get on with the work is education.
>
> ROBERT REDFIELD, *The Educational Experience*

One of the truly significant differences between adult education and the education of youth is in the relative freedom of the adult to choose the kind of program he is interested in or sees value in and, to some extent at least, his freedom to proceed at his own pace. A recurring theme in the literature of adult education is the desirability of the self-propelled leaner who does not need to be dependent on an instructor or a group or an institution.[1] If we tried to describe the ideal, our image might look something like this: a person who is curious about a wide variety of phenomena and is "cognitively open" in respect to them, that is, he is willing to entertain hypotheses about reality even if they clash with already established beliefs and values; he learns in many situations, from conversations, by reading thoughtfully, by observation; he has probably specialized in some field which interests him very much, be it naval architecture, Civil War battles, European politics, theater, baroque music, jazz, or any of the hundreds of subjects that American "buffs" are interested in.

There *are* people who approximate this image, fortunately. Adult education often serves them, in a lecture series or a special discussion program. That we ever have anything importantly to do with *developing* them is open to serious question; the structure of adult education, if the analysis in Chapter I is correct, is apt to produce more dependency by its concentration on adjusting people to specific role changes. There is a kind of inevitability about that focus, because most adult programs are self-supporting, most people seem to be attracted by highly specific, measured doses of education for which they do not have to do very much, and we are caught in a comfortable, if vicious, circle.

The problem of helping the adult to become more autonomous as a learner requires two different lines of development for its solution, though the two are interdependent. One is the existence of technical resources to help people learn by themselves; the second is help in acquiring the skills, in a most general sense, of learning. In relation to the first of these requirements, this chapter examines what may be the most important technical resource of the future, programmed instructional materials; the potential of our most important existing resource, correspondence programs; and the idea of the tutorial method as one deserving some attention in adult education. As for the second requirement, helping people acquire and refine the skills of learning themselves, one can only speculate about how it might be done, and the chapter closes on such speculation.

PROGRAMMED INSTRUCTION

Chapter II began with a remark by William James to the effect that sciences never generate arts directly out of themselves. In the same university that James honored by his presence, B. F. Skinner is coming as close as anyone has to making a direct application of psychological theory to educational practice. The discussion, early in that chapter, of Skinner's operant conditioning describes the basis for much of the current excitement in education over programmed instruction.

The key is in the behaviorists' principle that any live organism will tend to repeat a particular behavior if that behavior has been followed by a reward, that is, if it has been reinforced. The essential characteristic of programmed materials is that they arrange concepts or relationships which are to be learned in a series of short steps which require the learner to make appropriate responses. The material itself provides immediate reinforcement by telling the learner that he is correct. Stimulus, student response, and immediate feedback are the core of the method.

The complicated engineering involved in programmed materials of some types consists mainly in attempts to find ways of hiding the correct response until it is triumphantly produced as feedback. American love of gadgetry has produced in this field monstrous Rube Goldberg machines all in the service of this simple function. Those who have tried to work a considerable number of these teaching machines usually must deal with jammed paper rolls, gears which refused to mesh, and all sorts of other catastrophes. There are some really complicated and well-engineered machines which one must admire, and there is little doubt that children enjoy them, but repeated experimentation has failed to produce any evidence that hiding the answer in a machine helps learning any more than simply having it covered with a sliding slip of paper.

A more convenient presentation of "frames" is available in a variety of programmed texts, certainly a better format for adult education than the machine. There are two major approaches to the construction of items, each with many examples on the market (these are fundamental differences and apply to the machines as well). One is the *constructed* response; the other is the *multiple-choice* response.

1. The constructed-response approach uses much shorter steps and provides some way for the student to write the word or phrase which constitutes the correct response. Each frame has next to it the correct answer to the one which preceded it, and the student is prevented from seeing the answer by several methods. In the scrambled textbook, the frames are printed on different pages of the book; thus, Frame 1 is on page 1, Frame 2 on page 3, Frame 3 on page 5, and so on for a specified number of pages, after which the student is directed to turn back to page 1 to begin another sequence. In contrast to this horizontal arrangement, many texts use a vertical series of frames, with the correct responses on the right margin of the page hidden by a slip of paper or some such device which slides down to uncover the

relevant answer. This is much more convenient than turning pages constantly and appears to make no difference in effectiveness. To illustrate the constructed-response approach, here is a short sequence of frames from Markle *et al.*, *A Programmed Primer on Programming*;[2] this is a scrambled text, but for the sake of convenience the frames are presented in a vertical order.

Answer	Frame
	6. One condition which has been shown to facilitate learning is called "reinforcement." Programmed instruction employs techniques that facilitate learning. You might expect that programmed instruction uses ——— to facilitate learning.
6. reinforcement	7. In ordinary English, "reinforce" is a synonym of "strengthen." Something that strengthens behavior can be said, then, to ——— that behavior.
7. reinforce	8. To psychologists, behavior which is likely to occur, i.e., very probable, is "strong." (The behavior doesn't have to be noisy or forceful!) When a particular bit of behavior, a response, is strengthened by reinforcement, the response is more ——— than it was before being reinforced.
8. likely (to occur) or probable	9. Some consequences, i.e., events which *follow* a response, increase the likelihood of a repetition of the response. If the consequence makes the response more likely, the psychologists say it "r———s" the behavior.
9. reinforces	10. A response is reinforced by something which comes ——— the response occurs.
10. after	11. To psychologists, reinforcement is a "class of events" which comes ——— the response and which can be shown to make the response ——— to occur.
11. after, more likely or likely	12. Anyone who has taught tricks to his dog knows how to use reinforcement. In teaching the dog to "speak" he waits for the bark that follows the command "Speak!" As soon as the dog barks, the master gives it . . . . (in your own words)
12. a dog candy, a piece of food, a pat on the head, etc., or a reinforcement.	

It is worth noting a few more or less technical characteristics of this type of programming. Since the major objective of the method is to ensure a correct response from the student, and, consequently, the fewer the errors the better, frames are written with "cues" or "prompts" intended to elicit the response. At the early stages of a particular sequence, such cues are very prominent; they are then gradually withdrawn or "faded" until the learner is able to make important responses without them. More complex programs can lengthen the frame, introduce more material into each step, or present "panels," which are supplementary material in the form of diagrams, drawings, pages of exposition, or even a book. These latter opportunities for flexibility are important to keep in mind for a later consideration of the uses of programming in adult education.

2. The second major approach is the multiple-choice method, which arose out of the early work of Pressey during the twenties, in what was largely a testing program. Reasoning from experimental evidence that learning could be improved by giving the student immediate feedback on what he has understood and retained, Pressey invented a number of devices which the student could use to test himself immediately after he had finished studying a piece of material. The tests were multiple-choice in form and contrived in a number of ingenious ways to provide the right answer for each item once the selection had been made.

Pressey and his followers had high hopes for a technological revolution in the classroom, but the movement petered out, and not until the forties did Pressey become active again. On the basis of a number of informal comparative experiments, he is convinced that students of some maturity learn just as well from ordinary reading as they do from a constructed program based on the same material, if they are given guidance in the form of feedback. Detailed small-step, programming might be useful for young children, he suggests, but the learning of meaningful material by a person already somewhat knowledgeable makes different demands on learning theory. In developing a program for a self-instructional device, Pressey suggests the following steps:[3]

a. Pre-test at the beginning with a short-answer essay test, covering the essentials of the course;

b. Questions which are found to present any difficulty should be thrown into multiple-choice form, with the right answer carefully formulated to make clear why it is correct and the wrong answer representing common errors. These items can then be used as self-instructional materials for any future presentation of the course, assigned with the relevant materials for study. He finds that the most valuable items were those "of substantial difficulty, but presenting a clear and significant problem."

The advocates of the constructed-response approach criticize the Pressey method on several scores. First, the learner is not truly active in making his response—he merely selects one of two choices presented to him—a basic violation of Skinner's learning theory. Second, he may choose a wrong answer which is plausible; to permit this, Skinner would say, is out of place in the delicate process of shaping behavior, because it would strengthen unwanted forms.

Pressey's reply to the first of these criticisms, noted above, is that perhaps we need a modified learning theory for human learners above the level of small children. His answer to the second is: "Much has been made of the analogy that automation served like an able tutor. But surely a wise tutor does not all the time lean over a student's shoulder, continually asking very easy questions. Rather he sets tasks, asks questions stimulating discriminating thinking, gives the student assurance when he is right, guides him aright when he is wrong, and tries to help him increasingly to proceed on his own."[4]

A series of texts based on Pressey's principles have been issued under the name Tutortexts. Norman Crowder's *The Arithmetic of Computers*[5] is an excellent example of the Pressey method, and a copy of one section, with its relevant "right answer" and "wrong answer" feedback pages, is reproduced here to give some idea of how it works out. As you see, the text tries to duplicate the language of a human tutor. A comparable text in the constructed-response approach is Skinner and Holland's *Analysis of Human Behavior,*[6] a college psychology text which has been completely programmed.

Page 21

YOUR ANSWER: In the expression b^n, b is used as a factor "*n*" times.

Right. The letter "*n*" stands for the exponent, and this tells us how far to go in multiplying our base by itself.

It is necessary to know how the letters "*b*" and "*n*" are sometimes tossed around in discussing powers.

If, for example, $b=3$, then b^n means that 3 is raised to the "*n*th" power, or 3 is used as a factor "*n*" times.

If $n=4$, then b^n means that *b* is raised to the 4th power, or *b* is used as a factor 4 times.

Now we have defined the 2nd power of a base, b^2, and the 3rd power, b^3, and so on, but we have not defined the 1st power of a number, have we?

Do you know what we mean by the 1st power of any number, b?

ANSWER:

$b^1=b$. *page 15*
$b^1=1$. *page 27*
I don't know. *page 35*

Page 15

YOUR ANSWER: $b^1=b$.

You are correct. The 1st power of a number is defined as simply equal to the number itself:

$$3^1=3$$
$$10^1=10$$

and in general $b^1=b$.

This definition works both ways, of course. If we define $b^1=b$, then we also mean that any number may be regarded as its own 1st power; that is, that $b=b^1$. If we want to consider any number as a power of itself, we can consider it as the 1st power of itself:

$$3=3^1$$
$$10=10^1$$

and so forth.

Well, practice makes perfect. One of the groups of statements below contains an error. Which group contains the error?

ANSWER

$2^4=16$
the 1st power of 12 $=12$
$b^2=b \times b$
$5^3=125$
This group contains an error. *page 2*

the 2nd power of 1 $=1$
3 raised to the 2nd power $=9$
$2^3=8$
$5^2=25$
This group contains an error. *page 9*

the 3rd power of 3 $=27$
$9^1=9$
$6^2=36$
the 3rd power of 4 $=3^4$
This group contains an error. *page 38*

Page 27

YOUR ANSWER: $b^1=1$.

I'm afraid you don't understand all you know about this subject! There *is* a value of n such that b^n is always equal to 1, no matter what b is, but n in that case is *not* 1.

The 1st power of a number is simply defined as equal to the number itself. Thus,

$$2^1=2$$
$$10^1=10$$
$$b^1=b$$

and so forth.

We shall show later that this definition is consistent with certain operations that we perform with exponents, but for the moment you may regard it as simply an arbitrary definition.

Now return to Page 21 and choose another answer.

Answer to Self-Test Question 12, Lesson 1: $b^1=b$

Page 35

YOUR ANSWER: I don't know.

That's the spirit! If you don't know, speak up.

The 1st power of a number is simply defined as the number itself. Thus,

$$2^1=2$$
$$10^1=10$$
$$b^1=b$$

and so forth.

We shall show later that this definition is consistent with certain operations that we perform with exponents, but for the moment you may regard it as simply an arbitrary definition.

Now return to Page 21 and choose the right answer.

Some Relevant Questions about Programming

In an attempt to condense the most useful material for a field which is not particularly interested in technical problems but needs some assessment of how such problems stand, this section raises questions adult educators are likely to have about programmed materials and provides brief answers.

HOW EFFECTIVE IS PROGRAMMED INSTRUCTION? There is no solid, single answer to this one. What is surprising is that programmed instruction is not more unambiguously far better than it is, when compared with regular classroom instruction. It does with great precision what we have been trying for years to get teachers to do—carefully specify what the learning objectives are, present materials appropriate to those objectives, keep the learner active in practicing the skills specified, provide careful, consistent, and almost immediate reinforcement. Theoretically, at least, we should expect the method to have overwhelming superiority, which is hardly the case. Here are a few cautious generalizations:

a. Programmed instruction is, in most cases, *as* effective as ordinary classroom instruction and in some instances superior to it, as measured by achievement usually based on recall, but sometimes including much more complex skills. In fact, few studies are made these days comparing programmed instruction with human instructions; the programmers argue that they are not out to substitute machines or programmed texts for teachers, but to supplement, so there is no need for such comparisons. Even some of those who now advocate programmed materials consider them to be, at best, a superior form of textbook.

b. Most of the evidence available (and there is not as much as one would expect to find, given the severely scientific background of the enthusiasts) suggests a major gain in *time* for given amounts of learning achievement. There is not much doubt about this, although some of the studies demonstrating it are open to question. One such study showed that a group studying German achieved in 47 hours spent on programmed materials gains equivalent to a semester of German and scored on the average in the 80's and 90's on vocabulary and translation tests. A critic disputed the arithmetic of the researchers, who claimed that they bettered the 48 hours of a normal semester (regular classes, after all, are only 50-minute hours), but, more importantly, asked why only six students out of the 28 who originally started the instruction actually finished.[7] Programmed materials are supposed to be "stepped" so that very few students moving from one step to another should have any difficulty. But 22 of these students dropped out "at the most difficult lessons," which according to programming theory should not have been difficult at all.

c. Some fears during the early days of programming that much of the demonstrated effectiveness of programmed materials might be due to their novelty or to some variation of the Hawthorne effect appear to be groundless. On the whole, reports of groups using such materials over a period of six months or a year show little decrease in motivation or in effectiveness which might have been due to novelty.

d. There is a fair amount of evidence, though not of a thoroughly conclusive type, that there is less correlation between intellectual capacity and achievement in programmed instruction than in traditional situations. The child with a low IQ does better with programmed materials than we would expect him to. There are several suggestions in the literature, too, that upper-ability students find self-instruction techniques particularly useful, as one might expect; Briggs used

Pressey test-type materials with a group of upper-level students in college who met informally only once a week but did intensive work on their own. The group scored better on the standard tests for the course than matched controls taking the regular course.[8]

In summary, it seems clear that, although programming hardly has made a case for any revolutionary increase in teaching effectiveness generally, it has demonstrated that it can do some teaching jobs just as well as and perhaps better than a human teacher can, for some kinds of students.

WHAT LEARNING OBJECTIVES ARE SUITABLE FOR PROGRAMMING?

It is often very difficult to get a straight answer to this question from the experts, partly because the variety of programs actually tested is relatively limited. In general, everyone in the field is hopeful on the issue; they see no reason to believe, until proven otherwise, that one cannot program *any* learning objective in the repertoire. Writing a program forces one, at the very beginning, to specify in extraordinary detail the desired terminal student behavior: vocabulary, concept-recognition, knowledge of methods, problem-solving. As long as one can make that specification, programmers do not see why they cannot write a program for it. The reason for the present limitation is to some extent the profit motive; the commercial textbook publishers are the prime movers in this field, and they are interested in the big markets in the elementary and high school.

Most of the elementary materials do indeed put an emphasis on a sort of rote learning, and many of these programs look merely like aids to memorizing. But existing programs on the collegiate level already go considerably beyond the rote learning of simple materials; the Skinner and Holland text in psychology and the Crowder Tutortext in computer mathematics are good examples; there is a new text in statistics ready, and John Blyth of Hamilton College is working on programmed materials in logic. Crutchfield, at Berkeley, who can claim some eminence in psychology, is developing programmed materials aimed at objectives which most teachers have never even tried to achieve in the normal course of classroom teaching, and a statement of his perhaps sums up the highest of the expectations in the field:

> Indeed, it is dubious that most of what is now being taught by the currently available programs is sheer rote learning. Even the most simple mastery of curricular content as taught by methods of programmed instruction probably in fact requires the exercise of more complex mental functions of interpreting, hypothesizing, evaluating, etc.

My own research on the use of auto-instructive methods for the facilitation of creative thinking involves a radical departure from reliance on the processes of rote learning. We are undertaking to construct programs that will increase the flexibility and imaginativeness of the individual's thought processes, will sensitize him to subtler and more differentiated features of his environment, will equip him with a larger repertory of problem-solving heuristics, and will beneficially alter his conceptions and attitudes concerning the creative process.[9]

WHAT IS INVOLVED IN CONSTRUCTING PROGRAMS? Here is the point at which art enters the picture, in proof of James' insistence on the mediating ingenuity of the teacher. The process of developing an adequate program is a terribly time-consuming business and requires a considerable amount of expertise. Staff members of the Center for Programmed Instruction, who have had a great deal of experience in constructing a variety of programs, estimate that a finished program generally averages out to at least one hour of time per frame; since even a simple course entails at least several thousand frames, one's enthusiasm for attempting to program a course can be understandably dampened at the start.

An example will illustrate some of the difficulties involved. In a recent report, a description of the development of a program on the fundamentals of life insurance prepared for men training to become life insurance salesmen,[10] provides an opportunity of using an adult education program as an example. The final program totals 1,702 frames; the total number of responses to all frames is 3,159, of which 95 per cent are constructed responses. Here are the steps of development:

1. The Life Insurance Management Association provided a detailed, point-by-point outline of specific instructional objectives.

2. Each of the 239 topics covered in the program was categorized into one of four levels of behavior: recognition, recall, understanding and reproduction, and application to real situations.

3. Frames were constructed on 4×6 index cards with correct responses typed on the back. This, of course, is the heart of the process and requires a good deal of editing, usually by a number of people. The finished program was then tested on fourteen undergraduates of average capacity, who were paid on an hourly basis and worked about five hours a day. As the subjects worked through the frames, they reported every error they made to a monitor.

4. The initial program was tested on two subjects, then revised.

Each of the three revisions was tested with four subjects. The revisions were aimed at correcting items which were unclear or ambiguous and at re-writing frames which produced errors. The program itself included a criterion test of 77 items, so that each of the revisions was tested against the ultimate objectives of the course.

5. The error rate on each of the revisions was less than 5 per cent and on the third revision decreased to one-half of one per cent. On the final revision, errors on the criterion test were reduced to about 5 per cent.

This is one of the simpler of the developmental patterns. Many programs are field-tested on large numbers of students, entailing even greater resources for handling large amounts of data. Program construction is obviously not a process one can undertake light-heartedly with one's left hand.

There are, moreover, a number of highly technical issues involved in the process. Programming theory, at least of the constructed-response type, demands a very low error rate; what does one do about the wrong answer? There is much technical discussion in the literature about "branching" which is not worth going into detail about here but which at least deserves mention. The programmer can construct branching sequences which direct the student who has made an error to go through a series of remedial frames. If a particular error suggests that the difficulty consists in his having forgotten a previous section, the branch may lead him back to review previous frames; if the error indicates a lack in the background which the programmer has originally assumed he has in the subject, the branch might provide a sequence of remedial material.

Further technical questions arise in the construction of the frames themselves. According to Holland, a frame 1) must relate the response of the student to the critical content of the item and 2) must determine the response by providing adequate cues.[11] *Example:*

(correct version) A technical term for "reward" is reinforcement. To "reward" an organism with food is to ——— it with food.

(incorrect, not related to critical content) A technical term for "reward" is reinforcement. To "reward" an organism with food is to reinforce it with ———.

(incorrect, non-determined) A technical term for "reward" is ———. To "reward" an organism with food is to ——— it with food.

Finally, to provide some idea of the complexity involved in constructing programs, here is a classification scheme of the functions which frames are variously called on to perform.

Lead-in items—orient the student to a problem and prepare him for new information.
Augmenting items—supply new information, but not require any relevant response; responses merely insure that the student has read the item.
Interlocking items—require a student to review established skills while new information is presented.
Rote review items—present a problem identical to one earlier presented.
Restated-review items—require a rehearsal of a skill.
Delayed review items—allow for further practice distributed in time.
Fading items—require review, in which information is withdrawn from item to item.
Generalizing item—presents a verbal statement pointing to common characteristics of several specific problems previously presented.
Specifying items—exemplify a general rule in terms of specific cases.
Dovetailing items—require the student to make separate responses to separable stimuli that otherwise become confused.[12]

WHAT DIFFERENCES DO THE VARIOUS FORMATS MAKE? The conflicting claims based on conflicting research evidence and on theoretical issues cannot, at this point in the development of the art, be easily evaluated even by the experts. The best one can do is give impressions of several of the major controversies. There are some who insist that more is made of differences of opinion than the facts merit, that, for example, most programmers these days are using both constructed-response and multiple-choice items in putting together any particular program. One can hardly glance at the growing literature in the field, however, without being struck by a number of what seems to be crucial differences.

1. Several differences seem to be fairly well resolved by a considerable body of experimental evidence. There is little significant difference between machine presentation and text presentation of a program. Pressey seems to be still passionately addicted to the machine, but the major development in the future will most probably be toward the text.

2. There seems to be satisfactory evidence for assuming that there is no significant difference between the vertical and horizontal methods of text presentation. Having items follow one another on the same page, with the answers hidden by some sliding device, seems to work just as well as the scrambled textbook and is a substantially cheaper format to print.

3. The major argument between the constructed-response item and the multiple-choice appears to be unresolved. There is a good deal of evidence which undermines Skinner's insistence on the necessity for the student to make an overt response and his theoretical dislike for

permitting the student to select a wrong answer. Some research does demonstrate that constructed-response programs favor active recall (of language vocabulary, for instance), but other research also shows slightly better gains in other areas when *no* response is made. It is difficult to ignore the fact that the student *is* active, in a real sense, when he confronts a choice, even though the activity is covert. Crowder's approach seems to be confirmed by such research as Bryan and Rigney's, who found that explaining *why* the answer to a multiple choice is correct or incorrect is significantly better than just supplying a "right" or "wrong."[13]

The complex learning objectives which liberal adult education selects probably favor the multiple-choice approach using larger steps. Programs of this type are probably easier to construct and more easily adaptable to correlation with supplementary materials.

Programmed Instruction and Adult Education

Assuming that it is correct to suppose that even complex objectives are attainable by programming, what contribution can the method make to adult education, particularly for the cognitive objectives stressed in Chapter III? On the whole, it seems clear that if programmed materials show promise for public school education, they are even more likely to be useful here. The education of adults, for the most part, is either strongly influenced by university teaching or dispenses altogether with the professional teacher. University faculty notoriously encourage passivity in their students, and any method we can use to get the student active is an improvement; one of the programming experts, in an article suggesting steps in developing a unit of instruction, remarks, "Be wary of a college professor; he may never have seen a student learn." On the other end of the scale, informal discussion programs too often throw a group of adults on their own somewhat limited resources with some very complex readings to deal with and very little help in attacking them.

The following notes suggest some of the uses of programmed materials in the most common situations of adult education. They omit from consideration the issue of how feasible it may be to develop these materials; the amounts of time and energy required must obviously be financed on some special basis.[14]

SITUATIONS IN WHICH THE ADULT STUDENT WORKS ALONE. A distinctive characteristic of adult education is its incorporation to a much greater extent than any other level of education of settings which require the student to work at his own pace or with learning materials which do not permit him face-to-face interaction with an instructor.

1. Perhaps the most important of these situations is correspondence study, discussed in general terms later in this chapter. The standard pattern of the correspondence course requires that the student do reading and then some sort of exercise which reveals to his tutor the extent to which he has mastered the material or the skills for that particular lesson. There is no reason why, if it were financially feasible, correspondence study could not re-tool a large majority of its courses into programmed materials and gain a considerable advantage. The student would get immediate feedback, instead of waiting for work to return by mail, a considerable gain, theoretically; the instructor may save a good deal of time or at least more usefully employ that time by devoting his correspondence with the student to issues of judgment and values which cannot easily be handled by programmed set-ups.

For example, a course in English literature might assign a series of works to be read, with a supplementary programmed text covering each of the works, in the Tutortext fashion. The problems presented would involve interpretation and other basic skills of literary analysis. The student might first read the work, then go through the programmed text, then give himself a punchboard test on the work. This is one of Pressy's devices, in which the student answers a series of multiple-choice items by punching one of four holes on a particular row of a punchboard device. If it is the correct answer, the little awl goes through and pierces a piece of paper; if it is incorrect, the awl merely marks the paper. The paper can be sent back to the instructor as a record of how well the student did on the criterion test, but the student in the meantime has had immediate report on his achievement level and feedback on each question.

There are many courses, obviously, which could not fit this pattern. But, in general, these are likely to be ones which already demand active learning, such as English composition. Wherever there is a body of knowledge involved, and objectives which include comprehension and judgment, the pattern suggested, or some variation of it, should be useful in many ways. Not only would it set up a more effective learning experience, but also provide more motivation, an important consideration in a field with a very high proportion of students who do not finish courses they begin.

2. Another natural use for programmed materials is to replace

present materials sent to those who enroll in TV courses, a situation which differs from correspondence study in few important respects. The same arguments apply with even greater force, because in many cases the TV course does not provide as close a tutoring guide as correspondence divisions do.

But commercial TV suggests a more interesting and broader use for programming. Although there have been several attempts in the past to supplement mass media with materials which the reader or listener can use to go beyond the initial, often superficial, article or program, there has never been any real experimentation with the idea on a significant scale. Programmed materials provide an opportunity to develop attractive and useful packages which can be sent to viewers on request; it would be interesting to discover what proportion of a commercial TV audience would care to pursue further some area which a particular program or series of programs has opened up. Many of the TV programs most useful for such experimentation deal with issues or policy questions to which there are no "correct" answers. Can we develop programmed instructional materials appropriate to such a situation? Presumably it is possible, with branching sequences which could lead people on either side of an issue to consider the logical consequences of their positions as well as others and to cope with the problems of modifying their position to incorporate new material of which they may have been unaware. It may not be easy to construct this kind of program, but it would be worth a try.

3. Programmed materials might make the idea of an adult tutorial system more feasible. The most useful target for the tutorial idea does seem to be the mature, adult student of superior ability; everyone who has taught an adult non-credit class has probably been bemused about the problem of what to do with the one or two such people in every group. They are out of place among the merely curious dropper-inners, the dogged average, and the bright-eyed pure incompetents. They clearly are capable of doing high-level work on their own, with occasional encouragement and criticism in face-to-face sessions. Constructed-response programming would be obviously inappropriate for such people, but some form of self-testing might help them maintain interest and continuity between conferences with their tutor and would keep the tutoring sessions themselves free for discussion of important issues or of student-produced papers.

SITUATIONS IN WHICH AN INSTRUCTOR IS PRESENT. Adult education is commonly conducted in settings in which a responsible teacher, trained at least in the subject matter of the course, seminar, or institute, plans and conducts the learning experience. The administrative problems of introducing experimental materials, as we know from sometimes bitter experience, are greatly complicated by what ought to be the advantage of having an experienced teacher available. Yet, to look for a moment on the bright side of this somewhat gloomy picture, one extraordinarily useful outcome of attention to programming is that it trains the instructor to pay specific and close attention to significant features of the learning experience to an extent that few of us are ever compelled to do. Trainers of teachers are finding it very useful, for example, to assign their methods classes the task of programming a unit of work; the programs were technically inadequate, but the exercise forced the students to think through their objectives in terms they never before had found necessary and to dissect, as well, the structure of the particular knowledge involved.

Programming thus provides an excellent indirect route to the improvement of instruction, which may be taken as a stipulated auxiliary recommendation for most of the possibilities outlined below.

1. The most strongly patterned format under this general heading is, of course, the evening college and extension credit classes. Change in this sector may well come about through the utilization of programmed materials developed for regular college courses. If the statistics program is adopted by a day department, there seems no reason to suppose that it will not be used in the evening classes of that institution as well; a high school in the New York area recently resumed several adult classes in mathematics because the availability of programmed materials made it possible to allocate minimum amounts of scarce teaching resources.

Apart from this presumably normal process, which may well be the answer to the recently increasing threat of eliminating adult classes as undergraduate enrollments in the regular session soar, programming might be used to attack several of the persistent problems of the adult credit classroom: heterogeneity and time. Evening-class instructors have difficulty in many classes with the unevenness of both preparation and ability, often quite different from the accustomed standardization of day classes based on rigorous selective procedures. Special programmed materials for the student with inadequate background and for the slow learner is an obvious answer. Another complaint of the evening-class instructor is that the adult student does not have the time to do as much work as the day student and that valuable class time which might be used more profitably must be spent going over material or questions. If reading assignments were accompanied by self-administered Pressey-type quizzes, the need to devote class time to going over reading might be eliminated.

2. The non-credit area seems to provide a wide open opportunity for exploration and experimentation. Consider one possibility as an example of the type of innovation which might solve several problems. Instead of scheduling the course for one evening, one could list it for several nights, thus increasing the possibility of a larger enrollment. Each of the groups might be small, but taken together would be large enough to justify giving the course. Supposing that we do get two small groups for different nights; the instructor could meet with each group on alternate weeks for a seminar discussion. The group which is on its own would meet without the instructor and spend several hours with teaching machines, working solo but able to give each other aid and comfort.

Such a procedure would accomplish a number of objectives simultaneously. The instructor would meet a class only once a week but would be helping two groups. We would be doing something to solve the annoying problem of frequent absence, which results in students wandering in and feeling lost because the group is now using an unfamiliar vocabulary or series of concepts; the absentee can drop into the machine room at some other time during the week. The discussion sessions with the instructor would have a firmer base, can assume a similar level of sophistication in a particular area, and can be usefully devoted to a real look at issues or to the problem of application. Despite the previous depreciation of machines, in this case they are useful by providing a reason for the group to come together and ensuring continuity.

Programmed materials might similarly help solve a number of other difficulties in the non-credit area. There is reason to doubt that the educational impact of the large-group lecture, for example, is very large. If we can persuade some members of the audience for a lecture series to use follow-up programmed materials which might use the lecture itself as a "panel," we could help make it a considerably more effective experience.

3. The residential is a special instance of the non-credit program and deserves separate consideration. There are a number of ways in which programmed materials might make a useful contribution:

a. Sending quantities of threatening-looking reading in advance to help participants prepare for the experience often seems not to work out. Without some guidance, even those who do some advance reading are unlikely to do more than passively absorb. Advance materials in programmed form designed to provide the same background in the discipline for all the participants might be considerably more motivating and more certain in their affect. Such materials might usefully include some practice in the methods and assumptions of the discipline involved, as well as some basic conceptual framework.

b. If the residential is planned around a number of informal discussions, as is often the case, a brief programmed course in discussion methods sent in advance could scarcely do harm and might make the residential program considerably more effective.

c. The substantive material could be arranged to include a number of items which force the student to formulate for himself his positions on relevant issues to be discussed at the program. Seminar sessions can be considerably livelier if all the members of the group have already thought through some issues in a preliminary fashion.

d. The often-discussed need for follow-up materials for the intensive but brief residential experience suggests some further possibilities, but these are fairly obvious and might employ already-existing programmed texts which provide systematic entry into an area opened up at the residential meeting.

ADULTS IN GROUPS, WITHOUT AN INSTRUCTOR PRESENT. The most common form of this situation is, of course, the informal discussion group organized around a series of readings or other materials. Any lay-led discussion group trying to make sense out of Aristotle would be immeasurably improved if each participant, after he had done the specific reading, had the opportunity to work through programmed materials which enabled him to check his understanding of the complex texture of ideas and argument. A program for many of the Great Books readings could be constructed, for example, from the kind of questioning which the instructors in the Basic Program at Chicago have developed for their tutorial sessions on many of the same works.

At the other extreme, the materials provided for some community discussion groups often seem to be grossly oversimplified. It is easy to appreciate the reasoning that led to their present form, but the reading comprehension difficulties of the average adult might now better be taken into account by breaking the material into small steps. This is perhaps the one area in adult education for which the constructed-response type of programmed materials seems more appropriate than the longer-stepped multiple-choice item.

CORRESPONDENCE STUDY

Learning by some form of correspondence is a big business and yearly involves a large number of adults in the study of a wide variety of programs. A recent survey concludes that several million people each year are reached by correspondence programs; over 100,000 take college and university courses, private and armed forces programs account for over a million, and many more are enrolled in privately-sponsored industrial and business programs.[15] Thus, whatever figure one happens to choose for total adult education in the United States, it is clear that a significant proportion of those undertaking formal study do so by correspondence.

There are obvious reasons for the popularity of the format. A highly mobile population often finds it difficult to commit a relatively long-term and consistent amount of time to study in a particular place. Probably more important is the fact that we have no educational design which is as sensitive to individual differences in motivation and learning rate as the correspondence course. The student can proceed at his own pace; he can get attention to his individual, particular problems and questions; he is more apt to find that the program provides him with carefully developed, special materials in an organized syllabus; and the teaching is likely to be far more carefully thought through than the average.

Still, like most fields in adult education, correspondence study has developed unevenly and has begun only recently to experiment vigorously. Like most of adult education, it is overwhelmingly preoccupied with vocational demands, nor is this emphasis likely to shift in the future; it is a classic resource for job change and job improvement in this country. As the American economy speeds its automated shift from blue-collar to a dominantly white-collar work force, one wonders how much of a role correspondence study is playing in the shift. Enough, one suspects, to keep the private correspondence schools and most of the military activity in the field concentrated on programs devoted to work skills. The university sector of the field, however, seems now to be interested in expanding the application of correspond- techniques to a much wider range of activity.

Some Possibilities

The preceding section on programmed instruction suggested uses for correspondence methods in both the conference and institute field and educational television; it would be advantageous to have such materials programmed, but clearly not necessary. In the face of repeated suggestions of the value of follow-up correspondence work after an intensive residential institute or conference, the absence of any real experimentation with the idea is distressing. Educational television, on the other hand, has used a wide variety of correspondence techniques in its televised course programming; comment on these is reserved for a later chapter on the mass media.

Some of the most interesting possibilities lie in breaking through the relatively standard pattern for correspondence courses imposed, at the university level, by the credit course requirements. Correspondence methods have been used experimentally to enrich a high school program for bright adolescents, having them choose special projects of their own and providing instructions and help by mail. There is no reason why such flexible approaches should not work for adults: a current-affairs book club, for example, which not only sent a significant book every month, but, for an extra charge, provided some aid in reading it critically and reviewed and replied to a written essay from the reader on some issue raised by the book. Or a course on current issues based on home reading of selected magazines of news and opinion, with the student receiving each month an informal newsletter commenting on some major developments and posing an issue for him to analyze and mail in for critical evaluation.

Correspondence, if it were flexible enough, is an ideal aid to the American tendency toward absorption in a particular subject or field of interest. Hobbies are pretty well taken care of, but perhaps we could expand the interest of the Civil War buff into a genuine interest in history, the enthusiasm for railroads into an inquiry into the development of technology, and so on. One way of approaching this might be to develop a series of courses on scientific methods, in natural history, social sciences, history, and other fields; the course would start with some simple materials requiring evaluation of evidence and judgment in the particular field and move on to the point of assigning problems on which the student would be forced to collect his own evidence. Field work in the natural sciences, for bird watchers and rock hounds, for example, might demand collection or observation; in the case of history, some local historical event might be assigned, in which both documents and the evidence of living persons would have to be assessed. Such courses would demand considerable flexibility of the teacher, to be sure, but they would be fascinating to teach, too.

The Problem of Drop-outs

The correspondence equivalent of the drop-out in ordinary adult courses is the student who simply never finishes the total assigned lessons. The proportion of these students, though it varies from program to program, is excessively high, and perhaps the major methodological problem of correspondence study is to find ways of helping students finish what they begin, "although one factor working against reduction of drop-outs is the fact that most correspondence divisions, both proprietary and non-profit, would go bankrupt if the present drop-out rate were radically reduced."[16] What might help depends, of course, on the particular diagnosis of the problem:

1. A number of people in correspondence work suggest that an important source of non-completion is the student's discovery that what he thought he was interested in, in a course title or description, did not turn out to be quite what he expected. Counselling by mail is difficult and frustrating, and perhaps it is easier to let the student take the first several lessons and find out whether he is really interested. If the bulk of the non-completions were accounted for by this kind of sampling, perhaps one ought to institutionalize a sampling process, which would semantically shift the problem from "dropping out" to "deciding whether I like it" and reduce anxiety about failure. There ought to be more efficient ways of defining and measuring real interest, however, and the Center for the Study of Liberal Education for Adults is currently working on the development of an interest inventory which the inquiring correspondence student can administer to himself, send into the school for scoring and analysis, and get back a recommendation of the areas of study which he is likely to find most consistently interesting and rewarding.

2. Working on one's own is a lonely business, and the tenuous life line between the student and the instructor who reads and corrects assignments has, without question, an influence on whether the student continues. Most administrators caution instructors about the need to be supportive when they undertake correspondence teaching, and

many instructors are sensitive enough to student needs to come to this conclusion on their own. Whether they also have the skills necessary to make the relationship a supportive one for the student is another matter; it would certainly be interesting to analyze a random sample of lessons returned to students in any correspondence program in order to get some measure of what instructors really do. If we are to become serious about developing the autonomous learner, the nature of the helping relationship required is an extremely important matter to investigate and should constitute a research objective of high priority in adult education. Entirely apart from the problem of skill, moreover, is the question of whether the instructor can devote enough time to any student; if he is paid by the lesson, it is unlikely that he will. Only if he is paid for time, and generously so, could one hope to get consistent attention paid to each student's individual problems and potential.

3. It is likely that many adults choose correspondence because they may feel inadequate to the demands and pressures of the classroom; if they feel such inadequacy, the probability is high that it is a realistic one. There is a sad lack of research on the characteristics of correspondence course enrollees, but lacking evidence, it is probably a good guess to assume that such technical inadequacy accounts for some of the drop-out rate. Few of us are strong enough to persist at something we do badly. Low reading rate, low levels of reading comprehension, lack of skill in intellectual analysis, unpreparedness for the slow pace of complex learning—all of these act as constant negative reinforcers for learning. Administrators of correspondence study programs would do well to work together on producing a self-teaching manual on reading and study skills, including graded exercises. Several universities have tackled this problem on behalf of their undergraduates, with very ingenious results, so we have some models with which to work.[17] Perhaps the contribution of the correspondence field is to experiment with methods of discovering, without personal contact, which of their students need such help and with ways of persuading them to accept the aid before they get too discouraged.

4. Much of the recent experimentation in the correspondence study field has been with setting up groups of students, either sharing the same material or working separately and coming together occasionally for discussions. Wedemeyer and Childs describe three types of this hybrid:

a. Informal group study—the group organizes itself and submits either a group of individual assignments or a single one representing the results of a group discussion.
b. Informal group study, with occasional visits by the instructor—a form appropriate especially for university extension divisions who view a state as their community.
c. Directed group study—entire course under the direction of an instructor, who meets regularly with the group; each person does all the assigned work but meets with others for workshop or practice sessions.

All of these variations offer more or less group support for individual effort and thus attack the problem of drop-out. One could argue, of course, that once the group is formed, the real advantages of correspondence study are reduced; the student can no longer work at his own pace, and his self-direction as a learner is greatly modified. But it is likely that many people may be temperamentally unsuited to independent intellectual effort; they need the support of a teacher or a group in order to learn and cannot achieve the rewards of autonomous study anyway. By modifying the correspondence format in the ways suggested, we create new forms which may well be more appropriate for adults than many existing ones. Furthermore, these forms fit very well some already-developed methods; groups using correspondence materials will find the discussion model described in the preceding chapter an appropriate one for their purposes.

THE TUTORIAL

The provision of opportunities for guided independent study for adults has been a largely unexplored area in adult education; yet, as a proven methodology in other fields, it seems peculiarly appropriate for many adults who do not respond to established programs. There are, for example, many people who have sampled a number of adult discussion programs and become particularly interested in a special area; because most such programs are designed for breadth rather than depth, such persons must either turn to formal curricula or attempt to develop a systematic program of study on their own. There are probably even larger numbers of people who have university degrees, wish to pursue some avocational interest, but do not find existing discussion programs appealing because of the great variation in intellectual capacity among the participants.

There are a number of possible variations of the idea for an adult tutorial program, and in the current absence of any activity in the field any of them would be worth experimenting with. For example, many non-credit courses for adults must be cancelled because too few students register for them. One could propose to the three or four students who show up that they could work independently, conferring individually with the instructor occasionally and perhaps coming together once or twice to discuss their independent reading and reflection. Presumably many disappointed cancellees would prefer to enroll in a different course instead, but it is likely that some would find the idea of independent study appealing.

Or one could experiment with a more organized format and set up a regular tutorial program.[18] Such a program might aim at:

1. Freeing individuals from eternal dependence upon formal learning settings and the authority of the expert.
2. Giving students an opportunity to concentrate on their particular interest within an area, and providing needed guidance for such exploration.
3. Providing an opportunity for the exchange and testing of ideas acquired during independent study.

A group of perhaps fifteen persons interested in some general field or problem (peace and war, personality, the community) could be assigned to one or two instructors working together. A few meetings of the group at the beginning of a year would serve to identify individual issues or concerns of the participants and establish the general principles of work. Each student would then consult with one or another of the instructors on his own to discuss bibliography, to get help on special problems he may encounter, and to talk about preliminary drafts of any written work he is doing.

The tutorial group might meet in occasional seminars to present papers for critical discussion, to discuss a book they all have read, to exchange ideas about the field, or to meet with a visiting expert with something to contribute of general interest.

Such a program obviously presents many special problems. The tutors must be persons of considerable breadth and enthusiasm, interested in working with people. They would have to find a nice balance between giving too much of their time to meet the demands of the students and giving enough to be sufficiently helpful. It is, moreover, an expensive program, and students would have to pay substantial fees. But as the educational level in the society rises and educational needs become more specialized, some such format becomes more urgently needed.

LEARNING TO LEARN

Each of the three preceding forms represent devices intended to help people learn more effectively with less dependence on the teacher, working toward relatively formal learning objectives. Correspondence study is well-established and needs only to be expanded and improved; programmed materials will flood the market in the next few years; the tutorial for adults is still just a proposal and needs to be experimented with. Another possibility for increasing learning autonomy is not only at the idea stage but takes its departure from a radically different point.

Most adults spend a very small proportion of their time learning from reading or from structured discussion; they do learn an extraordinary amount from their daily experience, or at least they *could*, if they were "learning-oriented" to the structures and events about them and to their interactions with other people, if they became conscious of the meaning available in the world of experience. Suppose we asked, "How might we go about improving the general ability of the adult to learn from his own experience?" What methodological problems would we have to solve, and what educational format might reasonably emerge from the attempt? To answer these questions we would have to look first at the psychological factors which prevent people from learning from their experience and, secondly, at the kind of experience twentieth-century life provides.

Old saws to the effect that "experience is the best teacher" have tended to establish a general belief that people *do* learn adequately from experience. The image of the oldster, ripe with the wisdom of age and experience and delivering measured judgments, comes immediately to mind; but, of course, one is just as likely, or likelier, to encounter old fools. Neurosis tends to distort reality for the individual in the direction of some overwhelming personal need or anxiety and usually involves compulsive behavior of some kind, which makes it difficult for the seriously neurotic to learn from experience without help. But, apart from this difficulty, which therapy alone can do much about, there are a number of problems which occur normally in people in our society. The difficulties listed below are *personal* limitations to learning from experience.

1. People's interests and tastes are canalized very early, so that

they tend to pre-judge experiences in the same way in which many of us prejudge food. American norms, in addition, tend to reinforce such prejudices by discouraging an investigative or exploratory attitude toward the having of experience. One does what is the "right" thing to do in any given era, from how one spends vacation time to how one treats the children. The desperate search among middle-class mothers for prescriptions approved by their peers for the handling of children is a striking example of the unwillingness to experiment flexibly with structuring an experience, just to see what happens.

2. Many adults, of whatever age, do not have the necessary training to enable them to hold their opinions in check for the period necessary to consider another opinion or an event with at least some objectivity or to examine it for its meaning; that is, in regard to most experience, people tend to get their egos too intimately involved with the event to learn much except their feelings toward it. The process of discussing, itself, does not teach people to overcome this difficulty; they must be consciously trained to do so.

3. Many people tend to approach experience passively; they "let it happen." This passivity is surely to some extent due to the structure of the American family, just as it results partly from the urban environment to be discussed later. It would not occur to an American concertgoer to emulate the Frenchman who, at the premiere of an over-tympanic symphonic work, rose from his seat and solemnly and beseechingly waved his white handkerchief; nor in our era of changing urban neighborhoods does the threatened householder generally think of anything but flight to the suburbs.

4. The psychology of perception has much to say about the differential interpretation of experience because different aspects of reality are selected for emphasis by the individual. There is little one can do to stop this process from occurring, but there is a great deal one can do about sensitizing people to its existence. A study done several years ago of how a group of parents, high school students, and teachers perceived one another uncovered the fact that each group was acting on hypotheses about how the other two felt about it, guesses which turned out to be largely false. Establishing lines of communication among the three groups undoubtedly helped resolve that particular problem; what we need to do, however, is to help adults take the possibility of such perceptual error into account as an habitual evaluative device in all relevant experience.

There are other personal experience-distorters which might be added, but these will do as examples. The fact is that for these and other reasons, all of us learn poorly, lop-sidedly, and wrongly from some experiences, and not at all from others, because we do not know how to compensate for human frailties, how to frame the kinds of questions which can be asked about an experience to make it more meaningful, or how to look for connections and interrelationships which might be relevant to interpret experience.

The City as an Experience Context

The overwhelming majority of Americans now live in what the census classifies as urban areas, and there is every reason to expect that the trend toward urbanism will intensify as the tempo of change increases. Moreover, our national mobility ensures that many of us will live in more than one city. The experience of the adult who is part of such an environment bears inevitably the marks of large-scale forces, often unperceived and usually not understood by him; almost every waking moment is shaped in some way by the fact that he lives in a city or has been driven out of it into a suburban periphery. Transportation to and from work gives him a certain image of the city, depending on the route he takes and the frustration involved; the work itself is usually entangled in the urban context; the family problems he must face are shaped by it. What he is often largely unaware of, however, is that the city, as well as being a source of frustration and grievance, is also a tremendous resource for the enrichment of life. Only in places where the concentration of population warrants it has any society been able to build those institutions which create and store the cream of culture: the main currents of art, drama, music, architecture, thought, the clearly-focused microcosm of the society's conflicts and contradictions, the vanguard of movements into its future.

For many reasons, this most important dimension of the experience of the city dweller, the city itself, is largely unexplored and unused. We hear the weak echo of this assertion in the standard remark of the big-city dweller that he never "goes to see things like the Statue of Liberty or the Metropolitan Museum until relatives come to town." The awareness seldom goes deeper than that expressed by such a remark; the block between the individual and the city he inhabits goes much deeper and is due to complex causes.

To a sociologist like C. Wright Mills, people are "so sunk in the routines of their milieux that they do not transcend, even in discussion, much less by action, these more or less narrow milieux. They do not gain a view of the structure of their society and of their role in it. The city is a structure composed of milieux; the people in the milieux tend to be rather detached from one another; being more or less confined to their own rather narrow ranges, they do not understand the structure of their society. As they reach for each other, they do so by stereotype and through prejudiced images of the creatures of other milieux. Each is trapped by his confining circle . . . but (people) can transcend them—individually by intellect and education; socially by discussion and public action."[19]

One of the consequences of inhabiting narrow milieux is that people's experience, in an urban environment, is inevitably fragmentary and incomplete. The learner needs a sense of caution about the significance of individual experience and a knowledge of what is needed to supplement it. Most individuals, as anyone who has taught knows, tend to generalize wildly from bits of often typical experience.

In addition to being fragmentary, people's experience in the urban environment tends to be disconnected. It is easy for the primitive to see the relation between his family life and his economic life—the relation is often inescapable—or between his ritualistic life and his economic or sex life. But the abstractions which connect the various areas of life experience for the urban adult are too vast for him to perceive readily, and to connect the frustrations of his job with his temper toward his children is not easy. That the growth of industry and destruction of mosquito-breeding marshlands on one end of the city have anything to do with his frustrations over not being permitted to water his lawn is even more far-fetched.

Modern life gives greatest structure to the economic dimension of life experience, and other roles tend to pale into insignificance before the urgencies of making a living. The tiny area of the city in which one's economic role is acted out tends to thrust out of consciousness the enormous area and complex activities which exist around it.

Part of the difficulty may lie in the failure of any communication about things which are going on in the city to reach individuals. Newspapers focus on events often far away and of abstract interest; information about local activities must compete with high-powered saturation campaigns of various kinds, and the announcement of a Cézanne show at the Art Museum can hardly put up a fair struggle with the latest cold-cream soap. But even if the information comes through, the effort required to take advantage of the resources of a big city requires planning, time, and some money. Without some planning, it is considerably easier to give in to fatigue and the television set than to get dressed and venture out into bad transportation and uncertain weather, and to give the expenditure of energy necessary to participate in the cultural and civic life of the community.

A Program Proposal

On these assumptions about the life of the contemporary adult, it is not difficult to construct the outlines of a program whose objective is to train individuals to learn more effectively from their on-going experience and to encourage them to reflect on that experience. The program must be organized to provide two kinds of situations:

1. It must provide the participants with experiences as close as possible to the reality in the city in which he lives—its museums and galleries, its symphonies and theaters, its newspapers, its social dilemmas, political structure and problems, its families and social structure, its physical setting.

A day spent walking through an area of the city in which a nationality or racial minority lives, observing the style of life, the forms of social interaction, housing, and the like; arranged meetings with a local newspaper publisher, a political leader, a social worker, a police captain.

A weekend devoted to visits to all of the museums in the city, talks with curators, etc.

An auto tour of the city, with attention focused on its ecology, historical growth, economic advantages and disadvantages, etc., or on its architecture.

Observation over a period of time of a political campaign, perhaps concentrated on a single ward. Meetings with local campaign leaders to discuss issues, participation in a registration drive combined perhaps with a simple survey developed and carried out by the students, etc.

2. The problem of selecting and arranging such experiences is to make them significant foci for student learning, for the objective is not that they learn something about a political campaign but that they discover what questions need to be asked, how one overcomes one's own preconceptions, what kinds of inferences may safely be made in a given situation, and the habit of thoughtful reflection. The most important aspect of the program, therefore, consists of sessions which follow the experience in which two things must be done: the students must explore the meaning of the experience, the generalizations they form, the inferences they make, and their opinions about it; they need then to examine the *adequacy* of those conclusions and the process by which they arrived at them.

The success of the program obviously depends on how well this last process is carried through and, therefore, on the orientation and skill of the teacher. He must be willing to forego the pleasure of discoursing on his own field of expertness to concentrate relentlessly on the thought processes of the students, and he must be sensitive to the perceptual difficulties inherent in the situation. He plays the role of cognitive therapist, ready to disregard the particular content of a perception or a conclusion and to ask: what else did you see that was relevant, how did you arrive at that conclusion, what makes you think so, what other question should you have asked?

However large the student body is, most of these analytic and interpretive discussion sessions should be held in groups no larger than fifteen, to which an instructor is permanently assigned. Several purposes will be served by this arrangement: the smallness of the group and the fact that they will meet together often with the same leader is conducive to the development of a group cohesiveness which will hold people to the program and avoid the usual non-credit drop-out rate; second, the major goal of the program requires a situation in which all students can talk freely.

Because Americans tend to adapt fairly well to the "club" as a form of social interaction, it would be useful to set up as part of the program a "Commons" of which every registered student automatically becomes a member. One problem of city life is that people often live among those with whom they have little in common, and friends live far off through hours of traffic. Getting to see them for a good evening with some quiet conversation often is a real struggle and requires advance preparation and notice. The "Commons" would be an antidote to urban isolation from people with whom one can readily talk. Any evening a student cares to drop in, after dinner or after a movie, he will find some fellow students browsing among the books, or watching Brinkley, or listening to music in a special music room, or having a friendly argument in the corner over a drink. There will be occasional special showings of documentary films and once in a while a visiting eminent out-of-towner who agreed to drop in and for whom the program rounded up some students by phone or postcard.

Such a program would be expensive and difficult to staff and would require a considerable amount of administrative flexibility.[20] But the technical resources to carry it out do exist, and the experimental temper of adult education will, perhaps, someday encourage attempts to establish this program or others like it. Too much of what we do increases the adult's dependency on specialized institutions and on the expert; we should at least explore the possibility of training the independent learner.

NOTES

1. Cyril Houle, at the University of Chicago, has been much interested in the adult who goes on learning on his own and has done considerable exploration and encouraged his students to do more of this theme. His orientation has been mainly toward discovering what kinds of people they are, rather than toward what one ought to do for them or to develop them, which are the foci of this chapter.

2. S. M. Markle *et al., A Programed Primer on Programing* (New York: Center for Programed Instruction, 1961). Reprinted by permission. The field has recently decided arbitrarily to spell the word with one "m," presumably to avoid confusion with other kinds of programs. I have not followed that convention here.

3. S. L. Pressey, "Some Perspectives and Major Problems Regarding 'Teaching Machines'." This, and many of the articles cited below, have been collected in an excellent anthology of materials on programming by Arthur Lumsdaine and Robert Glaser, *Teaching Machines and Programmed Learning* (Washington: National Education Association, 1960).

4. *Ibid.*, p. 502.

5. Norman Crowder, *The Arithmetic of Computers* (Goleta: Western Design, a division of U.S. Industries, Inc., 1960), pp. 15, 21, 27, 35. Reprinted by permission.

6. James G. Holland and B. F. Skinner, *The Analysis of Behavior* (New York: McGraw-Hill, 1961).

7. C. B. Ferster and S. M. Sapon, "An Application of Recent Developments in Psychology to the Teaching of German," and the Commentary on it, page 592, in Lumsdaine and Glaser, *op. cit.*

8. L. J. Briggs, "The Development and Appraisal of Special Procedures for Superior Students" (abstract), Lumsdaine and Glaser, *op. cit.*

9. The quotation is taken from a letter published in the newsletter *Programmed Instruction,* Vol. I, No. 4 (February, 1962).

10. D. J. Klaus, H. H. Shettel, D. J. Glapp, and P. Welsh, *Development of Self-Instructional Materials on the Fundamentals of Life Insurance* (Pittsburgh: American Institute of Research, 1961).

11. James G. Holland, "Errors in Programming," *Programmed Instruction, op. cit.*

12. T. F. Gilbert, "An Early Approximation to Principles of Programming Continuous Discourse," a report to the Bell Telephone Laboratories, in Lumsdaine and Glaser, *op. cit.*

13. G. L. Bryan, J. W. Rigney, and C. Van Horn, "An Evaluation of Three Type of Information for Supplementing Knowledge of Results in a Training Technique" (abstract), Lumsdaine and Glaser, *op. cit.*

14. The financing problem is likely to be a real stumbling block in adult education. The expense of developing programs in many fields of elementary and secondary education and, to some extent, in undergraduate courses, will be willingly borne by commercial publishers because the markets are so large. Even if the adult market were large, it is hard to get at. Foundation support may be the only answer, as it has been in so much adult education experimentation.

15. Charles A. Wedemeyer and Gayle B. Childs, *New Perspectives in University Correspondence Study* (Chicago: Center for the Study of Liberal Education for Adults, 1961).

16. Personal communication from Paul Sheats.

17. A good example is the manual called *Learning to Learn,* produced by the University of Michigan for its undergraduate students.

18. This idea for a tutorial program is based on a proposal by James Whipple and Morton Gordon.

19. Reprinted by permission from C. Wright Mills, *Mass Society and Liberal Education, Notes and Essays No. 9* (Chicago: Center for the Study of Liberal Education for Adults, 1954), pp. 10–11.

20. This program idea was tried at Northwestern University, financed by the Center for the Study of Liberal Education for Adults, for one year. The experiment proved how difficult it is to try to get these kinds of educational changes, which surprised no one. The response to the announcement of the program was sizable, indicating some kind of interest in the idea (though, of course, the experimental nature of the program may well have had something to do with it). The difficulty, as one might suspect, arose mainly at the most crucial point—helping the students examine their own learning processes. The faculty team found it easy to be seduced by the interesting concepts involved in the experiences and seldom reserved enough time for retrospective discussion. With all its problems, it was a stimulating attempt to do something which had seldom been tried in adult education and indicated the worth of further experimentation with the idea.

8

THE LARGE GROUP: FROM LECTURE SERIES TO WORKSHOPS

The lecturer is one who talks in someone else's sleep.

WILLIAM KIRKPATRICK

The decade and a half since the end of World War II has witnessed the very rapid development of technical innovations in large group meetings devoted to some educational objective.[1] In a field where change often comes very slowly indeed, such rapid adoption of new techniques has been a surprising phenomenon and may be the result of the theatrical character of the large group session. A performer confronts an audience alone, but there is quite likely, as well, to be a person in the role of director who is planning the activity and to whom the performer is responsive. Change is consequently not altogether dependent on shifting the attitude of lecturers, as it is in the classroom, but can be induced externally.

It would be idle to deny, however, that the traditional ways of managing the large group educational setting are still with us. The firmly established nineteenth-century form, in which the traveling lecturer worked his way around the circuit, delivering a standard talk, is too deep-rooted to disappear easily. Its modern counterpart is still a lively part of the American national scene; most large universities have an active lecture bureau which books prominent persons for talks; one is just as likely to bump into Margaret Mead or Bennett Cerf in any medium-sized middle-western city as in New York. Similar bureaus provide the same or lesser talents to the clubs and associations of American cities to be served up with the creamed luncheon chicken.

Much of this activity can hardly be classified as education; it is a strange mixture of entertainment and the American love of celebrity. At the other extreme, however, some lecture series present important intellectual figures delivering serious and important views; New York University, for example, recently presented a series of four talks on existentialism by a brilliant Irish philosopher and was astonished to find a crowd appearing to hear her, and UCLA had to turn people away from a series of lectures on modern philosophy because their auditorium held only 1,700 persons. Between these extremes there is a mass of lecturing in the category of "expert on almost any conceivable topic talking to a group of people" who happen to be interested in it for some reason.

The social function of the latter, and dominating, type of lecture was, in the past, quite clear. At its best the format provided a humanization of knowledge, a way of filtering different perspectives and new life styles to a broader public. But it is difficult to explain why the form persists; radio, then television, and the development of mass circulation magazines, as well as the more recent spectacular success of the paperback, have all taken over the function previously performed by the public lecture and do it much more swiftly and efficiently. Perhaps some people feel the need for more personal confrontation of the expert, or perhaps the lecture is too firmly entrenched in associational habit patterns to wither easily. Adult educators report increasing difficulty in promoting some types of lecture series, and perhaps the format may be due to decrease slowly in prominence in the future.

Whatever its fate, however, the public lecture does not present methodological problems worth much attention. To put together a lecture series is a task rather like that of the librarian's: he selects already-packaged materials to suit his guess about the taste of a particular audience; occasionally he can exercise some creativity about finding a theme or problem to which several available packages relate. He has no control over the material, makes no attempt to find out what people learned from it, but merely makes it available.

When we confront the problem of the large group with a significantly educational intention, a wide variety of interesting alternatives arise. Adult educators, in experimenting with large group formats, have developed three general models which invite consideration in depth.

THE LECTURE WITH AUDIENCE INVOLVEMENT

The lecture presentation by an expert is not, whatever the discussion above might imply, a pointless educational instrument; it can, on the contrary, be very useful. Making it useful requires at least two conditions. First, we need to specify the audience; the public lecturer is talking to a mass audience, in the same sense that the television presentation does, and the fact that the bodies are all present in one space does not materially change the dynamics of the situation. Those present do not have any relationship to one another; least of all can we be sure that they share some purpose in being there. Only if the audience consists of persons with a common goal, or even a common concern, do we have a basis for hoping for educational consequences. Second, we must have some clear view of what use we want the audience to make of the material: a deeper understanding of some situation in which they are involved, an awareness of new concepts, re-examination of present opinions or values. A decision about the important desired outcomes of a lecture or lecture series will determine what kind of audience participation we must plan for.

It is crucial that this kind of decision precede the selection of method for obvious reasons; methodology otherwise becomes merely a matter of gimmickry and fashion. For a time, in adult education, one could hardly attend a meeting without finding oneself a member of a buzz group, whether the groups had anything useful to do or not. Most of the time, unfortunately, they did not. Involvement for its own sake makes no more sense than does the absolute audience passivity which the method intended to combat.

The report of an NYU program below excellently illustrates how both of the basic requirements can be met in making educational capital of a series of expert presentations. The audience was carefully controlled; the purposes were specified and translated into a design of audience participation which permitted their achievement.

The six-session Round Table program in Human Relations conducted by Liberal Arts in Extension of New York University in cooperation with the Teaneck Mayor's Advisory Committee on Community Relations dealt with the problems of individual and group relationships in a community undergoing rapid racial changes. New York University assumed the major responsibility for developing the outline and format, creating the Round Table discussion guides, training Round Table discussion leaders, and securing the consultants. The Mayor's Advisory Committee assumed the total responsibility for recruiting the participants.

In the preliminary meetings between members of the Mayor's Advisory Committee and New York University's coordinator,[2] it was agreed that the purpose and goal of the program should be to give leaders of Teaneck civic organizations:

1. A better understanding of the various forces now operating in our society in the area of race relations.
2. Some insight as to how different communities throughout the country had dealt or were dealing with the problem of racially changing neighborhoods.
3. An opportunity to apply the findings of social science research to the problems of racially changing neighborhoods in Teaneck
4. An opportunity to explore programs of community action with Members of the Mayor's Advisory Committee.

Moreover, it was hoped that it might help Teaneck community leaders who were opposed to the idea of open occupancy housing, or who were uncommitted to either side of the open occupancy debate, to re-examine their attitudes about open occupancy housing.

Accordingly, the program outline, as attached, was developed. The format for each session remained essentially the same: first, the presentation by a consultant of national developments of changing areas of race relations and problems of changing neighborhoods; second, Round Table discussions (led by members of the Mayor's Advisory Committee) relating the consultants' problems to the issues in Teaneck; third, a general discussion by the Reporters from the Round Tables (then joined in by other participants) led by the program moderator.

Attendance at the Workshop sessions varied from 90 to 100 persons, most of whom held leadership roles in one or more Teaneck civic organizations.

SUMMARY OF THE SIX SESSIONS

I. The national picture described by Prof. Dan Dodson and concurred in by Round Table discussants as accurately reflecting the situation in Teaneck and surrounding suburbia was:
   A. Suburbs are in a process of racial change arising out of the changes in Negro education, income, occupation, and expectations, and that these racial changes in suburban neighborhoods are inevitable;
   B. These changes bring in their wake a certain amount of racial tension and conflict;
   C. Conflict is part of the democratic process and has within it the possibility of personal and community growth, not available in static communities;
   D. "There is no place to hide." Suburbanites and urbanites are going

to have to learn to cope with the problem of changing neighborhoods.

II. Prof. Jeanne Noble cited various studies showing the changing nature of the Negro community, especially the rise of a new Negro middle class (the group which is moving to the suburbs) which has the same aspirations, hopes, and dreams as the white middle class. ("Too often, the Negro middle class tries to emulate both the faults and virtues of their white Protestant neighbors.") In general, the Round Tables recognized Teaneck Negroes in the description painted by Prof. Noble. Moreover, the Round Table participants agreed:

A. The percentage of Negroes in Teaneck who are active in civic groups, particularly the PTA, LWV, community chest, church, politics, boy scouts, etc., was about the same as for the white residents. (Both were too small!)

B. The fact that Negroes were relatively recent arrivals in the community meant that participation by them in community affairs at this time was more difficult. (There was divided opinion, by both white and Negro participants, as to the value of making *special* efforts to welcome Negroes into civic activity.)

C. Communication between whites and Negroes in Teaneck is poor, a situation which also exists between different religious groups.

III. The conflict and violence in Levittown, Pa., arising out of the move of Negroes to that community, was used as a case illustration by Prof. Marvin Bressler to illustrate the nature and growth of uncontrolled tension and conflict. Among the participants, however, there was agreement that as far as Teaneck was concerned:

A. There has been no violence arising out of racially changing neighborhoods. To the extent that tension and conflict do exist, it has been evidenced by whispering and rumor campaigns; over-sensitivity by both whites and Negroes; and finally, withdrawal by some from some community activities or, in extreme cases, moving away from the neighborhood to another section of Teaneck where no Negroes lived, or out of Teaneck altogether.

B. Interreligious conflict and tension is as great as or greater than racial conflict and tension.

C. There have been some real friendships established between Negroes and whites in Teaneck.

D. Standards in the changing neighborhoods, in schools, police, fire prevention, as well as in other municipal services, have been maintained.

IV. Mr. Theodore Leakes traced the history of anti-discrimination legislation and litigation in the housing area, and emphasized the use of law as an educative as well as enforcement device. Participants felt, however, that despite legislation and court action on a national and state level:

A. Anti-discrimination legislation has had no effect on the sale and purchase of homes in Teaneck. (With the exception of the pending state law, all prior legislation relates to public or publicly-assisted housing. Teaneck has few projects of this nature.)

B. The pending state law will be of great help in community education to combat discrimination, and may be of help in forcing realtors to show houses all over Teaneck to whites and Negroes.
C. Efforts to create "panic selling" by some real estate brokers have been partially successful and have contributed to community tension.
D. Pressure by neighbors (a kind of "gentleman's agreement") on sellers not to sell to Negroes has been a major factor in limiting sales to Negroes outside of the Northeast section of Teaneck.
E. Realtors have their own "gentleman's agreement"; viz., they will not show Negroes homes outside the Northeast area, and will not show prospective white purchasers homes in the area.

V. The most recent findings of what happens in integrated neighborhoods was presented by Eunice Crier. By and large, these findings indicate that there are fewer prejudiced attitudes by whites and Negroes in integrated communities than in non-integrated neighborhoods; that there is no consistent pattern of what happens to price patterns when Negroes move into a previously all-white neighborhood; that whites do not buy houses in an integrated area because of any "liberal" tendencies, but because the houses are the "best buys" they can get at the time. A major thesis presented by Mrs. Crier was that the outside forces were as important as the forces inside in determining whether a neighborhood would become all Negro.
In the Round Table discussions:
A. There was no agreement on which way prices in Northeast Teaneck had moved since Negroes moved in;
B. That if the Northeast section is to maintain a balance somewhere near its present level, the rest of Teaneck (and other surrounding areas) will have to open up to Negro occupancy.
C. That special efforts to attract white purchasers to the Northeast section of Teaneck can be made by maintaining the municipal services, and if possible, make these services models for the rest of the community.

VI. Mr. Henry Lipman summarized the findings of the first five sessions of the workshop. From these findings, a pattern of needed community action had been revealed; a pattern which included fact finding, education and social action. The responsibility for carrying out this program fell on all citizens, white and Negro, as individuals, as members of civic organizations, and as members of political parties. The Round Table participants agreed with the need in Teaneck for the three-part program, and their recommendations are included in the recommendations below.

RECOMMENDATIONS

1. Fact finding. A survey to be conducted under the auspices of the Mayor's Advisory Committee, but which will utilize the professional and personnel resources of community groups, to find out such essential facts (now not known) as: How many Negroes now live in Teaneck? Where do they come from? What is their occupation?

ices? What are the practices of
hat are attitudes of white families
vard having Negro neighbors?

2 nal program, to be conducted by
and other civic groups, which will
discussion of the survey findings;
discussion groups to consider the
g; establish and service a speakers
stribution of appropriate literature
roups; special programs for church,
merce leaders; and encouragement
dual groups.

on or statement, show that all groups
Teaneck; through individual civic or
th those responsible for panic selling;
and realtors show available housing
hites and Negroes; maintain a "listing"
ractice non-discriminatory practices;
persistent in their search for homes

ory Committee.

ariations

rogram was that the method it chose
was appropriate and relevant to its
citizens concerned about a particular
n gave them a chance to apply the
to their own situations. As one looks
le devices for enlivening large meet-
ther the criterion of relevance is often

y with problems of method in most
tion, must avoid the seductive trap of
t difficult to sidestep in the context of
s book has a central theme at all, it is
se, not determine it. There is no sense
rogram planner is not prepared to or-
lems which emerge; the mild exercise
nd to form buzz groups does not justify
ave a reasonable educational task.

large group procedure which follow,
rm which emphasizes the objectives for

VARYING PRESENTATION—THE PANEL[3]

Description: The most popular contemporary device for improving on the traditional single lecturer is the panel presentation, using three or four speakers and a moderator. Speakers may give brief, prepared talks, then interact, with a moderator as discussion leader; or introductory statements may be eliminated. Commonly ends with questions from the large group.

Objectives served: Clarifies differences of opinion, more challenging to a wide variety of views on a topic than a single speaker is likely to be.

Method: Staff, or a committee representing the group which will constitute the audience, must brief the panel some time in advance on the purposes of the session. The panel should have an opportunity to get together at a time reasonably close to the session to develop an informal outline of the discussion points. Such an outline may usefully be put on paper for them.

Comments: Panel members should represent really divergent views and had better be evenly matched for verbal ability or the discussion will be unbalanced; they must be firmly impressed by the time limits involved. If the moderator sees himself only as a figurehead, he will get trampled during the discussion, with sad results. Beyond this, *preparation is all*, and if not carefully managed, a single, well-organized speaker is more educationally effective.

VARYING PRESENTATION—THE SYMPOSIUM

Description: Two or more speakers talking on the same general theme or topic, with time at the end for some interaction with the group.

Objectives served: Information, increasing perspective by providing a broader spectrum of views.

Method: This is the least demanding of the variations, because the speakers are not required to interact freely. The major requirement is that they be selected carefully to present important facets of a topic or problem. The illustration given earlier of the NYU Round Table program might have been presented as a symposium if a one-shot program had been desired.

Comments: This form appears to be most popular for sessions dealing with fairly technical areas in which several views of a new development or theory are considered for the benefit of a professionally-trained audience; it is probably most useful in that role. If the topic involves sharp controversy, the panel is a more appropriate device.

VARYING PRESENTATION—THE FILM FORUM

Description: Film presentation, followed by audience discussion.

Objectives served: Getting people interested in a problem, dramatizing relationships.

Method: Film must be selected carefully with regard to the objectives of the session and should be previewed instead of relying on the often misleading descriptions found in catalogs and reviews. Petty details, such as whether one has a spare projector bulb or whether the sound lead is connected properly, take on considerable importance. Film is often hypnotic, and the group must have a clear idea of what use they are to make of it; use of one of the audience involvement devices is strongly recommended.

Comments: The worst feature of the film forum is that it is often used as a gadget to attract people to a mildly educational entertainment. "The newsreel goes dithering on," said Grierson," mistaking the phenomenon for the thing itself," and so do many educational films. It can be an extraordinarily powerful tool for examining personal and social relationships; it is a very inefficient way of conveying information; and as an arguer of causes, it must be used with care. If the film is making a case for something, or developing an idea, additional material should be provided; it can be too convincing.

INVOLVING THE GROUP—THE QUESTION PERIOD[4]

Description: At the close of the lecture, the group directs questions to the speaker.

Objectives: Clarification, understanding.

Method: The traditional method of opening the floor to any questions, without preparation, is usually unsatisfactory. One can do a great deal to get the group set for their role as listener: brief them before the lecturer begins on the kinds of questions they might keep in mind, even, perhaps, provide them with a few sample questions; distribute an outline, prepared by the speaker, of important things to listen for; pass out index cards to use in noting questions which occur to them during the talk; suggest to the lecturer that he pause for a minute at several appropriate points to give the group a chance to reflect and note any questions they wish to raise at the end.

Comments: Even these devices do not adequately overcome the passivity of the lecture, but they help. If the speaker is the kind of person who can take interruption, he can set up his own pattern of interaction with the group; even in a large group, if he is mobile and on the same level instead of on a platform, the lecture can be a very lively experience.

INVOLVING THE GROUP—AUDIENCE LISTENING PANELS

Description: Channeling audience reaction through representative panels, sitting either among the group or together next to the speaker.

Objectives: Clarification, understanding.

Method: The listening panel might be drawn at random—every fifteenth person who enters—or it may be selected as representing various interests among the group. It helps if they are given an outline of the lecture and a few sample questions to illustrate the form of the most useful questions to raise. If the room is formal, the panel is best seated together on the same level as the speaker; in an informal setting, they might be kept together in the first row. An alternative to the separate listening panel is to divide the audience into general areas and suggest that those sitting in a particular area listen particularly for some aspect of the topic.

Comments: If one must use the audience question device, and it is often the only practical form of response, the listening panel is probably the best device available. The general audience ought to be given a chance at some point to raise questions, of course.

INVOLVING THE GROUP—PROBLEM CENSUS

Description: Obtaining from the audience a list of the problems they perceive in a given area, or the questions they have about the subject the lecturer is to deal with.

Objectives: Making the lecture as relevant as possible to the needs of the group.

Method: The earlier this is done, of course, the better. A questionnaire can be sent to the group and the results given to the speaker weeks in advance to give him an opportunity to incorporate the results. Or a special program committee might get in touch with members more informally and pool the results of their interviews. The problem census may, on the other hand, be conducted during an early part of the session; have the audience, in informal buzz groups, state the two or three most important problems they see in the area, and report orally to the speaker before he begins.

Comments: This is a useful device if the speaker is willing to pay careful attention to the results of the census, a frustrating one if he does not. Only an adroit speaker can take advantage of the method if the material comes to him at the time of the session itself, but some people can do it.

INVOLVING THE GROUP—BUZZ GROUPS

Description: Dividing the group into small segments for a relatively brief period of time to engage in a task relevant to the topic or problem.

Objectives: Understanding, problem-solving.

Method: If the room is flexible, and the audience can be seated at small tables during the talk, each table can constitute a group. Some modern facilities provide a large lecture room surrounded by small conference rooms, and the audience can disperse to these after the talk, to reassemble later in the large room for reporting. Large auditoriums can be adapted to the method by asking people in odd-numbered rows to turn around to face those in the row behind them. Someone should instruct the groups to choose a reporter, remind them of time limits, and carefully outline the task, which might consist of applying some central concept outlined by the speaker to their particular situation or to suggest solutions to a problem he has anatomized. If group reports are briefly noted on a blackboard, the speaker can review and comment afterwards.

Comments: Above all, the task must be clear, restricted in scope, and relevant to the experience of the group. The method is admirably suited to involving people in learning activities, if the learning objective is well thought through.

INVOLVING THE GROUP—THE CLINIC

Description: The speaker, assisted by a panel, responds to problems raised by the group.

Objectives: Applying the results of experience, problem-solving.

Method: Adult education is often concerned with improving the individual's ability to handle practical problems in many areas, and this is a useful method. An expert with a good deal of experience, assisted by a panel of local people selected from the group for their backgrounds of experience, consider practical problems raised one at a time by members of the group. If the expert plays his role well, he will use it as an occasion to help individuals solve their own problems, by a line of questioning which implicitly forces the questioner to proceed himself with the problem-solving process, instead of providing pat answers from his own background.

Comments: It is surprising that this format is not more often used. Before the session, a staff member ought to confer with the expert to work out the most educationally useful consultant role.

THE CONTROLLED WORKSHOP

The dominant characteristic of the preceding form is the use of the lecture to provide the basic material for learning. Between that carefully controlled situation and the pure workshop format, some adult educators have developed an intermediate type of program which they usually call a workshop but which exhibits a considerably greater amount of pre-structuring. One finds it flourishing particularly in such fields as community relations, leadership training, executive development, and the like.[5] It is generally characterized by:

1. Flexible construction of the learning situations provided. There may be occasional lectures to feed in information or to review relevant theory, but these are supplementary rather than basic to its structure. The program is likely to include three or four different forms, scheduled to present a sequence of learning experiences which form an appropriate pattern for the particular objectives that the planners have in mind. Such workshops are usually run for one or two weeks, and in the course of the time the staff might decided to change their original schedule to adjust to events.

2. Some opportunity for skill training appropriate to the activity area of the group involved. During periods devoted to this objective, the group is usually divided into manageable smaller sections to which separate staff members are assigned to initiate or direct activity. The skills to be improved may be pre-selected by the staff or may arise out of discussion at the workshop itself.

3. An emphasis on active involvement of the participants. Although the program design permits the varied use of reading materials and lectures, the majority of the time is spent in small group activities which emphasize demonstration, role play, or special forms of discussion.

4. A closely cooperating staff, as the description of the preceding characteristics implies. This must be distinguished from a situation where a single director coordinates the activity of a number of staff persons or where he brings in appropriate resources at particular times. The workshop staff plans the design together, distributes roles among itself, meets together often during the course of the workshop to evaluate progress and decide on necessary schedule changes, and operates in general as a cooperating team.

It is clear from a look at these characteristics that this intermediate form goes far beyond the kind of program which depends on a series of expert views but does not go as far as the pure workshop in permitting activities to be designed basically by the participants themselves. The design presented below has been made deliberately general to permit some discussion of its applicability to several areas.

An Illustration

Here, first, is a typical day's activity for such a workshop, designed for a group of adults who are active in their local communities which are presently in the throes of urban renewal. Most of them hold office in some active community group which is attempting to solve problems raised by the breakdown of formerly segregated neighborhoods, potential racial conflict, or school deterioration. The major objective for the workshop is to make them more effective community workers by increasing understanding of the forces they are attempting to deal with, improving insight into their own role, and improving skills necessary for effective group action.

9–11 A.M. In small sub-groups of about 15 persons each, the participants explore the problems of making action groups more effective. The procedure is based on the widely known T-group methods originally developed by the National Training Laboratory, methods which require the group itself to develop its own tasks, deal with its own leadership problems, and in the process analyze what happens, in order to form its own generalizations about effective group operation and to gain individual insight into the members' own group participation styles.

The training-group procedure is applicable to any field whose personnel devote a significant part of their work time to managing or participating in the activity of groups, but it requires teaching skills of a very specialized order. Nor do all adult education staffs subscribe to its efficacy. A workshop of supervisory employees might devote a similar block of time to a somewhat more structured discussion of the participants' perceptions of their group roles and the problems they encounter in making groups productive, with the instructor taking a more active role in the discussion. The important general point is that this particular workshop activity ought to offer participants an opportunity to explore with considerable freedom one of their basic problems, using some method which forces them to confront the question of the adequacy of their own behavior and beliefs.

11–12 A.M. A theory session, in which some of the major problems which the sub-groups are discussing are selected for more general treatment at a more abstract level. If they have been struggling with leadership conflicts within their own groups, for example, one of the staff members might discuss some of the research on small-group leadership. However this kind of session is organized—and one can use straight lecture, panel, or some other variation—it should closely relate to the events in the free discussion which precedes it. If these are in the T-group form, one can predict with some confidence the kinds of problems which will emerge in the discussions; these groups have been exhaustively studied and exhibit uniformities of a relatively high order. Other types of discussion are likely to focus on a wider variety of problems, or somewhat more specific ones, in which case the staff can do less advance preparation.

1:30–3:00 P.M. Again the large group is subdivided, this time on the basis of a similar community or organizational function, perhaps, or by interest in a particular community objective, instead of randomly, as in the morning groups. The purpose of this session is the improvement of needed skills, which in the case of the community group might include decision-making, persuading other people to become active, chairing a meeting, or any number of other demands made on the community leader. Similarly, a group of supervisory personnel might be concerned with skills of resolving conflicts, helping work groups adjust to change, interviewing, and the like. This type of session will include a great deal of role playing, analysis of typical situations, and discussion of varying consequences of different courses of action. Instructors usually take a very directive hand in them, although the kinds of skills the group explores may be determined by the members in consultation.

3:30–4:30 P.M. A session devoted to content, or background, aimed generally at the question, "What do we need to understand about the broader context in which our work is done?" For the community relations group one might import an expert in city administration to discuss the functions of various city agencies or a sociologist to talk about neighborhood structure or urban ecology; or bring in a panel of the local elite, a real estate agent, a ward politician, a local newspaper publisher, to discuss their perceptions of urban renewal. Participants in a management program might look at organizational structure through the eyes of a sociologist or talk with a group of labor organizers.

Such a daily schedule, of course, may be varied, and usually is, to permit a number of special sessions. A favorite device is to devote several days to a mass role play for which the group is assigned various important roles to play in a fantasy community. Everyone is furnished with a description of the community: facts on its population, housing, schools, business, and the strengths and weaknesses of its associational structure. They are then assigned roles in various action groups: the school board, the executive committee of the PTA, the Chamber of Commerce, a neighborhood association, and others, depending on the kind of problem given to the group to handle.

Each of the groups meets briefly to get organized and to decide on their goals for the community generally. At this point the staff communicates an important event in the community which affects all of the groups—a gang fight, let us say—which motivates the neighborhood association to try to get community support for a large program of youth work. They may decide to send representatives to the other groups to ask for cooperation, and each of these meetings is played for the entire group. The idea for a special community council to handle the problem may emerge, and the organizational meeting of that body is role-played.

Management programs often utilize the same idea in organizational terms. The participants receive background data on a particular company and are assigned roles within its various key departments. The problem presented may be the making of some important business decision or the difficulty of dealing with some far-reaching economic event of importance to the company's life.

Whatever the context, the mass role play is a useful device, but it presents a number of challenges to the staff using it. They must exercise considerable ingenuity and ability to make impromptu decisions about what are useful next steps. They must sense when it is desirable to call a halt at crucial points to initiate analytical discussion of what has happened. They must, above all, be skillful in handling the feelings of participants that are expressed spontaneously in a situation in which they are playing at being someone else and therefore feel safe. This type of prolonged role play develops a great amount of enthusiasm, but it also encourages the acting out of submerged hostilities which can set off chain reactions.

THE PURE WORKSHOP[6]

A comparatively recent learning format, the workshop has probably suffered the greatest dilution of its essential meaning of all educational forms, including the seminar. It is applied indiscriminately to any session at which participants have a chance to talk or at which they engage in any activity, to the despair of the pure workshop enthusiasts. The corruption of the term is unfortunate primarily because in its original form the workshop is potentially the most effective method ever devised for group learning. It provides an opportunity for the student to learn what he is interested in learning instead of what someone else conceives that he should learn; it compels him to make his own search for meaning in a climate which maximizes group support for his efforts.

One can use the workshop for groups up to 200, or as few as 40 or 50, and for periods of time ranging from several weeks to several months or throughout a year; a minimum of three weeks is often claimed to be desirable, but smaller amounts of time are not impracticable. Workshops are often residential, and it helps if they are, but non-residential patterns for local groups work very well. The two essential elements are these:

Participants work together in small groups.
What is worked on and how to go about the work is decided by those who participate.

A typical workshop begins with a group who have some kind of shared interest. This may be a common profession or occupation; the form was originally a tool for teacher training and the improvement of public school administration and is now often used by social agencies and other professional groups. But it is equally applicable to any group of people interested in a common goal or involved in a problem. Those who agree to attend become actively involved in planning the general structure of the workshop during a period which may be fairly lengthy. At the beginning of the sessions themselves, these general plans are transformed into specific organizational schemes, specifying the membership and general goals of the work groups. These small groups then meet to lay out the pattern of their work and to agree on objectives and schedules and on the division of labor. Workshop activities alternate between working in small groups and participating in general sessions, objectives for which are also determined through consultation between staff and participants.

Workshops may successfully be structured around a complex activity, a theme, or a problem. In the first instance, one finds such topics as "Teaching the Handicapped Child" or "Improving Communication in the Organization." Groups often select such themes as "Barriers to International Understanding" or "The Role of the School in Child Development." Or most successfully, perhaps, workshops select problems like "Improving Human Relations" or "Resolving Community Conflicts." Whatever its focus, the workshop staff must face and solve a number of uniform problems if the program is to be effective.

1. *Planning.* In some cases this function includes defining the area or problem to be dealt with. That is, one can start with a group and seek the topic; at other times, one begins with both a group and a

general content. In either case, it is useful for the staff to explore for some period the areas within the general topic which the group will wish to work, general problems of organization and staffing, common concerns which may serve as common threads, and other such questions. Some of this can be managed by questionnaire; a more effective additional device, if the group is sufficiently localized, is forming a representative committee to meet with the staff over a period of time. The staff of the workshop illustrated at the end of the chapter did not engage in preliminary planning but chose to allot a fair amount of time to it at the beginning. If one has enough time, this procedure will do.

2. *Orientation.* The workshop is an unsettling threat to the expectations most people have about formal learning situations. They will be expected to work together and to make for themselves those decisions usually made without even consulting them. One can hardly do too much to counter feelings of strangeness and insecurity which are bound to arise. A simple manual describing workshop procedure, sent to participants in advance, can be useful, but it must be supplemented by adequate orientation on the first day or two of the workshop. Occasional general sessions might well be devoted to reporting on and discussing problems which the workgroups encounter. Most useful is a very early general session devoted to the process of small-group decision-making and planning.

3. *Flexibility.* Workshop success depends on several varieties of flexibility. The setting must be one which permits people to move at will from large group to small group, to individual library study or field trip. The staff must accept as a condition of life the changeability of schedules and of the structure set by pre-planning. If evaluation processes have been built in, both staff and participants should be prepared to drop some activities and begin on another task. If the staff is close enough to the workgroups to know what is going on, they can take appropriate action to meet difficulties as they arise. There is danger, to be sure, of going too far; people do need some secure anchorage points and enough stability to get some work done. This is a question of art and depends ultimately on the skill of the staff, as most educational questions do.

4. *Communication.* With a number of small groups working on different aspects of the same area, one inevitably faces the issues of how much ought to be communicated to the total group. Workshops continuing over a period of three or more weeks often produce a

mimeographed bulletin at intervals to keep everyone informed of progress. General sessions consisting of brief group reports are useful, particularly at the early stages when several groups working on related problems might discover the need to cooperate with one another. Forming service committees whose memberships cut across work-group lines is the best general device for maintaining adequate communication. Commonly these committees consist of:

Planning or steering
General sessions
Social events
Evaluation
Publications

5. *Materials.* An important part of staff preparation is to make sure that materials are available. In many cases this means that access to libraries has been cleared and that, if possible, a small library of basic materials is provided in some central location. Depending on the problem around which the program is structured, participants may also wish to consult with experts in the field or take field trips to operating agencies. The staff might wish to make sure that these resources are available in advance and provide participants with that information.

These general suggestions constitute only the barest minimum of considerations which workshop planners must be aware of. Adult educators who wish to taste the delights and despairs of including the pure workshop among their programs are advised to consult any of the numerous detailed manuals in the field.[7] For those who are unfamiliar with the process, the best way to get a sense of how these principles look in action is to consider a specific program. The account which follows is a fairly typical academic workshop, not too difficult to translate into other contexts.

An Illustration[8]

Two hundred workshoppers were chatting noisily as they waited in the auditorium for the summer workshop to begin. They had come from as far west as California, from Texas and Oklahoma, from the southern, the mid-western, and the eastern seaboard states. All in all, thirty-six states and five foreign countries were represented in the group. Some school systems had sent teams of as many as seven or eight to work on a particular project. Many of the two hundred knew no one and were self-consciously aware of their aloneness. These sat aloof, wondering, "What is this workshop all about anyway? Wonder why my adviser recommended this for me!"

All of the two hundred were enrolled in an enterprise called Workshop in Educational Leadership. The workshoppers had registered under several different course numbers. They would receive eight graduate credits for six weeks of intensive work. The workshop was housed in one of the public schools of the city, since University lacked adequate facilities. The staff of fourteen was composed of university faculty members representing seven different departments. Also there were several visiting staff members, most of whom came from active duty in the public schools.

At nine o'clock Dr. Andrews, who was the coordinator of the workshop and chairman of the department of administration and supervision, started the workshop rolling. He greeted the members, asked workshoppers to identify themselves by states, introduced the staff, and then said a few words about the workshop way of learning. It was discovered that only thirty had had prior workshop experience. The rest were very hazy about what to expect. Dr. Andrews explained that in a workshop as large as this one ways must be found to develop a feeling of at-homeness within the total workshop as well as to give workshoppers the opportunity to have a continuous and intensive experience in a group small enough for optimum working conditions.

The general assemblies held each morning at nine, the sociability of the lunch hour, and the other social activities were considered to be threads binding together the workshop. The work groups and the committee activities were working experiences having continuity and intensity. In addition, each workshopper was encouraged to tap the resources of the staff through conferences, visitation among work groups, and informal visits.

Workshoppers had received either through the mail or at registration a handbook describing the workshop way of learning. Reference was made to this statement in the first general assembly. A tentative schedule of a typical workshop day from nine to three was discussed. Workshoppers found out that the day was divided roughly into the following time blocks:

9:00–10:00	General assembly of total workshop
10:00–12:00	Work groups
12:00– 1:00	Lunch and relaxation
1:00– 3:00	Committee meetings, laboratory experiences in audio-visual and arts and crafts, library study, and conferences with staff members

Some questions were raised in the assembly. Answers were brief, friendly, and direct. Then workshoppers were instructed to meet in three sections to become organized into work groups. The ninety-seven who had registered under an elementary department course number constituted one section and met with the staff members from that department. Twenty-one workshoppers who had registered under a secondary department course number constituted another section which automatically became a work group because of its small size. The remaining eighty-two had registered under an administration and supervision department course number and constituted the section in administration and supervision.

And so another University summer workshop in educational leadership was on its way. This was the fifth summer. Each year the enrollment had increased until the numbers seemed to deny the possibility of realizing all of the dividends of workshop experience. The staff had faced this problem and had decided that with careful planning, a good deal of informality and flexibility could be maintained.

Since the same process was followed in organizing the three sections into work groups, let's follow one section through the process. The eighty-two people in administration and supervision left the auditorium and met in a room not quite large enough. But all of them did manage to squeeze in. One of the staff members, Dr. Hayden, chaired the meeting. He indicated that four staff members were available to work with this section and he stated briefly some of the major competencies and specialized interests of these four. He further stated that since the work groups are the heart of a workshop the participants should consider carefully the problem areas they wished to investigate during the summer.

This much orientation stimulated a lively discussion about why individuals had come. The beginning of a problem census was under way. By noon, the group realized that they had only scratched the surface of possible problems and interests. Someone suggested a continuation of the sectional meeting, but in a larger room, for the next day. Since no larger room was to be had, the group decided to return to the crowded room to finish the organization into work groups.

The next morning the discussion reflected the thinking that had taken place overnight. Most of the eighty-two had chosen a problem area they wished to investigate. About twenty wished to study school-community relations. Another twenty-five had chosen the curriculum planning and in-service education area. Fifteen wanted to investigate school building problems, and the remainder chose to study the role of the principal.

After the content areas of the work groups were agreed upon, one member of the staff became primarily responsible as a resource person for each work group. All understood, however, that the four members of the staff assigned to this section would work together as a team, that each work group could call upon any one of the four staff members for help or upon other staff members in the workshop, and that at times the entire section or parts of it might want to merge for discussion of a common problem. The schedule of the four work groups during the *fourth* week of the workshop shows how this flexible plan was implemented:

	Group 1 *Community Relations*	Group 2 *Curriculum*	Group 3 *Buildings*	Group 4 *Principalship*
MONDAY	Meet with Group 3 to discuss public support for building program	Regular meeting	Meet with Group 1	Regular meeting

TUESDAY	Regular meeting	Regular meeting	Meet in audio-visual room to learn techniques for telling a story of need	Regular meeting
WEDNESDAY	All groups meet together in cafeteria to discuss Initiating Curriculum Change			
THURSDAY	Meet with Group 4	Regular meeting	Regular meeting	Meet with Group 1 to discuss tenure and public relations
FRIDAY	Regular meeting	Regular meeting	Regular meeting	Regular meeting

You will note that Groups 1 and 3 met only twice in regular work group sessions during the week whereas Group 2 met four times in regular work group sessions.

After the work groups were formed, each group had the task of surveying the scope of its problem and deciding upon ways of working. The group of fifteen who were studying school buildings decided they wanted to learn as much as possible about three phases of the area. They wanted to see good buildings, read about them, and talk with architects who had designed some modern elementary-school buildings. They wanted to devise ways of interpreting building needs to the people who pay for the buildings. They wanted to learn as much as possible about building requirements for a modern program of elementary education. They decided that with only fifteen in the group, they would work as one committee for the most part.

The work group on curriculum planning, on the other hand, formed four subcommittees and agreed to spend at least half of their time working in these smaller groups of five or six people. The four subcommittees were on in-service education of teachers, initiating curriculum change, evaluating the program of a school, and using community resources to enrich the school program.

Each of the other two sections of the workshop devised similar plans and organization, so that by the end of the third day most workshoppers had a problem to study and had membership in a small group.

Let's turn our attention to the second general session of the workshop. On the morning of the second day, the workshoppers had begun to understand the degree to which this workshop depended on their planning and on their converting plans into action. Many felt a sense of adventure and were ready to pick up the reins immediately. Others felt lost. Nothing in their education experience had prepared them for this type of endeavor. They felt incapable of accepting the chance given them and were painfully aware that they were expected to go ahead on their own. They were plagued with feelings of guilt because they couldn't.

The second general assembly helped the workshoppers to face this problem. One of the staff members, a person who had much experience with group processes, made a few remarks about ways of working together. She encouraged confidence and relaxation by pointing out how little we know about ways of working together and how great is our opportunity in a workshop to find better ways. Each member was encouraged to be a co-operating pioneer in this endeavor. Then the question was raised, "What committees are needed to serve the workshop?" At this point the workshoppers were asked to "buzz" for a few minutes about the committees which were needed with six or seven others sitting close enough so that heads could be put together. After a few minutes of buzzing, each group suggested one committee and stated in a few words the function of the committee as the buzz group had discussed it. In fifteen minutes the following committees had been suggested:

- Planning Committee
- General Sessions Committee
- Library Committee
- Audio-Visual Aids Committee
- Folk Dancing Committee
- Evaluation Committee
- Lunchroom and Social Committee
- Publications Committee
- Trips Committee
- Bulletin Boards and Exhibits Committee

Workshoppers were asked to think about which committee they would like to join, and a time was placed in Wednesday's schedule for all committees to meet. Each committee had the services of at least one staff member as a consultant. One function of the staff member was to amplify and clarify the responsibilities of the committees. Some additional discussion was needed to clearly define the work of the planning committee. Time was placed in the schedule for a planning committee meeting each Wednesday afternoon. Each work group and each committee was asked to send a representative who would bring the plans and suggestions of the body he represented. All staff members attended the meeting, at which all the plans for the coming week were coordinated into a weekly schedule. *Providing enough structure to give unity and enough flexibility to allow for creativity was one of the toughest jobs in the workshop.*

From this description we see that by the end of the third day of the workshop the basic organization had been accomplished. Committees for special functions and short-lived groups sprang up as the need arose, but the permanent groups were formed and had begun operating. This came about by breaking the large group into smaller groups step by step, with a resulting common interest and manageable size, and by recognizing the need of the workshop for both unity and diversity and then step by step working out ways to achieve them.

Perhaps you are asking: "How were arrangements made for this workshop?" The summer workshops of University are the result of months of planning among departments in the School of Education. The Workshop in Educational Leadership is sponsored and conducted by three or more departments including Administration, Elementary Education, and Secondary Education. Each October the coordinator begins to plan budget and personnel needs with other departments. The budget which may be spent for instructional costs is limited to 75 per cent of the tuition paid by workshoppers. A maximum enrollment is decided upon and plans are made in terms of this number. Thus for a workshop of two hundred, carrying eight points of credit at $20 per point, the budget would be 75 per cent of $32,000, or approximately $24,000. This budget covers instructional costs, rental of building, and equipment and supplies.

The university assigns to the workshop one basic staff member for every twenty students. The staff must also include specialists in arts and crafts and audio-visual materials, a librarian, perhaps a person with a music specialty. All staff members are expected to be skilled in the use of workshop techniques and methods.

NOTES

1. Many of these innovations arise from attempts to make conferences and other such large planning and action meetings more effective. Although this area of activity is often considered to be part of adult education, I choose to view it as supporting rather than central to the educational function. Many national associations, for example, in addition to carrying out some educational activities, must solve problems of internal organization or decide on general policy in meetings and need help to make these gatherings more effective. I have attempted to keep this book focused on primary educational objectives and thus omit this area from consideration. There is a useful literature available on it, however; see, for example, the following issues of *Adult Leadership:* "Initiating Social Action," Vol. I, No. 9 (February, 1953); "The Group in the Community," Vol. I, No. 5 (October, 1952); and "Conferences That Work," Vol. II, No. 1 (May, 1953).

2. Henry Lipman, Assistant Director of Liberal Arts in Extension of New York University, coordinated the program and acted as moderator for all the Round Table discussions. This account is adapted from his report of the program, which he has graciously permitted me to use here. I have taken the liberty of dropping his use of the word "workshop" in the title of the program to keep the categories used in this chapter clear. See Note No. 6, below.

3. For more detailed descriptions of these methods, see the issues of *Adult Leadership* cited above, particularly Vol. II, No. 1 (May, 1953); also see Vol. I, No. 7 (December, 1952).

4. For more detail, see Leland P. Bradford, "Are There Any Questions?" and Bonaro W. Overstreet, "Speaking of Speakers," both in *Adult Leadership,* Vol. I, No. 3 (July–August, 1952).

5. The general method originated in the famous summer programs of the National Training Laboratory at Bethel, Maine. As I have suggested in previous notes, the quarrel about group dynamics within adult education is an unfortunate one, and those who disagree with what group dynamics stands for often direct their criticisms to the effusions of former participants in training groups rather than to the large body of research and the careful theorizing of the professionals. In part, the issue in the field is one of differing objectives: group dynamics, as a body of method, is interested primarily in directly changing role behavior, which is one of the most important aims in adult education, though not the only one. Few educators would claim, in the face of the evidence, that changes in fundamental attitude orientations or behavior can be brought about through traditional methods. The evidence is overwhelming that improvement in interpersonal skills requires methods which powerfully involve the participant. That such methods demand, on the part of the trainer, highly specialized skill and psychological knowledge, is difficult to deny and forms the basis for my judgment, expressed previously, that the methods of group dynamics are not likely soon to take a substantial position in adult education. Indeed, the one justified criticism of the field seems to me to be that enthusiastic but untrained people have often committed atrocities in its name.

There is a considerable and often technical body of literature on the pure human-relations workshop method, of which the example in the text is a modification; the interested reader might well begin with the National Training Laboratories pamphlet edited by Leland Bradford, *Group Development,* which is available from the National Education Association, and also look at Bradford, Gordon, and Lippitt, "Human Relations Training in Three Days," *Adult Leadership,* Vol. IV, No. 10 (April, 1956).

6. There are occasional cries of outrage at the degradation of the term; see, for example, P. R. Klohr, "So You're Having a Workshop," *New York State Education,* Vol. XXXVII (June, 1950).

7. The basic reference for the workshop form is still Earl Kelley's *The Workshop Way of Learning* (New York: Harper, 1951). Most theoretical and descriptive writing in this field is in the specific area of teacher in-service training, but the principles can be adapted to other areas easily enough. Bibliographies are easy to find, and the pamphlet cited below has a good annotated one.

8. The illustration is taken with permission from *The Workshop Handbook,* by Walter Anderson *et al.* (New York: Bureau of Publications, Teachers College, 1953). For a somewhat less rigorous view of workshop technique, from the specifically adult orientation, see the issue of *Adult Leadership* for January, 1956, Vol. IV, No. 7.

9

• • • • • • • • • • • • • • • • • • •

LARGE GROUPS: USING TELEVISION AND THE MASS MEDIA

> A film camera may be used indifferently to record the *Cruiser Potemkin,* an obscenity for exhibition at stag parties, a Hopalong Cassidy western, and *Henry V*. A television transmitter does not distinguish among the electronic patterns destined to materialize into the images of, say, Milton Berle, Bishop Sheen, Warren Hull, and Alistair Cooke. Distinctions of this sort are wholly a human function.
>
> MARTIN MALONEY

All mass media are, in a sense, educational, just as all stimuli to which we respond teach us by minutely reinforcing or modifying our notions about the world, our convictions, and our attitudes. As we skim the grocery ads in the paper, we make tiny adjustments in our sense of the current standard of living, or noting briefly the furniture pages, our taste for a new style may, by small increments, be brought closer to some new taste norm. The repeated stereotypes of television drama teach the current definitions of good guys and bad buys, the acceptable relationships between persons; the subtle choice of adjectives by news commentators reinforces established convictions or chips away at them.

The failure of the mass media to influence people in very specific ways, as in the fact, for example, that predominantly Republican newspapers are read daily by a predominantly Democratic public, should not be permitted to obscure the extraordinary general influence of the mass media on norms which are less securely anchored to salient group relationships. But the major channels of mass communication are far beyond the reach of conscious educational purposes and are likely to remain so in American society.

A small sector of the commercially-based mass media of radio and television does devote itself directly to programming which, on one level or another, is educational. A minor but significant aspect of this programming is carried on by FM radio stations in a number of large metropolitan areas and in a scatter of university towns throughout the country. The staple ingredient of these broadcasts is, of course, classical music, and the rise of such stations has coincided with the spectacular growth in the long-playing recording industry. Saturating the frequency-modulated air with first-rate music, and adding broadcasts of recordings of drama from Shakespeare to Ionescu, does not, in itself, constitute education, but it provides an exceedingly important element in the total educational effort directed toward raising the level of esthetic response in the society.

For as Margaret Mead pointed out some years ago, studies of education in a series of primitive cultures show that values and behaviors emphasized in education do not persist if the broader adult culture does not itself provide avenues for their expression.[1] The children of the Manus, unburdened by care or discipline, are happy and gay during childhood, but as soon as they achieve adult status, they become hostile unsmiling adults. American schools stress the virtues of honesty, independence, and cooperativeness, and send their students into a world where success often depends on quite opposing values. Little Manus grow to become adult Manus, and little Americans like big Americans. The application to FM is clear; only if music and drama are widely and easily available in the society generally are we likely to succeed at getting people interested in them and responsive to them at higher levels. The day's schedule of broadcasting, reproduced here in part, of Chicago's WFMT, is typical of stations like it across the country.

From *WFMT PERSPECTIVE,* Vol. 11, No. 5 (May, 1962).

Friday / 18

# indicates stereo

6:00 EARLY MORNING PROGRAM

8:30 NEWSCAST

HAYDN Sonata in G for Clavier—Wanda Landowska, hc. Fr RCA LM-6073 (2).

ALBINONI Sonata in A for Strings, Op. 2, #3 (arr. Giazotto)—Virtuosi di Roma; Renato Fasano, cond. Fr Ang 45019.

9:00 #BLOCH Concerto Grosso #1 for String Orchestra with Piano Obbligato—Eastman-Rochester Sym Orch; Howard Hanson, cond. Fr Mer SR-90223.

#DEBUSSY Sonata (#3) in g for Violin and Piano—Berl Senofsky, v; Gary Graffman, p. Fr RCA LSC-2488.

#FAURE Songs: "Aurore," Op. 30, #1, "Soir," Op. 83, #2; "Le Parfum impérissable," Op. 86, #1; "Le Don silencieux," Op. 92; "Le Secret," Op. 23, #3, "Fleur jetée," Op. 39, #2—Gerard Souzay, br; Dalton Baldwin, p. Fr Epic BC-1122.

#CHABRIER "Marche Joyeuse" for Orchestra—Philharmonia Orch; Herbert von Karajan, cond. Fr Ang S-35926.

10:00 THE STUDS TERKEL "WAX MUSEUM"

. . .*

12:00 NEWSCAST

#PUCCINI Excerpts from "Turandot"—Birgit Nilsson, s (Turandot); Jussi Bjoerling, t (Calaf); Renata Tebaldi, s (Liu); Giorgio Tozzi, b (Timur); supporting cast; Rome Opera House Cho, Orch; Erich Leinsdorf, cond. RCA LSC-2539.

1:00 BBC PRESENTS: SHAKESPEARE's play "TWELFTH NIGHT," adapted for radio by Peter Dews, with Dorothy Tutin (Viola); Geraldine McEwan (Olivia); The Shakespeare Memorial Theatre Company.

3:15 NEWSCAST (later than usual)

. . .

5:00 #POULENC "Gloria" in G for Soprano, Chorus, and Orchestra—Rosanna Carteri, s; French-National Radio-Television Cho, Orch; Georges Pretre, cond. Fr Ang S-35953.

. . .

8:00 #THE FINE ARTS QUARTET (Leonard Sorkin, Abram Loft, violins; Irving Ilmer, viola; George Sopkin, 'cello) IN A LIVE BROADCAST CONCERT, IN STEREO—HAYDN: Quartet in G, Op. 77, #1 ("Lobkowitz" #1); WOLF: "Italian Serenade" in G; MENDELSSOHN: Quartet #4 in e, Op. 44, #2.

9:15 BERTRAND RUSSELL delivering his Nobel Prize acceptance speech, "Human Nature and Politics." Audio Archives LPA-1202.

Today is Lord Russell's 90th birthday. For the next few days

*. . . indicates author's omissions. WFMT broadcasts uninterruptedly.

we will be broadcasting recordings featuring Lord Russell and his thoughts on a number of subjects.

10:00 NEWSCAST
"THE ART OF BRUNO WALTER"—
#BEETHOVEN Symphony #3 in Eb, Op. 55 ("Eroica")—Orch cond by Bruno Walter. Col MS-6036.

. . .

11:15 #BERNSTEIN "Jeremiah" Symphony—New York Phil; Leonard Bernstein, cond; Jennie Tourel, ms. Fr Col MS-6303.
#COPLAND Piano Fantasy—William Masselos, p. Fr Col MS-6168.

12:15 #SPIRITUALS sung by Marian Anderson, Contralto, with Franz Rupp, Piano—"Heavn'n, Heavn'n"; "Oh Peter, Go Ring dem Bells"; "Trampin"; "Hard Trials." FR RCA LSC-2592.

As the schedule shows, a minor portion of programming is devoted to more direct educational efforts in the area of social problems; sometimes this is done through lecture, often through the presentation of panels exploring an issue. Such programs are paralled by commercial television in various press sessions and panel shows and, at their best, in the developing television documentary, some of which are superb. Are these programs educational? To attempt to answer that question is to explore the problem of the adult educator's role in the mass media, and to suggest, by implication, some definition of his relation to educational TV as well.

One can set aside as a special case the various branches of journalism which seriously devote themselves to informing and enlightening the public: the magazine article writers, the popularizers, the political commentators, not because they are unimportant but because there is no role confusion between these people and adult educators. When an astute observer of American politics such as Theodore White publishes a brilliant account of a presidential campaign, there is little doubt that he has had an influence on the political understanding of the large group of people who have read it.[2] But Mr. White remains a political journalist, a part of a large press corps which controls, at an extraordinary number of levels, a flow of information and interpretation to the various publics in the society. Here, if we would admit it, the bulk of real adult education takes place: the business economist writing in the *Wall Street Journal* and the labor economist's piece in the *AFL-CIO News*, each applying the same analytical tools to the explanation of policy which suits the interests of his particular public; the psychologists who deluge newspapers and magazines with advice on raising children and keeping marriages together; the feature writers who invade slum and brothel and mental institutions to expose and recommend reform. Seldom does this river of print reach the remarkable objectivity and thoughtfulness that White's *The Making of the President* exhibits, but good or bad it constitutes the major penetration into the class- and group-segregated worlds of a pluralistic society, either directly or through indirect influence on opinion leaders.

But though adult educators see themselves as removed from this journalistic stream, they take a much more direct interest in film, radio, and television: in educational films, in early efforts to control educational radio, and in more recent and more successful attempts to establish educational television. It is in these fields that one feels the need for some role definition, for, as the educator tries to become film-maker and script-writer, he often not only produces some fearsomely bad results but relinquishes those objectives which truly distinguish his role.

It is easier to see this difficulty in film, perhaps, than in the other media. The serious film-maker is primarily interested, first, in the expressive use of his particular medium and, second, in making some significant personal statement about his material. In *Prater Violet*,[3] Bergmann, the film director, says to his new writer,

> I shall proceed to corrupt you. I shall teach you everything from the beginning. . . . Do you know what the film is? Bergmann cupped his hands, lovingly, as if around an exquisite flower. The film is an infernal machine. Once it is ignited and set in motion, it revolves with an enormous dynamism. It cannot pause. It cannot apologize. It cannot retract anything. It cannot wait for you to understand it. It cannot explain itself. It simply ripens to its inevitable explosion. This explosion we have to prepare, like anarchists, with the utmost ingenuity and malice.

If one looks at the really powerful documentaries, often used in educational programs, one sees what this means. One of the great American films, *The City*, uses the resources of its medium to great effect to argue eloquently for a new kind of community. It would have been a poor film, instead of the masterpiece it is, if it had stopped to debate the issues involved. That is why the "teaching film," ground out in quantity as a kind of visual textbook, is usually so dreary, as it wavers between being a film and being a teacher and ends by not being very satisfactorily either.

Ultimately, the film-maker is primarily interested in his subject and his medium, and the educator in what is happening to individuals, in what kind of growth is taking place in them. The case of the television documentary is in many respects similar to the film. The television program on the migrant worker produced by Murrow and Friendly is a striking piece of work, a grim, compassionate, angry study of a forgotten group of Americans.[4] It is effective because the producers are masters of their medium and because they wanted to move people to action on a problem which profoundly touched them.

The professional educator has his own complicated craft to master, and it is primarily focused on concerns quite different from the crafts developed to exploit the potentialities of the mass media. The answer to the question of how the educator ought to relate himself to a medium such as non-commercial television, then, is two-fold. First, we should exert every possible effort to encourage the development and training of those whose talents lie in the crafts of television and who are interested in the use of the medium for serious statement. As educational television increases in importance, there is a chance that we can make it a haven for people with considerable talent who would rather do something which interests them than desiccate in the vast wasteland of commercial TV. That this is not a misty goal is indicated by a recent review by *TIME* of two programs distributed by the National Educational Television and Radio Center (NET) and produced and directed by Denis Mitchell. *TIME* commented, ". . . natural, intimate, replete with insight—the kind of thing that television is uniquely equipped to do but which is seldom attempted and almost never so artfully achieved. At the end, viewers might have thought that they had just finished reading two brilliant novels."[5]

Even if we leave general programming to others, as an area beyond the scope of method appropriate to the adult educator, there is a second television field which fits squarely within adult education methodology. We can define that field by two basic criteria: the objective of the activity is some well-defined change in the individual viewer, instead of an interest in the theme or subject; and there is some opportunity for feedback from the viewer which modifies the pattern of one-directional flow of communication typical of the mass media in its true sense. Although it is hardly likely that we have yet developed the real potentialities of television within the bounds of those criteria, the two major lines of exploration thus far in which we have made technical advances of some interest are the use of television to multiply the effect of the single teacher and the development of communication nets within a community, using television as a flexible servant of the educational process rather than its determinant.

THE TV CLASSROOM

A significant proportion of adult education is carried on in formal classrooms at either the high-school or college level; if we could, without decreasing effectiveness, greatly expand the audience for our teachers, instead of bringing people in for a weekly meeting or sending the instructor out on the road, we would have a very potent instrument indeed for our work. A considerable amount of the activity of university TV stations of televised instruction parallels the growth of closed-circuit TV for resident undergraduates in many of the same universities. Unfortunately, with only a few exceptions, there has been little attempt at rigorous assessment of the effectiveness of TV teaching beamed to scattered adult audiences, most of such experimental work having been done with youngsters in closed-circuit conditions. The major exception, and an exciting one it is, is the excellently designed study of the Chicago TV College, which the following section will discuss in some detail. But a brief look, first, at the general findings of an extraordinary mass of experiments on closed-circuit television can be rewarding.

Some of the most interesting presentations of teachers have been on the commercial networks, but we have very little information about their effectiveness. Watching the superb showmanship of Leonard Bernstein on his famous *Omnibus* programs or his more recent Philharmonic broadcasts for children, it is easy to see his impact on the motivation of his audiences toward more varied experience with music. Beyond motivation, there was the possibility for real insight in, for example, his demonstration of the differences between drama and opera by having actors go through a scene without music and following it immediately with the actual scene from the opera. But Mr. Bernstein is not only a brilliant musician and an exceptionally magnetic person; he is in command of resources which permit him to wave his hand casually and summon up anything from a full symphony orchestra of the first rank to a jazz sextet composed of dazzlingly talented musicians to illustrate some point in his exposition.

Not quite as unreal in considering the resources of education are the "master teachers" for whom the commercial channels have on occasion made room. Perhaps the first of these to achieve national prominence was Frank Baxter, the Shakespearean scholar, followed by the great successes of the Continental Classroom programs, the most recent being that of Peter Odegard on American government. All of these men have been university scholars of great reputation, carefully selected for their winning personalities as well as for their vast erudition. They fit the generalized American image of the great teacher and the popular conception of what learning is.

It is interesting, and a little dismaying, that the university conception of learning is little more sophisticated than the popular one; if we look at what is carried by the closed circuits to full-time students within the university, we are likely to find bush-league Bernsteins and Baxters. The large body of evidence on the effect of this teaching is not only interesting but instructive.[6]

Does it make any difference whether the teacher is televised or live? The overwhelming answer of experiment after experiment is that it does not matter a bit. The statistician's formula of "no significant difference" is the verdict in so many of the studies which contrast the results of a televised class and a live class taught by the same instructor that the refrain gets boring. The ability of the students appears to have no effect on the results, nor does their attitude toward TV. Students who declare a preference for the conventional classroom situation perform as well in a TV course as their fellows who prefer the television setting. Although most of the studies concentrate on measures of achievement involving retention of information, the results are the same if one is interested in problem-solving ability in the particular field or in the ability to synthesize or apply information. Student attitudes *do* vary: acceptance is high at the grade school and adult level; mixed, but generally negative, at the high-school and college levels.

These are encouraging findings for television, if we are satisfied with the present level of teaching, at any rate. The sacred ratio of one teacher to thirty students, and the educational economics based on it, seem rather pointless. The findings, on the other hand, are most unsettling to our notions about conventional teaching. The convictions held by many teachers of the importance of their rapport with their classes, the great value placed on interaction with the master, and the opportunity to ask questions whenever the student wishes appear to be part of a great mythology when one gets tough-minded about it.

The results do *not* mean, of course, that there are no differences among teachers. Even a difference in attitude toward using TV may relate to differences in teaching effectiveness in the medium. This is not a clear-cut distinction, by any means; one could argue that those teachers who distrust the camera may well be lacking in the kind of flamboyance or love of drama which often distinguishes the most effective conventional teacher in the first place. Indeed, as one examines the researchers' definition of the ideal television teacher, one is reminded of the disconsolate remark by Ruth, in *My Sister Eileen,* as she reads the legend on the free sample of breakfast food: "delicious with strawberries and cream," declares the manufacturer, to which Ruth asks, "What isn't?" The television teacher should be proficient and enthusiastic, warm and outgoing, an eager talker but not a compulsive one, adaptable and flexible. We could use more of that kind in the classroom, too.

Shouldn't the unlimited ability of TV to blend special visual aids into the exposition make it more effective than the conventional classroom? It should, but surprisingly it does not. A group of experimenters at New York University presented a TV lecture with no frills at all, a "bare bones" presentation, and the same lecture supported by maps, graphs, models, film clips, and the like. No difference in achievement resulted from the full production; what difference there was favored the simpler, a finding which is supported by other similar experiments. Moreover, the students preferred the full-production lectures to the "bare bones" presentations and were sure that they learned more from them, evidence for an already very-well-documented truth that subjective judgments of students about their learning are highly unreliable.

The neutral impact of visual aids is puzzling and leads one to speculate that their exposure was perhaps too brief to serve their intended purpose. Or, more probably, students need an opportunity to work through relationships on such things as graphs by themselves for the aids to have maximum effectiveness.

How about discussion sessions after the TV presentation—do they increase achievement? The evidence is somewhat mixed, but fairly straightforward even so. The Pennsylvania State University experiments found that there was no difference in recall gains between groups provided with a discussion period and those who were not. But where the discussions were concerned with practice in related problem-solving and were supervised by section instructors, the discussion groups resulted in significant gains. Studies at New York University indicate that discussion sessions make a difference, but their effectiveness depends to a large degree on who the section leader is; furthermore, an important variable in determining his effectiveness is his attitude toward TV. The section instructor is "the Achilles' heel of televised instruction." [7]

The central tendency of these findings on instructional TV is fairly clear and very illuminating. So long as the dominant characteristic of college instruction is a one-way flow of communication from the teacher to the student, and the major objective is to have the student recall information and concepts sampled from that flow, the live presence of the instructor is not crucial. With modern techniques of storing images and sound on tape, there is no compelling reason why we cannot allow most university teachers to retire to their desks in the library and spend all their time on research, which they would rather do anyway.

For, returning again to the dominant theme of this book, what the instructor does is not a prime determinant of learning; the real question is what the learner does. As Carpenter puts it, after his series of investigations at Pennsylvania State University, "We begin to wonder if teachers have usurped from students their responsibilities for learning. Perhaps in our anxiety to teach well, we fail to make students aware of their prime responsibility in the learning process."[8] This is not to say, of course, that students enjoy this responsibility; many of them, both youngsters and adults, are dismayed and fearful in response to the demand that they engage in the search for meaning themselves.

We must distinguish, furthermore, between the kind of teaching which TV can do just as well and that for which the medium is totally inappropriate. A description of two very different teaching styles may make this clear:

1. Instructor One is an economist with an engaging easiness of manner, who likes to teach and is very confident of his teaching ability. He fits very well the ideal of the television teacher which the experts constructed and which is quoted previously. He is, in fact, a first-rate teacher of the conventional type. Here he is, teaching a session devoted to explaining the basic flow of goods and money to a group of adults. He constructs on the board a diagram showing the various relationships in the form of payments and expenditures between the producer and the consumer, defining each one slowly and carefully, using homely illustrations, stopping at intervals to make sure that the group has understood each step. Then he draws lines connecting both consumers and producers to the banking system and

points out how savings and loans create another circular eddy relating to the main flow and how by manipulating interest charges one can bring about changes in production and employment in the main stream. Finally, he diagrams the relation of the government to the whole system, indicating how government expenditure and taxes influence each of the separate free flows. Now he is ready to explore the operational meaning of events such as government deficit, how it affects the economy as a whole, and the policy questions involved in it.

The group has followed him raptly, asks interested questions, has learned a certain amount of basic vocabulary, and is probably better able than before to follow a newspaper or magazine discussion of economic policy as debated in Congress, although they will be inclined to accept their instructor's view as the correct one, since they have not themselves been forced to defend the view against others who disagree with it. In general, it is a faultless piece of exposition, and there is no particular reason why it cannot be just as effective on TV tape.

2. Instructor Two is a young legal scholar conducting several sessions on the problem of civil rights with the same group. He is witty and sardonic and has the manner of the classic prosecuting attorney. The class has received in advance a two-page mimeographed document which summarizes the first ten and the Fourteenth Amendments to the Constitution and presents briefly the case of an Arkansas law requiring teachers to list all of the organizations to which they belong. The intent of the legislation is ostensibly to give the state superintendent of education data on whether teachers are spending too much of their time in community activities; it also, clearly, will expose those teachers who are members of the NAACP to possible retaliation.

The instructor proceeded by selecting one student after another and addressing a series of questions to him, questions which asked first for a judgment, then forced the student to justify it under unmerciful grilling. Often the student would find that, unable to find justification which he himself could see as reasonable, he would have to reverse his original opinion. On the Arkansas case: Would you judge the law to be constitutional? Why not? Should the court begin with the presumption that it *is* constitutional, unless the teachers can prove otherwise, or presume that it is not? Why? Substantive due process means that the law does not violate due process if some reasonable man might judge that the goals of the state would be served by the procedure imposed by the law; do you think this law violates due process, then? Really? Then, anyone would have to be insane to think that such a listing of organizations is a legitimate way of getting administrative information?

The group was composed of union officials, and he turned next to union civil rights. Should a union be permitted to make a member declare his opinions? Should they be able to expel members for holding certain opinions? What about the case of a union member who is working for a state right-to-work law, which unions consider dangerous to them? Oh, if he votes for such a law, okay, but if he actively campaigns for it, get rid of him? Does it make any difference if the man cannot get a job in his trade if the union expels him? You don't think so? Do you think the *government* should be permitted to throw people out of the country if they have odd political beliefs? Oh, only if there is clear or present danger of revolution. Then you think that the unions can demand more discipline than the nation can? Why? And so on.

At the end of three hours the class had a considerably heightened respect for the complexity of the issues involved in civil rights questions and some understanding of the dilemma of preserving individual rights within the framework of organizational effectiveness, but they would have found it difficult to determine what position the instructor himself took on civil rights. Here, where the learner did all the work, television presentation would be totally inappropriate.

Clearly, although such extreme teaching styles as that of the instructor just described cannot be transferred to television, it is a reasonable hypothesis that we might make the medium even more effective than it is if we could utilize student response as an integral part of the telecast. Experiments at the University of Pittsburgh demonstrate that it can be done, at least for junior high school children. One method particularly appropriate for television, where the end result can be stored for re-use, involves airing a lesson to a sample studio audience, giving a quiz, and revising the lesson on the basis of the test results. Revised versions of science lessons produced significant improvements ranging from 6 to 26 percent. Another experiment, applicable to a wide range of situations, provided the students with teaching-machine devices which they used during the televised lesson to answer questions posed by the lecturer or to complete statements made by him. These, too, resulted in clear and significant achievement gains.[9]

The most reasonable answer to the question of student involvement in learning activities, however, lies in designing appropriate activities to supplement the telecast, and the most impressive evidence for the correctness of that answer lies in the remarkable success of the Chicago Junior College television experiment. The study included adults as well as college-age youngsters and is worth close examination by all adult educators.

Chicago's TV College[10]

In 1956, the Chicago Board of Education decided to experiment with presenting a complete junior-college curriculum on open-circuit television as a supplement to its regular junior-college activity located at centers throughout the city. The first three experimental years were financed by a grant from the Ford Foundation, and at the end of that time the program was so unreservedly successful that the Board voted to continue it on its own. During those first three years the average semester enrollment for credit was 1,261 persons, who registered for an average of almost 2 courses per person. The average enrollment of non-credit students per semester was 3,550, who took a total of 5,251 courses, or about one and a half each. The audience of individuals who did not register, but who tuned in to courses, averaged from 5,000 to 35,000 at any telecourse broadcast.

The median age of the students was in the low thirties, and two-thirds of them were women. Many were mothers of teen-age children and expected soon to go back to work, probably as teachers. The TV students were subjected to the same entrance requirements as regular students and were required to do approximately the same outside work and take the same examinations. They mailed in assignments, were permitted to call instructors by phone during specified hours, and could arrange face-to-face conferences if they wished.

Fortunately, the program financing included sufficient funds for an intensive and rigorous evaluation which compared the achievement at various times of the TV-at-home group with conventional day courses, with day courses which used some TV, and with conventional evening courses. The evaluation staff also studied such matters as retention and attitude toward the experience. Here are some of the major findings:

1. About two-thirds of the credit students finish the course they began, a surprisingly high proportion compared to ordinary adult drop-out rates. Moreover, the retention rate was higher in courses where interaction between students and teacher was increased or where the student had many opportunities to practice and test himself. Thus, Fundamentals of Music 111 used lesson-by-lesson mailing and return of assignments. Its instructor supervised the graders, sampling the papers to discover in which areas students were having difficulties, and devoted attention to those problems in subsequent broadcasts. The retention in that course was 73 percent.

2. Most students who took television courses at home said they liked them very much and would want to take more such courses. Experimentally-composed groups of regular day students who were provided with what were essentially TV lecture–discussion section courses liked them less well. Faculty acceptance grew with each year of the program and is clearly related to the degree of involvement in the telecourses.

3. Most previous studies comparing adult classes with regular day classes in the same institution report little difference in the mean level of achievement of the two groups and usually a somewhat greater dispersion among the adult classes—a disproportionate number of both higher and lower achievers. Evaluation studies during the first year of the experiment tended to confirm these earlier studies:

Comparing English, Social Science, Psychology, Shorthand: home TV vs. regular classroom, no significant difference.

Comparing home TV vs. evening class, in English and Physical Science: no significant difference.

Comparing home TV vs. regular classroom in Humanities, Biology, Physical Science: higher achievement in the TV group.

But in the third year, the picture is quite different, as is evident in the table reproduced on the opposite page. Such an overwhelming superiority of achievement results for the home-TV students is unlikely to represent any random variation in course type. Nor is the difference merely one of information recall. Many of the measures were of skill learning: the ability to write well, to speak well, to keep books, and so forth. In courses like Mathematics, ability to solve problems was measured. In the social sciences, a special study was done of improvement in critical ability, one of the most troublesome of educational objectives.

Some of this difference of achievement in favor of the home-TV student may possibly be due to motivation. No one would argue that the average junior-college youngster is anywhere near as highly motivated as a mature person in the thirties, particularly one with a well-defined goal, which many of the adult viewers had. No doubt motivation played an important role in the differences. But the TV group out-performed the evening classes during the third-year study, and evening groups are likely to have many adults in them. Furthermore, if motivation were overwhelmingly important, why was it not more critically significant in the first year?

1958–1959

Course:	*The Research Compared:*	*Result:*
Social Science 102	Home TV vs. Classroom	No significant difference
Social Science 102	Home TV vs. TV-in-Class	*More learning from TV-at-home*
Physical Science 101	Home TV vs. Classroom (North Side Center)	*More learning from classroom*
Physical Science 101	Home TV vs. Classroom (South Side Center)	No significant difference
Psychology 207	Home TV vs. Evening Class	*More learning from TV*
Psychology 207	Home TV vs. Classroom	No significant difference
Psychology 207	Home TV vs. Combined Day & Evening Classrooms	*More learning from TV*
Mathematics 103	Home TV vs. Evening Class	*More learning from TV*
Speech 141	Home TV vs. Classroom	*More learning from TV*
Speech 141	Home TV vs. Evening Class	*More learning from TV*
Humanities 201	TV-in-Class vs. Classroom	No significant difference
Humanities 202	TV-in-Class vs. Classroom	*More learning from classroom*

The answer probably lies in the intensive program of teacher orientation and training which we might expect would take a period of several years to become effective. Even the orientation procedures provided teachers with more opportunity for self-examination than they are accustomed to:

Preparation and presentation of a five-minute segment of course material, selected by the teacher, for closed-circuit kinescope recording.
Self-evaluation of the kinescope and critique discussion with the producer.

Preparation and presentation of an additional ten-minute segment, followed by further critique.

Presentation of a full lesson on closed circuit to give instructor an opportunity to learn about pacing, and to provide him with a general background for the work of outlining telecasts.

Of greater importance is the fact that the teacher was given a period of eight weeks, full-time, to prepare his course, during which he had considerable help in working through the problems involved. The report of the experiment fortunately provides us with a detailed picture of what went into that preparation:[11]

During the preparation period—the equivalent of eight weeks of full-time work—the television teachers had to meet a series of deadlines to insure adequate preparation of the course outline, of the teleclass study guide, and of lesson plans before broadcast time. The first deadline was for a statement of four or five main course objectives with a paragraph expanding the meaning of each objective. Explicit and concrete statements of course objectives were needed as a guide for selecting and organizing learning experiences, including assignments, and for devising means of evaluating student progress.

In the preparation of these statements of objectives, one of the great values of TV College to the City Junior College as a whole became apparent. Under the usual conditions of a full-time teaching load, a teacher seldom has time to make an explicit formulation of objectives for a course. The course tends to develop as he teaches it, following a vague outline of implicit objectives and often taking part of its shape from available textbooks and materials. Even multi-section courses developed by committees of teachers often evolve similarly, representing the results of collective past practice rather than the results of extensive theoretical planning. Also, since college teachers are usually content specialists, both by training and by interest, their courses tend to develop around organizing principles related to specific elements of content rather than around principles derived from broader behavioral goals.

But a teacher selected to prepare a TV College course was free to spend all of his efforts for eight weeks in thinking out a single course. For most of the teachers this was the first time in their careers that they had had such an opportunity. In addition, they had the counsel and assistance of the curriculum expert on the staff of TV College, a person who was trained in the principles of formulating objectives and selecting and organizing learning experiences and whose interest in behavioral goals of instruction perfectly balanced the teachers' content biases. Many TV teachers felt that the opportunity given them by TV College in planning and presenting a single course was of inestimable value in their subsequent classroom teaching. Many teachers who had not been directly involved in TV courses felt that they, too, benefited from the work that their television colleagues had done.

With time and expert assistance available to them, the television teachers developed considerable skill in formulating statements of objectives.

Early drafts of such statements often were too content-oriented, as in a mere listing of content-unit headings, too limited in behavioral type, tending usually to be the type involving recall of information, too much in terms of what the instructor was going to do rather than in terms of the behavioral changes desired in the student, and too general to have the same specific meanings for different instructors. But by the time of the deadline for these statements, the teachers were able to formulate objectives in terms of behavioral changes as well as content elements and in terms of attitudes, appreciations, and abilities as well as knowledge or recall of information. Many teachers became aware of the importance of critical thinking as a major objective. In addition, the teachers were able to qualify these statements in terms specific enough to indicate appropriate procedures to section teachers and control-class teachers and to aid the TV teacher himself in selecting and organizing learning experiences and in constructing pre-test, mid-term, and final examination exercises.

The second deadline that the television teacher had to meet in the preparation of his course was for the outline of telecast topics, the selection of textbooks and other student materials, and the selection of published materials and audio-visual aids to be used in the broadcast lessons. The outline and booklist were to be included in the promotional folder which was to be mailed several weeks before the opening of the broadcasts. Also, publishers had to be contacted to ascertain the availability of supplies to satisfy the expected demand. Cooperating bookstores had to be advised of adoptions of books, equipment, and materials so that they could stock their shelves before registration. And copyright holders had to be contacted to secure permission for use of published books, articles, films, and audio-visual aids which were to be used on a broadcast. Royalties had to be arranged when necessary.

The third deadline was for the preparation of a plan for assignments, conferences, examinations, and telephone conference hours. The television medium was relatively inefficient for communicating information relating to assignments, examinations, and the like. It was found far more effective to include all of this information in a bulletin distributed to credit students at the time of registration. This required advance planning to complete preparation and printing prior to registration. Circulating drafts of these bulletins to all persons involved, including the TV teachers, was an effective means of discovering desirable modifications and serious errors.

The fourth deadline was for the development of research designs and appropriate instruments to be used in controlled experiments. A basic plan was decided upon with the guidance of the coordinator of research, and pretests or questionnaires were constructed to be used in matching or checking the equivalence of control and experimental groups.

The fifth and final deadline was for the preparation of the teleclass study guide. Every student was provided with a study guide from thirty to a hundred pages in length. From the inception of TV college, the study guide was regarded as a means of integrating the televised instruction, the textbook, and the collateral readings and assignments into unified learning experiences for the TV student. Most of the guides followed a similar format, which included the following:

1. An orientation to effective learning via television.
2. A statement of objectives for the course.
3. An outline of the course.
4. A list of required readings, collateral readings, and other reference materials.
5. Sample test items and progress tests to acquaint the student with the type of examination to be used.
6. Clear statements of assignments and due dates.
7. Extracts of important readings which might be out of print or difficult for students to obtain.
8. A list of community agences where related information was available.
9. Workbook materials, which were sometimes used as mail-in assignments.
10. Evaluation or reaction forms.
11. Coupons for convenient purchase of allied learning materials or subscriptions for related periodicals or magazines. (In some instances, special offers were arranged with publishers.)
12. Charts, forms, or diagrams useful as bases for TV lessons in providing common material for the teacher and the student. (Notable examples of such materials were those distributed in the TV accounting and music courses.)

After the completion of the study guide, the instructor started to prepare the first ten or twelve telecasts. Several weeks before the first telecast, he began intensive work with his producer. About a week before the first telecast, he had a dress rehearsal of this telecast. All preparations for this rehearsal simulated the actual broadcast, but the signal was monitored only in a closed circuit within the studios. This gave the teacher, the producer, the director, and other personnel an opportunity to work together and to make suggestions for improving the studio situation and the presentation of the first lesson.

The major lesson of this report hardly needs to be underlined. From the demand at the start that the teacher specify his objectives in terms of desired student behaviors to the preparation of study guides which helped the student see what he must do, the emphasis was on what the student does in order to learn. The instructors teaching the control classes agreed to take over the objectives of the TV teacher and used the materials he developed; if they had been forced to work them through on their own, it is interesting to speculate on the possibility that the marked differences in achievement might not have resulted. At any rate, the TV College experience has much to say to all adult educators interested in methodology, whether or not they are specifically interested in the television medium.

TELEVISION AS AN INSTRUMENT OF INFORMAL ADULT EDUCATION

A large proportion of adult education activities proceed outside the classroom format. The first section of this chapter suggests that television's contribution to that sector lies primarily in the hands of the skilled writer and cameraman who have something to say about the human condition. Some recent imaginative work by adult educators indicates that there is an important role for educators to play as well, if we begin to explore the potentialities of the television medium.

Social critics of the mass media like to point out that they have added to the alienation of modern life, the individual feelings of lack of connection with and power over the forces which shape his life and his problems. But the very medium which perhaps most creates a sense of isolation can be made to serve the function that some social observers call "disalienation," a restoring of integration with the individual's social world, particularly in the cities where isolation and segregation are most extreme.

The most interesting example of this use of television in an organized adult education program is Washington University's Metroplex Assembly. It serves as a methodological model for experimentation with TV which ought to be going on at a much faster rate than at present it is. The Civic Education Center of the university conceives the Assembly as "a continuing inquiry by the people of St. Louis into the nature, the special problems and opportunities of modern urban life." The educational function of the staff is to organize the inquiry and find ways of making it educationally effective, and it utilizes television as a major instrument.

As an illustration, the 1962 Metroplex Assembly focused on the problem of housing and urban renewal and broadcast a series of Monday night programs over KETC, the educational channel. The programs included: a review of urban renewal projects in the area since World War II; an assessment of how well conservation, rehabilitation, and demolition have worked as tools of renewal; a study of the problem of relocation; a look at public housing as an answer to the problem of relocation; an examination of the issues of neighborhood design and how redevelopment affects neighboring municipalities; a general assessment of the impact of St. Louis' renewal program on the people it has affected.[12]

Each of the six programs, built around film and interviews with the people most directly involved in the problems, was broadcast in two phases. The first phase consisted of a half-hour program, from 8:00 P.M. to 8:30 P.M. During the next hour, participants, at Viewing Posts throughout the city, discussed the issues in small groups and telephoned questions arising out of the discussion into the station. During the second phase of the broadcast, from 9:30 P.M. to 10:00 P.M., these questions were discussed by a group of specialists, who had been present during the initial phase, in a broadcast back to the Viewing Posts.

The key element, clearly, is the organization of the small groups at the Viewing Posts, which included two to three thousand persons in several hundred groups. They were formed by the recruiting efforts of the Civic Education Center Staff, each of whom was assigned a specific population target—labor, neighborhood organizations, university alumni, and so on, in an attempt to sample all economic levels, all communities, and a variety of occupational, ethnic, religious, and racial groups. The recruiting was carried on by inviting organizations to co-sponsor the program and to assist in locating specific individuals who would assume the responsibility for establishing Viewing Posts. The methods and resources utilized in the general program are perhaps best revealed by the handbook prepared for those Viewing Post organizers, excerpts from which follow:

YOUR JOB AS HOST

As a host, you are one of a growing number of men and women who are establishing VIEWING POSTS for the METROPLEX ASSEMBLY. Your leadership in establishing a VIEWING POST will enable hundreds of other men and women of the St. Louis area to participate in the METROPLEX ASSEMBLY. Through your Post, the men and women of the area will be able to talk with each other, to question civic leaders and officials of public and private organizations, and to search for solutions to the problems that baffle the communities of this Metropolitan area as they do every other large urban area.

The purpose of these *Suggestions* is to help you get the greatest satisfaction from bringing together a group of men and women to talk about the important issues that will constitute the agenda for the METROPLEX ASSEMBLY and to enjoy each other's company. In addition to these *Suggestions,* the Civic Education Center of Washington University is ready at all times to give you any additional assistance you need.

Have you asked yourself, "What do I need to do to be a successful host to a VIEWING POST?" The answer to this is simple. Above all, you need to believe in the value of this kind of activity—bringing people together for a stimulating and profitable discussion. You need to believe that the issues presented to the METROPLEX ASSEMBLY are worthy of study and discussion, and that better solutions will be found for civic problems if the people are informed and interested in them. If you believe these things, you can be a very successful host at a VIEWING POST.

These *Suggestions* will answer most of the questions you may have about procedures and will refer you to additional services available to you and your group. You do *not* need previous experience in group discussion to be a successful host. You do *not* have to be an authority on any of the topics discussed. You *do* need to plan carefully for the development of your group; you *do* need to give this activity enough time so that important arrangements are completed.

As a host, your job is not to do everything yourself, but *to see that all necessary arrangements are made*. That is, you help the group come together, decide on its responsibilities and distribute them among its members. To help you in this work, you will have the services of a CIVIC EDUCATION REPRESENTATIVE (CER) from Washington University. If you need help at any time, your CER is there for that purpose. More information about the CER and other services are provided later in these *Suggestions*.

SERVICES FOR YOUR VIEWING POST

In addition to the help which your CIVIC EDUCATION REPRESENTATIVE is prepared to give you, the following services are available to help your group have the best possible experience.

Weekly Report and Discussion Guide. Each week—ahead of the discussion—you'll receive through the mail a roundup of interesting activities of other VIEWING POSTS, any necessary announcements, and a short guide for the use of the discussion leader for the next program.

Metro Poll. With the weekly mailing will come a supply of ballots for your VIEWING POST, one for each member. Each member should fill out his own ballot; they should not be signed. Return these Metro Poll Ballots in the self-addressed envelope which will be enclosed with each weekly mailing. The returns will be tabulated, along with those from other VIEWING POSTS, and forwarded to the appropriate public and private agencies.

Fact Sheet. THE CIVIC EDUCATION CENTER has prepared a FACT SHEET on each of the issues for the first series of the METROPLEX ASSEMBLY. You should try to see that each member of your group has a set of these *Fact Sheets*. It will improve the discussion very much. The *Fact Sheets* contain a brief summary of important information AND HELPFUL questions. A full set of seven *Fact Sheets* for the fall METROPLEX SERIES sells for $2. You can obtain them from your CIVIC EDUCATION REPRESENTATIVE or, call METROPLEX HEADQUARTERS, PA 6–3220.

Metropolitan Development Guide. For the past year, a group of outstanding authorities on different aspects of metropolitan development has been working with the Metropolitan Plan Association in preparing a comprehensive analysis of the major issues of the Metropolitan area. Through special arrangements with the Metropolitan Plan Association, METRO-

PLEX Headquarters is able to offer you a copy of this guide for the modest sum of $2. You may obtain copies from your CIVIC EDUCATION REPRESENTATIVE, or call METROPLEX Headquarters—PArkview 6–3220.

ESTABLISHING THE VIEWING POST

The Size of the Group

Experience has shown that groups meeting in homes will be most successful if they contain about 12 or 14 persons; if the group membership drops below eight, there may be too few persons for a successful discussion. Most living rooms cannot easily accommodate more than a dozen persons comfortably and side conversations tend to develop in large groups. However, full attendance on any one evening is unlikely because something is almost certain to prevent one or more members from attending. You can safely invite up to 16 persons without fear that the group will become too large.

Pick a group of people who will enjoy each other's company! Think over the people you know in your neighborhood, your church, your club, your place of work, and ask a group of people who you think will enjoy getting together.

What to Say to Potential Members

Of course you'll want to give them the facts about the METROPLEX ASSEMBLY. If possible, hand each person you ask a copy of the printed brochure on the Assembly; it will answer many of their questions.

Explain to interested persons that a VIEWING POST is a discussion group, that being in a METROPLEX group constitutes a new, exciting way for people to share ideas and reactions to important questions facing the people at the present time.

Call the attention of the people you invite to the 'talk-back' feature of the ASSEMBLY that will give each VIEWING POST an opportunity to present its views to the rest of the area.

Tell prospective members about the METROPLEX POLL—each person's opportunity to record privately his opinions on key questions. The BALLOTS will be tabulated and forwarded to appropriate agencies and also the results will be announced at the end of the Series.

Where to Meet

Living rooms in homes are fine places to meet. However, any room that is comfortable and quiet will be adequate as a meeting place. Club rooms in churches and faculty rooms in schools may be other good meeting places. If you meet in homes, plan on *rotating* meeting places among the homes of members unless you are willing to make your home available for all meetings.

Pace the Discussion

You need to pace the discussion so that it fits in between the two televised parts of the METROPLEX ASSEMBLY. You have one hour between 8:30 P.M. (when the first program ends) and 9:30 P.M. (when the second program—the VIEWING POST "TALK-BACK" begins.) Be sure to allow time in that period to formulate a question you want to present to the panel and to telephone it in. Please telephone the questions in *no later than 9:15* P.M. Your weekly discussion guide will contain detailed suggestions on procedure.

Agree beforehand how late the group will continue and then stop. You may want to continue meeting informally, but have a definite stopping time so that people can make arrangements to be back home and feel comfortable about leaving.

Selecting Leaders for the Meeting After the First One

After the first meeting, it will usually be worthwhile to pass the leadership around among group members. The question is, how can this best be done?

Here's a suggestion: During the first meeting or two, watch carefully to see which members seem most comfortable with the whole idea of group discussion and which members listen most carefully to the ideas of other persons and are most objective in their reactions to other people. After a meeting or two, approach one of these persons and ask him to try leading a meeting. In two or three weeks, it will be apparent how many people the group contains who can and will enjoy leading the discussion. If you have any problems, talk them over with your CIVIC EDUCATION REPRESENTATIVE.

ABOUT THE DISCUSSION

Discussion is a skill that people learn as they learn any other skill. It improves with practice. You will be pleased to discover how rapidly group members become skilled in the process and how much it increases their enjoyment of the activity. Your CER can help the group if you run into any particular problems. A separate short list of "Do's and Don'ts" for discussion is enclosed. Hand it on to whoever leads the discussion each week. If you want another copy, ask your CER.

From time to time, the sponsors of the program will conduct special discussion clinics at which specific difficulties that occur in carrying on discussion will be analyzed and worked out. Watch for announcements of these meetings.

VIEWING POST 'TALK-BACK'

The VIEWING POSTS will have an opportunity to 'talk back' every Tuesday evening from 9:30–10:00.

The 'talk-back' period has been established to give you and the other people at your VIEWING POST an opportunity to ask questions of a panel of people with special knowledge of the subject presented that evening. It's also an opportunity to present your views to the television audience and to hear views expressed by the other VIEWING POSTS.

Here's How to Participate in the 'Talk-back' Period

Telephone your question in to the studios of KETC. Special operators will be on hand to take your questions down and pass them on to the MODERATOR of the ASSEMBLY. Phone your questions in *before* 9:15 P.M. It won't always be possible to answer every question on the program, but the panel will do its best.

In this program adult educators may find a pattern for an important use of television in education in a variety of ways and for a range of problems. The growth of educational TV stations and the recent decision of Congress to require the technical changes in television sets necessary to permit reception of ultra-high frequency channels provide a challenge which will require the utmost ingenuity to meet. One can hope that Metroplex Assembly represents only a pioneer effort for the great deal of experimentation which must come in the future.

NOTES

1. Margaret Mead, *Growing Up in New Guinea* (New York: Morrow, 1930).

2. Theodore White, *The Making of the President 1960* (New York: Atheneum, 1961).

3. Christopher Isherwood, *Prater Violet* (New York: Random House, 1945), pp. 30–31.

4. *Harvest of Shame,* produced by CBS Television, Edward R. Murrow, narrator. Available from McGraw-Hill Text Films.

5. *TIME,* June 29, 1962.

6. *College Teaching by Television,* edited by John C. Adams, C. R. Carpenter, and Dorothy R. Smith (Washington: American Council on Education, 1958), reports a conference in which researchers and educators exchanged findings based on a good deal of experience. See also *Educational Television, The Next Ten Years,* a report of Stanford's Institute for Communications Research, published by the Institute in 1962. For the story of the development of educational television, see John Walker Powell's report, *Channels of Learning* (Washington, Public Affairs Press, 1962).

7. Adams, *op. cit.*

8. *Ibid.*

9. G. L. Gropper and Arthur A. Lumsdaine, *The Use of Student Response to Improve Televised Instruction: An Overview* (Pittsburgh: American Institute for Research, 1961).

10. Clifford Erickson and Hyman Chausow, *Chicago's TV College* (Chicago: Chicago City Junior College, 1960).

11. *Ibid.,* p. 19–22. Reprinted by permission of the City of Chicago Board of Education.

12. Eugene Johnson is responsible for the planning and operating of the Metroplex Assembly. The material quoted from the handbook for Viewing Post leaders is part of a variety of materials prepared by his staff. For further information or materials, write to the Metroplex Assembly, Washington University, St. Louis, Missouri.

10

MEASURING THE EFFECTIVENESS OF METHOD

In most social areas . . . we are still lacking objective standards of achievement. This has two severe effects: (1) People responsible for social management are frequently deprived of their legitimate desire for reconnaissance on a realistic basis. Under these circumstances, satisfaction or dissatisfaction with achievement becomes mainly a question of temperament. (2) In a field that lacks objective standards of achievement, no learning can take place. If we cannot judge whether an action has led forward or backward, if we have no criteria for evaluating the relation between effort and achievement, there is nothing to prevent us from coming to the wrong conclusions and encouraging the wrong work habits. Realistic fact-finding and evaluation is a prerequisite for any learning.

KURT LEWIN, "Group Decision and Social Change," *Readings in Social Psychology*

The demands of the evaluation process are often most clearly revealed in the conversations which attend the planning of a program, particularly if there is some need for assessing its effectiveness. The following conversation illustrates what often goes on; it assumes that an adult division plans to present an experimental program in public affairs education and that the administrator in charge has asked an acquaintance who is expert in educational evaluation to meet with him and with the political scientist responsible for the program curriculum.

ADMINISTRATOR: We're going to finance the program ourselves this year and probably take a loss, but if we can prove that it's successful, a local foundation might be interested in putting up some funds for us to run it every election year. So it's important that we have some convincing evidence that it was effective. Professor G. and I, consequently, are eager to do the best evaluation job we can.

EVALUATOR: I'll be pleased to be of any help that I can. I notice that you have the brochure already printed and that the program is scheduled to run on alternate Saturdays for about five months. Why don't you give me some idea of what you plan to do with that time?

POLITICAL SCIENTIST: I recommended that pattern, instead of the usual once-a-week evening session, because I think it's hard to cover the material you really need to in a brief couple of hours. Scheduling it on Saturday will permit us to run a morning session, break for lunch, and then come back for another period in the early afternoon. Each meeting will be devoted to a different problem the community faces: urban renewal, tax rates, schools, traffic, and so on. In the morning, I will present the data on the local aspect of the problem and then relate it to the national picture. In the afternoon, we'll bring in two or three people from the local community who have varying points of view on what ought to be done about the issue, let them present their views on a panel, and then I'll sum up.

ADMINISTRATOR: The group certainly ought to be able to vote more intelligently next fall after this much exposure to the major issues.

EVALUATOR: I see. It sounds like a very stimulating program. You obviously are interested ultimately in affecting voting behavior in some way, but tell me how you think the program will bring that ultimate objective about?

POLITICAL SCIENTIST: Why, it will give the students a much broader knowledge of the issues.

EVALUATOR: To be sure, but could you give me a little clearer idea of what you mean by "knowledge"? Do you mean more information about the issues, or better understanding, or what?

POLITICAL SCIENTIST: All of those things, of course. Young man, don't you know what *knowledge* means?

ADMINISTRATOR (hastily): We want to give them everything they need to come to intelligent decisions at the polls.

EVALUATOR: I understand, but does that mean that the program will be successful if the students vote a certain way? I assume that isn't your purpose. But it is crucial, if you want to evaluate your success, to decide what it is precisely that your end result should be; otherwise we would have no way of knowing what to measure. Now, it is clear that the local Democratic Club will evaluate its own efforts by how many of the people they have been in contact with go to the polls and vote the Democratic ticket, and the same goes for the Republican and Liberal parties. This is a nice, simple evaluation yardstick, but it is not an educational one. What I need to know, in order to be helpful, is what behavior of your students *you* are interested in affecting. As the program now stands, it seems to me that it assumes that if people have information about various solutions to local problems, they will be able to make intelligent choices among them.

POLITICAL SCIENTIST: That would be making a large assumption, indeed. No, in the morning sessions I will be giving them some basic principles which I would hope they will be able to apply in analyzing the arguments of each of the candidates.

EVALUATOR: Your objectives are becoming a little clearer, now. Would I be correct in saying, then, that your primary interest is in improving the political decision-making skills of the participants in the program, and that at least one part of that skill you consider to be the ability to analyze arguments and apply principles to specific instances?

POLITICAL SCIENTIST: That's right.

EVALUATOR: Let me go one step further. We would agree, I think, that it is possible for two reasonable men to come to different political decisions after analyzing the issue involved, and I assume that you are not primarily interested in having your students come to *your* conclusions.

POLITICAL SCIENTIST: Well, my political opinions are, of course, the only right ones, but I'll concede that they're not the only reasonable ones. Let's grant that if you start out with different basic values from the ones I hold, you could reasonably come to different, and valid, conclusions. What's important is that the students become conscious of the values they apply to political decisions or that they realize the values implicit in political positions which they are judging. That's the real problem.

EVALUATOR: This is very helpful, I think. We're beginning to get a fairly concrete idea of what it is that you want your students to be able to *do* when faced with a political decision. Do you think that we could work out a fairly systematic statement of these specific decision-making behaviors which you intend to influence?

POLITICAL SCIENTIST: Sure, given the time. There's been a lot of recent work by the political behavior boys which has a bearing on it—it would be interesting to see what would come out if we tried to construct a model of rational political decision-making.

ADMINISTRATOR: Well, that's interesting, all right, but how could you measure it?

EVALUATOR: It wouldn't be too difficult to work out a test to get at it. Even if we knew how they *vote,* come election day, it wouldn't tell us the important thing, which is *how* they came to that decision. But we could construct a test which would force them to make decisions about particular choice situations in a way that would reveal what principles they brought to bear on them, how conscious they were of values involved, and so on.

ADMINISTRATOR: But you know how adults hate to take tests; they get very anxious about them. In the past we've found it very useful to give them some kind of form on which they can express their reactions to the program—how they liked the lectures and discussions, how much they think they've learned, you know.

EVALUATOR: I know, but what can we learn from such an evaluation except that we have either pleased or displeased the student?

ADMINISTRATOR: Well, if you've ever tried to run an institution that depends for its existence on pleasing the clientele, you'd know how important it is.

EVALUATOR: Of course, I realize that, and I am not arguing against getting some evidence of student acceptance, if you wish. I would raise the question, though, of what this kind of evidence tells you about what they have *learned*. Learning implies some change in behavior, in this case, decision-making behavior in the political realm; and I would not find acceptable evidence for that change which depends on subjective perception, nor do I think an alert foundation would. I really don't think you have to worry about adult student reactions to taking a test—if it's an interesting test, and if the reason for their taking it is made clear, I've found that you get very little resistance.

ADMINISTRATOR: Well, okay, but we'd have to work it out carefully in advance. I'll think about it.

EVALUATOR: Of course. Now, there's another issue I'd like to raise before we go any further. It would be all very well for Professor G. to work out a test of political decision-making behavior to see whether the students really change the level of the skills which the professor thinks important —the question is whether we could expect such a change as a result of the program now planned.

POLITICAL SCIENTIST: Why not? In the morning sessions they'll be getting from me the important analytical elements that have to be applied and in the afternoons will be exposed to the important arguments on a particular issue. They'll have an opportunity to discuss all this, of course.

EVALUATOR: What kind of discussion do you propose having?

POLITICAL SCIENTIST: Well, they'll have the opportunity whenever they like of asking questions, addressed either to me or to the panelists. We'll probably even get into some hot arguments—I like to encourage controversy.

EVALUATOR: But would you expect someone to learn to swim better by watching you swim? They'll have a good chance to watch you practice the skills you're interested in improving in them, but will there be any opportunity for them to practice? I'm afraid that I don't see that they will.

POLITICAL SCIENTIST: Well, it's a little late in the day for me to change the way I teach. I'm the expert, and they're not, and I don't see any reason why they shouldn't learn by listening to me.

EVALUATOR: I suspect that if you assessed your graduate-school experience, though, you would agree that you learned most not from listening to your professors but from working through problems in the science on your own, wouldn't you say?

POLITICAL SCIENTIST: Perhaps, but these aren't graduate students.

EVALUATOR: But let's take a look at the decision-making behavior you want to influence in your students. I agree that it's useful for them to hear from you what principles should be applied and what data are valid in political problems, and to watch you modeling the decision-making behavior which you think is relevant. Perhaps we can also work out some activities for them, to give them a chance to practice the skills they are to learn. . . .

Perhaps it is best to draw a kindly veil over the remainder of the conversation. Depending on the skill of the evaluator, the background of the administrator, and the truculence of the instructor, such conferences can provide the groundwork for a really useful evaluation program or can end in a disastrous draw. It illustrates the major themes of the evaluation process, however, which can now be generalized from the specific context.

Evaluation is a process of assessing the extent to which some activity has succeeded in what we intended it to do. It is a vital step in the rational management of all social enterprise. A military commander who orders the destruction of a particular enemy point and does not follow the attack with some form of reconnaissance to obtain evidence for the degree of success or failure of the mission would foolishly endanger his men later.

But in many social enterprises, as Lewin points out, there is a remarkable failure to spend energy on reconnaissance of results, a generally confident assumption that because we are doing what seems to be the most reasonable thing to do we are achieving our purposes. As a result, much of our institutional life is devoted to routine activities, the consequences of which are seldom assessed, a state of things particularly true of those agencies whose purposes are not sharp and specific. A business enterprise which fails to maintain a certain profit level soon goes under; its evaluation is built in. But a social agency devoted to improving the climate of race relations in the society might go on forever, existing on the assumption that it must be doing some good.

By the nature of its structure and clientele, adult education has lagged behind other more formal educational institutions in accepting the need for evaluating its efforts. The imaginary conversation above indicates some of the reasons:

1. Administrators often confuse educational purposes with what are essentially goals of institutional survival. Typically, evaluation in adult education consists of asking the student whether he liked the program, a result which may or may not bear some relation to learning. Voluntary attendance at many programs creates further difficulties, as administrators assume that testing of any kind will alienate

students. But despite commonly expressed fears of "being evaluated," most people have even stronger desires to know how well they have done when they make an effort at achievement, and our fears of measuring progress deprive them of the opportunity of knowing where they are, as well as failing to provide us with data on the success of our own institutional goals.

2. Because adult education enterprises consistently employ leadership which is either untrained or imported from other institutional settings, we often confront the problem of dealing with conflicting or ambiguous purposes. If program objectives are left at a high level of abstraction, everyone can subscribe heartily to them and go on to do what he likes. As soon as we raise the question of *specific* purposes, we inevitably reveal differences of opinion which require considerable discussion to resolve, often a painful and time-consuming process to which people involved in adult programs are unaccustomed. Since any evaluation effort insists, first of all, on statements of specific and measurable objectives, it can be easily blamed for stirring up trouble in a previously serene situation.

3. Above the level of motor-skill training, adult programs exhibit such a variety of purposes, and often such complicated ones, that finding ways of measuring progress demands more technical resources than we often have available. At the elementary level, teachers not only pursue easily recognizable skills but have available an enormous pool of reliable instruments for measuring small gains in the mastery of those skills. The colleges, so long as they are content with transmitting the data and concepts of the recognized disciplines, can use any number of existing tests to measure achievement; if the college teacher is interested in improvement of such cognitive skills as problem-solving or judgment in his discipline, he can find tests for these as well. But a vast number of adult programs are constructed to meet such specific needs that they require especially-tailored measures of achievement.

4. In adult education our purpose in carrying on evaluation is somewhat different from that of most formally organized education. From elementary school through college, institutions are primarily interested in placing the individual on a scale of achievement to determine whether or not he measures up to some outside standard; can the child read as well as the average of his peers? Can the adolescent write an acceptable English sentence? Does this student demonstrate that he understands the fundamentals of economic analysis? Adult

programs, accepting a very wide range in ability and motivation, are more interested in growth as a result of specific effort, though individual rates of growth may be very different. The program, not the student, is on trial. It is particularly important, on this assumption, for program planners and teachers to apply the results of evaluation to improve the program. This inevitably means that teachers must be prepared to examine their methods and curriculum structure and be willing to experiment with new ones when the results of evaluation indicate the need.

Despite these special problems, adult educators are showing increased interest in careful and technically adequate evaluation procedures, partly due to the influx of foundation funds for experimental programs with its accompanying demand for measured results, partly as a result of the increase in the field of highly-trained professionals acquainted with the basic evaluation processes.

THE EVALUATION PROCESS

If we ask, "How well is this program of ours succeeding in helping people to learn what we intend they *should* learn?" the scope of program evaluation obviously goes far beyond the problem of measuring individual achievement; we need to know what goes into the program in the first place and what kinds of changes to make in it if it is not successful in helping students. The general process may be imagined as a circular one, involving three major elements which are so closely related that it is often difficult to work with any one of them separately; thus:[1]

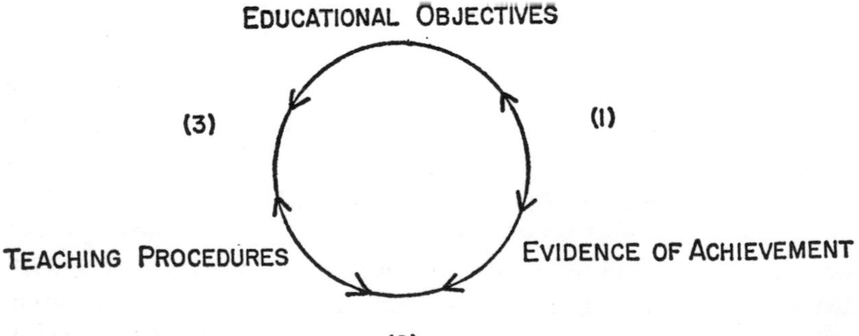

The major tasks which emerge from the relationship (1) between the objectives of the program and any attempt to gather evidence about how well we are succeeding in achieving the objectives are:

Defining the objectives clearly enough and specifically enough to indicate what devices can validly be used to measure their achievement.
Specifying the content aspect of the objective by indicating the areas in which the behavior we are interested in is to be practiced—"judgment" in politics, or in interpersonal relations, or in the arts, etc.
Developing valid ways of getting evidence that such behavioral changes in the students have actually occurred.

The major tasks which emerge from the relationship (2) between educational objectives and the teaching procedures which the instructor uses are those of discovering and developing those procedures most likely to change the students' behavior in the direction of the objectives which we have decided on.

The major tasks which emerge from the relationship (3) between teaching procedures and the educational objectives are:

Studying alternative teaching procedures to determine their relative effectiveness in helping students achieve the objectives.
Suggesting changes in teaching procedures to make them more effective than those currently in use.
Reassessing the reality of the objectives themselves and perhaps revising them in the light of the total process.

It should be clear from this formulation that evaluation and the teaching processes are inextricable and that, in talking about evaluating programs, we are merely shifting attention to a separate dimension of the teaching-learning process which has been the major theme of the book. A review of the early foundation chapters would be useful for the reader at this point, because they provide the background for the following development of the evaluation process.

Defining Objectives

How we state educational objectives largely determines our subsequent activity, whether the activity itself is directed toward setting up a series of situations for learning or toward developing means for gathering evidence of learning achievement. If the program planner has paid attention to the processes elaborated by the earlier chapters, the job of evaluation is relatively simple; we know what kinds of behavior the program aims to change, and we know it at a level of specificity which permits us to look for ways of measuring the changes in the participants.

Any educational aim, moreover, is embedded in a field determined by two separate dimensions:

Behavior: What should the student be able to do, or do better, as the result of the program? Recall more information? Apply concepts to concrete situations? Solve problems more efficiently? Make judgments more rationally?

Context: In what life areas, or fields of knowledge, do we want the behavior to be effective? We may possibly improve the act of judgment, for example, as a general activity of the person, but we are more likely to succeed in helping him improve *political* judgment, or *esthetic* judgment, at least at our present level of knowledge of the learning process.

In the illustration which began this chapter, the professor of political science had only a general aim of helping students become better voters. As the discussion proceeded, both of the major dimensions became more specific. The primary context was local politics, and the behavior he hoped to improve was the ability of the student to evaluate local candidates critically and come to more rational judgments of political merit. Obviously, one cannot restrict the program entirely to the local scene, as local politics often dramatically relate to the national picture and the international as well; but we know at least where to place the major emphasis. Similarly, one cannot make reasonable judgments without a great deal of information on crucial issues in the town, and the student must have an opportunity to acquire that information; but the program's major aim is not that he retain information but that he improve his ability to analyze and evaluate it in order to make judgments about the positions of local politicians. Thus, in testing, we will be more interested in gathering evidence for our major behavioral aim than in finding out whether the student has a great deal of specific information.

Gathering Evidence of Behavior Change

The evaluation process thus far parallels the program-planning process, but at this point, when we have adequately specified the program objectives, the two diverge. The programmer and teacher face the problem of helping the student become aware of the behavior models toward which he is expected to change, providing him with appropriate situations in which to practice the behavior, and ensuring that the practice is undertaken under conditions of proper reinforcement (see Chapter II). The evaluator must deal with some crucial problems of measuring behavior of widely different types. Fortunately, the behavioral sciences in general, engaged as they are in the primary task of measuring and recording all aspects of human behavior, have at least systematized the problems involved and have set some basic criteria for the adequacy of the measurement.

RELIABILITY. Whatever method we choose to gather evidence of the particular behavior we are interested in, an important concern must be whether our measure is reliable, that is, whether our measuring instrument provides an adequate and consistent measure. Take, for example, a simple kind of behavior; suppose we are interested in measuring how physically active a group of people are, to provide evidence, say, for some possible connection between activity and future heart disease. A direct measure of body activity is obviously the most reliable; if we could implant a mechanism under the skin, attached to the major muscles, which would broadcast continuous signals to a recording instrument, we would get a good measure of the intensity and duration of all muscular movements and be able to represent the general activity level of the individual. Such a measurement is probably at this point technically feasible, but we would have to persuade the subjects to submit to an operation, and the whole procedure would be enormously costly and only justified if precise results were exceedingly important.

At the next level, we might assign an observer to each of our subjects and instruct him to note as completely as he can each action of the person. To make his task simpler, we might provide him with a checklist of all common human activities and permit him to check items instead of writing them. The measure of activity we would get is likely to be not quite as accurate; there are, after all, some activities which people insist on carrying on privately, but it probably would give us an excellent approximation. But this procedure is not only also excessively expensive but somewhat impractical. The field of child study has recently taken to doing elaborate observations of child behavior over periods of days, but the procedure is unlikely to work as well with adults.

We might give our subjects a complex record form and ask them to record what they have done each hour of the day. As willing as they might be to cooperate, some will forget to make records for a time, while others will compulsively put everything down, and we are at a loss to know how to compare individuals within the group. If we send an interviewer around every day to gather information about the person's activities during the previous 24-hour period, subjects will have forgotten a good deal or will leave out things they think are unimportant or that they do not wish to reveal. Now, if at an even greater distance from the actual behavior, we ask the person during the course of an interview: "How active are you ordinarily—very active, fairly active, or not very active at all?" the reply might very well be worthless; in addition to the memory factor, we do not even know what the particular individual will use as criteria for such classification, what kinds of behavior he regards as "active," and so on.

The most convenient measures of behavior, consequently, are usually the least reliable. If one of the aims of our program is to increase the level and range of reading done by the participants, asking them what they have read is likely to be unreliable; they know what you wish them to reply, and the common human desire for approval may bias the answer. A paper-and-pencil test of problem-solving or judgment may provide evidence that the person has improved on the verbal level but gives no guarantee that he will do any better under pressure of the life situation. On the other hand, a person who has acquired some doubt about a formerly firmly-held value may be unwilling to voice his uncertainty in a group of his peers but might privately express the changed attitude on paper or to an interviewer.

The general problem for the evaluator is to sample the behavior he is interested in at a level as close as possible to the actual behavior and to take account of the influence of the measuring instrument itself. The requirements imposed by convenience and cost often dictate the use of a paper-and-pencil test, but these can be made much more reliable than they often are by raising the suggested issues of bias. Furthermore, adult educators, because they are usually uninterested in the question of individual certification, can use much more expensive ways of gathering evidence on a small sample of program participants; it is not necessary to test the achievement of every individual if we are interested primarily in finding out whether the program itself was successful.

VALIDITY. Difficult as the problems of reliability are, they are matched by issues raised by the requirement, in any instrument measuring behavior, that we measure what we are interested in and not some other behavior. A good example, from a field close to adult education, is the effort to get adequate measures of prejudice. Prejudice is not a definable behavior in the sense that "physical activity" in the previous illustration is; it is a *construct*, an invented concept which requires us to classify behavior according to some pre-determined scheme. Some people regard as prejudiced the telling of jokes about minority groups, others do not; on the scientific level, how one measures prejudice depends on whether one thinks of it as a feeling state of the individual, a predisposition toward certain kinds of overt behavior, or a dimension of the total personality. A group of eminent psychologists theorized that prejudice is one expression of an "authoritarian personality," a general tendency to view the world in rigid blacks and whites, an intolerance of ambiguity. The instrument they used to measure this personality, however, employed political items in such a way that right-wing political beliefs related to authoritarianism. Arguing that closed-mindedness, as a personality characteristic, may be found on the political left as well as the right, another investigator developed a measure which removed the influence of the specific political belief; it is, consequently, a more valid measure, measuring a "purer" form of authoritariansm.[2]

In the education of adults we often find ourselves gathering evidence which is not a valid indicator of program success. The most common example is our citation of enrollment, or holding power, as evidence of a successful learning experience. That a thousand people came to a series of lectures, returning each time, is evidence of their interest but not of their having learned anything. Participants in a program designed to increase sophistication of response to art objects may visit museums more frequently or buy more recordings and prints, but these behaviors are not necessarily indicators that they see or hear any better than they did before the program. That a person now has command over the basic concepts of economic analysis is no guarantee that he can apply them rationally to the understanding of some particular economic event.

Such examples can be multiplied indefinitely. The requirement of validity further emphasizes the need to specify as concretely as we can the objectives of the program; the more specifically we can frame them, the less likely are we to measure behavior irrelevant to the question of whether the program has succeeded in helping participants achieve the objectives.

OBJECTIVITY. Whatever measures of behavior we employ, a

further requirement is what we protect them as much as possible from personal bias. The emphasis in educational testing circles on the development of multiple-choice items is at least partly a response to this need; objectively evaluating a free response is a difficult job. To a considerable degree this is a technical matter, and the illustrations at the end of this chapter suggest ways of overcoming subjectivity in the construction of test items. It is sufficient here to raise the general caution and to suggest that one must critically survey any evaluation plan with the criterion of objectivity in mind.

TECHNIQUES OF GATHERING EVIDENCE. Because there is no well-defined curriculum in adult education, and a wide range of behavioral objectives, the task of gathering evidence is considerably more complex than it often is in more formal educational settings. As a basis for developing some generalizations about that task, here, again, is the framework originally used in the first chapter to clarify the objectives of adult education programs:

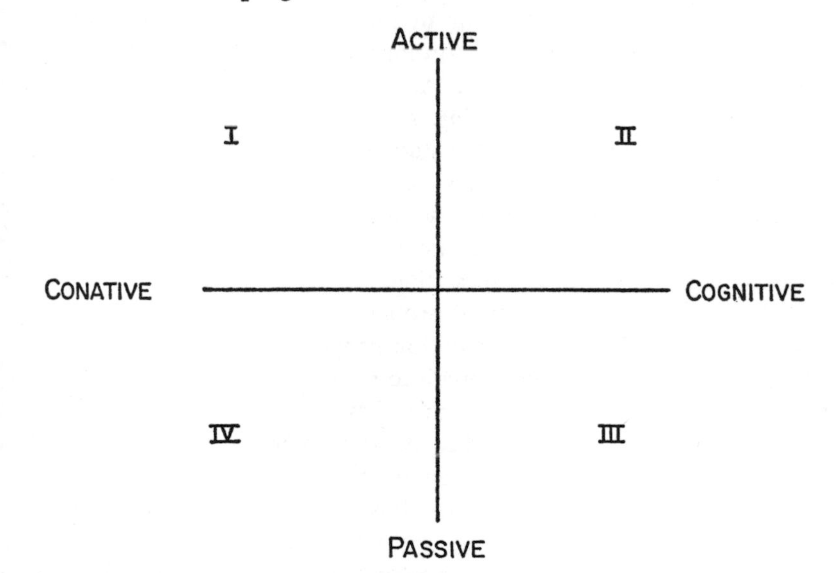

One dimension is somewhat different; the "conative-cognitive" continuum substitutes for the "adjustment-individual growth" one in the original formulation, because it is more appropriate for the evaluation problem.

I. This area includes those programs which aim at changing people's social behavior primarily based on strong feeling or belief systems: supervisory training, family life education, programs for the aging, and human relations training of all types. For this class of objectives, the problem of validity in measuring results is a serious one. It is often simple enough to show changes in verbal behavior in these areas but difficult to be sure that any really significant behavioral shifts follow in the life situation of the participant.

Nevertheless, the level of verbal change is often worth testing as an indicator of the student's understanding of the situational requirements for effective behavior. Attitude assessments can be useful, but one can get closer to the level of actual behavior by constructing little case problems to which the student must respond by formulating plans for dealing with them. The question of the reliability of such devices is a difficult one; if they are too similar to the materials used in the program, the student may base his responses on what he thinks the program wants him to do.

The valid test of behavior change, of course, would involve some kind of observation of behavior in the life situation toward which training is directed, which is ordinarily tremendously difficult to arrange or prohibitively costly. An alternative sometimes used in supervisory or executive training substitutes interviews with those who are in daily contact with the student, his superiors or employees, for instance. The reliability of such a procedure is often questionable, but it can nevertheless be a very useful device.

Or, without getting into the life situation of the student, one can simulate reality in the program setting by asking a sample of the participants to deal with a variety of problems in a constructed role-play. One of the most ingenious evaluation programs ever developed used role play in a way which was perceived as real by the student who was being assessed. A group of social scientists working in the general area of the reduction of race prejudice became interested in the problem of how to deal with the bigoted remark made in public places, as, for example, the person on a crowded bus who loudly announces, as a fellow passenger struggles up to the exit, "Just like a Jew—always pushing and shoving." The psychologists hypothesized that if a bystander replied to such a remark he might substantially reduce the reinforcement of general prejudice in the crowd present. A series of ingenious experiments confirmed the hypothesis and furthermore discovered the kind of reply which would be likely to be effective. A group of volunteers participated in a training program aimed at preparing them to reply effectively in such public incidents, in sessions which used role playing as the major training device.

The question of the effectiveness of the training now arose; would the participants in the training sessions actually perform as they should when they confronted the actual situation? A small sample of the trainees received a letter from a local radio station, inviting them to participate in a panel discussion and requesting that they come in at some appointed time for a preparatory talk with the director of the show. When the trainee appeared for the appointment, in response to this flattering invitation, he was asked to wait for a few minutes in the radio station's reception room. In the room were a number of "plants" ostensibly there on some business, one of whom, on a cue, made a suitably loud and bigoted remark. The proportion of trainees who made the appropriate answer in this situation, which *they* perceived as real (the percentage was satisfactorily high, in fact), constituted really adequate evidence of the effectiveness of the training program.[3]

We do not need to be this elaborate to get more valid evidence than we ordinarily rely on for the success of programs in this general category; however, as a model of what ingenuity can achieve in evaluating complex objectives so common in adult education, this procedure is worth thinking about.

II. The second quadrant includes those objectives which require cognitive activity, the skills of the rational and analytic mind: the acts of judging, of determining relationships, of problem-solving. Working in this area, the evaluator must be sharply aware of two basic demands imposed by the nature of the skills he is dealing with. First, they are complex, which means that we must have a reasonably precise picture of the different cognitive activities which compose them and the varieties of error which are probable. Second, they are active aspects of cognition, and we must not confuse them with mere recall of the results of someone else's cognitive activity; a student's ability to remember an analysis he read of the causes of juvenile delinquency is not evidence that he himself has the ability to unravel the complicated strands of cause and effect.

These skills are, nevertheless, fairly easy to evaluate, considerably easier than they are to teach. One cannot be certain, of course, that a person who can demonstrate his ability to analyze a problem on paper will be able to do so as well under the pressure of some real situation, but at least the cognitive processes involved in the paper-and-pencil test and in the life situation are the same. Thus, the question of validity in part hinges on our ability to make the abstract test come as close as possible to reality. The syllogism, for example, does indeed represent the thought processes in ordinary life, but people do not commonly think about things in syllogistic form; a person might be a whiz at detecting errors in syllogisms presented to him on paper but make the same errors in coming to a conclusion about some local political event. Consequently, unless we happen to be evaluating a course in formal logic, the closer to life we can make the materials of the test, the more valid it is likely to be. The test of judgment included in the illustrations at the end of this chapter is based on a fairly familiar problem in modern community life and on the things which ordinary people might well say about it.

A sizable difficulty in evaluating these complex skills, particularly in adult programs, lies in the relatively short exposure which most of our adult students have to the training. One cannot really expect a short course or an institute to modify these behaviors significantly, and the evaluator is consequently fairly often asked to develop complicated measuring instruments which seldom find gross enough changes to detect. Fortunately, much of what we do in adult education is focused on a particular task involving only simple models of such skills as judgment, as, for example, attempts to improve family budgeting skills in the illustration cited later in this chapter. The narrower the field of application, the more likely are we to find changes in cognitive abilities.

III. The third group of objectives are the most familiar and, in most respects, the easiest to evaluate. Some members of this category are on the lowest level of activity: for example, the ability to recall or recognize facts, principles, relationships. Others demand a somewhat more active role of the learner, particularly the ability to apply learned principles to new contexts, which is the best way of measuring understanding.

To evaluate achievement on the first of these levels, one can simply enough produce a multitude of items and put them together in a test. If, for some reason, actual *recall* is desirable, a brief statement with a blank left for the student to fill in is preferable; if, as in most cases, *recognition* of the correct information is sufficient, the common multiple-choice item is appropriate. A certain amount of skill is necessary to compose multiple-choice questions, but any text on testing includes a detailed analysis of the problems involved and provides adequate models.[4] The continuing controversy over the desirability of using this kind of item is at least partly a phantom argument. The critics who favor essay questions often have in mind quite different objectives from those that the multiple-choice item measures at its most efficient.

If we are interested in evidence of understanding, however, of the ability to *apply* knowledge, it is not so easy to avoid the argument, because the multiple-choice item can also be used for this purpose, as the section of illustrations indicate. In general, the demands of both reliability and objectivity are better served by the multiple-choice item: because the student can answer such items much more quickly, one can use a greater number of them and thus include a wider sampling from the broad universe of possible items, or one can give the student an opportunity to demonstrate his ability to apply knowledge a number of times; the interpretation of the essay-question response is, of course, subject to considerably more bias than is the multiple-choice item. Many instructors and students, however, continue to distrust the multiple-choice measure, arguing that it restricts the student's response too sharply and does not allow for the original or the nonconforming answer. Those who share this view ought at least to bow in the direction of objectivity by making their interpretation of the free response considerably more structured than it commonly is; a model for this procedure is included among the illustrations.

IV. The final group of objectives, those basic feelings or attitudes which may or may not be directly evident in behavior, presents in many ways the most troublesome measurement problems. The earlier chapter on objectives raised the question of whether the educator should, indeed, even *adopt* the objective of changing people's feelings, and it is not necessary to recapitulate the issue here. Even if we do not set out to do so, we are often very interested in finding out if a program has, as a by-product, managed to change some primary orientations of the student.

The concept of *attitude* has been a battleground in the behavioral sciences for decades, but despite constant attacks on its validity it has proved too valuable a notion to give up. The critics on the extreme wing of behaviorism charge that what a person *says* about how he feels makes little difference; his behavior in a particular situation may well contradict his verbal expression, a contention difficult to deny. Nevertheless, most people exhibit a general, if qualified, underlying consistency of orientation and behavior, and change in verbal behavior may well relate to hypothesized change in overt behavior. So long as we are cautious about interpreting the significance of verbal change, there seems to be no real reason for rejecting such evidence out of hand.

The Likert scale, one which provides the respondent with a series of statements of attitude and the opportunity to indicate agreement or disagreement on a five-point scale, may well be the most common form of attitude measurement. It can be scored objectively, it can include a large enough quantity of items to ensure reliability, and it lends itself easily to detailed item analysis as well as single scoring.[5] In some areas of attitude it is possible to get much more subtle measures of the meaning which particular concepts or people have for the student; the *semantic differential* is the most ingenious paper-and-pencil device for measuring such responses and holds a good deal of promise for this area of evaluation. It, as well as the Likert attitude scale, is illustrated in the later section.

THE EVALUATION PROCESS IN ACTION IN ADULT PROGRAMS

The wide variety of objectives in adult education, as well as the great differences in format, results in evaluation problems of considerable complexity. Although there is a great deal of overlap in the objectives of separate programs, the task of identifying the areas of overlapping objectives and developing common methods of gathering evidence has only begun.[6] It is still necessary to approach each program as though it represents a special evaluation problem with its own specific measurement demands. A brief look at several different programs to assess the problems they present to an evaluator may illustrate the challenge the field presents.

The Domestic Skills of Rural Women

At one end of the range, a useful example of adult programs is in the work of Cooperative Extension in improving the skills of home management. Let us suppose that a particular state has decided to conduct a program in each of the counties aimed at helping the women it serves do a better job of budgeting and has instructed the home demonstration agents to devote one of their monthly meetings to that end. The understanding and skills involved in such an objective appear, on the surface, to be relatively simple. But are they? Assuming that the home demonstration agent is interested in getting evidence of the effectiveness of the meeting and goes to the trouble of specifying the objective, she might come up with such particular competences as:

Awareness of the need to keep accurate records of income and expenditures.
Awareness of the need for long-range planning for family needs.
Ability to make wise consumption judgments, to apply family values to consumption choices, to weigh alternatives in the allocation of funds, etc.
Skill in dealing with family conflicts over expenditures.
Simple bookkeeping skills necessary to maintain accurate records.

As an evaluator, the agent has now confronted herself with a problem in her role as program planner. In one session of several hours with a resource person from the home economics department of the university, can she hope to achieve these aims? Perhaps the first two, and the last, but she is not likely to succeed in the other objectives, whose achievement depends on complex practice, discussion, role playing, and the like. She can either modify the objectives and select the ones appropriate to a restricted schedule, or she must expand the program. Assuming that she decides on the latter course and includes, in an extended series of sessions, activities designed to improve the behaviors she has specified, what kinds of evidence should she seek? Here are some possibilities:

Simply ask the participants, several months after the completion of the meetings, how many are keeping records.
Ask them to bring in the budgets they are keeping, and review them for detail and clarity.
Present them, on paper, with a number of short cases presenting buying choices that are likely to be common ones for that particular group and that require them not only to come to a decision but indicate their reasons;
Some time after the program is over, make a point of interviewing a sample of the women informally about any recent family conflict over an expenditure, and get an account of what they did to resolve the conflict.

Whether one wishes to devote this much energy to evaluate the particular program depends, of course, on how important one considers the objectives to be. In fact, these steps are not extraordinarily complicated ones and, if planned in advance, can be accomplished easily, with the exception of constructing the paper-and-pencil device. This device should be worked out far enough in advance of the program to enable the agent to use it both as a pre- and post-test.

A Liberal Education Program for Labor Officials

One such program currently in the planning stages consists of a year-long series of courses, developed cooperatively by universities and the education staffs of unions, which require attendance several evenings a week. The general objectives of the program are to help the participants gain a broader view of the problems of the labor movement in the 60's, to enable them to think more analytically and objectively about those problems, and to help them develop the attitudes and skills required for creative problem-solving in their organizations. Here are objectives of a very different order from those in the first example; not only is the field of phenomena more complex, but the cognitive skills required are on a very much higher level.

The evaluation of a program of this kind is quite likely to fall into the same trap which awaits its program planners, the delusion that the program should turn out modified amateur economists, political scientists, and labor historians. If the evaluator sidesteps the trap but the program planners do not, program activities may well have only slight relevance to measure of achievement; it is crucial, therefore, to have planning and evaluation proceed together and cooperatively.

Supposing that those who are constructing the sessions agree that they are unlikely to succeed in making professional scholars out of labor officials in one year, even if it were desirable to do so, they might well emerge with some objectives which, though more realistic and legitimate, provide far greater difficulty for the evaluator. For example, the students are men who face extraordinarily complicated organizational problems; they need to comprehend some of the basic concepts of organizational structure and function, but above all, to be able to apply these concepts to problems familiar to them. They are functioning members of an institution which seems unable to adapt to new circumstances and a different clientele and tends still to reach for old solutions to problems which are no longer the same; they need to practice examining the whole range of possible solutions and the values which stand in the way of adopting some of them. They cannot themselves become expert economists, political scientists, or labor historians, but they need insight into the role of the expert: what one must accept from him and what one can and should question.

Should the program adopt objectives such as these and provide experiences for the students which have some relevance to them, the task of devising instruments to measure their achievement would have to start from scratch. One could measure the verbal ability to apply organizational concepts by devising a fairly large number of items which sample union organizational problems, then asking the student to select from a series of statements of relationship the one which best explains the difficulty or describes it most meaningfully. Or, after a period of something like six months after the end of the program, one could select a random sample of the participants and interview them, asking them to talk freely about specific problems arising in their job in the recent past, how they reacted to them, and how they solved them. The evaluation might attempt to measure improvement in solution-finding by providing a specific familiar problem and asking the student to supply as many possible solutions as he can; both a quantitative and qualitative analysis of the answers might be significant. One could test the student's ability to use the expert wisely by developing items somewhat like those in the test of judgment presented at the end of this chapter (note particularly section 2.2 of the test).

A Residential Workshop on Supervision in Industry

As a third example which poses some very different problems of evaluation, consider a one-week workshop in supervision. The planners might have any of a wide variety of objectives, but the aim is most likely to focus on human relations training, often recently described as "sensitivity training."

The task of the evaluator in this kind of program is considerably simpler than in the preceding program. Problems of cooperation with planners and instructional staff are seldom very complicated here; the staff is usually test-sophisticated and has a very clear picture of the kind of behavior it is trying to change in the participants. At the same time, in one week even a well-constructed program is unlikely to change to any significant extent behavior so related to deep levels of personality; the kind of change one might look for is on a fairly superficial level.

The problem of measuring what are likely to be relatively small changes is chiefly one of making whatever measures one is using reliable enough to pick up small differences. An advantage of the residential setting is that it permits us to get observational evidence of social behavior which is very difficult to get otherwise, and it is easy, too, to construct controlled situations if it is important to note spontaneous reactions to a particular circumstance. The reliability of any final assessment increases as we use such a variety of evidence; we may increase it still further, in any paper-and-pencil device which attempts to measure sensitivity to specific aspects of human relations, by using as many items as possible.

A most useful evaluation technique for this type of program is to obtain some evidence about the performance of the participant in the life setting which the program was designed to improve in some way. One might accept a range of evidence bearing on the improvement of a supervisor's insight into human relations—lowered grievance rate, turnover rate, or other indicators of general morale—but the question of their validity is a serious one. The reaction of the supervisor's immediate superior is often used as evidence and is considerably more valid. Even if the evaluator can interview a sample of back-home superiors, however, which is probably the best way of getting at the subtle judgments involved, there is some utility in supplementing the interviews with a rating-scale device.

The rating scale may well be the most flagrantly abused evaluation device now in use. There is a good probability that any conference we attend will present us with a slip of paper with a scale such as, "This meeting has been: excellent–very good–better than average–okay–poor," and ask us to circle one. Anyone with supervisory responsibility faces pages of evaluative scales on employees: "This person's general work habits are: excellent, good, fair, poor." The problem of interpreting responses to scales as vague as these is an enormous one; there are bound to be different individual perceptions of what "work habits" involve, and very different views of what constitutes "excellence." Constructing a useful scale demands primarily that we separate the important dimensions of the quality we are rating; thus, work habits may involve such dimensions as punctuality, responsibility, thoroughness, originality, or other very different qualities. A good rating scale will identify those of the greatest importance to the particular situation and ask for ratings of each one separately, making the scale responses as specific as possible, for example:

Punctuality

______The person is always, or almost always, on time.

______The person is occasionally late to work or to appointments, but is almost always on time when it is important to be.

______The person cannot be depended on to be on time even to important meetings.

______The person is completely unreliable and seldom on time.

Separate scales might follow, dealing with specific categories for responsibility, originality, and so forth. Another type of scale presents the rater with a real continuum, with specific anchoring points suggested; for example:

Punctuality:	1	2	3	4	5	6	7
	Always, or almost always, on time.			Occasionally late, but usually on time when important to be.			Completely unreliable.

Rating scales, if they are well-constructed, are a very useful evaluative device for many kinds of educational objectives, and the principles of good construction are, as these examples indicate, easy enough to follow.

THE ADULT EDUCATOR AND THE EVALUATION PROCESS

This book has addressed itself much of the time to the teacher of adults, who often does not consider himself to be primarily an adult educator at all, and on occasion to the full-time administrator who is in a position to plan programs and hire teaching staff. This final note is directed to all administrators of adult education who, whether or not they get involved in program planning, often find it difficult to define an *educational* role for themselves. It is one thing to master the strategy of space assignment, the technique of promotion, and the political skills of dealing with other parts of the institution, if, as most adult educators are, one is part of a more encompassing organization. Necessary as these activities are, some administrators of adult education enterprises seek to balance them with a more creative connection with the teaching-learning process.

A possible role for many administrators is in curriculum policy, the development of distinctive approaches for adults to standard disciplines and problems. Some find another role in creating new and more appropriate formats for adult learning, applying techniques for making large groups more active in learning, or finding new uses for television. A third role is seldom adopted, though it is an essential one usually missing from most adult education programs—the expert in the process of evaluation.

As knowledge becomes more specialized, all educational administrators find it more difficult to function as more than a coordinator in the development of curricula, and many of them turn to the technical and non-substantive area of format development. But administrative concentration on the evaluation process, this chapter suggests, makes it possible to work cooperatively with experts in fields in which one is not himself an expert and opens the way not only to assessing institutional effectiveness but to improving instructional practice. Surely an administrator would have difficulty finding an activity more important than these two, and he might well consider becoming skilled enough in the evaluation process to play the role of evaluator in his own institution or to direct evaluation activities.

What skills are needed? Some the good administrator already has, others he can develop easily enough, still others he might have to acquire the hard way through study or purchase them through consultation.

1. A group of skills of primary importance is involved in working with instructors on the task of defining the aims of their program. Basically, the administrator needs to know what questions he must confront the instructor with, the skill of presenting them insistently, and above all, patience.

2. The task of gathering evidence presents very different problems. Assessing the adequacy of evaluation instruments presents a series of technical problems, as does the handling of data after one has gathered it. This is an area in which the administrator, convinced of the importance of evaluation, might well decide to acquire competence himself. Or he can make sure that one of his staff has some technical background in the field of educational measurement. Or he can call on a local expert for consultation. His own experience will soon begin to build some rule-of-thumb beliefs about evaluation of adult education, as contrasted with other educational settings: that the heterogeneity of adult experiences makes pre- and post-testing essential; that evaluation devices need to be interesting to the subject and as close as possible to life; that objectives of adult programs, to be attainable, must often be stated in limited terms.

3. He needs the human relations skills, which hopefully he already has, necessary to deal with the results of an evaluation effort. How does one handle the reactions of the instructor or instructional team to negative findings? It is considerably easier to say, "Well, that group is just resistant to change," than it is to say, "What can we do the next time which will increase the possibility of getting more positive results?"

One can do very little in a book, at least, to help people acquire some of these skills; motivation, experience, and reflection are necessary to their acquisition. Some of the more technical aspects of evaluation are another matter; it may be helpful to look at some examples of devices appropriate for getting evidence of the kinds of change adult educators tend most to be interested in. The section below presents some models of instruments but does not, of course, pretend to completeness; the reader interested in going beyond these suggestions must consult any of a wide variety of specialized works on educational measurement.

SOME EVALUATION INSTRUMENT MODELS

Testing Recall of Information or Principles

The most efficient form for testing this objective is the multiple-choice item, particularly if all one is aiming at is recognition rather than active recall of material. This kind of item can do a very complex measurement job if, for example, each of the incorrect alternatives offered represent a different type of error. The sample items below would be appropriate for any number of courses in industrial psychology, a favorite adult education offering.

When we say that a person accuses others of having the same faults that he has, we are talking about (1) regression, (2) fixation, (3) hostility, (4) spontaneity, (5) projection.

Which of the following is *not* an ordinary cause of frustration: (1) difficulty of a task, (2) lack of knowledge, (3) conflict of goals within an individual, (4) emotional response, (5) inadequate reward.

When the Western Electric studies were started, the investigators were interested mainly in the effects of: (1) physical working conditions, (2) group process, (3) supervisory behavior, (4) prestige ranking, (5) difficulty of task.

The score that most people get on a test is known as the (1) critical score, (2) mode, (3) median, (4) mean, (5) standard score.

A mature person is one who (1) seeks problems to solve, (2) avoids situations that are likely to result in problems, (3) helps others to solve problems, (4) recognizes problems when he sees them, (5) solves problems by concentrating on his goals.

Which of the following is *not* a common result of frustration in the job situation: (1) spontaneity, (2) aggression, (3) sickness, (4) absenteeism, (5) anxiety.

In the Scanlon plan, the union and the workers (1) tell management how to distribute the profits; (2) bargain with management about distributing the profits; (3) have nothing to say about distributing the profits; (4) take part in committee action with management in deciding how to distribute the profits; (5) vote on distributing profits.

Which of the following is *not* an example of a negative approach to morale: (1) improving lighting; (2) removing safety hazards; (3) adjusting complaints; (4) stimulating discussions between union and management; (5) transferring complaining employees.

If a supervisor believed in the "satisfaction" or "contentment" approach to morale, he would be most likely to be concerned with (1) getting the right worker into the right job, (2) increasing participation of workers in management decisions, (3) installing incentive systems, (4) improving working conditions, (5) removing bad foremen.

Testing the Ability to Apply Principles or Generalizations

The student's ability to apply a principle to a concrete case is evidence of understanding. The examples given below illustrate two different approaches: the multiple-choice item and the free response to a case or problem.

a. Multiple-choice items:

Under which of the following conditions would you expect the *greater amount of social discontent and irrationality among proprietors of small business?*

_____When there is an effectively competitive free private enterprise economy.

_____When the degree of monopoly is high and rapidly increasing in the economy.

_____Social discontent and irrationality among proprietors would be about the same whether there's a lot of competition or a lot of monopoly.

_____You can't really say, we just don't know enough about the relation, if any, between irrationality and the economy.

Under which of the following conditions would you expect the *greater amount of social discontent and irrationality among members of the lower classes?*

_____When the opportunity and hopes for improving one's position in life are about like they are now in the U.S.A.

_____When the real opportunities are very small, and when there's very little hope or desire to improve one's position.

_____Social discontent and irrationality among members of the lower classes would be about the same when things are like they are now and when there's no hope and no opportunity to improve one's position.

_____You can't really say, we just don't know enough about the relation between discontent and opportunity or expectations.

Under which of the following conditions would you expect the *mobility of labor* to be greater?

______In an all-around perfectly competitive labor market.
______In a labor market where employers have a lot of monopoly power over the hiring of labor.
______Mobility of labor would be about the same whether you had a lot of competition or a lot of monopoly in the hiring of labor.
______You can't really say; we just don't know enough about the relation between mobility of labor and the nature of the labor market.

b. Free response.[7] Note that the case composing the test is followed by a rating scale used in scoring the answers, an illustration of a method for eliminating some of the ambiguity and bias which inevitably enters the evaluation of such questions. If one can have several persons do the rating independently, so much the better.

A friend of yours asks for help in a problem he faces in his community. The situation, as he outlines it for you, is briefly this:

He has lived for several years in a government housing project which includes about 1,200 families. The community maintains such services as a co-operative grocery, a community church, a co-operative nursery school, and a systematic car pool for getting into town. The Community Center is busy with meetings of volunteer clubs which put out a weekly newspaper, provide amateur theatricals, take care of the library, etc., and also serves as meeting place for a number of social, political, and religious groups. The residents have formed a Community Council by electing a volunteer representative from each block, and this informal body functions fairly smoothly in dealing with the housing administrator on such problems as getting needed repairs made, preventing health hazards, etc.

Recently a number of Negro families have moved into the project, and, although the surface of community life seems calm, rumors are beginning to fly. "People say" that: (1) some white families are moving out; (2) the housing administrator is placing most Negro families in one area, with the intention of maintaining segregation; (3) a white woman has been frightened by a Negro resident and called on the police. (Your friend adds, from his own knowledge, that the police had questioned the man, decided that the woman had been mistaken, and released him.)

The council, of which your friend is a member, does not feel that it can do anything about the situation, but he feels that if it is allowed to go on, a very nasty community conflict may develop. He is interested in finding ways in which tension can be reduced, and any conflict avoided.

What suggestions can you make that may be helpful to him? Your answer, as long or short as you like, should be written out to hand in next time.

Your comments will not be "graded" or held to your credit or discredit in this course. Instead of signing your name, put at the top of your paper a number representing your birthday (*e.g.*, 715 would mean July 15) so that your paper can be compared with one you may be asked to do later in class.

Rating Scale for Judging Responses

1. How aware is the student of the complexity of the problem?
   a. Sees the situation personally in terms of vague threat, or as very confused.
   b. Sees only the immediate problem of the mistaken accusation.
   c. Perceives the problem simply in terms of Negro vs. white, or in some other bi-polar sense.
   d. Sees the situation as complicated, but is not aware of the specifics which make it so.
   e. Aware of the variety of different perceptions possible in the situation and of the interaction of numbers of groups with differing motivations.
2. To what extent is the student oriented to a solution of the problem rather than to his personal feelings about it?
   a. Devotes most of the essay to denouncing some group involved in the situation; strong tone of moral indignation.
   b. Somewhat more interested in expressing personal opinions than in analyzing the problem.
   c. Interested in dealing with the problem, but his personal feelings interfere with solution-finding.
   d. Expresses personal feelings about the situation, but primarily interested in finding a solution to the situation, and seems able to search without undue interference from his own affect.
3. To what extent is the student aware of group-process factors in the situation?
   a. Seems to attach no importance at all to the description of the group structure of the community, and does not utilize it in his suggestions.
   b. Seems aware of the importance of group structure in a general way, but makes no specific use of the phenomenon in discussing the situation or solutions.
   c. Seems sharply aware of the importance of group structure and processes in the situation, and tries to make use of it in his suggestions, but not very successfully or specifically.
   d. Sharply aware of the importance of group structures and processes, and makes creative use of them in both analysis and suggested solutions.
4. How realistic and mature is his solution to the problem?
   a. Solution depends mainly on vague hopes or on idealistic conceptions of human behavior; or, rejects any possibility of solution.
   b. Solution built around the Council taking an essentially public relations approach to the situation.
   c. Makes some attempt to construct a general plan for action, with some involvement of existing community structure, but solution remains somewhat general in its suggestions.
   d. Constructs a general plan for action, with involvement of existing community structures, including a number of specific suggestions for activities within such a plan.

Measuring Interest in Some Activity Area[8]

It is not difficult to specify the dimensions of an instrument which would gather evidence of change in interests.

1. To obtain evidence on the *pattern* of interests, the items should consist of simple statements of activities, including mental ones, which people who have an interest in the subject area might be presumed to engage in. Each group of items can sample a variety of different types of human activity. The following classification may prove useful in establishing the range of activities which should be included:

Items that imply a primary concern with THINGS.
Items that imply a primary concern with THOUGHTS.
Items that imply a primary concern with WORDS.
Items that imply a primary concern with ACTION.

Obviously, any activity may involve more than one of these, but let us assume that we can construct items in a way which makes clear which one is emphasized. An orientation toward *things* involves such activities as collecting, buying, and displaying. An orientation toward *thoughts* or ideas may be interpreted as an interest in the theoretical aspects of a problem or issue or process; toward *words,* an interest in the descriptive or structural aspects; toward *actions,* an interest in the applied or practical aspects.

2. We need to have, in addition, some notion of the *intensity* of interest. We can ask, for each item, whether the person has engaged in this activity *in the past month* and looks forward to doing so often again, has done it but *not in the past month,* has never done it but thinks he *might like to,* or has never done it and *doesn't want to*. This would provide us not only with some indication of the importance a given pattern of activities has in the leisure-time life of the individual, but also with some measure of his exploratory drive and curiosity.

3. We need to sample not only intensity of interest but *level* of interest. People will read articles about Khrushchev in the newspaper as a consequence of a superficial interest in him as a "ham." Reading about him out of a concern for estimating his intentions is quite different. This is the kind of change in level which might reasonably be expected as an outcome of educational activity.

Since such an instrument is usually administered to participants both before and after a program, the results will provide a considerable amount of information about the effectiveness of the program in changing the pattern, the level, and the intensity of student interests in this area. For example, a person whose interests are mainly in action items before participating in some social affairs program may afterward reveal increased interest in items of the "thought" character. Such a change is ordinarily regarded as a desirable outcome of a university program. Similarly, an increase in the number of items he marks as things he would *like* to do, even if no change in the pattern of activities has occurred, would also normally be interpreted as favorable. In general, this design gives some promise of measuring small changes, as well as gross ones; and this is an important characteristic of any instrument intended for use in a variety of programs.

Sample Test Items.

Instructions: For each of the following activities, circle the letter

A – if it describes something you do often and would like to continue doing;

B – if it describes something you have done in the past month and would like to continue doing;

C – if it describes something you have done at some time prior to the past month but would not like to do again;

D – if it describes something you have never done, but think you would like to do;

E – if it describes something you have never done, and don't particularly want to do.

1. Read newspapers and magazines which deal with current world and domestic issues. A B C D E
2. Wonder about what makes a particular person tick. A B C D E
3. Collect clippings about particular social issues you are interested in. A B C D E
4. Read columnists in the papers who try to deal with life problems people write in to them about. A B C D E
5. Participate in local political party activity around elections. A B C D E

Testing the Ability to Make Rational Judgments

The following example presents a general model for constructing an instrument for testing judgment utilizing simple case materials of the kind one often encounters in daily life.[9] Note that a part of the model consists of items which give some picture of the way the respondent applies values to the particular case; if one is interested particularly in change in values, this type of device could, of course, be used separately.

In constructing cases such as the one illustrated below, it is important to pick a situation (a) which admits of differences of opinion even among experts; (b) which nevertheless involves the application of certain principles on which experts do agree; and (c) which is the subject of widespread misconceptions among the uniformed or prejudiced.

Secondly, in constructing the statements following the case it is important to include some statements which are wrong or may be wrongly applied so that progress can be measured in terms of the participant's success in avoiding these crude, but common, types of errors.

Third, it is important to construct the statements in such a way as to provide apportunity for individuals to reveal a consistent critical and analytical approach despite differences in their basic value position.

Fourth, it is necessary to construct the statements in such a way that it is possible to interpret the meaning of any response *no matter how much or in what way it diverges from the expected or desired response, i.e.,* so that it is possible to score every possible response in terms of (a) the value position it represents and (b) its logical correctness or incorrectness, and, if incorrect, the nature of the logical fallacy involved in the response.

Fifth, the statements should sample all the behaviors specified in the list of behavioral objectives, though any program may wish to use only one or a few parts of several cases.

Finally, each individual's response should be scored as follows:

A. Logic:
   1. Number of statements correctly marked;
   2. Crude errors: number of statements marked as supporting one position when they should have been marked as supporting the opposite position;
   3. Failure to see relevance: number of statements left blank that should have been marked;
   4. Failure to see irrelevancies: number of statements marked that should have been left blank.

B. Attitudes and Values: Range of considerations regarded as decisive. (Each statement will be coded for the value position it represents, and the number of each type that a student selects will be reported.)

C. Sensitivity to motivation of others.

D. Flexibility in taking into account new factors in a situation.

Illustrative Model: The Johnstown Case

One of the members of the Johnstown School Board has charged that the art teacher is a Communist. Various people have testified—see Exhibit A below. One board member stated he would not hire this Communist to pump gas. Another pointed out that you should not fire people because of their political beliefs. The teacher's record shows that he formerly belonged to three Communist organizations on the Attorney General's list. Tonight the Board will vote on a motion to recommend that the Principal dismiss him.

What do you think should be done in this case?

Exhibit A

Those who reported a ground for suspicion were asked to tell what the ground was. Below are some sample responses.

"He is always talking about world peace."

—Housewife

"He does not attend church and talked against God. He is always against local politics."

—Housewife

"I suspect it from his conversation and manner. He was well educated and had a high disregard for the mentality of others."

—Lawyer

"I saw a map of Russia on a wall in his home."

—Locomotive Engineer

"His activities in distributing literature about the United Nations."

—Housewife

"He wrote his thesis in college on Communism."

—Dentist

"He aimed all his talk toward betterment of people through government ownership of property."

—Foreman

"He is a radical who wanted to change everything in the country—it fits the picture."

—Farmer

"Just his slant on community life and church work. He is not like us."

—Bank Vice-President

"He was strongly in favor of the Hollywood group who were taken up as Communists and objected to their conviction."

—Stockbroker

"I just knew. But I wouldn't know how to say how I knew."

—Farmer

"I saw a CP Membership card in his wallet."

—Prostitute

"He didn't believe in Christ, heaven, or hell."

—Building Contractor

"He brought a lot of foreign-looking people into his home."

—Housewife

"He's against almost everything done in the United States. His ideas are not those of a liberal but a fanatic. He voices ideas with abandon."

—Accountant

"When I was collecting for the United Fund Drive and asked a man for a donation, he began raving about war and Korea."

—Housewife

"He avidly defends the underdog and explains the reasoning behind Communist moves."

—Manager of Business

"During World War II, I used to say Russia was our enemy and he got mad at me."

—Merchant

"He gave me a radical-sounding paper to read—that we should all be equal such as the leaves on a tree are equal."

—Housewife

"Very aggressive along certain lines. Wanted to be a leader but not interested in money."

—Insurance Agent

"He had a foreign camera and took so many pictures of the large New York bridges."

—Housewife

1. *To test the ability to identify crucial issues:*

Pattern

Include 10-12 items testing 1.1 *the ability to scale various statements of issues according to their relevance.* (Items should range from statements of central issues to peripheral and irrelevant, (a) including some quite wrong statements that only a very badly-informed person would select and (b) including a range of value positions. As constructed it includes a test of *the ability to exclude irrelevant issues* and *the ability to identify the central issue.*

Illustration

1.1 Directions: The following statements could conceivably be challenged and debated in connection with this case, but some are more important than others. *Check the five statements* you think it is most important for the School Board to discuss in making its decision.

_____ 1. Capitalism is superior to Communism as an economic system.
_____ 2. Communists should not be allowed to teach in our schools.
_____ 3. Communists should be free to express their opinions, like anyone else.
_____ 4. Communist doctrine has definite implications for art and art theory.
_____ 5. Any community has the right to restrict the activities of members it considers dangerous to its security.
_____ 6. The Attorney General's list is undemocratic.
_____ 7. There is an important difference between a "fellow traveller"

(deeply interested in Communism) and a member of the Communist Party.

_____ 8. Our children should not be taught by atheists.

_____ 9. Youngsters cannot be expected to detect and see through the propaganda of a trained Communist.

_____10. Our nation is founded on the principle that there is a God.

_____11. The teachers of our youth should be typical members of their community, above suspicion of any kind.

_____12. Membership in the Communist Party implies a dedication to the violent overthrow of the American Government.

_____13. The School Board has the right to dismiss any teacher, or any other employee, for any reason it considers a good one.

_____14. A public-school teacher is a government employee and can expect to keep his job only as long as he agrees with government policy.

_____15. No person should be dismissed whose competence is proved.

1.12. Statements 1-15 above are all relevant, in some sense, to the present case. Discussion of some of them, however, would not help very much in making an intelligent decision on this case. Which *three* would you consider *least* important to *this* case? (Write the numbers in the blank)

Statements number: _____, _____, and _____.

1.13. In determining whether or not the teacher should be dismissed, which of the following questions is the most important to be answered? (Check one)

_____16. Is he a Communist?

_____17. Is he interested in Communism?

_____18. Does he preach Communism to his students?

_____19. Is he good at teaching art?

_____20. Does he discharge his total responsibilities as a teacher satisfactorily?

_____21. Is he unpopular in the community?

_____22. Is he a reputable person?

Pattern

Include 3-5 items testing *1.2 the ability to identify assumptions which must be made in order to accept a particular statement as the crucial issue or problem:*

Illustration

1.2 Consider the statement of issues in Column I below. Before each statement in Col. I write the number of the one or more beliefs in Col. II which a person would have to accept in order to make that statement of the issue.

Col. I – Issues	*Col. II – Beliefs*
_____A. "The real issue is whether or not the man is competent."	23. Communism is not dangerous.

______B. "The most important question is to decide whether or not he's a good artist and can teach art."

______C. "The real question is whether or not this teacher has un-American ideas."

24. A teacher's beliefs don't have any real influence on students.
25. A Communist has prejudices that prevent him from being really competent.
26. A teacher's qualifications for a particular job are the most important factors in deciding to hire or fire him.
27. A teacher's knowledge of the subject matter he teaches is the most important factor to take into account in deciding to hire or fire him.
28. Communist doctrine has definite implications for art theory and art.
29. Parents have a right to protect their children from contact with things they don't believe in.
30. Teaching is different from other kinds of jobs, a teacher has to be like Caesar's wife—above suspicion.

Pattern

Include 3-5 items testing *1.3 the ability to identify assumptions which must be made in order to accept a particular statement as evidence for a particular conclusion.*

Illustration

1.3 Each statement in Column I below could be used *as a reason for dismissing the teacher,* provided that a person accepted one or more of the beliefs in Column II and regarded it as obviously true and not in need of discussion. Before each question in Column I, write the number of the belief or beliefs in Column II which a person would have to accept in order to offer the statement in Column I as a reason for dismissal.

Col. I – Reasons

______A. "I wouldn't hire this Communist to pump gas."

______B. "He wrote his thesis in college on Communism."

______C. "His ideas are not those of a liberal but of a fanatic. He voices ideas with abandon."

Col. II – Beliefs

31. Our children should not be taught by atheists.
32. The teachers of our youth should be typical members of their community.
33. The art teacher is a Communist.

_____D. "He does not attend church and talked against God."

_____E. "He explains the reasoning behind Communist moves."

_____F. "He brought a lot of foreign looking people into his home."

34. There is a God.
35. There is no important difference between being interested in Communism and being a member of the Communist party.
36. Communists should not be allowed to teach in our schools.
37. A public-school teacher must agree with government policy to keep his job.
38. Something can be told about a person's political beliefs from his appearance.
39. Anyone who associates with foreigners is a Communist.

2. *To test the ability to analyze an argument:*

Pattern

Include 10 items testing *2.1 the ability to identify the relevance of evidence for a particular issue.*

Alternative Method

Relevance to the broad issue may be tested by directing the student to identify, by different symbols or by checking in two different columns, arguments for, and those against, a proposal. This differs from the illustration below in that the illustration enables the tester to specify each issue more narrowly, whereas the alternative may be a little more economical in allowing the tester to include all arguments that are necessary in part 3 below.

Illustration

2.1 Check any of the following statements which you think help in judging whether or not the teacher is a Communist.

_____40. "I saw a map of Russia on a wall of his home."—Locomotive Engineer

_____41. He was well educated and had a high disregard for the mentality of others.

_____42. "I saw a Communist Party membership card in his wallet."—Prostitute

_____43. He objected to the methods employed in convicting known Communists.

_____44. Three times he has won the award as the best teacher in our school system.

2.12 Some of the arguments below favor dismissing the teacher, some favor dismissing him only if he is proved to be a Communist.

In the blank before each statement write:

A – if you think it is a reasonable argument in favor of dismissing the teacher without further investigation;

B – if you think it is a reasonable argument against dismissing him on the basis of the evidence against him so far:

(Leave other statements blank)

_____45. Capitalism is superior to Communism as an economic system.
_____46. Communists should be free to express their opinions like anyone else.
_____47. Any community has the right to restrict the activities of members it considers dangerous to its security.
_____48. There is an important difference between being deeply interested in Communism and being a member of the Communist Party.
_____49. Youngsters cannot be expected to detect and see through the propaganda of a trained Communist.
_____50. The teachers of our youth should be typical members of their community, above suspicion of any kind.
_____51. Membership in the Communist Party implies a dedication to the violent overthrow of the American government.
_____52. A public-school teacher is a government employee and can only expect to keep his job as long as he agrees with government policy.
_____53. Three times this teacher has won the best teacher award in our school system.
_____54. A teacher's qualifications for a particular job are the most important factors to consider in deciding to hire or fire him.

Pattern

Include 15 items testing *2.2 the ability to judge the validity of evidence,* of which 5 items test *2.21 the ability to distinguish fact from opinion.*

Illustration

Instructions: Some of the statements in the preceding group are facts that everybody could agree are true, and some might be proved false. However, there might be considerable disagreement about other statements because they are really matters of opinion that cannot be proved either true or false. In the blanks below, write the number of any statements which you think are matters of opinion that can never really be proved either true or false.

Statements No. _____, _____, and _____.

Alternative Method

The student could be asked to identify by different symbols or by checking in different columns statements which illustrate different kinds of fallacies. (Note that in either method the statements should include some errors or irrelevancies to give participants who do not think clearly an opportunity to "go wrong.")

Pattern

In the 15 items testing *2.2 the ability to judge the validity of evidence,* include 5 items which test *2.22 the ability to evaluate the source or authority of particular evidence.*

(Note: In this exercise, items testing 2.22 and 2.23 appear in the same group so that the student is not made too conscious of the crucial element to look for. In that way we can evaluate better the kinds of errors he makes.)

Illustration

2.22 and 2.23 Instructions: In each of the following pairs of statements check the statement which you think is the more damaging evidence that the teacher is a Communist. Leave both statements blank if you think one is just as damaging as the other or if neither one is really damaging.

_____55. A locomotive engineer says, "He was in favor of Communist government for this country."
_____ A professor of political science says, "He was in favor of a Communist government for this country."

_____56. A housewife, "He is always talking about world peace."
_____ A building contractor says, "He didn't believe in Christ, heaven, or hell."

_____57. A prostitute says, "I saw a Communist party membership card in his wallet.
_____ A banker says, "He wrote an article advocating government ownership of industry for a magazine."

_____58. A neighbor said: "I saw a map of Russia on his wall."
_____ A fellow teacher said: "He was well educated and had a high disregard for the mentality of others."

_____59. A worker said: "He aimed all his talk toward betterment of people through government ownership of property."
_____ A lawyer said: "He has been very active in distributing literature about the United Nations."

Pattern

Include 5 items testing *2.3 and 2.31 the ability to identify gaps in the argument.*

(Note: An alternative technique for testing this skill consists in asking the respondent to select from a list the particular things it would be most important to know about in order to make a thoroughly reasoned judgment on this case. Such a list should, of course, include several quite irrelevant items.)

Illustration

2.3 Instructions: For each of the following statements of evidence write:

A – if it is important as it stands;

B – if it might be important if more were known about the subject of the statement;

C – if it could not be important no matter how much more were known about the subject of the statement;

_____60. "He wrote his thesis in college on Communism."

_____61. "I saw a CP membership card in his wallet."

_____62. "He does not attend church and talked against God."
_____63. "I just knew. But I don't know how to say I knew."
_____64. "He was strongly in favor of the group of actors and artists in Hollywood who were convicted as Communists and he kept objecting to their conviction."

2.31 Instructions: Which two of the following would you find most decisive in deciding whether or not statement 64 above was really important evidence? (check two)

_____65. He has been very active in certain clearly subversive groups.
_____66. He criticized people who thought members of this group should be fired.
_____67. He objected to the method used in convicting this group.
_____68. He has objected to practically every conviction of alleged Communists on the ground that Russia and Communism really are not threats.
_____69. He has criticized the Congressional Investigating Committees on the grounds that their procedures destroy basic rights.
_____70. He has openly advocated government ownership of railroads.

Pattern

Include 5 items testing *2.4 the ability to identify alternative hypotheses to account for a given situation* and 5 items testing *2.5 the ability to identify probable consequences of a given situation or policy.*

Illustration

2.4 and 2.5 Instructions: Below are some conclusions that readers of this case have arrived at. For each conclusion write

A – if you believe that it is a sound conclusion and is supported by the material presented in the case;
B – if you believe it is not a sound conclusion in light of the material presented in the case;
C – if there is not enough evidence to decide whether it is sound or unsound.

_____71. The art teacher is actively disliked by a number of people in the community.
_____72. The art teacher is very aggressive in stating his views and beliefs on a great many issues.
_____73. The art teacher is a very intelligent and mature individual.
_____74. The art teacher probably is an authority on Russia and Communism.
_____75. Many people in this community identify Communism with issues and actions which they dislike.
_____76. The art teacher is a very poor classroom instructor.
_____77. If the teacher is dismissed on this flimsy evidence, people with liberal views in the community won't be so ready to express their ideas freely.
_____78. If teachers like this are dismissed on account of their ideas, civil liberties will be threatened for others.

______79. If the teacher is kept, his ideas will corrupt some of the most impressionable students.

______80. If this teacher is dismissed on the basis of the case against him so far, it will probably be harder to hire good teachers in this community.

______81. If this teacher is kept, other teachers in this school are likely to pay less attention to the opinions of parents and the rest of the community.

3. *The ability to arrive at a conclusion consistent with his own analysis:*

Pattern

Include opportunity for the student *3.1 to support his own position with valid evidence* and *3.3 to identify the major arguments against his own position.*

Illustration

3. If you had to decide this question on the basis of the information so far, would you vote in favor of (check one)

______82. dismissing the teacher

______83. keeping the teacher

3.1 In your opinion, which of the following are the most persuasive arguments *in favor of dismissing* him. (Check one or more)

______84. Communists should not be allowed to teach in our schools.

______85. Communists should be free to express their opinions, like anyone else.

______86. Any community has the right to restrict the activities of members it considers dangerous to its security.

______87. Youngsters cannot be expected to detect and see through the propaganda of a trained Communist.

______88. No person should be dismissed whose competence is proved.

______89. A Communist has prejudices that prevent him from being really competent.

______90. Teaching is different from some other kinds of jobs; a teacher has to be like Caesar's wife—above suspicion.

______91. There is no important difference between being interested in Communism and being a member of the Communist Party.

______92. Three times he has won the award as the best teacher in our school system.

______93. A locomotive engineer says, "He was in favor of Communist government for this country."

______94. A prostitute says, "I saw a Communist party membership card in his wallet."

______95. He has been very active in certain clearly subversive groups.

______96. He has objected to practically every conviction of alleged Communists on the ground that Russia and Communism really are not threats.

3.3 Which of the *above* statements (84–96) are in your opinion the most persuasive arguments for keeping the teacher?
Statements No. _____, _____, _____, _____.

4. *The ability to deal with non-rational elements in a problem situation:*

Pattern

Include 5 items testing *4.1 the ability to identify and classify these elements.*

Illustration

4.1 Each of the types of testimony makes use of a particular form of appeal. Read each of the following statements and mark it:
A – if it represents "Guilt by Association";
B – if it generalizes that disliked people are guilty of other things;
C – if it condemns people because they are different and strange;
D – if it represents a bandwagon effect;
E – if it equates Communism and progressive or radical views;
F – if it assumes guilt without evidence.

______ 97. He didn't believe in Christ, heaven, or hell.
______ 98. He's against almost everything done in the United States.
______ 99. He voices ideas with abandon.
______100. I saw a map of Russia on a wall in his home.
______101. I just knew. But I wouldn't know how to say how I knew.
______102. I would not hire this Communist to pump gas.
______103. He belonged to three organizations on the Attorney General's subversive list.
______104. He brought a lot of foreign looking people into his home.
______105. Just his slant on community life and the church work. He is not like us.

Pattern

Include 5 items testing *4.2 the ability to manipulate these elements.* One could ask the student to indicate the most probable reactions of different people and the most probable explanation of their reactions. Alternatively one could ask the student to indicate which one or more of the arguments he would use if he were arguing the cast before a particular type of audience.

Measuring Beliefs and Attitudes

a. The instructions and sample items below are a common form of attitude scale using a five-category set of responses. For some respondents the uncertain middle category can be very seductive; one can either eliminate it entirely as a category or suggest in the instructions that it be used only as a last resort. The "uncertain" category does have value in a test given both before and after an educational experience; the objectives of a course may well include either the desirability of crystallizing a particular group of tentative attitudes or of making people less dogmatic about a set of beliefs.

This inventory consists of statements which range over a wide variety of topics. As you read each statement, you are asked to indicate quickly your agreement or disagreement with it in terms of the key given at the top of each page. People have a different reaction to these various statements. This is not a test in which there are "right" and "wrong" answers. What is wanted here is your own quick personal reaction. You should be able to finish taking the inventory in 30 minutes or less.

KEY: SA. I strongly agree or accept the statement.
A. I tend to agree or accept the statement.
? I am uncertain, or have no opinion.
D. I tend to disagree or reject the statement.
SD. I strongly disagree or reject the statement.

SA A ? D SD 1. Chicago is the ugliest city in the world.
SA A ? D SD 2. Any censorship of the presumed morality of books and movies is highly undesirable.
SA A ? D SD 3. You can't believe anything you read in the newspaper.
SA A ? D SD 4. Modern paintings have both beauty and purpose.
SA A ? D SD 5. The people get the kind of movies they demand.
SA A ? D SD 6. The lack of planning accounts for the ugliness and inconvenience of our large cities.
SA A ? D SD 7. The big newspapers are really run by the advertisers.
SA A ? D SD 8. No art work is worth more than a few minutes of the viewer's time.
SA A ? D SD 9. There are basic principles of good art, which a person must learn before he can judge art works.
SA A ? D SD 10. The best of the worthwhile magazine articles can be found in *The Reader's Digest*.
SA A ? D SD 11. Chicago could quickly revive and cleanse itself if it had an honest fighting newspaper.
SA A ? D SD 12. The plans for a house should be approved by the city officials for its beauty as well as for its structural features.
SA A ? D SD 13. The newspapers really encourage crime and corruption by the attention and space they give to this.
SA A ? D SD 14. Architects should return to the types of homes built by the founding fathers.
SA A ? D SD 15. Since the experts often cannot agree about the worth of a painting, it is useless to expect lay people to be able to discriminate between good and bad art.
SA A ? D SD 16. No one should be allowed to live in the city who doesn't have proper standards of conduct and morals.

SA A ? D SD 17. Recent congressional investigations have proven that gangsters are really in control of city politics.

SA A ? D SD 18. People are dishonest because government officials set a dishonest example.

b. There are many more complicated ways of approaching the measurement of values, only one of which is suggested here, the semantic differential.[10] The theory behind the device is based on some very sophisticated notions of communication, but its rationale for measuring the meaning a concept has for a person is simple enough:

> Ordinarily, if we want to find out what something *means* to a person, we ask him to tell us. What does a POLITICIAN mean to you? "Well, it is someone who campaigns and does or does not get elected. It's usually a hearty, husky, good-natured guy who's always on the 'go'—but also a 'glad-hander' and liable to be untrustworthy, a double-talker. Not as good as a statesman, of course. . . ." What does SOPHISTICATED mean? "Well—I know what it means, all right, but it's hard to put into words. It's being clever and wise about people and things—knowing the ropes, so to speak. It's sort of smooth, and polished, graceful, but not awkward . . . poised, 'savvy', you know. . . ."

But most people are not articulate enough to provide these resonances which concepts set up for us and which capture their meaning for us. The semantic differential is a device which *presents* the respondent with a series of adjectives from which he can choose the ones which for him resonate to a particular concept. A great deal of preliminary research established the three most important dimensions of this view of "meaning"—*evaluative terms,* words which express for us some kind of goodness or badness; *activity terms,* words which express feelings of fastness or slowness and the like; and *potency terms,* words which carry implications of power or weakness.

Those interested in the scoring methods and in the ingenious picturing of "semantic space" which Osgood and his collaborators have developed should consult their major work on the instrument already cited. The simplicity of the device itself is illustrated below by a copy of the instructions commonly used and a sample sheet. The test consists of as many such sheets as the number of concepts one wishes to get a response to; each sheet is headed by a single concept.

Typical Instructions

The purpose of this study is to measure the *meanings* of certain things to various people by having them judge them against a series of descriptive scales. In taking this test, please make your judgments on the basis of what these things mean *to you.* On each page of this booklet you will find a different concept to be judged and beneath it a set of scales. You are to rate the concept on each of these scales in order.

Here is how you are to use these scales:

If you feel that the concept at the top of the page is *very closely related* to one end of the scale, you should place your check-mark as follows:

fair __x__ : ____ : ____ : ____ : ____ : ____ : ____ : unfair

OR

fair ____ : ____ : ____ : ____ : ____ : ____ : __x__ : unfair

If you feel that the concept is *quite closely related* to one or the other end of the scale (but not extremely), you should place your check-mark as follows:

strong ____ : __x__ : ____ : ____ : ____ : ____ : ____ : weak

OR

strong ____ : ____ : ____ : ____ : ____ : __x__ : ____ : weak

If the concept seems *only slightly related* to one side as opposed to the other side (but is not really neutral), then you should check as follows:

active ____ : ____ : __x__ : ____ : ____ : ____ : ____ : passive

OR

active ____ : ____ : ____ : ____ : __x__ : ____ : ____ : passive

The direction toward which you check, of course, depends upon which of the two ends of the scale seem most characteristic of the thing you're judging.

If you consider the concept to be *neutral* on the scale, both sides of the scale *equally associated* with the concept, or if the scale is *completely irrelevant,* unrelated to the concept, then you should place your check-mark in the middle space:

safe ____ : ____ : ____ : __x__ : ____ : ____ : ____ : dangerous

IMPORTANT: (1) Place your check-marks *in the middle of spaces,* not on the boundaries:

THIS NOT THIS

____ : ____ : __x__ : ____ : ____ : ____ x ____ : ____ :

(2) Be sure you check every scale for every concept— *do not omit any.*

(3) Never put more than one check-mark on a single scale.

Sometimes you may feel as though you've had the same item before on the test. This will not be the case, so *do not look back and forth* through the items. Do not try to remember how you checked similar items earlier in the test. *Make each item a separate and independent judgment.* Work at fairly high speed through this test. Do not worry or puzzle over individual items. It is your first impressions, the immediate "feelings" about the items, that we want. On the other hand, please do not be careless, because we want your true impressions.

Concept: *Politician*

kind	____:____:____:____:____:____:____	cruel
clean	____:____:____:____:____:____:____	dirty
light	____:____:____:____:____:____:____	dark
healthy	____:____:____:____:____:____:____	sick
strong	____:____:____:____:____:____:____	weak
hard	____:____:____:____:____:____:____	soft
heavy	____:____:____:____:____:____:____	light
masculine	____:____:____:____:____:____:____	feminine
constrained	____:____:____:____:____:____:____	free
stable	____:____:____:____:____:____:____	changeable
active	____:____:____:____:____:____:____	passive
hot	____:____:____:____:____:____:____	cold
fast	____:____:____:____:____:____:____	slow

NOTES

1. This statement of general framework is adapted with permission from a similar section in Harry L. Miller and Christine H. McGuire, *Evaluating Liberal Adult Education* (Chicago: Center for the Study of Liberal Education for Adults, 1961).

2. For a discussion of this particular problem of validity, see the early chapters of Milton Rokeach, *The Open and Closed Mind* (New York: Basic Books, 1960).

3. The study cited was done by the Commission on Community Interrelations of the American Jewish Congress. A more detailed account of the project and the evaluation may be found in Claire Selltiz *et al.*, "The Acceptability of Answers to Anti-Semitic Remarks," *International Journal of Opinion and Attitude Research,* Vol. IV, No. 3 (Fall, 1950).

4. There are, of course, a large number of useful texts in the field of educational measurement. An excellent one, not too complex, and readable, is R. L. Thorndike and Elizabeth Hagen, *Measurement and Evaluation in Psychology and Education* (New York: Wiley, 1961).

5. There are several more or less complicated methods for constructing attitude tests, the simplest being to pool a fairly large number of relevant attitude statements and examine answers for shifts from pre- to post-administration. If one is interested in assigning a meaningful single score to an attitude scale, much more complex developmental procedures are necessary. For some methods of doing so, see L. L. Thurstone, *Measurement of Values* (Chicago: University of Chicago Press, 1959).

6. The project reported in the Miller and McGuire monograph cited in Note #1 above is a long-range effort, initiated by the Center for the Study of Liberal Education for Adults, which aims eventually to produce evaluation instruments developed especially for adults and relevant for a wide range of adult programs.

7. The case, and part of the rating scale, is taken with permission from H. L. Miller, "Evaluating Courses—Not Students," *School and Society,* Vol. LXXVII, No. 1996 (March 21, 1953), p. 182. The article describes evaluation procedures used for an experimental adult course and the results of applying them.

8. This note on an instrument to measure adult interests is adapted from Miller and McGuire, *op. cit.,* pp. 49–51.

9. *Ibid.,* pp. 64–76.

10. See Chapter III, Note #8 for a previous reference to the semantic differential. The instructions are taken with permission from Charles E. Osgood, George J. Suci, and Percy H. Tannenbaum, *The Measurement of Meaning* (Urbana: University of Illinois Press, 1957), pp. 82–84; see Chapter 3 in that work for instructions for using the test.

Index

INDEX